$\mathcal{S}$INS

OF THE $\mathcal{S}$PIRIT,

$\mathcal{B}$LESSINGS

OF THE $\mathcal{F}$LESH

ALSO BY MATTHEW FOX

BREAKTHROUGH:
Meister Eckhart's Creation Spirituality in New Translation

THE COMING OF THE COSMIC CHRIST:
The Healing of Mother Earth and the Birth of a Global Renaissance

CONFESSIONS:
The Making of a Post-Denominational Priest

CREATION SPIRITUALITY:
Liberating Gifts for the People of the Earth

HILDEGARD OF BINGEN'S BOOK OF DIVINE WORKS
WITH LETTERS AND SONGS (editor)

ILLUMINATIONS OF HILDEGARD OF BINGEN

IN THE BEGINNING THERE WAS JOY

MANIFESTO FOR A GLOBAL CIVILIZATION
(with Brian Swimme)

MEDITATIONS WITH MEISTER ECKHART

NATURAL GRACE:
Dialogues on Creation, Darkness, and the Soul in Spirituality
and Science (with Rupert Sheldrake)

ON BECOMING A MUSICAL, MYSTICAL BEAR:
Spirituality American Style

ORIGINAL BLESSING:
A Primer in Creation Spirituality

PASSION FOR CREATION:
The Mysticism of Meister Eckhart

THE PHYSICS OF ANGELS:
Exploring the Realm Where Science and Spirit Meet
(with Rupert Sheldrake)

THE REINVENTION OF WORK:
A New Vision of Livelihood for Our Time

SHEER JOY:
Conversations with Thomas Aquinas on Creation Spirituality

A SPIRITUALITY NAMED COMPASSION
and the Healing of the Global Village,
Humpty Dumpty, and Us

WESTERN SPIRITUALITY:
Historical Roots, Ecumenical Roots (editor)

WHEE! WE, WEE ALL THE WAY HOME:
A Guide to a Sensual Prophetic Spirituality

WRESTLING WITH THE PROPHETS:
Essays on Creation Spirituality and Everyday Life

LESSONS FOR

TRANSFORMING

EVIL IN SOUL

AND SOCIETY

THREE RIVERS PRESS

NEW YORK

Sins of the Spirit, Blessings of the Flesh

Matthew Fox

Published by Three Rivers Press, New York, New York.
Member of the Crown Publishing Group.
Random House, Inc. New York, Toronto, London, Sydney, Auckland
www.randomhouse.
Three Rivers Press is a registered trademark and the Three Rivers Press colophon
is a trademark of Random House, Inc.
Originally published in hardcover by Harmony Books in 1999.
Printed in the United States of America

Book design by Donna Sinisgalli

Library of Congress Cataloging-in-Publication Data
Fox, Matthew, 1940–
Sins of the spirit, blessings of the flesh/by Matthew Fox.—
1st ed.
Includes index.
1. Deadly sins.   2. Chakras.   I. Title.
BV4626.F68   1999
233—dc21   98–40312
ISBN 0-609-80580-0
1   3   5   7   9   10   8   6   4   2
First Paperback Edition

This book is dedicated to the many wonderful teachers of my life, some in books, some in the flesh, all in the spirit. Included are Buck Ghosthorse and Jose Hobday, M. D. Chenu and Thomas Berry, Brian Swimme and M. C. Richards, Clarissa Pinkola Estes and Thomas Aquinas, Martin Buber and Erich Fromm, Howard Thurman, Joanna Macy, and Diane Ackerman. And many more, including those acknowledged in the footnotes.

It is also dedicated to those visionaries who are helping the University of Creation Spirituality and the Howard Thurman Ritual Center with its Techno Cosmic Masses happen. Among these coworkers are: Ben Yee, Mary Ford Grabowsky, Marlene DeNardo, Fred Matzer, Bishop William Swing, Linda Lowrance, Mel Bricker, Jo Sanzgiri, Dorsey Blake, Ana Perez, Aileen Donovan, Jill Martin, Ed Smith, Dominic Flamiano, Clare Ronzani, Deborah Martin, Mary Franklin, and our faculty, staff, board, and benefactors.

PERMISSIONS

Sins of the spirit are more grievous
than sins of the flesh.

—ST. THOMAS AQUINAS

Grandfather, look at our brokenness,
We know that in all creation
Only the human family has strayed from the Sacred Way.

—OJIBWAY PRAYER

TABLE OF CONTENTS

Introduction: A Species Wanting Attention   1

PART I

BLESSINGS OF THE FLESH: THE SACRED FLESH   19

Chapter 1   Redeeming the Word *Flesh*   23
Chapter 2   Universe Flesh   42
Chapter 3   Earth Flesh   57
Chapter 4   Human Flesh   69
Chapter 5   The Seven Chakras: Further Blessings of Our
Human Flesh   94

PART II

SIN IN CONTEXT: THE EVOLUTION OF SIN AND ITS MEANINGS   117

Chapter 6   What the Mystics Say About Sin, Including Rumi,
Kabir, Julian, Eckhart, Jesus, and Paul   121
Chapter 7   Meanings of Sin from Theologians and
Biologists   137

PART III

SINS OF THE SPIRIT: THE SEVEN CHAKRAS AND THE SEVEN CAPITAL SINS   161

Chapter 8   Misdirected Love in the First Chakra:
Acedia, Arrogance   167

Chapter 9   Misdirected Love in the Second Chakra: Control, Addiction, and *Lust*   209

Chapter 10   Misdirected Love in the Third Chakra: Victimization, *Anger,* and Violence   234

Chapter 11   Misdirected Love in the Fourth Chakra: Fear, Avarice, and Resentment   250

Chapter 12   Misdirected Love in the Fifth Chakra: Gluttony and Consumerism   275

Chapter 13   Misdirected Love in the Sixth Chakra: Rationalism, Reductionism, and Pessimism   293

Chapter 14   Misdirected Love in the Seventh Chakra: Envy and Resentment   315

CONCLUSION: THE BLESSINGS OF
FLESH *AND* SPIRIT AND THE LAUNCHING OF
A MORAL WAVE FOR OUR FUTURE   328

Appendix A: Hitler as a Religious Figure   339

Appendix B: Synonyms for *Sin* in English   348

Appendix C: Paul Ricoeur on the Evolution of Sin   350

Notes   355

Index   381

ACKNOWLEDGMENTS

I am grateful to all those authors and thinkers through the centuries who have thought about the topics of goodness and transgression. A special thanks to those who are developing a new, grace-based cosmology today including an appreciation of our holy bodies. I have tried to acknowledge all these thinkers by taking their thought seriously in this book and by recognizing their contributions in the text and in the footnotes. Hopefully, by presenting their research in the light of the history of spirituality, the spirit-dimension of their deep work will receive the attention it deserves.

Also, I am grateful to my agent, Ned Leavitt, whose encouragement has never faltered, and to my editors at Harmony Books, Shaye Areheart and Leslie Meredith. Shaye's support in particular has been invaluable. A special thanks to the Eugene Yee family, who lent me their summer home as a retreat in nature where I was able to study and write significant parts of this work. And to Julie Anglin for her illustrations. And to Mary Ford Grabowsky and Christian de la Huerta for their editorial suggestions.

INTRODUCTION:

A SPECIES WANTING ATTENTION

A year ago, following a lecture I gave in Hawaii, a young man approached me with a story. "I have AIDS," he said, "and the day I was diagnosed you came to me in a dream wearing the white coat of a doctor and you said to me, PWA does not mean a person with AIDS. PWA means 'a person wanting attention.' This dream changed my life." He explained how he was, for the first time, taking care of himself and his heart issues, had moved from Boston to Hawaii to live a gentler lifestyle, and was feeling strong and joyful for the journey that lay ahead.

I believe this story can be adapted slightly to apply to all of us. The acronym I suggest is SWA, our "species wanting attention." In the wars and violence of the industrial age, our species has been neglecting our heart needs. We have also neglected the needs of other beings with whom we share this planet. We need to probe more deeply and more communally into who we are as a species: our strengths and our weaknesses, our power and our misuse of power. Paying attention includes going into our capacity for destruction and self-hatred, our resentments and our avarice, our envy and our listlessness, our despair and our cynicism, our addictions and our projections, our arrogance and our malice—in short, for lack of a better word, our sins. This book is an attempt to set out on such an exploration.

As our species evolves spiritually, we must take another and harder look at our complicity in evil and at how our spiritual traditions may assist us in growing beyond our violence. Spiritual advancement is not restricted to increasing light in the world; we need also to increase awareness of those shadow forces with whom we must wrestle. If we don't, we will pay a price. Scott Peck, in *People of the Lie,* speaks of the issue at hand:

The major threats to our survival no longer stem from nature without but from our own human nature within. It is our carelessness,
our hostilities, our selfishness and pride and willful ignorance that
endanger the world. Unless we can now tame and transmute the
potential for evil in the human soul, we shall be lost.[1]

Yet Peck warns that "the naming of evil is still in the primitive stage."[2]
Martin Buber, in his book *Good and Evil,* raises the question, What
should be the "point of attack for the struggle against evil?" And his
reply is, "The struggle must begin within one's one soul—all else will
follow upon this."[3]

THE METHODOLOGY FOR THIS BOOK

Clearly the issue is not so much *whether* to explore or talk about human
malice but *how* to talk about it. In that regard I have chosen a very specific methodology for this book. First, in Part I, I talk about goodness,
specifically the blessing of the flesh—all flesh, the flesh of the universe
and of earth as well as our human flesh, and the seven chakras that name
some of the blessing-energy inside all of us. Unless we ground ourselves
in our capacity for goodness, we will be in no position to consider our
capacity for wrongdoing. To assist in this grounding, I include a litany
for each blessing of our flesh—cosmic, earthly, and human.

Next, in Part II, I explore briefly what mystics East and West have
said about human sinning, and then what theologians and biologists say.
And in Part III, I focus on the ancient Middle Eastern and Western tradition of the "seven capital sins" and the "sins of the spirit" and relate it
to the Eastern tradition of the seven chakras. The link between the two
traditions can be found in the Jewish understanding of sin as "missing
the mark" and in Thomas Aquinas's definition of sin as "misdirected
love." Is sin, then, not an energy (chakra) that is off center or missing
the mark? Is sin not a love energy (chakra) that is misdirected? Might
the chakra tradition of the East not shed light on what we in the West
call sin? And might our understanding of sin also contribute to a deepening of the meaning of chakra?

In Part III, when I discuss the seven capital sins and their "offspring" at some length, I conclude each chapter with a brief discussion of the traditional sacrament that corresponds to the chakra at issue and I offer practical exercises that persons can do to cleanse themselves of the "misdirection" associated with the particular chakra.

Rabbi Solomon Schimmel, in his study *The Seven Deadly Sins: Jewish, Christian, and Classical Reflections on Human Nature,* argues that "the seven deadly sins—pride, anger, envy, greed, gluttony, lust, and sloth—are with us every day" and that our primary purpose in studying them is to learn "what it means to be human and humane and the responsibilities that we have to fulfill if we want to be considered as such."[4] In this book I adapt slightly the list of the seven cardinal sins and mix them with the sins of the spirit. But I agree with Rabbi Schimmel that these sins "concern the core of what we are, of what we can become, and most importantly, of what we should aspire to be."[5] The great twelfth-century mystic and healer Hildegard of Bingen agreed when she wrote that "the knowledge of good and evil represents, so to speak, the innermost part of the soul."[6] Aleksandr Solzhenitsyn says something similar when he observes that "the line dividing good and evil cuts through the heart of every human being. And who is willing to destroy a piece of his own heart?"[7]

Sin is a heart issue, a soul issue; to explore our heart and soul is to explore our capacities for sin. Hildegard taught that the pursuit of true joy implies an understanding of sin, for "we can never find true joy in sinning." In fact, "the soul accomplishes in joy its good deeds of a heavenly nature; in sadness and sorrow it accomplishes evil deeds of an earthy nature."[8] Thus to explore the seven capital sins is to shed new light on our inner lives.

RECONTEXTUALIZING EVIL

All sin has a history and a context. In this book I try to recontextualize evil and humanity's complicity in it within a postmodern worldview, one that begins with a scientific cosmology and a creation-centered spirituality. Thus the section on "Blessings of the Flesh" precedes that on "Sins of the Spirit." The context ought to be set right at the beginning. This century has been marked by the realities of the Holocaust and of technological marvels put to use for destruction. The culmination of those modern scientific and technological achievements has rendered our species dangerous to ourselves and to other beings on this planet beyond any possibility previously imagined. Perhaps the reality of our time was best summarized in a sentence by J. Robert Oppenheimer, when the first atomic blast was successfully detonated in the New Mexican desert: "Now we know evil," he said.

Yes, the modern age has assured us of a knowledge of evil. Yet theology has not kept pace with our demonic powers. We need to examine anew our traditional sources of spiritual insight, which might tell us not only about evil but more importantly about ways beyond it. As Thomas Aquinas warned, one human being can do more evil than all the other animals on the planet. As ecological catastrophe threatens our existence as a species and many others with whom we share this planet, we need to revision how we can lend help, healing, and transformation.

By examining the sins of the spirit and the blessings of the flesh, we are paying attention to the wisdom of our ancestors, whose awareness of spirit-sin was in many ways far more nuanced and developed than the moral agenda that has come to us during the modern era. Life in the premodern era was lived closer to the earth and closer to the flesh. The mechanistic consciousness of the Newtonian era effectively removed the living flesh from the universe, assuring us that only humans and the food we ate were flesh. Today's cosmology, on the other hand, reintroduces us to the "fleshiness" of existence—all beings, even stars and galaxies, live, die, and resurrect in their fashion, and all are made of similar elements or stuff. The new creation story has enlarged the meaning of the word *flesh*. Much more is flesh because much more exists and dies than we had ever imagined and all things are connected, animate to inanimate.

In a dream I received a year ago, a very clear sentence said: "There is nothing wrong with the human species today except one thing—we have lost the sense of the sacred." To recover the sacred would be to recover our humanity. We are sacred and part of the sacred, but we have the capacity to choose and act otherwise. Indeed, Rabbi Abraham Joshua Heschel defines sin as "the refusal of humans to become who we are."

Recently I coauthored a book with British scientist Rupert Sheldrake on *The Physics of Angels*. A postmodern worldview allows angels to return, but to admit the angelic is also to admit the demonic. Angels or spirits, like humans, have a shadow side and a potential for negativity—at least, that is the traditional teaching. Today we don't call angels by names such as Satan and Lucifer and Beelzebub. Rather, the names might appropriately be Anthropocentrism, Racism, Sexism, Arrogance, and so on. These realities are spirit-beings that seek to inhabit our souls and, like the parasites they are, feed there.

To talk about the sacred is to talk about evil. An appreciation of the former renders one more vulnerable to the latter. It is not unlike the experience of being in love. I remember when I was first deeply in love, the reality of death hit me stronger than it ever had before. For to be in love is to want never to lose the beloved. But death is such a loss, and so death looms great in the context of love. So too with the sacred and evil. As one tries to deepen one's appreciation of the sacred, evil looms great. For the sacred is always in jeopardy, at least when humans are around. French philosopher Paul Ricoeur, based on his extensive study of myths from religious traditions around the world, makes the following observation in *The Symbolism of Evil:* "It is, in fact, because evil is supremely the crucial experience of the sacred that the threat of the dissolution of the bond between man and the sacred makes us most intensely aware of man's dependence on the powers of the sacred."[9] I disagree with Ricoeur that evil is "the crucial experience of the sacred"—I believe that awe is. Yet no one can deny that today, with humanity's exploding population, with extinction occurring among species the world over, with the destruction of 26 billion tons of topsoil annually, with the warming of the planet, with despair and potential violence among the young, with the growing gap between haves and have-nots, a "dissolution of the bond between man and the sacred" looms before us. This situation presents us with a need to reexamine our understanding of sin and ways of liberation from it.

THE RELUCTANCE TO TALK ABOUT SIN

As I was checking out an armload of books on sin at the library of the Graduate Theological Union in Berkeley, a student who was at the checkout desk moaned, "Ugh, sounds dreary."

Few people want to talk about sin today.[10] There are many good reasons for this, and one of them is that we do not wish to bore one another with the obvious. Some people call sin a disease; New Agers bathe themselves blissfully in the light; certain feminists say evil and good are patriarchal categories (which sounds an awful lot like a new category for sinfulness). Yet most of our news on television and in print involves sins of some kind or other, and our species seems perfectly willing to engage in sinful activities.

Our reluctance to talk about sin may stem from the fact that organized religion has ignored the deep traditions about the sins of the spirit in favor of superficial, even titillating sins of the flesh and has divorced sin-talk from its appropriate context of goodness. As process theologian Norman Pittenger puts it, "a great deal of Christian talk has been sin-obsessed.... The distortion has been appalling."[11] My book *Original Blessing* addressed this awful one-sidedness in the guilt-ridden conscience of Western religion. Pittenger believes that the notion of sin has reached such a low point that "either [it] has no meaning at all, save as a piece of religious jargon, or it is almost entirely misunderstood in respect to its basic significance."[12] This perceived irrelevance of sin-talk may underlie the Brazilian feminist theologian Ivone Gebara's observation that "today we are experiencing a world-wide institutional crisis where the old religious sanctions and admonitions are simply exhausted. Nobody listens to them anymore."[13] The exhaustion of western religion certainly is closely connected to its excessive preaching about sin: morality over spirituality. A fundamentalist theology that ignores the Holy Spirit *and* the Creator by being overly zealous about redemption and Jesus-olatry ends up trivializing sin.

Theologians and popular preachers, too, have vitiated the term *sin*. On the right, fundamentalists are running away with the word and the concept and in the process are rendering progressive theologies flat and flaccid. Some on the left say that good and evil do not exist, but if that is so, then we must empty our prisons of all the rapists, wife beaters, child molesters, murderers, and thieves.

We need a theology of spirit, a practice of spirituality, to deal with sins of the spirit. But religions may be so cut off from spirituality and spirit now that they have little to offer. As a result, the secular media are left "to instruct" us about sin, and the planet is in profound decline. Cynicism reigns. Churches are emptier than ever. No battles are waged there any longer. Even sin has become boring. In the Scriptures sin is not trivial. Sin is about battles. It is not sanitized or domesticated, as our shopping mall culture has so often rendered everything around us.

Another reason many of us do not want to talk about sin is that greater visions await our souls than to dwell on the negative. The Sufi mystic poet Rumi put it memorably when he said:

Out beyond ideas of wrong doing,
and right doing,
There is a field.
I'll meet you there.[14]

Most of us yearn for such a field, in which we can run and play and lie down with our beloved. Something far vaster, far more beautiful, awaits us and beckons us, and we feel an urgency to meet it heart to heart in the field beyond. That field is a soul-place, a spirit-place, that beckons our deepest selves. That call inspires us and moves us to go beyond ethics to being, to encounters with the beloved. Nevertheless, not even Rumi said that discussion of wrong-doing and right-doing is never needed—only that we ought not get bogged down in that particular corner of our souls.

In my opinion we do need to talk about sin today, but not in the same way we talked about it in the past. Sin evolves, as culture evolves. Our capacity for destruction and alienation, self-hatred and social resentment, luxurious living among gross injustice, evolves. We must talk about sin again because not to do so perpetuates our problems, just as any kind of denial invariably creates more complex problems. (Think of an alcoholic who insists he is only a "social drinker." The denial launches still more abuse.) We must talk about sin again because while our news is filled with it, we would be fools to let newscasters and jour-nalists be our surrogate theologians; because the earth is dying due to human transgressions; because our hearts are sad and we are without energy; and because elders have a responsibility to show the young where boundaries lie. Indeed, the ecological disasters of our time, whose reality appears daily in our news reports, have reintroduced sin—by whatever name—to our awareness.

DEEP ECUMENISM AND SIN

In this book I call on the wisdom of the East by way of the chakra tradition because our times are unique for their pluralism, bringing
together East and West, North and South. No culture is without its
insight or experience of sin. No tradition holds all the answers or even
many answers. Because we all face the precarious future of our planet
and of our species together, it seems appropriate to discuss the dangerous side of human nature together. Thus I write in the spirit of what I
call Deep Ecumenism, wherein we search from the depth of our various spiritual traditions for wisdom in a difficult time.

Part of a postmodern cultural context is recognizing diversity and
realizing how pluralistic a world we live in. Deep Ecumenism[15] is the
coming-together of world religions around common themes and the
drawing-out of their deep wisdom to address those themes. Surely sin
is such a theme. Surely all cultures, all religions, all spiritual disciplines
worthy of the name deal with what the Vietnamese Buddhist monk
Thich Nhat Hanh calls the "seeds of violence" and the "seeds of divine
peace" in every human. Martin Buber, working out of the Jewish tradition, teaches something similar when he says that humans have "two
urges" and that we must "harness both urges together in the service of
God." Our task "is not to extirpate the evil urge, but to reunite it with
the good."[16] Psychologist Erich Fromm wrote of the "life-affirming syndromes" that include love, solidarity, justice and reason which are in
conflict with the "life-thwarting syndromes" of sadomasochism,
destructiveness, greed, narcissism, and incestuousness.[17] Surely Jesus
and Lao-tzu, Buddha and Moses, Chief Seattle and Gandhi, were dealing with such issues. To explore more carefully the deeper traditions we
hold about sin is to draw ourselves more closely together, at a time
when the planet is urging us to unite for the sake of common survival
and earth survival.

Sin is part of what makes us human. Its ambiguity, its hidden attractions (and those not so hidden), its allure and deceits, its false promises
and letdowns—all are everyday fare for every human being. Sin "excites
attention by its very character as a scandal," observes Paul Ricoeur.[18] We
are all subject to sin and its wiles. The principle of interdependence—

long held true by mystics and only recently approved by Western science—holds that we are all in this together. We are all implicated in evil, and we share the negative as well as the positive in life—the pain and the pleasure, the suffering and the joy. Too much distancing of ourselves from evil can in fact contribute to evil, as Erich Fromm warns us: "As long as one believes that the evil man wears horns, one will not discover an evil man. The naive assumption that an evil man is easily recognizable results in a great danger: one fails to recognize evil men before they have begun their work of destruction." He warns that to deprive even Hitler of his humanity "would only intensify the tendency to be blind to the potential Hitlers unless they wear horns."[19] Perhaps this is one reason why ancient stories about evil picture evil as faceless. Evil is faceless because it can take over any one of our beings. No one is exempt from the possibility of evil. The reality of evil calls for alertness.

Sin is surely one of the daily happenings we all have in common, something we can all identify with. It is a battle to win or lose. Morton W. Bloomfield, who wrote the classical work on *The Seven Deadly Sins,* calls these sins "the real enemies of humanity."[20] To come together in opposition to these vices to which we are all prone would be to wage a war that matters.

Harder than coming together around the reality of sin, however, is coming up with ways out of sin: liberating ways to freedom. These ways constitute the good news and grace found in all spiritual traditions. In drawing on the Western tradition of the capital sins and the sins of the spirit, as well as today's cosmology and the Eastern treatment of the seven chakras, I hope to employ the wisdom of deep ecumenism.

In the concluding chapter I bring to the fore seven positive precepts and a single virtue, around which our species can gather today to usher in a new era of human morality. These seven precepts derive from the seven chakras and the seven principles of Creation Spirituality—and they represent the light that shines behind the darkness of the seven capital sins. The virtue of generosity, as I indicate, summarizes our practice of cosmology, creativity, and magnanimity.

There is a rich Western tradition of artists wrestling with the seven sins. Not only Chaucer and Dante but William Langland's poem *Piers Plowman,* and Edmund Spenser's *Faerie Queen* all treat these sins. Satires of humanity through the prism of the seven capital or cardinal sins are numerous and can be found on medieval French cathedrals as well as in English literature. (Somehow the ten commandments do not lend themselves to rich satirization.) I have often felt that our times deserve much richer satire than they are receiving. Perhaps if humanity could agree on the seven basic sins presented in this book, then our capacity for satirizing them in ourselves and in our institutions, and for spreading this satire around the world swiftly by way of common art, entertainment, and electronic communication, might contribute mightily to lessening the gap between rich and poor, powerful and powerless—in short, to liberation from these very sins (surely this effort will generate good work for artists).

COSMOLOGY, THE CONTEXT FOR SIN-TALK

In this book, and especially in Part I, "Blessings of the Flesh," I am attempting to put sin-talk into its proper context. Will acknowledging this proper *context* allow us to talk about sin more honestly and to challenge it more effectively? The context ought to be the following: (1) cosmology and history; (2) blessing or goodness, including the existence and powers and vulnerability that make even sin possible; (3) creativity—every sin being a choice and therefore a certain act of creativity; (4) the quest for goodness and blessing inherent in all our choices, even in sinful ones (Aquinas believed that every choice we make is in some way based on love); (5) a sociopolitical context—sin does not rupture just personal relationships but also social, ecological, and political relationships.

Humans have been sinning for a long time—at least, from our perspective of time. But from the perspective of the history of the universe, we have been at it for only a short time. We have been here only a brief time, around 2 million years. Do other animals commit sin? That would be grist for another book, no doubt by an author more schooled in animal behavior than I, but this much can be said: If they do, they aren't very good at it! Their efforts are so minuscule that they pale in comparison to humanity's! We are the experts at sin—due, I believe, to our amazing capacity for creativity and imagination, a power that needs bridling if it is to serve the larger purpose of our existence.[20]

It is that larger picture that holds and embraces an examination of our capacity for malfeasance. Cosmology is an essential part of an understanding of evil, because evil is understood as a rupture in creation.

The biblical tradition treats sin as a *cosmological event*. The Jewish scholar Jon D. Levenson, in *Creation and the Persistence of Evil,* tells us that in apocalyptic literature, Israel's struggle is against "cosmic forces of the utmost malignancy. Their evil reaches everywhere, even into the human heart, and their defeat requires nothing less than a cosmic transformation—a new cosmogony, a new creation."[22] Chaos happens when evil happens; it constitutes the undoing of creation. The Israelites believed that community worship guaranteed the victory of order over chaos—ritual puts creation back together again. Martin Buber proposes that humans need a "bridge" to awaken them to how psyche and cosmos struggle in tandem. "Man knows of the chaos and creation in the cosmogonic myth and he learns that chaos and creation take place in himself, but he does not see the former and the latter together; he listens to the mystery of Lucifer and hushes it up in his own life."[23]

The early Christian church also understood the struggle with evil to be cosmic in nature. The writer of the Letter to the Ephesians warned that "our contest is not against flesh and blood, but against powers, against principalities, against the world-rulers of this present darkness, against spiritual forces of evil in heavenly places" (Ephesians 6:12). Mark's gospel begins by placing Jesus' struggle in a cosmic setting, while the Essene community of Jesus' time envisioned their struggle as a cosmic one.

Our culture is frankly bored with the word *sin,* and one reason is that we are bored with everything. We are a species made for cosmology, yet our culture has rendered us passive couch potatoes and shopping and entertainment addicts. In short, we have been cut off from the big universe, and consequently we are bored, boring, and violent. We have even managed to render sin boring!

BLESSINGS OF THE FLESH:
A POSTMODERN CONTRIBUTION

The modern era was a *textual* era—it began with the invention of the printing press. The postmodern era is a *contextual* era. It began with the breakdown of the modern society in the 1960s and the computer, electronics, and multimedia explosions of the 1970s. In Latin, *textere* means "to weave," and *contextere* means "to weave together."

In this book I *weave sin together with blessing* and *the human with the more-than-human*. Human decision-making and action need to be woven together into the larger tapestry of the universe's activities—that is, set in a cosmological context. This context has been missing in our theological, educational, and professional life for centuries. Without cosmology we have no shared ethics—only lawyers (civil or religious) arguing over man-made *texts*. We have text but no context.

In addition to weaving blessing (cosmology) and sin (human choice) together, I weave together East and West, the seven chakras and the seven capital sins and seven sacraments. I also weave together the mystics of both traditions, for they always work from a context that is creation-centered. *Creation* is another word for cosmology, isness, wholeness, being, universe, all our relations, spirit, self, and the Kingdom/Queendom of God.

Part of the *context* of human iniquity at the end of the twentieth century is horror of the Holocaust. A postmodern time is neither innocent nor naive—"tragic optimism" is the way Charles Jencks names a postmodern attitude.[24] The tragic is omnipresent. Theologian Robert Funk describes a post-Holocaust theology as one that realizes that "we can no longer trust the authority structure of an ecclesiastical tradition that learned, at several crucial junctures in its history, it was unable to resist the ultimate compromise."[25] He includes in these critical moments black slavery and the Spanish Inquisition.[26] A post-Holocaust theology requires that we educate ourselves to the issues of morality and immorality.

Morton Bloomfield, in his fifteen-year study of the seven capital sins, points out that sin and vices were much more attractive to medieval authors and lay readers than were virtues. The same is true today. Sin fascinates. It sells newspapers and tabloids, it deposes presi-

dents and potential presidents, ministers and sports heroes, and it mes-
merizes people in front of their television sets. The popular press traf-
fics in it. Our species is more attracted by vice than by virtue. In that
regard we have evolved very little from medieval times. And that is why
meditating on the blessings of the flesh is such an important exercise
today. Given a new cosmology, one that is intrinsically alluring, can we
be seduced, loved, inspired—if not by human virtue, in this cynical
time—by cosmic beauty? Glory? Awe? Blessing?

The title for this book deliberately confronts a taboo in Western
theology. A few years ago, when I was working on *Sheer Joy,* my book on
the thirteenth-century saint and theologian Thomas Aquinas, I came
across this sentence: "The sins of the spirit are far graver than the sins
of the flesh."[27] How amazing I found this sentence to be, since over the
years so many papal preoccupations and those of religious preachers
have stressed the "sins of the flesh." The overidentification of sin with
sex is still part of an obsession among many ecclesiastics and is found in
our language itself, when we say unmarried persons are "living in sin."
At times I have felt that the sixth and ninth commandments in the
Decalogue referring to adultery and coveting another's partner were
the "two commandments" that Jesus left behind. Most practicing
Christians can readily list sins of the flesh, but how many of us can name
sins of the spirit?

Sins of the flesh are more than sexual peccadilloes. The deeper sins
of the flesh include those that destroy children and adults, forests and
other creatures. Most economic decisions concern the survival or the
destruction of flesh. Perhaps our ancestors made too much of the distinction between sins of the flesh and those of the spirit. David Korten's
When Corporations Rule the World[28] and William Julius Wilson's *When Work
Disappears: The World of the New Urban Poor*[29] show us what is at stake with
the neglect of flesh. To deny someone decent work or wages, drinking
water or health care, shelter or safety, is to curse their existence.
"Curses on the flesh" might most aptly name the new system—using
new technologies but old imperial slave/master relationships to destroy
flesh—human and more-than-human—in the name of global profi-
teering. It is in our flesh that we bear the curses of spiritual sins—
the poor suffer from more diseases and live shorter lives than the
wealthy.

Recently, when I read David Korten's book, I wrote the following entry in my journal:

> How amazing to read a book on the history of the seven sins on Monday and a book on corporate power on Thursday. All the sins of history are laid out in this book—only on a global scale affecting the quality of life of the planet and billions of people today. A spiritual crisis, indeed!
> NOT "Word was made flesh," but the "Devil is made fleshless." Yes, a Devourer of Flesh—of the flesh of rainforests and indigenous peoples, of ordinary citizens, of the future. When this system collapses it will make the S&L failures look like a dime store romp. They are the Flesh Eaters, a new breed of Flesh Eaters. They lack incarnation. They are angels—bad angels, unfortunately. As in the Book of Revelation, there is only one question here: Who rules the universe: economic fleshless imperialists or the incarnated ones? There is no democracy without flesh. The oligarchy is antidemocratic at every level.

Three ancient spiritual traditions—the chakras and Creation Spirituality and the seven capital sins—may have something to say about the God incarnate in flesh, and about the God being crucified anew by impersonal, rational, abstracted, mostly fleshless powers and principalities. Theologian Dominic Crossan makes the distinction between flesh-lovers (sarcophilia) and flesh-fearers (sarcophobia, from the Greek word for "flesh," *sarx*). He asks whether "the history of Christianity and especially of Christian theology [represents] the long, slow victory of sarcophobic over sarcophilic Christianity?"[30]

Learning about the new cosmology as well as the chakras is a way to celebrate our flesh, our living bodies, our ensouled bodies. Knowing our chakras helps us to love ourselves, to embrace our flesh. Therefore the study of the chakras makes possible Jesus' admonition to "love your neighbor as yourself."

Christianity and its doctrine of *continuous Creation and continuous Incarnation* means that God has become incarnate—made flesh—not just in the historical Jesus and certainly not just in the two-legged creatures but in all of us. All of us are incarnations—home and dwelling-places for the Divine—all people, the poor no less than the comfortable. All races, all religions, all sexes, all sexual orientations, and all beings—four-legged, the winged, the rock people and tree people and cloud peoples—all are dwelling places of the Divine. That is the depth to which a "blessing of flesh" theology takes us.

SINS OF THE SPIRIT

Modern philosophy has been so *unspirited* that it is not well equipped to talk about sins of the spirit. Sins of the spirit, after all, offend spirit. They constitute an obstacle to it and prevent it from flowing. But spirit also heals sins of the spirit. There can be no awareness of the sins of the spirit without awareness of spirit.

In treating the sins of the spirit, I have chosen to follow the tradition of the seven capital sins handed down from the monks dwelling in the Egyptian desert and from medieval, premodern theologians. But I have adapted them considerably to our own experience and language. By invoking the chakras, I am practicing what I preach in Part I: that we must ground our sense of sin—as well as our sense of awe—in the body.

Blessing must be the context for any authentically human endeavor. For any act of waking up, recovering a consciousness of praise and goodness, of blessing and gratitude, of what the mystics call the *via positiva,* is paramount.

Sin, most believers have been taught, means sins of the flesh. But the body does not sin, as Aquinas observed—it is the soul that sins. And the soul's most grievous sins are less sins of the flesh than sins of the spirit. These spirit sins get us in our deepest trouble with self, relatives, spouses, earth creatures, and future generations—in other words, with all our relations, and with all flesh.

HOW SIN-TALK AND FLESH-TALK DIFFER

The energy difference in talking of sin and talking of blessings of the flesh is observable. As I read works on "blessings of the flesh" such as Diane Ackerman's *The Natural History of the Senses* and David Abram's *The Spell of the Sensuous,* my own energy is very different from when I read literature devoted to sin and evil. Works on "blessings of the flesh" create an expectancy and have an element of pleasure and fun and won-der. Sin-talk, by comparison, is drudgery. And that is *the whole point.* Talking of sin without talking of blessing ignores *context,* for all sin takes place in a larger context of blessing or goodness. Without this blessing of existence, we couldn't do anything, including sin. Motivation is pos-itive, not negative, and requires a blessing context.

The energy loss I felt on reading theologians is not due, I realize, merely to the subject matter. It has to do with the inherent anthro-pocentrism, textism, and moralism of the writers. Consider this quo-tation from the Lutheran Augsburg Confession of 1530:

> Since the fall of Adam all men who are born according to the course of nature are conceived and born in sin. That is, all men are full of evil lust and inclinations from their mother's wombs and are unable by nature to have true fear of God and true faith in God. Moreover, this inborn sickness and hereditary sin is truly sin and condemns to the eternal wrath of God all those who are not born again through Baptism and the Holy Spirit.[31]

John Calvin wrote: "Original sin...seems to be a hereditary depravity and corruption of our nature, diffused into all parts of the soul, which makes us first liable to God's wrath, then also brings forth in us those works which scripture calls 'works of the flesh.'"[32] I wrote in a journal, at the time I came across these texts: "Such talk drags one down and sucks the air out of one's lungs, the light out of one's heart, the life out of one's body."

One wonders if these authors had lost entirely Paul's observation in his Letter to the Romans: "Where sin abounded, grace did much more abound" (5:20). As Rabbi Zalman Schachter has put it, "There is more good than evil in the world, but not by much." Or as Paul Ricoeur puts it, "However radical evil may be, it cannot be as primordial as good-ness."[33]

Sometimes the news is so grim that humans seem almost exclu-sively malicious. One thinks of the Oklahoma City bombing or the Holocaust or the slave ships. Or the destruction of indigenous peoples on American soil and elsewhere. Then the pessimism of ancient Greece comes forward wherein, we are told, a catechist asks an acousmatic,

"What is the truest saying? That men are wicked."[34] It is one more reason for getting the context right.

Rabbi Solomon Schimmel talks about "the persistence of sin."[35] Iniquity is not something that the human race has yet outgrown; it belies the modern myth that "progress" is everywhere. Human sinlessness gives little evidence of having arrived along with the abundance of highways and electronic gadgets and television channels. In fact, one could make a good case for the opposite: that technology has increased our capacity for destruction, violence, cruelty, injustice, and inhumanity. For one thing, it has birthed more potential sinners and kept them alive longer because it has increased the number of humans on the planet. In addition, it has put into the hands of potential sinners untold powers of destruction, from Uzi machine guns to nuclear and biologic weapons to the capacity to bulldoze in a day forests that nature and God took ten thousand years to create.

The main reason for writing this book is not to name or even redefine sin. It is to heal sin, to show liberation or redemption or *ways out of sin,* or as Martin Buber puts it, "to deprive evil of its power."[36] An increased awareness of the blessing of the flesh and an upsurge in gratitude is one way to deprive evil of its power. Erich Fromm observes that

> Love of life or love of the dead is the fundamental alternative that confronts every human being. Necrophilia grows as the development of biophilia is stunted.... Severely necrophilous persons are very dangerous. They are the haters, the racists, those in favor of war, bloodshed, and destruction. They are dangerous not only if they are political leaders, but also as the potential cohorts for a dictatorial leader. They become the executioners, terrorists, torturers; without them no terror system could be set up.[37]

Psychologist Carl Jung predicted that the Age of Aquarius would be a time when evil would be on the table. We would all know what it is. The moral issue would be whether we had the will to do something about it. Hopefully, this book will help us put evil on the table to look at. Whether we do something about it, as always, is our choice.

PART 1

BLESSINGS OF THE FLESH:
THE SACRED FLESH

*I*n our times a new creation story and a new cosmology have vastly expanded the meaning of *flesh*. No previous generation has been taught that the universe is hundreds of billions of galaxies large and still expanding. Ernesto Cardinale, in his poem on the new cosmology, celebrates that the news of the expanding universe is the "most important discovery of the twentieth century."[1] If the universe is expanding, so too is flesh, for the universe is fleshy. Flesh is matter, and matter is flesh. This insight is implicit in Einstein's establishing the interchangeability of matter and energy (isn't flesh energetic matter?), just as it is explicit in Thomas Aquinas's definition of spirit as "élan" or vitality.

The news from today's physics is not just that matter expands but that matter is intrinsically energetic, vital, organized and organizing, busy, dancing, vibrating, seeking, moving, and finding order in the midst of chaos. All things in motion—isn't this Aristotle's definition of soul, as that which produces locomotion from within?

The boundary between animate and inanimate, like so many other boundaries today, is rapidly fading. Medical doctor and scientist James Lovelock writes that "there is no clear distinction anywhere on the Earth's surface between living and nonliving matter. There is merely a hierarchy of intensity going from the 'material' environment of the rocks and the atmosphere to the living cells."[2] Recently a car mechanic told me this story: He was depressed at work but stuck with his job because of family responsibilities. Then he encountered a Sufi teacher who said to him, "Each time you turn the ratchet as you repair a vehicle, speak the word *Allah*." The mechanic did so, and his whole life changed, the whole relation with his work changed. "Now," he said, "I love my work. I love cars. They are alive. It is a mistake to think of animate versus inanimate. A car will tell you, if you listen deeply enough, whether it wants to be repaired or whether it wants simply to be left alone to die."

In the context of evolution, all things have animate-like qualities. Mountains grow and shrink in the context of aeons of time. Soil breathes and rises and falls, as do entire continents and the sea with its tides.

Cosmology fascinates us and restores awe and excites us. The earth context—the animals and plants, the flowers and forests, the fauna and landscapes, the birds and fishes, the creepy-crawly things that burrow in our gardens and compost piles—fascinate us and bless us. They too have something to tell us, indeed something to reveal to us about our failures, about our sins, and about our capacity for beauty and blessing.

Our own bodies, with their 15-billion-year histories (they carry hydrogen atoms that were birthed 14 billion years ago, with their stunning achievements of eye and ear, of heart and lung, of bladder and liver, of sexual organs and larynx—our bodies too have something to reveal to us about beauty and reverence, gratitude and awe, and their opposites.

The proper context for talking about sin is cosmology, the evolution of our world, indeed the evolution of flesh. For the evolution of the world *is* the evolution of flesh. Flesh, we now know, has a history. (Not long ago we were taught, *à la* Aristotle, that species were eternal.) For most people, the blessing that flesh is and has been constitutes the ordinary entry into wisdom and into the temple of the sacred. As Ricoeur puts it, humanity "first reads the sacred *on* the world, *on* some elements or aspects of the world, on the heavens, on the sun and moon, on the waters and vegetation. Spoken symbolism thus refers back to manifestations of the sacred, to hierophanies, where the sacred is shown in a fragment of the cosmos. . . . First of all, then, it is the sun, the moon, the waters—that is to say, cosmic realities—that are symbols."[3] As our biblical ancestors knew well, *the universe is God's temple,* and the temple is a microcosm of the universe depicted in cosmic terms that recall the language of creation.[4] "He built His Sanctuary like the heavens, like the earth that He established forever" (Psalms 78, 69). Our bodies are also temples, as Paul insists. Through the temple of the body celebrating in the body of the temple, chaos becomes creation, and evil is transformed into order.[5]

The purpose of Part I of this book, "Blessings of the Flesh," is to get us to accept the *awe* of our 15-billion-year-old fleshy universe more fully. This universe so deserving of praise comes in at least three layers: the cosmic flesh, the eco-flesh, and the human flesh.

It is striking that the most ancient creation story in the Bible, Psalm 104, so full of praise of the fleshy creation of God, in celebrating the same for 34 verses, only at the 35th verse, and only in the context of praise and joy, raises the question of human sin.

> I will sing to the Lord as long as I live,
> all my life I will sing psalms to my God.
> May my meditation please the Lord,
> as I show my joy in him (her)!
> Away with all sinners from the earth
> and may the wicked be no more!

Bless the Lord, my soul.
O praise the Lord.

In putting praise before sin and blessing before curse and flesh before sins of the spirit we are following in this ancient tradition.

CHAPTER 1

REDEEMING THE WORD *FLESH*

Thomas Aquinas did not blame sin on our flesh. "Our flesh in its nature is good," he declared,[1] and "flesh is not a sufficient cause of actual sin."[2] Unfortunately, this message is not the one most often passed on by Christian writers or by modern philosophers.

WHAT EVER BECAME OF FLESH?
THE MODERN AGE'S STRUGGLE AGAINST FLESH

The modern age deadened us to matter, teaching as Augustine had sixteen centuries ago that matter and spirit are separate entities. It withdrew soul from animals, plants, mountains, birds, the land, the waters, the forests, and even from the human body from the forehead on down. (Our soul is in the pineal gland, said Descartes, eliminating six chakras in the process.) By teaching us that the universe is a machine, other species' bodies are machines, and our bodies are machinelike, modern philosophy took the life out of matter. Inert matter became the object of our senses. Subjectivity and intersubjectivity were eliminated. So-called "objectivity" reigned. Science became "frightfully estranged from our direct human experience" and the myth of objectivity "led to an almost total eclipse of the life-world."[3]

The modern era's "objectivity," in fact, has carried a great bias against the flesh. As society became more and more urbanized and people became less and less in touch with soil and sun, seasons and beings other than the human, this anti-flesh bias deepened. Biologist Rupert Sheldrake summarizes the scientific worldview of the modern era when he says that the notion of a mechanistic universe rendered the world

> inanimate and purposeless. Inanimate literally means "soulless." Purposeless means "without any internal purposes." The whole course of nature is supposed to be pushed by causes from behind rather than drawn by attractions or motivations from ahead, moving toward goals.
>
> In the seventeenth century, matter became mere dead, unconscious stuff, made up of inert atoms. The Earth was thought of as a misty ball of rock hurtling around the sun in accordance with Newton's laws of motion; it had no life of its own.
>
> The whole course of Nature was thought to be determined. Everything went on inexorably, mechanically, and was in principle completely predictable. The kind of knowledge that scientists had of the world was essentially disembodied.[4]

"Essentially disembodied." That phrase might serve not only to name what scientific knowledge has been about but also as an epitaph on a civilization: A disembodied civilization is not thankful for bodiliness or for living flesh, whether that be the flesh of a rainforest or the flesh of animals or the flesh of the ozone layer or the waters or even one's own flesh. Thus, we are driven to live vicariously—to pursue the symbols of flesh that our culture holds up as supreme and of merit, especially those that our advertising culture holds up as models. The industrial revolution, with its preaching of obedience and the sinfulness of pride, also denigrated the body, as is clear from slavery, child labor, stinking and dangerous working conditions in factories, and the multiplication of slums. One might say that the economic system was acting out the basic physics of the day: that matter is lifeless and must be pushed and pulled to the shape of those in charge. A fleshless and purposeless universe served the purposes of the masters of industry and commerce, who certainly had *their* designs in mind. Religion, bogged down by Augustine's dualistic and shame-ridden philosophies from the fourth century, hardly uttered a word in protest. "Incarnation" meant the capacity to suffer and die; it seldom meant the capacity to live and flourish. Religion was in no mind-set to redeem the word *flesh*.

Living matter—i.e., flesh—was a contradiction in terms. Mysticism was killed. Awe was deadened. Flesh died. And our senses were dulled. French philosopher Merleau-Ponty said, "We have unlearned how to see, hear, and generally speaking, feel, in order to deduce . . . what we are to see, hear, and feel."[5]

Now flesh had only a danger side to it, awe without the wonder, fear without the power. The notion that divinity could love flesh and even take it on was practically anathema. No one could love flesh. It stank, as the influential French cardinal Bossuet put it in a sermon in Paris in the seventeenth century. "Cursed be the earth, cursed be the earth, a thousand times cursed by the earth from which rises continually that dark fog and those black vapors which ascend from these dark passions and hide heaven and its light from us and draw down the lightning and rays of divine justice against the corruption of the human race."[6]

When Galileo, in his quest for more truth about the universe, reduced knowledge to mathematics, he severely restricted our awareness of fleshiness and our love of it. The philosopher Whitehead says that now the cosmos has become "a dull affair, soundless, scentless, colourless; merely the hurrying of material, endlessly, meaninglessly."[7] In a word, fleshless. Academia since Galileo has done very little to return flesh to education. The result is that we have separated education from learning and much of academia is at war with itself and produces graduates who make war on the planet.

THE SUSPICION OF FLESH: A POLITICO-ECONOMIC EXPLANATION

Diane Ackerman holds out for a political-economic explanation of why Christians were initially suspicious of flesh. Dissipation is a class issue: some buy it, and others sell it. Christianity's uneasiness with the flesh, she believes, came in part from the abusive class warfare that was being waged by the Roman Empire when Christianity was young. In Roman debaucheries handicapped and deformed people were made to perform sexually, while gladiators fought at dinner tables for the emperor Caligula, splashing the food with their blood and sweat. Slaves were often sadistically treated. Christians, many of whom were of the slave class, preferred to emphasize self-denial, restraint, discipline, and the poor inheriting the earth. Pleasure, as the early Christians observed it, was a kind of hell. Jerome wrote, "Let your companions be women pale and thin with fasting." In this way, says Ackerman, "the denial of the senses became part of a Christian creed of salvation."[8]

Ackerman does a great service by telling us this story. Persons and groups fighting for their very survival often take on asceticism because they need to have the vigilance of the warrior and because they critique the prevailing value system of their opponents. The lower classes do not have the luxury to spend time or money on extravagances, indulgences, frills, or amenities. Their agenda is *survival*. A parallel story could be told about the Jansenists in seventeenth-century France. They were also politically critical of the ruling classes but were spiritually very ascetic. Unfortunately, as has happened often in Western history, when their worldview was exported to other places and generations, their critical policies were omitted but not their antiflesh attitudes. Indeed, subsequent ruling classes employed their negative attitudes about the body against the poor. Today many of the powerful decision-makers in the world are Westerners. How much of the subjugation of the poor in the Southern Hemisphere at the hands of the World Bank and other Western institutions is a continuation of the denigration of the flesh?

One reason this pattern of flesh-oppression seems to persist in the West is that the first Christian theologian left very equivocal language around the word *flesh*.

PAUL AND THE THEOLOGICAL AMBIGUITY AROUND *FLESH*

The very first published Christian theologian, Paul, whose letters constitute the oldest of the Christian Scriptures, set a very dangerous precedent in his negative use of the term *flesh*. Paul stood at a four-directional cultural crossroads, which made his life and thinking very complex. He was Greek-educated and wrote in Greek; he was a Roman citizen when the Roman Empire ruled the Western world; he was a Jew and indeed a very zealous Jew; and then he was also a follower of Christ (though he never met Jesus or read the gospels, which were written after his death).[9]

What does *basar* (the Hebrew word for "flesh") mean? It "stands for the whole life-substance of men or beasts as organized in corporeal form."[10] In Hebrew any body part can be used to represent the whole. While the Greeks pitted body against soul, the Jews did not. "Man does not *have* a body, he *is* a body. He is flesh-animated-by-soul, the whole conceived as a psycho-physical unity: 'The body is the soul in its outward form.'"[11] At death the soul does not survive the person as an immortal entity. It is emptied or poured out at death. The dead are not souls but shadows, and death is not extinction but "the weakest form of life."[12] While matter was a principle of individuation for the Greeks, for the Hebrew the "personality [was] essentially social" and flesh did not separate creatures from one another. Instead it united them. It united human to beast in a wonderful communion. "The flesh-body was not what partitioned a man off from his neighbour; it was rather what bound him in the bundle of life with all men and nature, so that he could never make his unique answer to God as an isolated individual, apart from his relation to his neighbour."[13]

What flesh (or *sarx* in Greek) meant to Paul is the flesh-substance common to humans and animals: "All flesh is not the same flesh: but there is one flesh of men, and another flesh of beasts, and another flesh of birds, and another of fishes" (1 Corinthians 15:39). For humans, flesh means "the whole body, or, better, the whole person, considered from the point of view of his external, physical existence."[14] Flesh means the person. Flesh also represents man in his weakness and mortality. God is the "God of all flesh" (Jeremiah 32:27), yet God is Spirit and not flesh.

Paul contrasted living *according to the flesh* and living *according to the spirit*. But he did not pit matter against spirit when he did so. That would have been a Greek way of seeing things. After all, when he listed fifteen "works of the flesh," only five had anything to do with sensuality (Galatians 5:19–21). He spoke, for example, of jealousy and strife:

> It is important to understand exactly what this living "after the flesh" means and why the "carnal" can thus stand for what is sinful (e.g., Rom. 7.14). It cannot be overemphasized that this is not because, as in Greek thinking, matter or the material part of man is inherently and irremediably evil, in contrast with the soul or spirit.

When Paul says that "the flesh lusteth against the Spirit, and the Spirit against the flesh" (Gal. 5.17), he is not referring to the conflict familiar to Greek ethics, between man's reason and his passions.[15]

According to Ricoeur (and Robinson), flesh for Paul was decidedly *not* about bodiliness or sexuality. Rather, "the flesh is myself alienated from itself, opposed to itself and projected outward. Now if I do that which I will not, it is no more I that do it, but sin that dwelleth in me. . . . It is, then, I myself who by reason serve a law of God and by the flesh a law of sin" (Romans 7:20, 25).[16]

"Flesh" is humans living *in* the world, but sinful flesh is living *for* the world. A person of the world allows his whole self to be governed by the world, to be taken over by the powers of "the belly" or "lust" or "indulgence" or "covetousness," in a kind of idolatry (Co. 3:5)—a making of God out of ordinary things.[17] The flesh in its negative sense is about human self-sufficiency.

Paul also honors the body: "Your body is a temple of the Holy Ghost. . . . Glorify God therefore in your body" (1 Corinthians 6:18). The body ties us to each other and binds us to the rest of creation.[18] As *body* we inherit the kingdom of God and we experience resurrection (1 Corinthians 15:50). The body stands for the human personality.

Paul's concept of the body formed the keystone to his theology, bringing together its principal themes:

> It is from the body of sin and death that we are delivered; it is through the body of Christ on the cross that we are saved; it is into His body the Church that we are incorporated; it is by His body in the Eucharist that this Community is sustained; it is in our body that its new life has to be manifested; it is to a resurrection of this body to the likeness of His glorious body that we are destined.[19]

Platonically tinged Christian philosophers have often ignored the complexity of Paul's thought around "flesh" and "body," and the result has been a toxic message—one that carries us far from the mainstream Hebraic tradition and that of the historical Jesus. Dominic Crossan believes that Paul's Hellenistically influenced attitude toward the flesh contradicts both the historical Jesus and the Gospel of John that revels in the fact that "the Word was made flesh." When Paul says that "flesh and blood" cannot enter the kingdom of God, a gulf in sensibility opens up between him and Jesus."[20] Furthermore, the earliest expressions of Christianity contradict Paul's attitude as well. "The traditional Judaism that begot both the historical Jesus and earliest pre-Pauline Christianity did not separate spirit from flesh or flesh from spirit. Neither, therefore, did it separate religion from politics, ethics from economics, or divinity from humanity."[21]

Rabbi Solomon Schimmel comments on how un-Jewish is Paul's ambiguity toward the flesh: "In the Hebrew Bible the enjoyment of physical pleasure is not considered sinful. . . . Life is not viewed as a continuous struggle between the flesh and some 'higher' part of us. This attitude of the Hebrew Bible towards the body contrasts sharply with Plato, Paul, and Augustine's negative view."[22] The rabbinical tradition teaches that we can control our impulses, but Paul "despaired of our ability to control the evil within us, and so he opted instead for reliance on God's grace through faith in Christ."[23]

PLATO AND CHRISTIAN THEOLOGIANS ON THE FLESH

With this attitude, Paul goes along with negative Platonic views of the body. Plato declared in the *Phaedo,* "It seems that so long as we are alive, we shall continue closest to knowledge if we avoid as much as we can all contact and association with the body, except when they are absolutely necessary; and instead of allowing ourselves to become infected with its nature, purify ourselves from it until God himself gives us deliverance."[24] To know truth, we must withdraw from the body, Plato proposed, and he praised "the man who pursues the truth by applying his pure and unadulterated thought to the pure and unadulterated object, cutting himself off as much as possible from his eyes and ears and virtually all the rest of his body, as an impediment which by its presence prevents the soul from attaining to truth and clear thinking."[25]

This "abstract" kind of knowing seems to have found a certain culmination in the "value-free" ideology of modern science as well. In the *Phaedo* the body is said to "trouble the soul and prevent it from attain-

ing truth" (66a). Ricoeur believes, as did Plato, that teaching that philosophy consists "in the death of the body, in order to 'behold things
themselves with the soul itself' (66d); the body appears to be pre-
eminently the locus of evil: 'our soil is mixed with an evil thing' (66b),
it is delivered up to the 'dementia of the body' (67a)."[26] In this context
Christianity identified the fall with a fall into our bodies and regretted
its bodiliness. Christianity

> will, so to speak, breathe the air of the dualistic myth. In its ascetic
> form as well as in its mystical form, Platonizing Christianity adopts
> the opposition between contemplation and concupiscence, which,
> in turn, introduces the opposition between the spiritual soul
> and the moral and raving body; the old fear of defilement and
> the old fear of the body and sexuality are taken over by the new
> wisdom. . . . It might be said that Christianity will tend towards the
> identification of evil and the body (without, it is true, ever reach-
> ing that limit).[27]

Mix Plato's denigration of the body with an uncritical application
of Paul's notion of *flesh* as sin, and you have a negative cocktail that has
haunted Christianity for centuries. What theologian James Nelson calls
the "ambivalence" and inconsistency in Paul does not go away, as for
example in his interpretation of marriage as a concession to human
weakness. (Granted, he did think the world was coming to an end
soon.) In this regard, as Nelson confesses, "Paul was a Hellenist,"[28] as he
was when he accepted both slavery and the inequality of women. A few
centuries after Paul ambivalence disappeared altogether from Christian
theology—the body was for the most part negatively conceived.
Jerome actually said, "I praise marriage and wedlock but only because
they beget celibates."[29] Augustine was so negative toward sexuality that
for him, "for a couple to copulate for any purpose other than procreation was debauchery." Augustine's understanding of sexuality "was
almost exclusively concerned about [its] genital aspects."[30]

While the Hebrew love song in the Bible called the Song of Songs
celebrates our sexuality as a revelation of the Divine, Augustine linked
original sin with sexuality. Indeed, the Roman Catholic Church in particular still follows Augustine's prejudice against the body in its teach-

ing on birth control, for example, since Augustine taught that every sexual act must be legitimized by being capable of producing a baby.

Christian theologians like Origen projected the dualism upon the Song of Songs. In his commentary on that biblical book, Origen interjected Plato's distinction between sensual and spiritual love: "There is a love of the flesh which comes from Satan, and there is also another love, belonging to the spirit, which has its origin in God; and nobody can be possessed by the two loves. . . . if you have despised all bodily things . . . then you can acquire spiritual love."[31] Origen practiced what he preached and had himself castrated rather than trust his fleshy existence to stay God-focused.

REDEEMING *FLESH*

It is unfortunate and a source of profound pain in Western history that Paul chose to use the word *flesh* to denote his acedia, his spiritual pain at being part of a deadening law of consciousness and being outside the spirit of a life-oriented consciousness. His choice encouraged other pessimistic theologians to blame their burdens on the body and the part of our existence that we happily share with other creatures. It has contributed surely to the denigration of the earth's flesh and the flesh of other creatures with whom we share this holy planet, including women and slaves.

This denigration constitutes a scandal and a shame. It diverts us from the truth and from the path of God's holy creation set up in the first chapter of Genesis. Our one-sided language needs cleansing and renewal. We need to extricate our sin-language from this misbegotten terminology—terminology that far too few Western theologians have resisted strongly enough. Such a purification of the term *flesh* can happen only in a new context: in the context of creation or cosmology, the context of the holiness of all flesh.

This brief look at early Christian theologians and their Hellenistically influenced philosophy shows how important it is to *redeem the word flesh*. As we now know from studying his words, the historical Jesus, unlike Paul and other Christian theologians, had no animosity for the flesh. An awareness of the historical Jesus and how he differs from

Paul can also assist our extrication from Paul's ambiguous language and teaching about flesh. We shall consider Jesus' attitude toward flesh in Chapter 6. Here we shall attempt to redeem the word *flesh* by employing the new cosmology.

A year ago I asked a young artist what came to his mind when he heard the word *flesh*. His answer was "Earth." That earth and flesh are the same thing is an ancient notion. At least one twentieth-century philosopher, Maurice Merleau-Ponty, tried to regain that sense when he wrote about "the collective 'Flesh,' which signifies both *our* flesh and 'the flesh of the world.' By 'the Flesh' Merleau-Ponty means to indicate an elemental power that has had no name in the entire history of Western philosophy."[32]

Contemporary philosopher David Abram, in *The Spell of the Sensuous,* tries to dispel the modern philosophical bias against sense-knowledge that is a carryover of the Platonic prejudice. Abram explains our relationships with other creatures in the following manner:

> Each of us, in relation to the other, is both subject and object, sensible and sentient. . . . I am not just a sentient subject but also a sensible object, even an *edible* object, in the eyes (and nose) of the other. . . . The perceiver and the perceived are interdependent and in some sense even reversible aspects of a common animate element, or Flesh, that is *at once both sensible and sensitive.*[33]

A creation story like the new creation story, which demonstrates that all beings in the universe derive from the same origin, also demonstrates how connected we are to one another: and it is precisely our flesh that constitutes this holy connection.

> We are organs of this world, flesh of its flesh, and . . . the world is perceiving itself through us. . . . If we dwell in this forest for many months or years, . . . we may come to feel that we are a part of this forest, consanguineous with it, and that our experience of the forest is nothing other than the forest experiencing itself. Such are the exchanges and metamorphoses that arise from the simple fact that our sentient bodies are entirely continuous with the vast body of the land, that "the presence of the world is precisely the presence of its flesh to my flesh."[34]

Indigenous people who were once one with the land, the animals, and vegetative life know these things. They were aware of the sacredness of this one-ing. Abram calls on us today to "return to our sense" and to rediscover that we are part of countless other bodies, from streams to slopes to birds to soil. Years ago I was living on a farm in southern France, in the mountains of the Basque country, a sheep-herding region, while writing my doctoral thesis. I used to walk the mountains when I took breaks and invariably I felt a connection from my feet to my head with the land on which I walked. I felt I was walking on women's breasts. I was. It was Gaia, our mother. Abram says the world has now been revealed as a "profoundly *carnal* field."[35]

The Dutch artist Willem de Kooning first painted human flesh in the form of large and fleshy women; later he painted earth landscapes; and still later he combined the two, recognizing no difference between them. Flesh is flesh. Earth is flesh. All of us creatures on and in the earth, with the earth in us, are flesh. In many ways his contributions to art speak to the twentieth century's gradual rediscovery of the relationship of our flesh to the rest of flesh in nature—and to its glory. "Flesh is the reason why oil painting was invented," de Kooning said.[36] It made it possible to depict the luminosity of the skin. He used to eat oil paints, and his work progressed from women pictures and human lust to a deep pansexuality. It has been said that there was a "great democracy of flesh in his work." He committed himself to painting flesh—and perhaps to redeeming the experience of flesh for the rest of us. Georgia O'Keeffe is another twentieth-century artist who displayed the blessing that flesh is. Her special interests were in rendering the flesh of dried bones and flowers, leaves, fruit, barns, and landscape.

Dancer Gabrielle Roth, in her recent book called *Sweat Your Prayers,* tells of growing up Catholic with strict nuns who taught her she had a choice of being a virgin or going to hell. This is from a chapter called "God, Sex and My Body":

> I hated my hunger, hated my body for betraying me, and in this dumb moment I swore I would never let my appetite get the best of me. . . . By thirteen I was a wreck. My body was blossoming; every day some new part of me turned on that had to be turned off. My breasts moved from triple a to double a overnight. I was scared to death of the woman emerging from deep within my bones, her

irrational desires and insatiable appetites. . . . I prayed for the strength to withstand temptations of the flesh, to become pure spirit. I prayed to God to take my breasts back and turn my period off. I wanted to repress all that messy, uncontrollable feminine stuff; to be a good girl.[37]

But Roth never fully accepted the antiflesh message of her church. "I yearned to be a lover too, body and soul, and I didn't understand why, if God made my body and my body wanted sex, that could be wrong. Someone had taken sex out of God and God out of my body. I wanted to put myself back together again."[38] It was dancing that saved her from Christianity's antiflesh message: "Rock n' roll became my savior." She found that dance and sweating are as good a way to pray as any other.

To sweat is to pray, to make an offering of your innermost self. Sweat is holy water, prayer beads, pearls of liquid that release your past, anointing all your parts in a baptism by fire. Sweat burns karma, purifying body and soul. Sweat is an ancient and universal form of self healing, whether done in the gym, the sauna, or the sweatlodge. I do it on the dance floor. The more you dance, the more you sweat. The more you sweat, the more you pray. The more you pray, the closer you come to ecstasy.[39]

Recently I went to the countryside and saw two very young fawns and their mother in the backyard next door eating. They pranced about, chasing birds and ducks into the water as puppies would. They wandered into my yard and scampered like bunnies as they practiced their jumping skills. Mother deer stayed where she was eating intently but also watched them closely as they scampered into a third yard to play. She was always on the lookout, her ears straight and tall. The fawns returned regularly and sucked at her titties. It was a holy scene. A holy family. I was privileged to behold it. Is this what makes it holy? Its preciousness. I had never seen fawns at play before, frolicking like puppies, only with more elegance and less foolishness. It was a scene of *holy flesh*. Of the blessing that life is and flesh is. The flesh of deerdom. How beautiful, how graceful, how sacred. How elegant. How holy. What a blessing.

Some people will say, "But deer multiply too fast and eat our straw-berries and are a nuisance." To this I say, humans multiply faster and eat far more than strawberries and leave far more garbage behind! We can accommodate deer habits, and they ours, I suspect.

What is flesh? The clouds are flesh. The mountains clinging to this gray morning are flesh. The green trees nodding slowly in the light breeze are flesh. The sun that is not yet visible is flesh. The waters of the still lake are flesh. The birds singing their morning cantatas are flesh, as are the ducks quacking loudly about whatever it is they have on their minds. The pebbles are flesh, and the ancient rocks. All is flesh. All fits. All connects. All is blessing.

And we too—with our eyes, ears, skin, fur, hearts, lungs, spleen, gallbladder, liver, genitals, breasts, feet, hands, necks, heads, hair, limbs, thighs—we are flesh too. Blessed flesh.

What is *not* flesh? That might prove a simpler question to answer. Angels. The deceased. I hesitate to say ideas or ideals, because the for-mer begin with the senses and lead to them and the latter raise goose bumps on our skin and in our hearts.

Finding our common ground in the flesh with other flesh creatures is at the heart of the pleasure that community grants us. After reading *A Natural History of the Senses* and *Creation and the Persistence of Evil* one day, I relaxed in the cool breeze of sunset on the back porch and a fam-ily of deer—two fawns, an adolescent and two parents—filed by. A kayaker also paddled by with sun at his back. The lake was quiet and still. The pleasure I found in such sights and sounds and relations revealed to me that community is possible—provided we respect one another's differences. Harmony happens—as does grace. They are already here. There is more good than evil in the world—though not by much. Blessing exists.

THE PRECIOUSNESS OF FLESH

One thing about flesh is its transitoriness. All flesh dies. Like the grass, as the Scriptures say. This means all flesh is only with us for a while—one more reason not to ignore it or take it for granted or fail to take delight in it. Flesh is for joy and wonder and delight. This is Sabbath—

to take note of flesh in all its abundance and uniqueness and softness and firmness and color and sound and sell and taste. To enjoy it—which is not the same as exploiting it or controlling it or abusing it or making a pleasure-object of it. The object is to enjoy it. To pay attention.

Recently I received news that a young nephew of a coworker of mine was accidentally killed on his family farm. My journal entry follows:

Flesh. How precious it is, how fragile and precarious. I have just received a phone call from a close faculty member telling me how her four-year-old nephew was killed in a tragic accident on the family ranch. Suddenly gone, a radiant boy. His father held him in his arms as he died, having been run over by the family truck. His mother is eight months pregnant. What a lesson in the brevity of life, the preciousness of it. No sin is involved. Not on humans' part, at least.

> *The universe, has it sinned?*
> *The earth, has it sinned?*
> *God, has she / he sinned?*

Who knows. The tears flow. Flesh is precious. Don't ever again tolerate anyone putting it down.

Flesh. The flesh of a child. A living, loving, warm, cuddly, laughing, needy child. Now cold, no longer flesh, no longer living. The blessing that flesh is. That children are. Sharing our gratitude. Not forgetting to touch the child and love the child every day. And the child's maker. All its makers and co-creators—parents and grandparents, ancestors all, sky and food chain, soil and rain, sun and siblings— thank them all—dance his praises—while flesh lives among us.

And the word was made flesh and dwelt among us and we saw God's glory and grace in this flesh. Amen.

Death is real and will not be trivialized. Death's reality is what makes flesh so real as well—real, though short-lived.

Flesh is so vulnerable. Humanity has to recover the sacredness and blessing that flesh is before it is too late. The ecological crisis is a *flesh crisis.* It is about our home *(eikos* in Greek) being invaded, being toxic and unhealthy for our flesh. Consider the air, for example. In South-

Central Los Angeles children have one-third less lung capacity than children in the rest of the United States. What are the implications for their physical and mental health, which is interdependent with the health of the brain? I recently heard from a Thai citizen that Thailand has a law that schoolchildren must take a bus to school because of the awful pollution in the air. Seemingly children are better off in a bus than walking to school. When this man was a child, he could walk to school in twenty minutes—but instead he was forced to take a bus, which took three and a half hours for the same trip! He had to get up at five A.M. to go to school. It is a story about flesh. Flesh is in grave danger in our present world. That is what is at stake in the eco-crisis, and in the crisis of unemployment in inner cities and the so-called Third World, and in the despair of young people.

THE CARNAL IN INCARNATION

I wonder how many Christians have been invited to meditate on the fact that the word *carnal* is at the heart of their primary doctrine of *Incarnation*. Our culture, having been poisoned by negative attitudes toward flesh, is ill at ease with the notion. Indeed, a religious faith that claims to believe that "the word was made flesh" actually denigrates flesh and has turned "flesh" over to the pornographic industries rather than sanctifying it and including it in our spiritual practice. It is time for this ambivalence toward flesh to cease. Either flesh is sacred or it is not. Either the divine is present, *incarnated* (which literally means "made flesh"), or it is not. If it is, it is time that worship and education became enfleshed, incarnated, in order to provide a proper home *(eikos)* for the Divine, which is clearly biased in favor of flesh, having, after all, made it. Our very language is biased against the flesh: *Webster's Dictionary* says that the antonym or opposite of *carnal* is *spiritual* or *intellectual*. Here we are, two thousand years after the Incarnation of Jesus, and our language still doesn't get it: that flesh and spirit are one.

It is this making of flesh, the coming-to-be of flesh, the history and creation of flesh, that will redeem it and render it sacred and a blessing in our awareness once again. What can be more ecstatically positive about flesh than Jesus' words: "The Kingdom/Queendom of God is among you"? That the *basileia* or kingdom we know of as creation is also the dwelling place of God? That the fleshy world is the Kingdom of God? Why don't Christians follow Jesus' teachings more, and let go of Paul's and Augustine's negativity toward the flesh? Only cosmology, only a creation story, will reset the context by which flesh can once again be experienced as holy. And that time is upon us.

The beautiful naming of marital love in Genesis, the promise that "the two shall be one flesh," is a reminder of the blessing-oriented understanding of flesh that our Jewish ancestors celebrated. Anyone in a long and successful marriage knows that that struggle is part of the process of marital commitment. "Becoming one flesh" is a lifetime journey—a journey together and at the same time a journey singularly, insofar as a certain amount of solitude and self-knowing must accompany any prolonged friendship, any true relationship. The promise is that we become "one flesh" in ways other than sexual ways. Indeed, sexual love is a sign, a symbol, indeed a sacrament for a union of living beings. To promise that lovers can be "one flesh" is much more than a sexual promise. It is a promise of heart, mind, *and* body. And from that union more sacred flesh enters history.

COSMOLOGY REDEEMING FLESH

Cosmology gives us a *context* again for appreciating flesh. The *textual* revolution that marked the modern era, which began with the invention of the printing press in the fifteenth century, has not been kind to flesh. Text is not fleshy, but context is. Flesh's brilliance is not easily illuminated on the printed page. Flesh is too colorful for that, too tactile, too full of breath, too soft and yielding to the touch. During the modern era flesh became denigrated in whole new ways—its glory is not of a mathematical and quantitative kind. Flesh is qualitative. Body counts soared during the modern era. Flesh became expendable: human flesh in human wars but also animal flesh and bird flesh and whale flesh and fish flesh and soil flesh and forest flesh.

As the modern era's preoccupation with text yields to a postmodern concern for context, perhaps flesh can score a comeback. Perhaps humans can learn to love their flesh anew—and with it the flesh of others on whom we are so dependent and interdependent.

Jesus said: "Love others as you love yourself"—that is, love the flesh of others as you love your own flesh. Flesh breathes. One of our creation stories in the Book of Genesis describes the human's coming-to-be as Adam's nostrils filling with the divine breath. To breathe is to breathe God's breath—*ruah,* or spirit. Breathing is the first act we commit on entering the world, and it is our last act on parting from it. Hildegard of Bingen defined prayer as nothing more than breathing in and breathing out the one breath or *ruah* or spirit of God. There is no dualism between flesh and spirit. Spirit breathes through flesh, and flesh receives its existence from spirit. We call all this breathing *life,* and the mystic Thomas Aquinas said, "God is life, per se life."

The medieval Jewish mystical work called *Zohar* teaches that the union between God and humanity occurs through the medium of the breath. Indeed, David Abram suggests that the name YHWH is an exercise in breathing in *(yah)* and out *(weh)* and that the Greek alphabet, in which the New Testament is written, destroyed this link between breath and divinity. The Greeks took the breath out of psyche, rendering it "not just invisible but utterly intangible. The Platonic *psyche* was not at all a part of the sensuous world," says Abram, "but was rather of another, utterly non-sensuous dimension. . . . a thoroughly abstract phenomenon now enclosed within the physical body as in a prison."[40] As Christian missionaries encircled the globe, they took the Greek-based alphabet with them and denuded native peoples of their link to the breathing of other creatures and their sense that the shared breath was holy: "Wherever the alphabet advanced, it proceeded by dispelling the air of ghosts and invisible influences—by stripping the air of its anima, its psychic depth."[41] The animistic world of nature was left without a voice. Spirit and nature were separated. Flesh was no longer holy. The notion that "the world around us is a continual, ongoing utterance" was lost.[42] Meister Eckhart also saw that "every creature is a word of God and a book about God,"[43] but that kind of creaturely book has been displaced by the modern textbook.

Abram indicates by the title of his book, *The Spell of the Sensuous,* that a magic and a kind of spell surrounds our senses.[44] Yet contemporary cosmology is opening the doors of our perception onto a universe more vast, more dynamic, more intelligent, more ancient, more organic, more colorful, more in process than ever we have dreamed of. Yesterday the Pathfinder landed on Mars, and today we are receiving wonder-filled pictures of the *flesh of Mars* in color in our living rooms. Does this not signify an expansion of flesh in the human consciousness? A new language is opening up. In deconstructing and reconstructing our language, we may be able to rid ourselves of some human arrogance. Flesh is not restricted to the human.

THE SACREDNESS OF FLESH

Instead of the "fear of flesh" that guilt and patriarchal regrets instill in us, a new cosmology can teach us the *awe of flesh* and with that awe the *sacredness of flesh*. Awe is what Thomas Aquinas called "chaste fear"—a fear that leads to reverence and gratitude, rather than a servile fear that renders us afraid and masochistic in the presence of bullies. A pleasure is built into what is awesome. Pleasures contain beauty and beauty is goodness. The needs of the flesh are pleasurable and good. We eat to stay alive and preserve our health but also because food is good and delicious.

Why do we make love? Out of duty? I hope not. So that the world will have more babies? It hardly seems to need more at this time in history. We make love because it is good—a built-in attraction. Why do we do ritual? Is it to please God? Thomas Aquinas said that God does not need worship but we do. We do ritual because it is delightful to us at a deep level. It satisfies our deep need for community and celebration and healing. Why join the environmental revolution? Out of duty or because it is good, natural? It fits our appetite to fight for what we love, to defend beauty against greed and rape and pillage, to pass something of beauty on to future generations. "The zeal of your house has eaten me up," say the Scriptures. Because we are eaten up by beauty, we defend it when it is in peril.

Our new creation story teaches us that all flesh has a 15-billion-year history. Only if we know that history can flesh become a *redemptive force*. When we know it, we become *grateful* and *reverent* toward our bodies, food, flowers, forests, soil, other animals and birds and fishes, and other human beings. Gratitude and reverence heal. They redeem. They cure us of diseases of soul and mind and heart and body.

Flesh redeems because it awakens awe and wonder and delight. Awe is redemptive, returning us to our origins—every baby is easily awestruck. This is the positive side to vulnerability—to be struck by awe, spellbound. Mystics promise that we can return to the state of vulnerability and awe, to the "unborn self,"[45] as Meister Eckhart said. And we can be free there. We can start over there.

This "return" is redemptive. It heals us of sin—our own, our culture's, our enemies' sins against us. Salvation is a return.

CHAPTER 2

UNIVERSE FLESH

When Pathfinder landed on Mars and sent back pictures, one of the headlines was "Mars: Beauty and Mystery," and the story proceeded as follows:

> The video images showed a rock-strewn floodplain, local hills, a distant crater, and a dark, mysterious object resembling a couch.
>
> The crystal-clear pictures looked like a tourist's snapshot from the Southwestern United States, with one key difference: Everything was bathed in a reddish-orange hue—even the salmon-colored sky, tinted by reddish, wind-blown dust.[1]

We are beginning to reach out, to touch the flesh of other planets, the flesh that the universe is. This is part of our creation story today—that we all participate in the same flesh, all derive from the same origin, and that all flesh is connected. Now technology allows us to transmit live photos in color from the planet Mars into our living rooms, and from the edges of the universe via the Hubble telescope, cosmic flesh is coming ever closer to our own. Flesh meets flesh. Our souls are being stretched by these encounters, for as Paul Ricoeur warns us, "to manifest the 'sacred' *on* the 'cosmos' and to manifest it *in* the 'psyche' are the same thing."[2] And as Aquinas put it, every human is *"capax universi,"* capable of the universe. We yearn for the universe—for proof that our lives are not trivial and not meaningless. The unique stretching that we are undergoing today as a species is a powerful thing: It is a time for soul enlargement. Everything we consider in this chapter and will cover in the next could be taken as an exegesis of one line in John's Gospel: "And the word was made flesh and dwelt among us."

When you look at a star, you may be looking at a being that died a long time ago. We are seeing the light it beamed before it died. To look into space is to look into time. This is new! Early in this century we thought—even Einstein thought, until Hubble—that the universe was static. All flesh was essentially static. But flesh is old, evolving, full of the scents of time and of space. Flesh has a long story to tell. Every flower contains that story, every body, every peach, every blade of grass, every face.

THE AWE OF COSMIC FLESH

Instead of fear of flesh and flight from flesh and dogmas against flesh, it is time for the awe of flesh. This is about rediscovering reverence, respect, awe, and wonder—and therefore, the Sacred. Paul Ricoeur cites the Jewish teaching that fear is the beginning of wisdom, but in typical anthropocentric Protestant consciousness, he confuses the fear of awe (which is holy) with the fear of dread. They aren't the same thing! *The new cosmology gives a whole new meaning to flesh*—and a whole new sense of wonder and miracle. Celtic bard Walt Whitman caught that sense in the last century, when he wrote a poem called "Miracles:"

Why, who makes much of a miracle?
As to me I know of nothing else but miracles,
Whether I walk the streets of Manhattan,
Or dart my sight over the roofs of houses toward the sky,
Or wade with naked feet along the beach just in the edge of
    the water,
Or stand under trees in the woods,
Or talk by day with any one I love, or sleep in the bed at
    night with any one I love,
Or sit at table at dinner with the rest,

Or look at strangers opposite me riding in the car,
Or watch honey-bees busy around the hive of a summer
forenoon,
Or animals feeding in the fields,
Or birds, or the wonderfulness of insects in the air,
Or the wonderfulness of the sundown, or of stars shining so
quiet and bright,
Or the exquisite delicate thin curve of the new moon in
spring;
These with the rest, one and all, are to me miracles,
The whole referring, yet each distinct and in its place.
To me every hour of the light and dark is a miracle,
Every cubic inch of space is a miracle,
Every square yard of the surface of the earth is spread with
the same,
Every foot of the interior swarms with the same.

To me the sea is a continual miracle,
The fishes that swim—the rocks—the motion of the
waves—the ships with men in them,
What stranger miracles are there?[3]

Whitman's worldview of the *wonder* of our cosmos has been confirmed in the twentieth century by science but long before that was available to all who connected to nature with their hearts and not just their heads. In the modern era, so beholden to interventionist and redemptive ideologies that interrupt the orderliness of a machine, miracles were treated as events that interrupt God's absolute laws. In today's cosmology, miracles are everyday. Every breath we breathe is a miracle. As John Muir put it:

I used to envy the father of our race, dwelling as he did in contact with the new-made field and plants of Eden; but I do so no more, because I have discovered that I also live in "creation's dawn." The morning stars still sing together, and the world not yet half made becomes more beautiful every day.[4]

What Muir's poetic soul intuited is scientifically accurate: The world is still being made, still being created. The ancient Aboriginal phrase *yorro yorro* means "continual creation." An Aboriginal elder explains its meaning: "Everything on earth is brand new and standing up. *Yorro* is . . . renewal of nature in all its forms."[5] All is brand new and standing up; all is in the act of being created. That is ancient wisdom, and it is today's science. Speaking from the African-American spiritual experience, Dr. Howard Thurman also speaks from the point of view of cosmology when he writes in his classic *The Search for Common Ground:*

> The most natural question that comes to mind therefore, whenever men reflect or try to rationalize their experiences of life is: How did life get started? What was the beginning of it all? . . . It is natural that man should concern himself with beginnings. This is a part of the curiosity of the mind. Without it there would be no exploration of the world and there would be no growth. . . . Contemplation concerning origins is a part of the curiosity of the race. . . . We want to know how the world began, where we came from, and what the meaning of life, and Life, is.[6]

Thurman's own exegesis of Adam's fall in the Genesis story concludes that he fell from "his sense of community with the rest of creation."[7] The Hopi people, he feels, never underwent that fall. But both they and the biblical community seek a return to a climate of community such as we once experienced. When I worked in the Philippines a year ago, I met a Catholic sister who had worked among the rainforest dwellers there. She asked them, "What is the single biggest mistake we Westerners have made working with you indigenous people?" They thought the question was a good one, and they went off to discuss it as a tribe for several days. Upon returning, they had a consensus. "You Westerners, you put God in a little white house. And the rest of creation you treat however you want." Locking God up in a little white house; de-Divinizing creation; having no cosmology—in their eyes, that is our greatest mistake.

When we do this, our own souls shrink. Madge Midley in her book *Beast and Man* puts it this way: "We need a vast world, and it must be a world that does not need us; a world constantly capable of surprising us, a world we did not program, since only such a world is the proper object of wonder."[8] Our wonder depends on a vast world that we do not control, one that can still surprise us. Awe requires cosmology. To return to awe is to return to praise, and praise, as Rabbi Heschel points out, "precedes faith." None of our faith traditions—no matter how many people we have killed or sent to hell in this life or the next in its name—is anything without praise. Don't tell me what you believe or what your dogmas are. Tell me first *what you praise and how you praise.* That is the implication of Heschel's teaching, and it could go a long way in eradicating our tired mind-sets and in resuscitating our tired souls.

When the Chinese Scriptures, the *Tao Te Ching,* say, "Just realize where you come from, this is the essence of wisdom," they are also invoking cosmology. Cosmology tells us where we come from, what our origin is, and therefore perhaps where we choose to go. This choice constitutes our morality, our shared ethics. There is no shared ethic without a shared creation story. When people lack a cosmology, they turn to lawyers for ethics. They turn to books for ethics or to religious conscriptions. Eco-psychologist Theodore Roszak comments on the breakthrough inherent in the new cosmology when he writes that "in the course of the last generation, we have passed into a postmodern cosmos as significantly different from the universe of Copernicus, Kepler and Newton (or even Einstein, Hubble, and Shapley) as theirs was from the cosmos of Ptolemy."[9] The discoveries of background radiation, the quasar, the Big Bang, and black holes "rapidly coalesced with quantum mechanics and Einstein's relativity to produce a radically new world picture. We now know that HISTORY is a characteristic of everything, not only living things."[10] The universe we know is not eternal after all. Nor are its "laws," as scientist Rupert Sheldrake points out, eternal. Is all history flesh? Is all flesh historical? It would seem so.

Playwright and president of the Czech Republic Vaclav Havel recognizes the new cosmology as the sign of hope for our species.

> We are not at all just an accidental anomaly, the microscopic caprice of a tiny particle whirling in the endless depths of the universe. Instead, we are mysteriously connected to the universe, we are mirrored in it, just as the entire evolution of the universe is mirrored in us. . . . The only real hope of people today is probably a renewal of our certainty that we are rooted in the Earth and, at the same time, the cosmos. This awareness endows us with the capacity for self-transcendence.[11]

Self-transcendence can happen when a sense of the cosmic connection returns. This cosmic connection is the cosmic flesh that we share. This flesh, in the context of a cosmology, will itself prove to be *redemptive*. Yes, flesh redeems. Flesh itself dispenses grace and healing, liberation and forgiveness. Spirit is at home in flesh and loves to dwell therein. Spirit makes her home there and sets up a tent there.

WONDERS OF THE FLESH OF THE UNIVERSE: A POSTMODERN LITANY

There is a cascade of awe-filled evidence that flesh is a blessing. This is true of the flesh of the universe, the flesh of our planet with its many creatures and systems, and the flesh of our bodies. Here we will explore the blessings of the flesh that the universe is. The universe is God's flesh, says the poet Rainer Maria Rilke:

all this universe, to the furthest stars
and beyond them, is your flesh, your fruit.[12]

- Matter is frozen light (David Bohm).
- An atom is a vast region of empty space in which incredible tiny particles called electrons orbit around a nucleus. Blow an atom up to be the size of the dome of St. Peter's Basilica in Rome, and the nucleus would be the size of a grain of salt.[13]
- Light and matter are ultimately interchangeable. "There is no ultimate physical substance to matter."[14]
- "Matter is nothing but gravitationally trapped light."[15]
- The afterglow of light from the original fireball of the universe is so significant that "for every one atom of ordinary matter in the Universe there exist 1 billion light particles."[16]
- While most of the energy of the universe resides in matter, almost all particles in the universe are those of light.[17]
- For every particle of matter, there are 1 billion particles of light.[18]
- "Matter is just a minor pollutant in a Universe made of light" (Ilya Prigogine).
- At the origin of the universe, all the light of the universe was compressed in a volume smaller than the point of a needle.[19]

- Sixty percent of the matter of our bodies is hydrogen atoms, and all of them were once constituents of the Big Bang.[20]
- All the other chemical elements of our bodies (40 percent of the atoms of our bodies) were forged in the interiors of stars. They are "recycled star dust."[21]
- Light is a vital ingredient in all atoms and in molecules and life-forms (including human ones) that are made up of atoms.[22]
- The human body stores immense amounts of light: The 100 trillion atoms in each of our 100 trillion cells together store at least 10^{28} photons. This is enough light to illuminate a baseball field for three hours with 1 million watts of floodlights.[23]
- Hydrogen atoms are so prevalent in the universe that there are approximately 10,000 of them for every carbon, nitrogen, and oxygen atom in the universe, and there are 100,000 hydrogen atoms for every magnesium, calcium, and iron atom. Yet carbon, nitrogen, oxygen, magnesium, calcium, and iron make up the stuff of living creatures. Thus we must say that "the stuff of life itself is a second-order minor constitution of the Universe."[24]
- All nine planets began with the same elements, spun by the same star and burned with the same energy.[25]
- But on Mercury, Venus, Mars, and Pluto, all geological activity slowly came to a halt within a billion years.
- On Jupiter, Saturn, Uranus, and Neptune, things hardly evolved at all from what they were when the solar system began.
- Only Earth was the proper size so that a balance between gravity and electromagnetic energy happened, allowing a temperature range to develop where complex molecules could form.
- Amino acids formed on Earth and throughout the Milky Way galaxy. Yet "to get atoms in the universe to bounce together haphazardly to form a single molecule of an amino acid would require more time than has existed since the beginning, even a hundred times more than fifteen billion years."[26]
- The solar cloud that eventually birthed the sun was 5 million times the diameter of the sun.[27]
- The daily output of solar winds from the sun amounts to 20 billion tons of protons.
- A full moon is 9 times as bright as a half-moon.[28]

- The moon causes not only tides to rise twice a month but continents too. North America, for example, rises 6 inches during the new and full moons.[29]
- If the moon were only 50,000 miles closer to the Earth, tidal forces would flood coastal regions of the world under hundreds of feet of water.[30]
- The footsteps left on the moon by Apollo astronauts will remain visible for at least 10 million years.[31]
- The oldest rock on Earth is one brought back from the moon. It was dated at 4.6 billion years—1 billion years older than the first single-celled microorganism that lived on Earth.[32]
- On the average the menstrual cycle of women is exactly the same duration as the lunar month—29.5 days, and the human gestation period is exactly nine times the lunar month. More babies are birthed during full and new moons, when the gravitational influence is the strongest.[33]
- Every day 100 million meteors rain into the Earth's atmosphere, and most burn up and come to Earth as dust—4 million tons per year. Thus some of the dust we breathe or touch each day is ancient, as old as the solar system itself—4.6 billion years.[34]
- In orbit around the sun, we are spinning 64,800 miles an hour. The solar system itself is moving at 43,200 miles an hour along its course; and we spin at about 836 miles per hour around the Earth's axis.[35]
- The fastest that humans have traveled in space is 24,791 miles per hour, but comets travel at speeds of more than 1 million miles per hour.[36]
- If our sun were a basketball in New York City, the solar system would have a diameter of under 2 miles. But the next star would be a basketball 5,000 miles away in Honolulu, Hawaii.[37]
- The sun contains 99.86 percent of all the substance in the solar system. The Earth contains only 1/332,000 of the sun's mass. The sun is 1 million times larger than the Earth—one million Earths can fit inside the sun. The moon's entire orbit around the Earth can fit inside the sun.[38]
- Flying at 500 miles per hour, it would take 21 years to reach the sun from Earth, which is 93 million miles away.

- Ancients considered the sun eternal, but it was born about 5 billion years ago and will die in about 5 billion years.
- The sun is composed "of the same substances as the Earth and, in fact, the Universe as a whole." An intensely hot sphere of gas, 78 percent of the sun is hydrogen and 20 percent is helium.
- The temperature on the interior of the sun is about 29 million degrees Fahrenheit.
- The sun emits more energy in one second than humankind has consumed in the whole of its history. One second of the sun's energy is 13 million times the annual mean electricity consumption of the United States.[39]
- The Earth receives only 2 parts per billion of the sun's total energy output—but this is 10,000 times greater than the total energy presently consumed by the human race.
- 99.98 percent of all energy passing through the atmosphere originates in the sun's core. (The remainder is from starlight, cosmic rays, and tidal and geothermal energy.)[40]
- Wood and coal are stored-up solar energy; wind and ocean currents originate from the sun's radiation, as does our food.
- When coal burns, hibernating sunlight that was imprisoned for millions of years emerges.
- Solar neutrinos that stream out of the sun shoot through your body—100 million million of them every second.[41]
- Sunlight takes about 8 minutes to travel from the sun to Earth, but previously it took 20,000 years to emerge from the sun to travel into space.
- Photons (or sunlight) take 100,000 years to cross from one edge of the Milky Way galaxy to the other.
- The Milky Way is spiral, and in this kind of galaxy a kind of creativity happens that is absent from elliptical galaxies. Generation after generation of stars recycle the interstellar medium and build increasingly complex chemicals along the way.
- Venus is too hot for living things, and Mars is too cold for people. Earth is just right (most of the time).[42]
- Stars fill only 1 part in 100 million of the volume of space.
- Stars' lifetimes range from 1 million years for the largest supergiants to a possible 100 billion years for the smallest.[43]

- If stars were closer together than they are, invisible high-energy radiation would kill most life-forms living within 2 or 3 light-years.[44]
- The Milky Way is one of maybe 100 billion galaxies in the universe and one of 30 billion spiral galaxies.
- The Milky Way represents one trillionth of the universe—compare a small metal screw to the mass of a 100,000-ton ship.[45]
- Our galaxy was born from the pristine elements of the Big Bang, hydrogen and helium.
- If you fit our solar system into a coffee cup, our galaxy would be the size of North America. Our galaxy is at least 80,000 light-years in diameter, or 480 million billion miles.[46]
- Our sun and solar system lie about 30,000 light-years from the center of our galaxy. A car traveling at 100 miles per hour would take 201 billion years to drive to the center of our galaxy—which is about 20 times the age of our galaxy.[47]
- Every 18 days our galaxy gives birth to a new star.
- Every 11,350 years a habitable planet forms around one of these stars.
- Every half second a human birth occurs on Earth.
- A conservative guess is that there are 900,000 habitable planets in our galaxy (of a total of 100 billion planets).
- The energy of the Big Bang may have equaled the total energy of 10 million billion quasars, each of which equals 300 billion suns in light energy alone.[48]
- When the universe was younger than one trillionth of a second old, its radius was just over 3 feet.
- At the Big Bang the temperature was 100 billion degrees.
- One second after the explosion, the temperature had dropped to 10 billion degrees Celsius.
- Three minutes after the explosion it was 1 billion degrees.
- 700,000 years later it was 2,700 degrees Celsius (4,900 degrees Fahrenheit).
- Helium constitutes about 25 percent of the universe. With little or no helium, the universe would have no stars, no light, and no life.
- If helium were 30 percent of the universe instead of 25 percent, our sun would be dying now, and life would not have happened on

Earth. If the intense backround radiation had been less during the first second of the universe, this would have happened.[49]

· At the beginning of the universe, light was trapped and did not escape for hundreds of thousands of years.

· Several hundred thousands of years after the Big Bang, the universe cooled enough that electrons married nuclei and created little hydrogen and helium atoms. From these were born galaxies, stars, planets, and us.

· The universe at 4 minutes was as dense as iron; at 11 minutes, as dense as water; at 5 hours, as dense as air.

· After 1 second the radiation era began.

· Matter did not exist until 700,000 years after the Big Bang. At the beginning of the universe, only radiant energy that was 10 million times more dense than matter existed—no atoms, no atomic nuclei—only subatomic particles and antiparticles such as protons, neutrons, electrons, and neutrinos.

· At the 700,000-year mark, the radiation era ended and matter separated from radiation and hydrogen was created. In a few billion years, hydrogen and helium formed the first galaxies and stars.

· Hydrogen is the "blood of the universe."[50]

· When the universe was 9.6 million years old, it was expanding at 1.98 million miles a second—or 10 times faster than the speed of light. Thus space, not matter, was doing the expanding. A spaceship traveling this fast could get from Earth to Pluto in less than 25 minutes.[51]

· The oldest fossil in the universe was a fossil of radiation discovered in 1965. Coming from every direction of the universe, it was a remnant from 1 million years after the Big Bang cataclysm.[52]

WORDS MADE FLESH

If the universe is a machine, it is not flesh. It is not animate or alive or growing or sensual or tactile or edible or wonder-filled.

But if the universe is like an organism—a tiny zygote-like being that grows and expands and births realities anew—then the universe *is flesh*. And it is flesh that gets eaten, chewed up, and transformed. If stars die, are they not flesh? Eucharist. Divine food. A thank-you meal with each repast. "This is my body." All things are my body. My body is all things.

Recently I heard that NASA has consulted theologians to learn what the theological take would be should NASA discover intelligent life elsewhere in the universe. We know a lot more about flesh today than we did 1900 years ago when John recorded: "And the word was made flesh and dwelt among us." We also know a lot more about what *us* means. *Us* means all creatures in the universe—for we are all interconnected by gravity, by electromagnetic energy, by light, by energy. *Us* means hundreds of billions of galaxies, each with hundreds of billions of stars. *Us* means 15 billion years of birthing and coming to be and arrival time. And *flesh* is that which binds all visible beings together. The Gospel does not say: "The word became human flesh exclusively" but that "the word was made flesh." In our experience and that of those who encountered the Christ in the historical figure of Jesus, that was exceptional. But Jesus himself taught—as does the Christ in John's Gospel and elsewhere—that the word is made flesh in all of us.

Anthropocentrism is not necessary to understand the Gospel message. Indeed, given what we now know of our universe and "us" in it, anthropocentrism interferes with the Good News—the news that the universe is indeed filled with the spirit and the presence of God, the Source of it all. That Divine intimacy and care are integral to the workings and labors of the unfolding creation. That Divinity too is flesh and therefore edible and able to be consumed (as in "this is my body, this is the cup of my blood," and as in *"consummatum est,"* the last words attributed to Jesus as he died on the cross). The sun is edible after all and is flesh of our flesh, bone of our bones. And so is the Son—and all other sons and daughters of Divinity. All of *us*—as in "give *us* this day our daily bread." Bread includes planets and stars, galaxies and supernovas, atoms and neutrinos, sun and soil and rain and earthworms. All life is related and interdependent. This is our daily bread. It is holy. And we depend on it.

In offering this Litany of Wonders of the Flesh of the Universe, I have worked with scientists—but seldom *as scientists*. One young scientist whom I consulted about these blessings told me that he had been forbidden to ask such questions in his years as a student of science. Awe was not on the curriculum. James Lovelock, in *The Ages of Gaia,* challenges a scientific educational system that excludes awe when he writes about a kept scientific establishment:

> In fact, nearly all scientists are employed by some large organization, such as a governmental department, a university, or a multinational company. Only rarely are they free to express their science as a personal view. . . . They have traded freedom of thought for good working conditions, a steady income, tenure, and a pension. . . . In recent years the "purity" of science is ever more closely guarded by a self-imposed inquisition called the peer review. This well-meaning but narrow-minded nanny of an institution ensures that scientists work according to conventional wisdom and not as curiosity or inspiration moves them. Lacking freedom they are in danger of succumbing to a finicky gentility or of becoming, like medieval theologians, the creatures of dogma.[53]

Then Lovelock speaks from his own experience: "As a university scientist I would have found it nearly impossible to do full-time research on the Earth as a living planet." He challenges scientists with a twist of the phrase from Karl Marx: "Fellow scientists join me, you have nothing to lose but your grants."[54]

On the other hand, in religion's corner, by choosing to remain stuck in its anthropomorphism, religion is deliberately encouraging ignorance—ignorance of creation and therefore even of the Creator. Thomas Aquinas warned seven centuries ago that "a mistake about creation results in a mistake about God."[55] Have religions been making many mistakes about both God and creation for centuries? Hopefully the litanies offered here will assist religion itself in becoming redeemed—that is, in starting over again with spirituality and the experience of awe and wonder. After all, the two etymological meanings of *religion*, "to bind back" and "to read a second time," both refer to cosmology and to nature. Cosmology is a binding-back, a renewal of our understanding of our origins, and cosmology is about reading a second time because when one understands one's creation story, one sees all of one's relationships in a new light and a new perspective. Indeed, the argument could be made that the two etymological meanings of the word *religion* are about cosmology in the following sense: cosmology as space, and cosmology as time.

SPIRITUAL EXERCISES APROPOS OF UNIVERSE FLESH

I propose the following exercises apropos of this chapter:

1. What do you think of when you hear the word *flesh*?
2. If you are a scientist, tell the story about your vocation. When did you first feel the call to be a scientist? What were the circumstances? What did it feel like? (This story may be told in words or in poetry or in drawing, painting, clay, dance, rap.)
3. If you are a scientist or just a human being, report what you feel of *awe* on hearing this Litany of Wonders of the Flesh of the Universe. Which of the facts given excite you and amaze you? Why do you think that is? Dance this awe or paint it or sing it.
4. If you are a religious person, connect some of the facts in this litany to Scriptural passages that you know.
5. Add other facts to this litany that are not included.
6. Create a ritual around this litany.
7. Chant this litany with others.
8. Translate this litany into language or images for the following groups:
   a. Children under five
   b. Children five to ten
   c. Teenagers
   d. Young adults
   e. Elderly people
   f. Dying people
9. If you are a churchgoer, introduce your pastor and congregation to this litany. How do they respond?
10. If you belong to a self-healing group such as AA, introduce them to this litany. How do they respond?
11. Meditate on the paintings of Willem de Kooning or Georgia O'Keeffe for their celebration of the flesh of the cosmos. Do the same with another artist of your choice. What do you learn about the holiness of flesh from that experience?
13. In the past the cosmos was considered to be spiritual only. More recently it was considered to be matter only. What difference does it make to you to learn that the cosmos is flesh?

   a. Difference in your relationships?
   b. Difference in your parenting or grandparenting?
   c. Difference in your work?
   d. Difference in your citizenship?
   e. Difference in your values?
   f. Difference in your prayer life?
   g. Difference in your use of leisure time?

14. Have you had experiences like the one described by the indigenous tribe of the Philippines, in which God was in effect restricted to a "little white house"? Discuss the implications of that teaching.

15. In light of the teachings about light and life in this chapter, comment on Christ's sayings "I am the light of the world" and "This is my body, this is my blood" and "Do this in remembrance of me" and "the Kingdom/Queendom of God is among you (or within you)."

16. Create a prayer of Thanksgiving for these cosmic blessings, upon which we depend so thoroughly for our very existence.

CHAPTER 3

EARTH FLESH

In her poem "Wild Geese" poet Mary Oliver captures the truth of the fleshiness of the earth and of its relation to the fleshiness of the universe and our own flesh. Wild geese were the symbol of the Great Spirit for the Celts as well as Siberians and some Scandinavians.

You do not have to be good.
You do not have to walk on your knees
for a hundred miles through the desert, repenting.
You only have to let the soft animal of your body
    love what it loves.
Tell me about despair, yours, and I will tell you mine.
Meanwhile the world goes on.
Meanwhile the sun and the clear pebble of the rain
are moving across the landscapes,
over the prairies and the deep trees,
the mountains and the rivers.
Meanwhile the wild geese, high in the clean blue air,
are heading home again.
Whoever you are, no matter how lonely,
the world offers itself to your imagination,
calls to you like the wild geese, harsh and exciting—
over and over announcing your place
in the family of things.[1]

That geese and other earth creatures "announce our place in the family of things" is good news. It is evidence that grace exists, that the world does not depend on us, that our task is a cosmological task: to fit into the family of things. To relearn how trustworthy our body is—indeed, the "soft animal of our body"—to love what it loves is also good news. And while despair and brokenheartedness and loneliness are real, so too are the gifts of the earth—its sun and rain and land and trees and mountains and rivers and wild geese. In addition the world is revelatory—it gifts our imaginations to reconnect to what counts: our place in the family of things.

The "family of things" is especially close kin here on earth. We all live under a shared canopy that we call the "blue sky." This blue sky extends about ten miles into space. Within this stratosphere we and other organisms can breathe and carry on our lives. But beyond it we are dead. Ten miles is not a long distance—we could drive it in ten minutes and walk it in a few hours. A hundred miles below us on this earth that we like to think is solid there lie a thousand miles of molten fire. It is in these fires, which percolate onto the earth's surface from time to time in the form of volcanoes, that life on this planet apparently began. There we have it: Ten miles above us and a hundred miles below us, death and extinction await us. The earth's flesh is precious—and precarious—to a great extent.

Did life happen 3.5 billion years ago on earth by chance? Scientists Fred Hoyle and Chandra Wickramasinghe calculated the odds that life could have happened by chance in a kind of primordial soup in the oceans. Limiting the issue to a sequence of twenty or thirty key amino acids in the enzymes of a cell, they concluded that the odds were one chance in $10^{40,000}$.[2] Christian de Duve worked out a combined probability for the spontaneous origin of life in a series of necessary steps taking place in the right order. The result "borders on the miraculous: 10^{300}."[3] Scientist Arne Wyller, who was a Royal Swedish Academy professor in astrophysics for twenty years, comments that what makes these statistics so important is that "the number of chance trials available is not infinitely large." He concludes that "the Darwinian principle of chance creating genuinely new gene structures fails miserably."[4] If we ignore the more than 200 different types of body cells in the human being and the complexity of the brain and of the eye, and concentrate solely on the humble bacterium *E. coli,* this bacterium alone requires more than two thousand different enzymes, each made up of several hundred amino acids. Life is not simple! Flesh does not come easily into the universe—nor by chance, apparently.

Wyller believes that an "astounding" amount of high-technology information has gone into the creation of life: "There simply has not been time enough, in the mere 600 million years it has taken to create a conservatively estimated 100 million different species, for this knowledge to accumulate by the Darwinian notions of chance and natural selection."[5]

How then did life come about? Wyller speaks of "an invisible Planetary Mind Field that pervades the entire Earth." The creative activity of this Mind Field "is responsible for the appearance and evolution of all forms of life on planet Earth." Only this reality accounts mathematically for "the sophisticated information put into the genetic blueprints of all multicellular life that has existed on this planet within the last 600 million years."[6] For 99.9 percent of the time of life on earth, humans have not existed, but today the mind field is reaching out to include humanity. To connect to it, a sense of the whole, a quest for the beauty that cosmology brings, is required of humans once again. The specialization that is so common in our piecemeal academic systems can be keenly felt by scientists. Nobel laureate biologist Albert Szent-Györgyi tells his own story:

> I entered biology to understand the beauty of life. I started with the ecology of animals, but that wasn't quite right, so I went one level deeper, to the study of tissues, then to chemistry, and finally even dabbled in the depths of quantum mechanics. Yet when I got there, I saw that the wonder of life had somehow slipped through my fingers along the way.[7]

If the quest for the beauty of life can be so easily lost even by one committed to scientific research, how much are we ordinary laypersons in danger of losing it? What can we do to stay true to our quest for life's beauty? One answer might be found in the experiences of those who have left Earth behind—the astronauts and cosmonauts.

ASTRONAUTS AND COSMONAUTS ON
THE WONDER OF THE EARTH

It is not only scientific thinkers who recognize a need to see the bigger picture of the Earth system. Those few fortunate ones who have left the Earth also respond with a sense of the sacred when they see the whole picture. Astronaut James Irwin, who walked on the moon on the Apollo mission, said afterward about looking back at the earth: "That beautiful, warm, living object looked so fragile, so delicate, that if you touched it with a finger it would crumble and fall apart. Seeing this has to change a man, has to make a man appreciate the creation of God and the love of God."[8] About his walk on the moon, he commented: "I felt in a way as Adam and Eve must have felt, as they were standing on the Earth and they realized that they were all alone. I talk about the moon as being a very holy place."[9] The moon was a "world of no sound, no smell, no sense," said Irwin.[10] Edgar Mitchell commented: "On the return trip home, gazing through 240,000 miles of space toward the stars and the planet from which I had come, I suddenly experienced the universe as intelligent, loving, harmonious."[11] On his view of Earth: "My view of our planet was a glimpse of divinity."[12]

Taylor Wang, another American astronaut, commented on his first experience in space: "A Chinese tale tells of some men sent to harm a young girl who, upon seeing her beauty, become her protectors rather than her violators. That's how I felt seeing the Earth for the first time. I could not help but love and cherish her."[13] Cosmonaut Boris Volynon talked of what seeing a sense of the whole did to his own psyche. "During a space flight, the psyche of each astronaut is reshaped. Having seen the sun, the stars, and our planet, you become more full of life, softer. You begin to look at all living things with greater trepidation and you begin to be more kind and patient with the people around you. At any rate that is what happened to me."[14] And from this Dutch space traveler, Wubbo Ockels: "Space is so close: it took only eight minutes to get there and twenty to get back."[15]

Warnings abound from those who have left our planet, such as cosmonaut Vladimir Shatalov: "The 'boundless' blue sky, the ocean which gives us breath and protects us from the endless black and death, is but an infinitesimally thin film. How dangerous it is to threaten even the smallest part of this gossamer covering, this conserver of life."[16] Or this from Ulf Merbold of the Federal Republic of Germany: "For the first time in my life I saw the horizon as a curved line. It was accentuated by a thin seam of dark blue light—our atmosphere. Obviously this was not the ocean of air I had been told it was so many times in my life. I was terrified by its fragile appearance."[17] The eco-flesh is indeed in jeopardy. That is one more reason for cherishing it and falling in love with it—for allowing its awe to fill our hearts.

EARTH AS GAIA

In the 1970s scientist James Lovelock was working on NASA's original probes of Mars and Venus and was struck by how these planets were so similar and yet so different from Earth. The difference was the presence of life. He came to an awareness that Earth is a special being—indeed, the largest organism—and that this alone explained its remarkable achievements, such as its ability to maintain a regular temperature hospitable toward life even when the sun increased its temperature by 30 percent: "To me it was obvious that the Earth was alive in the sense that it was a self-organizing and self-regulating system."[18] He proposed the Gaia hypothesis. How do organisms keep oxygen at 21 percent and the mean temperature at twenty degrees Celsius? Being a kind of organism, Earth deserved a name. Thus, "Gaia."

Evolution concerns Gaia and not just individual organisms in adaptation. Gaia is a kind of gestalt way of looking at things on Earth: It is the bigger picture within which smaller parts such as species make sense. Biologist Lewis Thomas agrees with Lovelock when he talks of Earth as a "coherent system of life, self-regulating, self-changing, a sort of immense organism."[19]

Lovelock names four dimensions to Gaia, "the largest manifestation of life" and a "tightly coupled system of life and its environment":

1. Living organisms that grow vigorously, exploiting any environmental opportunities that open.
2. Organisms that are subject to the rules of Darwinian natural selection: the species that leave the most progeny survive.
3. Organisms that affect their physical and chemical environment.

Thus animals change the atmosphere by breathing: taking in oxygen and letting out carbon dioxide. Plants and algae do the reverse. In numerous other ways all forms of life incessantly modify the physical and chemical environment.

4. Constraints or bounds that establish the limits of life. The environment can be too hot or too cold; a comfortable warmth in between is the preferred state. It can be too acid or too alkaline; neutrality is preferred.[20]

If Earth is alive, if Earth is Gaia, then Earth is also *flesh*. It is impossible to deny that we eat Earth. The soil's nutrients that make the carrot nutritious—or the cow's milk or the orange on the orange tree or the wheat—we are eating Earth and drinking Earth daily. Is this not the work of flesh? Is Earth not our food? Rightly, then, we can talk about earth flesh and the blessing that it is. (What distinguishes Mars from Earth, according to Lovelock, is that you cannot garden on Mars.) From a biblical perspective the Gaia hypothesis fills in the meaning of blessing. It underscores the Hebrew understanding of the word *blessing*, as theologian Sigmund Mowinckel defines it when he writes: "Blessing included that which we call material as well as the spiritual. But first and foremost, blessing is life, health, and fertility for the people, their cattle, their fields. . . . Blessing is the basic power of life itself."[21] Earth is truly a blessing, truly good, truly a gratuitous grace, truly the matrix through which our life is possible and all Incarnations of Divinity are possible. Visiting the Hawaiian volcanic park this winter, I was privileged to see the hot lava as it meets the sea with a large hiss. This lava is continuing to build up the island of Hawaii. All of the Hawaian islands were born this way. Earth is still being born there. Earth is alive; flesh is being formed of fire and rock and water, and very soon grasses and insects and trees will find their niche there. Blessing of the flesh indeed!

EARTH INVENTS THE EYE

Among the miracles of Gaia's inventions is the eye. Scientist Lyall Watson comments on the perfection of the vertebrate eye: "The transparent cornea of our eye could hardly have evolved through progressive trials and errors by natural selection. You can either see through it or you can't. Such an innovation has to be right the first time or else it just does not happen again, because the blind owner gets eaten."[22] Four families have developed eyes: fish, squids, insects, and other vertebrates. About 550 million years ago the lancelet, an ancestor of the fish, had no eye, only a light-sensitive spot. "The first eye must have been invented over a period of a mere 100 million to 150 million years, an astoundingly short period of time for such a complex development," says Arne Wyller.[23] Darwin himself saw the eye as too supreme an invention to have happened by chance when he wrote:

> To suppose that the eye with all its inimitable contrivances for adjusting the focus to different distances, for admitting different amounts of light, and for the correction of spherical and chromatic aberrations, could have been formed by natural selection seems, I freely confess, absurd in the highest degree.[24]

EARTH FLESH LITANY

David Abram points out that given today's science, "the life-world has been disclosed as a profoundly *carnal* field. . . . It is, indeed, nothing other than the biosphere—the matrix of earthly life in which we ourselves are embedded."[25] Ancient traditions among indigenous peoples relate that at one time animals and humans all spoke the same language and indeed that the whole landscape speaks. But we have to learn the language of the landscape. We live in "a world that speaks," as Abram puts it.[26] All of nature is a kind of revelation, every being is "gladly doing the best it can," as Meister Eckhart put it,[27] to reveal the divine to us. Just what is the world saying when it speaks? Diane Ackerman listens to the trees and hears the following:

> Because trees can't move to court each other or to defend themselves, they've become ingenious and aggressive about their survival. Some develop layers of strychnine or other toxic substances just under their bark; some are carnivorous; some devise flowers with intricate feather dusters to touch pollen to any bug, bird, or bat they have managed to lure with siren smells and colors. Some orchids mimic the reproductive parts of a female bee or beetle in

order to trick the male into trying to copulate, so it will become dusted with pollen. One night a year, in the Bahamas, the *Selenicereus* cactus flowers ache into bloom, conduct their entire sex lives, and vanish by morning. For several days beforehand, the cactuses develop large pregnant pods. Then one night, awakened by a powerful smell of vanilla, you know what has happened. The entire moonlit year is erupting in huge, foot-wide flowers. Hundreds of sphinx moths rush from one flower to another. The air is full of the baying of dogs, the loud fluttering of the moths that sounds like someone riffling through a large book and the sense-drenching vanilla nectar of the flowers, which disappear at dawn, leaving the cactuses sated for another year.[28]

What else is the air full of? James Joyce said of the air in Dublin, "The air without is impregnated with rainbow moisture, life essence celestial, glistening on Dublin stone there under starshiny coelum, God's air the Allfather's air, scintillant circumambient cessile air. Breathe it deep into thee."

Additional wonders of animal nature include the following:

- The Gila monster stores fat in its tail and can live for more than 2 years without eating a thing.
- The arctic tern migrates from the Arctic to the Antarctic and back every year, covering a distance of 16,000 miles.
- The cheetah can run up to 62 miles per hour over short distances.
- The fastest living creature is the peregrine falcon, which dives through the air for prey at speeds up to 112 miles per hour.
- One female ocean sunfish carried 300 million eggs.
- The banded yellow mouthbrooder protects its young by holding them in her mouth and spitting them out occasionally so they can feed.
- Termites build mounds up to 5 meters high. The mounds are oriented to the sun and face east-west in order to catch morning and evening warmth while minimizing noonday heat. They contain elaborate ventilation systems. The air-cooling chimneys of certain rainforest species look like multiroofed pagodas; the layering provides protection from tropical downpours.

- The jawfish builds a nest by digging a well-like tunnel up to a meter long, with a chamber at the bottom for turning around. They reinforce their wells with stones and shells.
- A plover with a nest of eggs or chicks will lure a predator away from the nest by putting on a "broken-wing display" and mimicking an injury in which a wing or two or the tail is held in an abnormal position that suggests an injury.
- Herons sometimes do bait-fishing: They toss an object like a twig or a piece of bread into the water, then lunge at any fish that rises to the bait.
- When a wildebeest calf dies, its mother loses interest in just minutes. But when a juvenile baboon dies, that mother's behavior undergoes great change. She becomes morose and withdrawn and may carry her dead child around with her for weeks on end.
- A chimp named Kanszi was part of a language learning project. He fooled a zookeeper by flattening himself on his bed, covering his body with blankets, and lying completely still for twenty minutes. Then he emerged laughing. He also hid a tool from his keepers and feigned to help them look for it, to no avail. When they were not watching, he found the tool and let himself out with it.
- There are many reported cases of dogs and cats who have adopted orphaned skunks or piglets.
- Year-old beavers help their parents take care of younger siblings.
- Elephants seem to make allowances for the weak ones in the herd. One African herd always traveled slowly because one of its members had never fully recovered from a broken leg as a calf. Another herd was very solicitous of a female that carried a small calf that had been dead for several days. She would place it on the ground whenever she ate or drank, and she traveled very slowly, but the others would wait for her: "This suggests that animals, like people, act on feelings as such, rather than solely for purposes of survival. It suggests that the evolutionary approach is no more adequate to explain animal feelings than human ones. . . . It raises questions that biologists have yet to face. There appears to be so little survival value in the behavior of this herd, that perhaps one has to believe that they behaved this way just because they *loved* their grieving friend who loved her dead baby, and wanted to support her."[29]

- The cow has four stomachs; the sea cucumber discards its belly and grows another one; the spider and the starfish digest their food outside their bodies.
- The salinity of the blood of whales, humans, mice, a shrimp called Artemia, and most fish is essentially the same.
- Recently a shaman told me that the animals are very worried about humanity these days and have had councils to decide how to help us, including entering our dreams more fully.

Some wonders of the soil, plants, and trees include the following:

- The top 1 inch of forest soil contains on an average 1,356 living creatures for each square foot. Among them are 865 mites, 265 springtails, 22 millipedes; 19 adult beetles; and various other kinds. Also in one teaspoonful of soil there are: 2 billion bacteria and millions of fungi protozoa and algae.[30]
- The top cubic foot of the soil contains about 40,000 living visible animals.
- Topsoil is 50 percent air and the soil actually inhales oxygen and exhales carbon dioxide down to several feet of depth. The soil down to five inches in depth is completely renewed every hour by this process.[31]
- Trees each year create 99 percent of their living parts from scratch.
- Water going up tree trunks travels at one hundred and fifty feet per hour.
- In summer an average-size tree gives off a ton of water every day.
- In a single season a large elm tree makes about six million leaves.
- The bark of a sequoia tree is almost as fireproof as asbestos.
- The orchid Tricoceros parviflorus will grow its petals to imitate the female of a species of fly so perfectly that the male will attempt to mate with it and in doing so pollinates the orchid.
- There are over 500 varieties of carnivorous plants that eat any kind of meat from insect to beef and use many cunning methods to capture their prey, including tentacles, sticky hairs, and funnel-like traps.
- Even as a child, George Washington Carver was known for his

ability to heal sick plants and to discern what plants could heal sick animals. He said, "All flowers talk to me and so do hundreds of little living things in the woods. I learn what I know by watching and loving everything." He created hundreds of products from the peanut and the sweet potato, including peanut butter, axle grease, cosmetics, and printer's ink. He said, "If you love it enough, anything will talk to you."

- The total length of roots and root hairs of a single rye plant is seven thousand miles. The roots grow over 3 miles per day in search of microorganisms.
- There are prairie grasses in the Midwest whose roots are 10,000 miles long.
- A single eucalyptus tree that is 45 feet tall will transpire over 80 gallons of water a day.
- A willow tree will transpire 5,000 gallons of water per day.
- A single tree can provide the same cooling effect as ten room-size air conditioners working twenty hours per day.[32]
- Bamboo can grow 3 feet in twenty-four hours.
- The winter rye plant, in four months, puts forth 378 miles of roots (3 miles per day) and has 14 million different roots. Also, it gives birth to 14 billion root hairs. In a single cubic inch of soil the length of the root hairs total 7,000 miles.[33]
- The roots of a larch tree are recorded to have split a 1.5-ton boulder and raised it a foot in the air.
- Squashes have been measured to exert a lifting force of 5,000 pounds per square inch.[34]

It is reported that a Hasidic master once said: "When you walk across the fields with your mind pure and holy, then from all the stones, and all growing things, and all animals, the sparks of their soul come out and cling to you, and then they are purified and become a holy fire in you."[35] For those who are alert and looking for holy fire, this would seem to be everyday fare.

SPIRITUAL EXERCISES APROPOS OF EARTH FLESH

To assist a heartfelt response to this discussion of earth flesh, I propose
the following exercises:

1. Make a list of the facts in the litany that most moved you. Why
   do you think they moved you? Draw a picture or create a poem
   about them.
2. What other facts can you add to this litany?
3. Share these facts with your family or with your coworkers. What
   is their response?
4. Create a ritual around this litany: one in celebration, and another
   in grief for what we are losing.
5. Talk to scientists you know about their mystical experiences as
   scientists.
6. Talk to clergy you know about their mystical experiences. Were
   they trained in mystical practice at all in their seminary? Why or
   why not? Has this changed since their time? Why or why not?
   What can you do to bring about change?
7. Meditate on the statement by the Hasidic master. Has this happened to you? How often? Under what circumstances? Share
   your answers to these questions with others.

CHAPTER 4

HUMAN FLESH

Wendell Berry says that eating is more than a merely sensory or appetitive stimulation; it is the last act of an agricultural drama.[1] It is still more than that: It is a last act in a *cosmological drama.*

Life on earth is a latecomer to this drama. It was very generous of Divinity to come here and join in on the action: "This is my body, this is my blood." Earth bounty and generosity and diversity have raised the possibilities of good food to new heights. Poet William Carlos Williams writes:

> There is nothing to eat,
> seek it where you will,
> but the body of the Lord.
> The blessed plants
> and the sea, yield it
> to the imagination
> intact.[2]

As we saw in the last chapter, our universe is flooded with light, and light is far more prevalent in the universe than is matter.

A flood of light dominates our Universe today and...matter is numerically insignificant in the stuff of the universe. For every particle of matter there are 1 billion particles of light. As Nobel Prize winner Ilya Prigogine puts it, matter is just a minor pollutant in a Universe made of light. Perhaps there is more to the phenomenon of light than meets the eye of the physicist. At the moment of almost ultimate compression, this light of the whole Universe was able to fit into a volume much smaller than the point of a needle.[3]

It seems that the very food we eat is light.

It is interesting that the creation story in Genesis says that light was the first of the creations of God, paralleling a major finding of today's science: that the universe began as a fireball. The creation story in Psalm 104, which is older than the creation stories in Genesis, also talks of light. It begins with the awakening of psyche and cosmos together:

Bless the Lord, my soul:
O Lord my God, thou art great indeed,
clothed in majesty and splendor,
and wrapped in a robe of light.

Divinity comes "wrapped in a robe of light." Is light the primal gift, the radical expression of the Divine presence, of the creative power or fire in the universe? Is this what lies behind the creation story in John 1, where it is said that Christ is the "light of the world" and the light and life within all existing things of the universe? If Divinity comes wrapped in a robe of light, then is penetrating light a way to penetrating Divinity? Is photosynthesis a special creation that carries on the light-making properties of the universe and of its maker? When we eat and drink the sun, which is seized in fruit and vegetables, coffee and orange juice, are we imbibing Divinity? Is all food a holy Eucharist—an eating of the flesh of the Divine One? The Food of the Beloved?

In Psalm 104 the majesty, splendor, and special robes of Divinity are about the Creator God who, like a King, runs the universe. The universe is subject to the justice of this King. The poet knows God is great because God's creation is so great, as the rest of the poem goes on to recount: the heavens, the waters, the clouds, the wind, the flames, the earth, the sea, the rains over hills and valleys, the wild beasts, the wild asses, the birds that sing among the leaves. Grass for cattle, vegetation that becomes bread and wine, oils, storks, mountain goats, rock badgers. The moon, the sun, the darkness, the night, the beasts, including young lions, "seek their food from God." And humans join this great work, for they "work until evening."

"Countless are the things thou hast made, O Lord. Thou hast made all by thy wisdom; and the earth is full of thy creatures, beasts great and small." (Ps. 104.24) Teilhard de Chardin said: "The cosmos is primarily and fundamentally living. . . . Christ, through his Incarnation, is internal to the world, . . . rooted in the world, even in the very heart of the tiniest atom."[4] Human ingenuity in the form of microscopic photography has opened up the amazing wonders and blessings that our bodies are. In his classic work *Behold Man,* Swedish photographer Lennart Nillson has made available the beauty and workings of the body that move us to awe. His book, as he confesses in the introduction, "is most unabashedly designed to catch the wonder of the human body. It is a look at the extraordinary things that are happening inside your body every day of your life, and how they affect the way you feel and act." There is no longer an excuse, he points out, why "learning about how the body really works has to be boring."[5] Just as we created a litany of wonders of the cosmic flesh and the earth flesh above, let us proceed with a litany of the wonders of our human flesh.

HUMAN FLESH: A LITANY OF WONDERS AND BLESSINGS

- Over 60 percent of the atoms in our material bodies were once inside the flaming inferno of the cosmic fireball. Every single hydrogen atom in our bodies was once part of the Big Bang itself. Forty percent of the atoms in our material bodies came from older stars. "This cosmic connectedness is shared by all life forms on this planet, be they horses, flowers, fish, or insects. It is also shared by rocks and stones and water and air—all the nonliving matter."[6]
- Humans are naturally radioactive, and every minute a few million potassium atoms undergo radioactive decay in each one of us. We need radioactive potassium in order to live; were it replaced by the similar element, sodium, we would die instantly. Potassium is

a long-lived radioactive nuclear waste of the supernova explosion, as are uranium and thorium and radium.[7]

· One human body contains a hundred times more cells than there are stars in the galaxy. There are 100 trillion cells in your body and about 200 different kinds of cells, ranging from the tiny sperm cell the size of a pinpoint to the nerve cell connecting the spine and the toe, which is three feet in length. Cellular materials range from bone protein to hair or muscle cells to the liquid molecules of egg and sperm cells. Your 100 trillion cells are all "orchestrated into one magnificent whole—they communicate with each other for the sake of the whole body."[8]

· Human chromosomes are 6 feet in length but fit crumpled up into a tiny ball of a cell that is 0.1 millimeter in diameter.[9]

· Each minute 300 million of the body's cells die. If they were not replaced, we would die in about 230 days.

· In each cell lies our DNA, the keeper of all codes, infinitely complex in its variations, and unique to each of us. The DNA directs the cellular growth in every organism on Earth. If the DNA in our bodies' cells were uncoiled and laid end to end, it would reach to the moon and back 100,000 times!

· On the strand of DNA are 50,000 genes, which constitute a blueprint for reproducing the cells.

· The heart weighs only half a pound and is the size of a clenched fist. A normal heart does the daily work equivalent of lifting a ton from the ground up to the top of a five-story building. In a lifetime it beats about 4 billion times—once for every man, woman, and child on earth. Expanding and contracting, the heart delivers oxygen and nutrients to the cells of hungry tissues and organs.

· Blood takes 16 seconds to travel from heart to toes and back again.

· The circulatory system in each of our bodies is 60,000 miles long. If laid end to end, the body's blood vessels would encircle the Earth more than two times.[10]

· Each red blood cell circuits the entire body up to 300,000 times over a 120-day period before it wears out and dies.

· Three million replacement cells are manufactured in bone marrow each minute.

· Once per minute the heart pumps the body's entire blood supply through the lungs. Exhaling gets rid of the carbon dioxide, a waste product. Fresh oxygen turns the blood red again and goes back to the body to feed hungry tissues.[11]

- The heart is our most faithful muscle and clings to life to the very end, when all the rest have relaxed permanently.
- The ventricle in the heart is the most exceptional muscle in the body. It pumps more than half a million tons of blood in a lifetime without fatigue or rest.
- The mitral valve in the heart looks like a fragile sail in the wind. In fact it is very strong, opening and closing about 5,000 times per hour, encouraging the blood to flow in only one direction. Blood flows like a river, nourishing the soil of our tissues with the oxygen, nutrients, and hormones that we need. Cleansing where it flows, it builds our immunity and defenses. Blood evolved directly from ancient seawater.
- Our flesh is liquid—two-thirds water—and our skin holds it in one piece.
- The average American eats one ton of food and drink per year— 74 tons in a lifetime. To process this food, the adult stomach has 35 million digestive glands. Stomach acid is so powerful, it can dissolve razor blades in less than a week. The stomach produces a new lining every three days to protect itself from its own acid. This means the lining must shed and regenerate about 500,000 cells every minute.[12]
- The kidneys clean and reclean 40 gallons of blood per day and maintain an exact proportion of water in the blood as well as a strict mineral and chemical balance in the salty blood. It coordinates with the work of the lungs, heart, liver, pancreas, and more.
- The female breast houses a system of 18 little rivers of milk, each with thousands of tributaries that combine into the nipple. It exchanges blood for milk.
- Fat is 88 percent carbon and hydrogen, which makes it chemically very close to gasoline and other hydrocarbon fuels.
- There are 3 million sweat glands throughout the body; on an average summer day they will pump out about 2 quarts of fluid; in a desert climate 2.5 gallons of perspiration.[13]
- The average person has about 100,000 hair follicles on their head

and about 5 million hairs on the body. Hairy skin is thinner than skin without hair and is therefore more sensitive than smooth skin. We lose between 50 and 100 hairs a day through brushing our hair.

· A hair will grow from 2 to 6 years, rest for a few months, and die. Eighty-five percent of our hair is growing and fifteen percent is resting. Some hair is dying, and hidden hair is being birthed anew.

· Bones are the living architecture of the body. We are made of more than 600 bones. They are stronger than steel but very light-weight and porous in their internal structure.

· Forty-five percent of bone is mineral deposits, especially calcium phosphate. Thirty percent is living tissues, cells, and blood vessels, and 25 percent is water.

· Bones are "one of the strongest building materials known to man, one that can withstand stresses of 24,000 pounds per square inch or about 4 times that of steel or reinforced concrete."[14]

· Bones are alive and grow back when they are broken. Within bones both red and white blood cells are formed. Bone is the hardest expression of connective tissue in the body—its mineral combination is like that of many sedimentary rock formations, yet it possesses the elastic strength of the collagen fibers.[15]

· Bone tissue is constantly being destroyed and replaced. Every seven years the body grows the equivalent of an entirely new skeleton. "The mineral content, porosity, and general makeup of human bone is nearly identical to some species of South Pacific coral"—so much so that some plastic surgeons are now using coral to replace lost human facial bones.[16]

· Bones need to be exercised to maintain their thickness and strength. Marathon runners have among the thickest and strongest bones.

· Our muscles move. We have 656 muscles throughout the body. Voluntary muscles are attached to the skeleton by tendons and aid the body in conscious movement.

· Involuntary muscles line the internal organs and contract auto-matically to regulate the heart, lungs, intestines, blood vessels, and glands.[17]

· Muscle makes up between 70 and 85 percent of the body's weight and is one thing that sets animals off from plants. Our musculature is the largest and most metabolically active organ of the body.[18]

• Muscle tissue has a liquid crystal quality to it that allows it to be watery, elastic, wiry, or solid. Muscle tissue "has developed the ability to shift its sol/gel states almost instantaneously to conform to the needs or whims of the moment. It can lengthen, shorten, soften, or harden all at the snap of a finger, creating an ever-changing kaleidoscope of structural conditions and movements. . . . Muscle tissue produces all of the postures, gestures, and qualities of flesh of which we are capable."[19]

• Muscle is utterly interdependent with other systems of the body. For example, it depends on the digestive system to supply it with glucose and on the lungs for oxygen to burn the glucose to replenish the supplies of ATP (adenosine triphosphate). The circulatory system delivers the glucose and oxygen to the individual muscle cells, and the nervous system provides electrical signals to begin or end the contractions of the muscles. The connective tissue organizes muscle fibers into directions of pulling and anchors them to the bones.[20]

• Simply to raise one's right arm, the following must occur:

> The fibers in the deltoid, the supraspinatus, and the upper trapezius will contract to produce the primary motion, while the fibers of the pectoral major, the pectoral minor, and the latissimus dorsi must simultaneously extend to allow it. But the contraction of the right trapezius will not only raise the right arm, it will also tend to pull the neck towards the right; therefore the left trapezius, along with other muscles of the neck, will have to contract as well in order to stabilize it. Furthermore, the extended right arm will overbalance the torso to the right, so the erector spinae muscles on the left side of the spine must contract to brace the whole torso and keep it erect. And since this contraction of the left erector spinae set will tend to pull the left side of the pelvis up as well, the gluteus medius and minimus of the left side must also brace to hold the pelvis level. Since not only the torso, but the body as a whole is threatened with tipping by the overbalancing weight of the extended arm, the right leg must brace as well, using fibers in the hip, the thigh, the calf, the feet, the toes. And of course our subject continues to breathe, so all of the muscles which cooperate

to fill and empty the lungs must now make the necessary asymmetrical adjustments to continue their rhythm without disturbing the pose. . . . It is clear that muscle fibers from the occiput to the toes, and from both sides of the body, all must cooperate to "raise the right arm."[21]

If raising an arm is this complicated, imagine what the act of swimming entails, or having a baby, or ballet dancing! How grateful we need to be daily that the body knows how to do these things without our intervention! Also, a hint is given here as to why we do not yet have an entire theory on how Gaia or the universe works— we cannot even get clear how the body works so well. But it does work. There is the miracle; therein lies the grace of it all.

LITANY OF BLESSING OF THE SENSES

Our senses are gateways through which the world reveals itself to us. Revelation happens through the senses. We ought not take them for granted but delight in them daily—that is our thanksgiving for their powers and gifts. We ought to feel awe in them as well. We shall consider some of the awesome aspects of our senses.

1. *Smell.* Smells awaken our memories. I remember a lilac bush near our house, when I was little, and whenever I smell a lilac, my entire childhood returns to me. That is not so unusual. Our sense of smell, it is said, can detect more than 10,000 odors![22] Each day we breathe about 23,000 times and move around 438 cubic feet of air. It takes five seconds to breathe—two seconds to inhale and three to exhale. To breathe is to smell. Says Diane Ackerman in *A Natural History of the Senses,*

> Smell is the most direct of all our senses. When I hold a violet to my nose and inhale, odor molecules float back into the nasal cavity behind the bridge of the nose, where they are absorbed by the mucosa containing receptor cells bearing microscopic hairs called cilia. Five million of these cells fire impulses to the brain's olfactory bulb or smell center. Such cells are unique to the nose. If you destroy a neuron in the brain, it's finished forever; it won't regrow.

If you damage neurons in your eyes or ears, both organs will be irreparably damaged. But the neurons in the nose are replaced about every thirty days and, unlike any other neurons in the body, they stick right out and wave in the air current like anemones on a coral reef.[23]

Smells not only last for a lifetime; they also stimulate learning and retention. Perfume is a kind of "liquid memory."[24] We get tongue-tied and short of adjectives when we try to describe the plethora of different smells we encounter. Ackerman believes it is the very ineffability of smells that renders them mysterious and magical and nameless and "sacred."[25] Smells affect us biologically and actually produce hormonal changes in women. For example, women who sniff musk (animal musk is close to human testosterone) develop shorter menstrual cycles, ovulate more often, and find it easier to conceive. Flowers smell good because their sex organs are "oozing with nectar."[26] Smell happens only when volatile particles go airborne. Not all things give off smells or have volatile particles to entice our sense of smell. Ackerman calls the Song of Songs the "most scent-drenched poem of all time," as it sings of human love through perfumes and unguents, myrrh, camphire, honey, and milk: "The smell of thy garments is like the smell of Lebanon."[27] Interesting that a book of the Bible runs away with the Oscar for Smell. We each have our own unique odor, and part of kissing is smelling. I remember that Maori people in New Zealand greeted us at a traditional ceremony by rubbing noses. Helen Keller's sense of smell was so keen that she could tell by smells what work a person did and what room—whether kitchen, garden, or sickroom—a person had emerged from.

When we were sea creatures, smell was essential to our survival, for we found our food through smell. Indeed, smell gave birth to our thinking, according to Ackerman. "Smell was the first of our senses, and it was so successful that in time the small lump of olfactory tissue atop the nerve cord grew into a brain. Our cerebral hemispheres were originally buds from the olfactory stalks. We *think* because we *smelled*."[28] The ocean helped to carry smells: odors dissolve into watery solutions where our mucous membranes can absorb them for smelling.

Those of us who are dog lovers and have often wondered why our dogs go on walks, but prefer stopping and smelling to walking, get a useful answer from Ackerman. A dog

> sniffs at curb, rock and tree, and so on senses what dog has been there, its age, sex, mood, health, when it last passed by.... it's like reading the gossip column of the morning newspaper.... *Jackie, 5:00 P.M. young female, on hormone therapy because of a bladder ailment, well fed, cheerful, seeks a friend.*[29]

Many mammals are born blind and must find their way to their mother's nipple by way of smell. Mother bats find their young through smells, as do seals and cows seeking their calves. Even human mothers recognize their newborns by smell and vice versa. We humans have 5 million olfactory cells, but a sheepdog has 220 million and can smell 44 times better than we can.[30] The bloodhound's sniffing organ is 50 times larger and thousands of times more sensitive than a human's. A silk-worm moth can detect sexual attractants up to seven miles away; male butterflies can smell a female miles away, and salmon return to their home place to spawn by smelling distant waters.

It is interesting how many perfumes are named after sins, an apparent lesson in how smell takes us to the edge. Consider Obsession, Tabu, My Sin, Opium, Indiscretion, Decadence, Poison. In interviewing a perfume maker, Ackerman was told the following: "When I first saw Picasso's *Guernica,* it was disturbing, but also deeply moving. Perfumes do that, too—shock and fascinate us. They disturb us. Our lives are quiet. We like to be disturbed by delight."[31]

2. *Breathing.* In Chinese *breath* and *wind* are the same words. The air we breathe is essentially "an altered form of sunbeams" because photosynthesis converts solar energy into nutrients for plants, which in return release oxygen into the atmosphere.[32] The body requires 8 quarts of air per minute when lying down; 16 when sitting; 24 when walking and 50 when running. We breathe about 75 million gallons of air in an average lifetime.[33]

The first lungs were invented by the fish. We breathe with our lungs, inhaling healthy air and exhaling waste of carbon dioxide and other materials. The total surface area of the lung is about the size of a tennis court—300 billion capillaries are contained there. "The purpose of breathing is to bring oxygen into contact with blood.... The exchange takes place almost entirely in the alveoli which are so fine that the red blood cells must slither through them in single file."[34]

What is breath made up of? What is the invisible air that we call wind or breeze? One ounce of air contains 1,000 billion trillion atoms—some hydrogen, others oxygen or nitrogen, all containing electrons, quarks, and neutrinos. "The air is always vibrant and aglow, full of volatile gases, staggering spores, dust, viruses, fungi, and animals, all stirred by a skirling and relentless wind."[35]

What is the sky? Do not be deceived. It is not above us—it is all around us.

> You are standing in the sky. When we think of the sky, we tend to look up, but the sky actually begins at the earth. We walk through it, yell into it, rake leaves, wash the dog, and drive cars in it. We breathe it deep within us. With every breath, we inhale millions of molecules of sky, heat them briefly, and then exhale them back into the world.... Air works the bellows of our lungs, and it powers our cells. We say "light as air," but there is nothing lightweight about our atmosphere, which weighs 5,000 trillion tons. Only a clench as stubborn as gravity's could hold it to the earth; otherwise it would simply float away and seep into the cornerless expanse of space.[36]

3. *Touch*. Our skin weighs 6 to 10 pounds and constitutes about 16 percent of our body weight, covering an area of 20 square feet in an average adult male. Just one square inch of human skin contains 19 million cells, 625 sweat glands, 90 oil glands, 65 hairs, 19 blood vessels, 19,000 sensory cells, and more than 20 million microscopic animals. The skin has been called the largest organ of the body and the key organ in sexual attraction. It produces vitamin D, keeps our bodily fluids inside us, cools us and warms us, protects us from injurious microbes and rays, regulates our blood flow, heals itself when necessary, and houses our sense of touch. Our skin is a door to the outside world: when it is open, it brings the world in, when it is shut, it protects us and gives us our identity and form. Self-containment is key to all living protoplasm, whether a creature be plant or animal, single or multicelled. Membrane is essential for the process of life to occur, both

at the cellular level and at the level of the whole organism. Skin interacts with the outside world at the same time that it keeps the inner world alive and healthy. It must excrete wastes as well as take in nourishment. Our skin has approximately six hundred and forty thousand sensory receptors that are connected to the spinal cord by over half a million nerve fibers; tactile points vary from seven to one hundred and thirty five per square centimeter.[37]

Skin is thinnest on the eyelids, the lower abdomen, and the external genitals; it is thickest on the palms of the hands and the soles of the feet. From babyhood to old age, our skin adapts and changes, grows and dies, changing its shape and contour. Like plywood, it is made of several layers. On the outside or epidermis there are no blood vessels. It takes twenty-seven days for an entire cycle of new skin cells to live and then die off. The bottom layer of the skin contains blood and lymph vessels as well as hair follicles, sebaceous glands, erector muscles, sweat glands, and most of the skin's nerve endings. The connective tissue is produced by cells called fibroblasts; they come to the aid of the skin by way of the blood when it is injured. There they fill in the wound by giving birth to connective tissue.

It is through skin that we touch and are touched. Helen Keller learned about the world almost exclusively through the sense of touch. To block out touch is to invite emotional and physiological breakdown. Eight tactile nerve endings have been detected so far in our skin, but no doubt more will be discovered. The skin plays a prominent role in the development of the central nervous system and has a special link to the brain. "Skin and brain develop from exactly the same primitive cells. Depending upon how you look at it, the skin is the outer surface of the brain, or the brain is the deepest layer of the skin."[38] We are learning that the brain is not just in the head but runs throughout the body. "The skin is no more separated from the brain than the surface of a lake is separate from its depths. . . . The brain is a single functional unit, from cortex to fingertips to toes. To touch the surface is to stir the depths."[39]

Neglecting touch is as damaging as neglecting food. The symptoms are similar as well. Sensory deprivation often results in retarded bone growth, failure to gain weight, poor muscular coordination, immune deficiencies, weakness, apathy, and lack of maturation of the central nervous system and other parts of the brain. In studies of rats that were isolated and rats that were fondled, all these symptoms appeared in those that were not touched. Emotional and behavioral responses followed suit. The fondled rats were "much calmer and less excitable, yet they tend to be more dominant in social and sexual situations. They are more lively, more curious, more active problem solvers. They are more willing to explore new environments (untouched animals usually withdraw fearfully from novel situations) and advance more quickly in all forms of conditioned learning exercises."[40]

Tactile stimulation is necessary for the healthy development and survival of the individual organism. This is especially the case for infants. Orphanages in the nineteenth century often had a 90 to 99 percent mortality rate for one-year-old babies until it was discovered that the key ingredient of holding and fondling was missing because the caregivers were too few and overworked. There is no substitute for affectionate bonding with an infant. Massaged babies gain weight 50 percent faster than unmassaged babies and are more alert to their surroundings. They are also calmer and less irritable, and they cry less. When a mother dog licks its pup, it is not doing so to clean the puppy so much as to stimulate it by touching it. Among monkeys who have not been touched adequately, brain damage has been demonstrated. Fetuses touch and are touched in the womb by the liquid warmth of amniotic fluids. Nursing is a touching of the nerve cells in the lips, and "swaddling clothes" give a baby the kind of warmth it was used to receiving in the womb. The mother touches the child, and the child learns that touch is possible in the world as well as in the womb. The world becomes the womb, and the womb has grown into the world.

Touch, as Ackerman points out, is the oldest of the senses "and the most urgent. If a saber-toothed tiger is touching a paw to your shoulder, you need to know right away."[41] Research has shown that simply touching someone's arm or hand lowers their blood pressure. One study of victims of heart attack found that pet owners survived the longest: petting and stroking a pet was the most calming thing a patient or former patient could do. As with mother and child, the one doing the touching is affected as much as the one being touched.[42]

4. *The Tongue and Taste.* We have 9,000 taste buds on our tongue. (Cows boast 25,000 and rabbits have 17,000.) Our taste buds make possible our enjoyment of life's many foods and drinks—but they

also motivate us to hunt for food, prepare food, eat in convivial settings, and even experience holy rituals. Consider the Catholic mass or the Jewish seder; the ancient Egyptians swore their oaths on an onion. Each tiny taste bud contains about 50 taste cells, which alert a neuron, which in turn alerts the brain as to what is being tasted. Taste buds reside not only in the center of the tongue but also in the palate, pharynx, and tonsils. Some taste buds tell us about salty tastes, others about sour, others about sweet, and others about bitter. We can taste saltiness in one part in 400; sour in one part in 130,000; bitterness in one part in 2 million. This helps us to avoid poisonous food, which often tastes bitter.[43] Taste buds live only 7 to 10 days, after which they are replaced. A baby has far more taste buds than a middle-aged person, whose palate needs more stimulants to be satisfied. Tasting begins with saliva, which helps us dissolve the food. Everyone has their own unique and distinctive saliva. Often it is the smell of an apple pie or soup cooking or bread baking that awakens our salivation. Smell comes first and fastest to us from afar, whereas tasting is up close and personal.

The mouth evolved early. All insects and animals, even one-celled animals like paramecia, have a mouth. In the human embryo the mouth develops very early during gestation. The tongue is the strongest muscle in the body; without it we would not only starve but we could not speak or kiss. As infants our intensely enjoyable experience of our mother's milk no doubt sets the pace for our appetites for the rest of our lives. Even at our mother's breast we are being made strong as well as pleasured. Antibodies for mumps, polio, influenza, vaccinia, salmonella, streptococcus, herpes simplex, and Japanese encephalitis are all passed on to the newborn's immune system through the breast milk of the mother.[44]

While food is a necessity for survival, bringing food to the table is something we have to accomplish. It is not involuntary like breathing. There may be as many as 20,000 edible plants growing in the earth. Ackerman reports that the first restaurants were created by the Chinese in the T'ang dynasty (A.D. 618–907). Food, too, has a history. One person I know says his father taught him a basic lesson in life: "If you want to eat, you've got to work." There is a relation between eating and working. As a species, most of our work during our 2-million-year presence on Earth has been in hunting and gathering. We turned to agriculture only ten thousand years ago. And only very recently did we begin shopping for our food. No doubt we have much to learn as we grope with new ways to feed ourselves, and we have much to remember that we have forgotten or are in danger of forgetting. Our appetites for food are fundamental to our survival. Our stomach tells us when we are neglecting it. Pleasure is built into the process, lest we forget our needs.

The pleasure of sex is related to the pleasure of eating. First: "Food is created by the sex of plants or of animals; and we find it sexy. When we eat an apple or peach, we are eating the fruit's placenta.... We use the mouth for many things—to talk and kiss, as well as to eat. The lips, tongue, and genitals all have the same neural receptors, called Krause's end bulbs, which make them ultrasensitive, highly charged."[45] The sexual appetite also renders us "hungry" and eager to "taste" and "lick" and "devour" a lover.

5. *Hearing*. Molecules of air, stirred up by any being at all, create waves of a certain frequency that we hear as pitch. Sound moves at only 1,100 feet per second, whereas light moves at 186,000 miles per second. Fortunately, we do not hear all sounds—otherwise we would be preoccupied with the music of our stomach digesting its food or our eyelids closing and shutting, and we could never get our work done. Hearing has a history, as Ackerman observes: "The act of hearing bridges the ancient barrier between air and water, taking the sound waves, translating them into fluid waves, and then into electrical impulses."[46] The eardrum vibrates from the wave of disturbed air molecules. This rattles the three tiniest bones in the body, which press fluid in the inner ear against membranes, which in turn move tiny hairs that trigger nearby nerve cells, which send a message to the brain. Adults are hard of hearing at the level of low frequencies, but when we are young we hear almost ten octaves or 20,000 cycles per second. Men speak at about 100 and women at 150 cycles per second. Humans hear frequencies as high as 20,000 hertz (vibrations per second)—higher than the sound of a piccolo—and as low as 20 hertz, lower than a bass fiddle. But vampire and fruit bats hear pitches as high as 210,00 hertz, ten times higher than humans. Dolphins hear 280,000 hertz.[47]

Some humans hear better than others. African Bushmen, for example, can hear the sound of an airplane approaching from as far as 70 miles away.[48] Deepak Chopra has pointed out that our skin is actually an extension of the ear, and Ackerman concurs. She says that "we listen with our bodies...a musical note is just pulsating air stimulating the organs in our ears. It may have various qualities, like volume, pitch or duration, but it is still just pulsating air. That's why the deaf often enjoy music, which they perceive as attractive vibration."[49] Helen Keller would hold her fingers against Caruso's lips and throat as he sang. She would hold a radio during a symphony concert and feel the different instruments as they played.

No doubt there is far more music in the air and in the world than our limited hearing can pick up on. Other animals hear far more than we do. But wherever there is vibration, there is music, and wherever there is music, we vibrate—yes, we dance! How much dancing the atoms and galaxies and stars and earthy creatures are doing daily! Hopefully we are not wallflowers in the dance hall of life. As Ackerman puts it, "our cells vibrate; there is music in them, even if we don't hear it.... Perhaps a mite, lost in the canyon of a crease of skin, hears our cells ringing like a mountain of wind chimes every time we move."[50] Hopefully that is the case. If so, it may be the reason our species is so drawn to beat a drum or carve a whistle or blow air into a hollowed stick or sing a melody—perhaps our *true* vocation has everything to do with praise and with encouraging others to dance and celebrate and with saying thank you for being part of the dance, part of the drama that is our shared existence: holy as it is, interconnected as it is, ongoing and open-ended and surprise-laden as it is, not unlike Divinity itself.

6. *Speaking.* Most mammals have their voice box high in their throat, so they can breathe while they eat. We humans are different. We can't eat and breathe at the same time, which is why we choke more often. Our larynx lies low in the throat, and our vocal cords are more fully developed than those of any other animal. No doubt a responsibility accompanies this unique gift of speech and singing. Are we the species assigned the task of praising? Of elaborating song? Of speaking soothing words? Of seeing words and language as revelation? To chant is to make bones and cartilage vibrate, massagelike, as all atoms are vibrating. Chanting puts us on the same vibratory highway as other beings. Other species have languages, but ours seem more diverse and more elaborate and may even be more necessary for our survival.

7. *Seeing.* Seventy percent of our bodies' sense receptors are housed in the eyes. Eyes are prominent not only in our heads but for what they bring in from the world around us. Light, the basis of all matter, finds its special home in us through the eyes. A home in Technicolor, a home with details of form and shadow, color and shade. I am often struck by how many shades of green are contained in just one glimpse of a forest, for example. How many shades of sunset or of ocean blue—or is it black? Or is it green? Or is it aqua?

Television's ubiquitous conquest of our world today may have a lot to do with the increased appetite of the eye. It is not just that television, the light machine, draws attention to our eyes whenever it is on in a room. More to the point, *television is an extension of our eyes*—it allows us to *see* what is going on where we would not otherwise be able to. Our recent sojourn to Mars is a good example, as is the Hubble telescope's picturing of the edge of the universe. It also takes us to ball games, ballets, battlefields, and presidential assassinations. The list goes on and on. For better or worse, television extends our eyesight. It is not kind to our sense of smell or touch or taste, but it feeds our eyes and ears.

Our eyes (like almost everything else in our bodies) began in the ancient seas—thus we still constantly bathe our eyes in salt water. Early dwellers of the sea developed patches on their skin that were sensitive to light. These lancelets, as we have noted, lived about 550 million years ago. The first eye was probably invented over the next 100 million to 150 million years, and over a period of tens of millions of years, lenses and mirrors were added to the basic design of the eye. The eye detected light by means of retinal cells, then sent nerve impulses to the brain for central processing. The eye of the trilobite evolved into the mosaic eyes of insects. Fish were different because they had paired eyes to protect their sides, as well as a third eye on top to protect them from attacks above them. (This third eye became the pineal gland in humans.) Fish that operate near the surface have color vision, while others—such as the shark—do not see colors.

Unlike humans, trilobites had 180-degree vision, and their "high-definition" eyes had as many as 15,000 crystalline lenses. Some developed a doublet lens, which allowed vision underwater at low light levels—their eyes had both a convex and a concave lens. The scallop boasts 50 eyes within its shell, and each of them has a compound opti-

cal system of a parabolic mirror and a correction lens—a modern telescope uses the same design. "The trilobite's eye required optical engi-
neering knowledge of considerable sophistication. Can chance
accidentally hit upon knowledge such as this? It is hard enough to envi-
sion a single lens being built by chance."[51] Most flying insects have 360-
degree vision, which is why flies are hard to swat. The ant has only 6
ommatidia (the "basic element of the insect's compound eye or little
eye"). The housefly has 4,000, and the dragonfly has 28,000. Humans
can read out 16 images per second; the housefly can read out 200. The
compound eye does not have to adopt its focus because it builds up a
mosaic image of dots of varying brightness. Flies and dragonflies "have
perfectly sharp vision."[52]

Still, according to Arne Wyller, "the vertebrate eye, in particular
the human eye, is the supreme seeing device created by Nature. In many
ways, humans still have not been able to duplicate the entire system. In
the vertebrate eye, for example, the lens can change its shape, so that it
has a variable focus to see clearly whether the object in view is far or
near."[53]

How many times a day do we express gratitude for our eyes? Or do
we take them for granted—until we have an accident or even get
blinded? Ackerman puts it this way: "Both science and art have a habit
of waking us up, turning on all the lights, grabbing us by the collar and
saying *Would you please pay attention!* You wouldn't think something as
compactly busy as life would be so easy to overlook."[54]

The eyeball is made up of three layers of different tissues. The first
lets light into the eyeball; the second provides nutrients for the living
cells of the eye. (Mitochondria live inside each of the eye cells.) The
third and innermost layer of the eye, the retina, is made up of rods and
cones. The eye is not a simple single-lens system but an optically complex two-component system. Three pairs of muscles operate the eye—
one moving the pupil up and down, another sideways right and left, and
another rotating it. A second layer is the ligaments of the eye lens,
which relax to bulge the lens and bring near objects into focus. When
they tighten, the lens thins down and brings distant objects into focus.
Dilator and sphincter muscles open and close the pupil size to let in varied amounts of light: "That design is completely analogous to the workings of a camera but is done with living cells and is automatically

regulated by the brain. As we so often find in our beautifully constructed human form, simple actions that we take for granted, like
focusing our eyesight on near or distant objects, involve a vast number
of secondary processes to achieve."[55]

The human retina contains 100 million rods and cones. (The most
sophisticated panoramic detector systems of astronomers contain only
1 million individual detectors.) The human eye can respond to light
over a range of *1 trillion to 1,* whereas the detectors we have made so
far have a range of only 300 to 1. Ordinary camera film gets overex-
posed at a factor of 1 to 10. A candle burning 10 miles away can stimulate our eye: "The human eye can see both in bright sunlight and on a
starlit night when the illumination is a trillion times fainter."[56] Eyes
work in room temperatures, while astronomers have to cool their CCD
machines to −196 degrees Celsius to detect some light. "The pupil of
the eye, the blackest part of most people's bodies, is actually the part
that lets in the most light to the interior, being the aperture through
which you see the outside world."[57] As for the molecular levels of the
eye—enzymes, proteins, and the like—we have barely begun to understand the complexity that makes the eye so useful. Among human
beings, our capacity for sight varies significantly. African Bushmen can
see four moons of Jupiter with the naked eye.[58]

8. *Thinking—the Brain.* What about our brain? Our human
brain is composed of 1 trillion cells, of which 100 billion are nerve cells
that connect with each other in up to 100 trillion ways. In addition,
each cell contains 100 trillion atoms that are bound together electri-
cally in various ways. The nerve cells transmit signals or messages. The
mechanism at the molecular level displays an astounding beauty and
elegance. One neuron receives signals from as many as 10,000 other
nerve cells.

Wyller compares the human brain to the collective linking of 100
billion microcomputers. Most synapses in the brains of mammals are
chemical, while those in most invertebrates are electrical. The chemical synapse is capable of "fine-tuning" a nerve network—where electrical synapses can identify only "on" or "off," chemical synapses can
discern "almost on" or "almost off" kinds of responses. As Wyller points
out, sensory organs and locomotive organs like fins, limbs, and inset
eyes come in a variety of forms and cell structures, but "the brains of

all life forms are basically built up of the same type of cells, the nerve cells (or neurons). The jellyfish, a very primitive type of life, uses the same type of nerve cell as the sophisticated human being."[59]

The nerve cell and its signal transmission mechanism was first laid down in the nervous systems of creatures like the jellyfish 600 million years ago. The bee's brain contains only 7,000 nerve cells, but its instinct is strong. The hardness of insect bodies placed limits on their brain growth. Humans have the most brain cells, 100 billion of them. The fish brain includes highly developed optical lobes and olfactory lobes, but the cerebrum or "thinking part" of the human brain exists only embryonically in fish. The reptile brain had to develop areas for processing balance and muscle coordination on land as well as a fight-or-flight response and a center for coordinating smell and vision. The largest dinosaur had a brain only the size of an orange—while its body weighed 100 tons, its brain weighed less than half a pound. Today the humpback whale, also weighing 100 tons, has a brain that is 18 inches long and weighs 10 pounds.

About 200 million years ago, our small mammalian ancestors developed brains in new ways. The smelling part of the brain grew in order to seek food at night. Controlling body temperature internally, providing prolonged parental care for offspring, and expanding vision for operating in the daytime (once the dinosaurs left the scene)—all this meant expanding the cerebral cortex or the outer part of the cerebrum: "It is the cerebrum that has grown explosively in the last few million years, making the mammalian brain the fastest-developing organ in evolutionary history. During the last 4 million years, the protohuman brain has tripled in size."[60] Humans have by far the largest brain-to-body-weight ratio. The human brain is 50 times heavier than the rabbit's, if a rabbit were as large as a person; 10 times that of the wolf, and 3 to 4 times that of the ape.

Living in trees, as our ancestors did, demanded that the brain's coordination of eyes and limbs develop more fully. Flexible and supple hands were part of such a development. In the past 2 million years, the cerebrum doubled in size and weight. In the last million years, one pound of gray matter was added to the brain. In light of evolutionary history, we can see how the human brain is a very unique organ: "It is, in evolutionary terms, a jumble of things. It is not a streamlined tool like the human hand, eye or ear but rather a patchwork of grafts."[61] The fish and reptilian brain are present on the spinal cord; the limbic mammalian brain is grafted onto the reptilian brain; and the simian-human brain is grafted onto the two others: "The human brain is the culmination of at least 400 million years of evolution in three major stages. First came the reptilian brain (aggression, survival instincts), arising out of the brain stem. The mammalian brain (caring and nurturing emotions) was added some 65 million years ago, and finally the large cerebral cortex (abstract mental thought) emerged only a few million years ago."[62]

In the human brain an immense amount of data input and processing is handled by billions of nerve cells without our being consciously aware of the process. "This is an absolute necessity for not overloading the conscious parts of the brain," which are the cerebellum and the cerebral cortex, the newest parts of the brain.[63] To optimize the brain's information-processing capacity, the outer layer of the new brain that began evolving 100 million years ago developed crinkled folds that can pack more brain surface area into the space of the skull.

The cerebellum is the center for coordinating body movements, including sports activities and driving a car. The earliest mammals, mouse-sized creatures, had brains 5 times that of the giant dinosaur *Tyrannosaurus rex* and 20 times that of the plant-eating dinosaurs. Wyller praises the human brain in this way:

> With the development of the human brain, we have moved into the area of Nature's grandest design scheme. In the creation of the human animal, 2 billion years of primitive cell development and 800 million years of multicellular life form development culminate—though with a spectacular brain development (the cerebral cortex) that took only a few million years.[64]

Adding the extra pound of gray matter involved growing more than 30 billion new nerve cells, capable of providing more than 30 trillion new neural connections. During a 1-million-year period, this growth had to coordinate with the nerve tissue from the older part of the brain. It is this process that "provides a unique tool capable of creating civilization and culture, which define the essence of human beings and set the species apart from all others."[65] Wyller concludes that the brief time span in which this jump occurred eliminates chance as a proper cause. "The most difficult creative achievement in evolutionary history took place in an 'instant'—a flash of generations. To have the gall to claim, as the Darwinists do, that this was the product of chance and natural selection is utterly nonsensical."[66] Since the brain of the human has not altered in the last 4,000 years, Wyler rejects the idea that chance could account for the appearance of human intelligence, creativity, and mind.

Each second more than 100,000 chemical reactions occur in the brain. This process draws a lot of stored energy from the body, so we need to feed the brain with oxygen. Exercise can increase the brain's oxygen supply by 30 percent.[67] The brain produces more than 50 psychoactive drugs that affect memory, intelligence, sedation, and aggression. For example, endorphin is like the painkiller morphine but is three times more powerful. Running and laughing produce these natural painkillers.[68]

9. *Sexuality*. As scientist Guy Murchie points out, sex is not the same thing as reproduction. Dandelions reproduce prolifically without sex. "Sex has its usefulness, for it increases variables and adaptability by its exchange of genes. . . . Sexual conjugation is a randomizing process, a shuffling of the genetic 'cards.'"[69] At the very beginning sex was without gender. In pre-Cambrian times, about a billion years ago, there was no such as thing as male or female anywhere on Earth.

Sex cells are very persistent. Murchie calls them "practically immortal." They live on generation upon generation "without dying, being passed 'down' from parent to child."[70] Not only are our sex cells demanding and persistent—they are also very numerous. The largest cell in the body is the ovum. A woman releases about 450 eggs in her lifetime. The smallest cell, on the other hand, is the male sperm. Fifteen billion sperm cells are manufactured each month, and 400 million are released in a single ejaculation. Given the great powers of generativity and beauty that sex includes, it is difficult to imagine that the Creator would have relegated sexuality to a less than sacred activity. Surely the ecstasy that sexuality gives and receives is evidence of a divine bias in favor of spirit operating through our sexuality.

HUMAN FLESH: SPIRITUAL PRACTICES TO AWAKEN AWE AND WONDER FOR OUR BODIES

Having considered nine dimensions to our fleshy existence as human and sensate beings, we can now make an effort to deepen our spiritual relationship to our bodies. Feel free to answer these questions not just with words but with drawings or poems or dances or...

1. Which of the facts or stories told awaken wonder and gratitude in you?
2. Which of these senses have you most been taking for granted? How will you cease to take them for granted in the future?
3. Which of these gifts means the most to you?
4. To further appreciate the wonderful gift of our senses, consider the following exercises:
    a. What are you smelling (or seeing or hearing or touching) right now? If nothing, go find something to smell (see, hear, or touch). What memories come to you as a result of this smell (sight, sound, or touch)?
    b. Recall a great smell (or sight or sound or touch) from your recent past.
    c. Recall a great smell (or sight or sound or touch) from your childhood.
    d. Do you feel grateful to be alive? To be able to smell, see, or touch? To be able to breathe?
    e. How do you express your gratitude for being alive and being able to smell, see, or touch?
    f. Do you know people who cannot smell? Have you experienced a loss of smell, sight, hearing, or touch? What was that like?
    g. What stories can you relate from your own autobiography that tell of your senses as saving you from harm? or leading to love or extending love of any kind?
    h. What stories recall your awakening to smells? To sights? To sounds? To sensual awakenings?

5. Gather a group of people, and discuss each of these nine gifts and graces in turn.

6. Rabbi Abraham Heschel tells us that there are three ways to respond to creation. We can exploit it, we can enjoy it, or we can *accept it with awe.*

   a. How do you exploit your body or allow others to?

   b. How do you enjoy your body?

   c. How do you accept your body with awe?

   d. How has this chapter encouraged you to accept your body with awe more fully?

7. Jesus was a human being, truly a person of flesh and spirit combined. What stories of his existence or sayings from his teachings parallel teachings in this chapter about wonder and gratitude for our own incarnated existence?

HUMAN FLESH:
GETTING THE CONTEXT RIGHT

Getting the context right is very important for dealing with sin. Too many theologians have derided our goodness in favor of railing about our evil. In doing so, they paint an inaccurate picture of *who we are* and *what we are.* And they pull us totally out of context, oblivious to *where we come from,* forgetting the creation story that in the Bible itself begins with praise. (Psalm 104 is all about the praise of creation, while Genesis itself begins with the stories of the *goodness* of creation and culminates in the *very goodness* of it.) My experience reading about the goodness of the body and its marvelous organs and capacities, then reading theologians about sin, confirms the methodology of this book. Consider, in light of reflecting on sin, the words of the poet Rilke: "Walk your walk of lament on a path of praise." The lament we rightly feel for our transgressions as individuals, as groups, and as a species must itself be contextualized by a deep meditation on our goodness. Praise what is good about us, *then* work on how to heal the imbalance.

Even in writing this chapter, I had an experience that confirms what I am saying. When I went to bed after writing about the muscles and the eyesight and the skin, I lay thinking how wonderful my body is and how much blessing it has offered me and offers the world—and how wise it is, how little brainpower it requires of me to operate so efficiently and well. It just goes about its job, like so much else in nature. Surely this is the meaning of grace, of unconditional love. I meditated on the goodness of my flesh, all the good things my eyes and ears and cells and muscles are doing even while I sleep. I slept more peacefully that night, having ended the day with praise and gratitude. Hopefully, a similar experience might befall some of the readers of this book.

There are still more blessings of the human flesh and spirit: chakra blessings. Once we have recognized them, then—and only then—will we be ready to go on to the sins of the spirit (Parts II and III).

CHAPTER 5

THE SEVEN CHAKRAS: FURTHER BLESSINGS OF OUR HUMAN FLESH

The chakra system is a way of understanding our energy system physiologically, emotionally, and spiritually. *Chakra* is a Sanskrit word from ancient India that means "wheel" or "disk" or "spinning vortex." A chakra is a place of intersection and can be any coming together of energy forces, be it a fingertip, a flower bud, a spiral galaxy, or a traffic jam. There are different traditions about chakras and about their numbers in our bodies—some speak of 32 chakras or 16 or 9. But the most common tradition speaks of seven primary or master chakras. I will be employing this tradition in this book.

The lotus flower is often used as a metaphor for a chakra because it bespeaks the unfolding of flower petals. A chakra, like a lotus flower, unfolds. It can open or close, live or die, and like the lotus it is grounded in the water and slime of earth, from which it derives its energy. Kundalini energy has been conceived as sap growing up the tree of our spine.

The Western mystical tradition also images our existence in metaphors of vegetation. The Christ in John's gospel speaks of himself as a vine and we as his branches. And the Epistle of John (1 John 3:9) talks about the "seed of God" in us. Meister Eckhart developed this theme in the fourteenth century when he wrote: "Now the seed of God is in us. Now a hazel seed grows into a hazel tree, a pear seed into a pear tree, and a seed of God into God."[1] But he cautioned that for this growth to take place, care and cultivation are needed.

FIRE AND THE CHAKRAS

Sometimes the seven chakras are compared to a coiled snake (kundalini energy) that is yearning to rise in our spinal cord and thus awaken, enliven, and enfire us. In the West both the Jewish and the Christian mystical traditions develop the fire metaphor on the basis of the *ancilla animae,* the spark of the soul. We are all born with the divine spark in us—a fire that can never be extinguished—and our life's task is to turn the spark into a flame and then into a conflagration, the fire that compassion brings. Meister Eckhart equated the spark of the soul to the place where God is birthed in us and to the Holy Spirit itself. In the spark of the soul, Eckhart said, "God glows and burns with all the divine wealth and all the divine bliss."[2] Indeed, in this spark "is hidden something like the original outbreak of all goodness, something like a brilliant light that glows incessantly, and something like a burning fire which burns incessantly. This fire is nothing other than the Holy Spirit."[3] This spark houses the image of God that each of us is: "In the soul there is something like a spark of divine nature, a divine light, a ray, an imprinted picture of the divine nature. . . . Here is located the image of God that [we] are."[4]

Hildegard of Bingen equated fire with Divinity when she wrote, "I, who am without beginning, am the fire by which all the stars are enkindled."[5] And again: "I (God) remain hidden in every kind of reality as fiery power. Everything burns because of me in such a way as our breath constantly moves us, like the wind-tossed flame in a fire. All of this lives in its essence and there is no death in it. For I am life."[6]

The Christian tradition expresses the fire-energy as that of the Holy Spirit, in its story about Pentecost and the fire that came over the fearful disciples of Jesus after his death, and in an ancient prayer that invokes the spirit in this way: "Come Holy Spirit, fill the hearts of your faithful and enkindle in them the fire of your love." This invocation to bang loving fire to the heart, to the fourth chakra, is a reminder of the connection between fire and spirit, just as the Pentecost story tells of the overcoming of fear by fire.

Fire is powerful and can be very much a blessing. It warms the heart, melts divisions, moves us out of iciness and coldness of heart, and heals. Thanks to fire we can cook, stay warm, get clean in baths and showers, and smell aromas like bread baking and soups simmering and pies awaiting our sensory desire. We gather around fire in the *hearth*, which is the *heart* of family or community, where we feel together in the deepest sense.

Each of the chakras can be envisioned in relation to its being a fireplace. The first chakra is firelessness—no fire. The fire is out, smothered, ashen. The second chakra reminds us of the fire of passion and lust and the yearning for unions of all kinds—the generative fire. Third is the fire of power and anger. The fourth fire names com*passion,* the culmination of all our passions in the fire of love. The fifth chakra is the fire of truth-telling, the opportunity to share the fires lit in our hearts and minds. The sixth chakra denotes the fire of wisdom, the coming together of intellect and intuition in mind, in the third eye, and in the bold fires of creativity, intuition, and hope. The seventh chakra actually emits fire and sends light waves out into the fires of the universe to link up with and connect with other photon-filled beings, who have their fires to offer to our own.

Fire has a dangerous and even destructive side as well. It can destroy. One thinks of the fires of war, the fires of bombs and napalm and nuclear weapons, as well as the fires that burn down our houses, destroying even our photographs if not our memories. This negative aspect to awakening fire energies in the chakras is one reason that staying asleep is so tempting. Fire brings with it responsibilities, as Prometheus learned all too well.

Fire is an apt metaphor for the chakras and for sin as well. When fire gets ignored or strays out of its hearth, it becomes dangerous. It needs tending, stoking, and tempering. It can rise up and help us or rise up and destroy us.

Fire needs water to temper it, even to put it out at times. The yang of fire needs the yin of water and of meditation and of process. Fire without water is an unbalance; sin is like that too.

Rumi, the great Sufi mystic who was a contemporary of Meister Eckhart, wrote about the fire in our souls:

Ah, once more he put a fire in me,
And once more this crazy heart is craving the open plains.
This ocean of love breaks into another wave
And blood pours from my heart in all directions.
Ah, one spark flew and burned the house of my heart.
Smoke filled the sky.
The flames grew fierce in the wind.
The fire of the heart is not easily lit.[7]

Because "the fire of the heart is not easily lit," an awareness of the chakras might help light our divine fires and make known what is "hidden" within us.

CHAKRAS: A BODY-BASED ENERGY SYSTEM

Studying the chakras can help us redeem our relationship to our bodies. We shall see that the chakras as understood in the East share a curious parallel with the endocrine system as understood by Western medicine today. As Doctor Richard Gerber puts it:

The endocrine glands are part of a powerful master control system that affects the physiology of the body from the level of cellular gene activation on up to the functioning of the central nervous system. The chakras are thus able to affect our moods and behavior through hormonal influences on brain activity.[8]

Chakras are about not *sins of the flesh* but *powers of the flesh*. Each chakra represents a power, a potential, a blessing that we have every right and responsibility to develop. (It is interesting that the Hebrew word for *blessing* is defined by Sigmund Mowinckel as a "power."[9]) Chakras represent our powers in the flesh, and the blessing of the flesh.

To bring blessing back to our awareness of body is to bring power back—healthy power, not power-over or power-under but power-with. Because each chakra is about power—getting it right and taking it back—chakra work is very political. We are all meant to share in the power that chakras are about—we all have bodies with spirit-energy yearning to be unleashed in them. There is something democratic about this common unfolding of common power.

If we fail to develop this blessing or power either as individuals or as a culture, then we are only half alive. Young people, in particular, have a right to having their chakras nurtured. Chakra work is about awakening our spiritual and physical energy—together.

THE SEVEN CHAKRAS AND SEVEN PRINCIPLES OF CREATION SPIRITUALITY

By learning the chakra tradition, we're doing Deep Ecumenism. When we consider the seven chakras in light of the seven principles of Creation Spirituality, we can bring the wisdom of the East together with the wisdom of the West. As we saw above, both the vegetative image and the fire-energy associated with the chakras finds its parallel in Western mysticism and in Middle Eastern Sufi mysticism. The organs of our endocrine system and the hormones its glands secrete correspond to the location and function of the chakras and their energies. We can bring the wisdom of the East together with the wisdom of the West as represented in the creation spirituality tradition when we consider the seven chakras in light of the seven principles of Creation Spirituality. These principles follow as a subtitle to each of the chakras.

In Part III we will apply the ancient tradition of the sins of the spirit to the tradition of the seven chakras, thus bringing East and West together around that experience we share in common and which Thomas Aquinas called "misguided love" or sin. Might another name for sin be "misdirected chakra power"?

FIRST CHAKRA: COSMOLOGY

The first chakra is called the "root chakra" or *muladhara* (which means "root" in Sanskrit). It is located at the perineum, midway between the anus and the genitals. It corresponds to the lower part of the spine called the coccyx and the coccygeal spinal ganglion. Minor chakras or subchakras connect the root chakra to the knees and feet, grounding us to the earth. The root chakra's base is often identified as the *sacrum,* which literally means in Latin "the sacred bone." The sciatic nerve is like a root for our nervous system as it travels from the sacral plexus down through the legs. It is the largest peripheral nerve in the body and is almost as thick as the thumb. This chakra is so important because it is the base chakra. All the other power centers depend on this one being engaged and alive, open and flowing. In the KundaliniYoga tradition, the kundalini is pictured as a goddess coiled like a snake at the base of the spine. To open the first chakra is to release this energy to rise up the spine. Kundalini is often envisioned as the caduceus, the winged staff with two serpents coiled around it—interestingly, the symbol that the medical profession has taken for its own.

It is said that when the root chakra is in balance, "we feel secure, alert, full of active energy, stable and warm."[10] We also feel grounded. This chakra grounds us to the earth, connects us to the depth of things. It is invoked by dances that lead us into the earth: indigenous dance is based on first-chakra awareness—the bent knees and the open feet connect us to the earth. A color and a musical note is associated with each chakra—our bodies are tuning instruments. The first chakra's color is red—a deep, vibrant red, the color of beginnings, of blood, of the longest wavelength and slowest vibration in the visible spectrum. The color red gives off strength. In an experiment at the University of Texas, the grips of individuals being tested became 13.5 percent stronger when they were looking at the color red.[11] The musical pitch associated with the root chakra is C.

FIRST CHAKRA AS COSMOLOGICAL

In the Creation Spirituality tradition, I associate this chakra with vibratory energy and with cosmology. Why? Because in this chakra we hear deeply. Indeed, a strong case could be made that animals that still have tails at their sacrum or holy bone are actually picking up sound and vibrations with them—the tail is a kind of antenna. This is one reason four-legged animals are often more alert than we are. To engage this chakra, making deep sounds of "om" is very useful. Getting in touch with the sounds of the universe, pulling sounds in, is one way to awaken this chakra. What we now know about the universe is that *all beings make sound, all atoms make sound, because all atoms are vibrating.* Vibration, as scientist Stuart Cowan points out, is the simplest way for a system to behave. Every atom is vibrating, and all atoms want either to be in their vibrational mode of being or to rest. This is called an eigenvalue or an eigenfunction—it has to do with a tuning relationship for which all beings yearn.

If every atom is vibrating and we can tune in to the sound, or vibration, that atoms emit, then when we are talking about the first chakra, we are clearly talking about the *whole* or cosmology. (*Kosmos* is the Greek word for "whole.") To put it inversely, to the extent that we are unconnected to the whole or lack a cosmology, we are lacking in first chakra energy. To bring cosmology alive is to bring the first chakra alive and vice versa. To the extent that we are unconnected to the whole or lack a cosmology we are lacking in first chakra energy. The endocrine system associated with the first chakra lies in the adrenals, which are about strength; they emit adrenaline to deal with fear, with stress-filled or dangerous occasions.

Tellingly, in the Eastern tradition, the first chakra is symbolized by the four-petaled lotus flower. Four is the cosmic number: four directions, four winds, four directions of the cross. The tetragon symbolizes the whole or the cosmos. To talk about the cosmos is to talk about the earth—"ecology is functional cosmology," as Thomas Berry likes to say. Thus, this chakra grounds us in the earth *and* connects us to the heavens. Indeed, our bodies are both earthly and cosmic since their elements were birthed in a supernova explosion 5.5 billion years ago (except for those hydrogen atoms we carry in our bodies from 14 billion years ago!)

Hearing takes place in our lowest chakra. We hear, as we learned in Chapter 4, with our entire body. Because the ear is the first organ to be developed in the young fetus, the brain is properly an extension of the heart, and the skin is an extension of the ear. At times we hear with the skin—we actually feel vibrations on it. What makes the ear work, after all, is a bone tinier than a grain of rice; surely our tailbone, wedged into our bums, is also a kind of ear, picking up vibrations. In the first chakra, we hear the whole, hear the music of all beings singing and vibrating and dancing: no wonder the bone that picks up this cosmic music for us is called holy. Music from all holy flesh flows through it. Such an orchestra! Are we listening?

Is it just coincidence that ancient spiritual traditions talk about beginning the spiritual journey with sound? "In the beginning was the sound," says Hinduism. "In the beginning the Creator *sang* every creature into existence," say the aboriginals of Australia. "In the beginning was the Word," says the Gospel of John, which is par excellence the gospel of Sophia and the Christ. Mahatma Gandhi said, "To become divine is to become attuned to the whole of creation."[12] The first chakra takes all the sounds of creation in and attunes to all the beings singing about their presence in the world. Truly cosmology is alive here. It begins everything—even the journey of the chakras.

SECOND CHAKRA: FEMINIST PHILOSOPHY

The second chakra is the sexual chakra. The endocrine glands associated with this chakra are the ovaries and testicles, which produce eggs and sperm respectively.

Few would question that the West, under the influence of Neoplatonic thought and Augustinian sexual neuroses, has not dealt positively with sexuality. Indeed, the great psychologist and cultural critic Otto Rank suggests that from the fourth century to Freud in the early twentieth century, the West identified the soul and the quest for immortality with sexuality. For those with inheritances to pass on, proving one's offspring to be legitimate was a preoccupation, and this excessive seriousness about sex so burdened our awareness of it that we lost altogether the sense of play and eros with which the world's indigenous people approach the subject. Sexuality became something negative and heavy, a burden,[13] and for many Christians like Augustine, a regret.

The biblical tradition, as I have pointed out elsewhere,[14] is not so negative about sexuality. Jesus himself has very little to say about it, and when he does speak, he speaks on behalf of those who have been belittled by society, whether it is the woman caught in adultery or the woman who was a prostitute, or the denigration of women in a society where men but not women could divorce over adultery. The Song of Songs, an entire book in the Bible, is dedicated to celebrating human sexual love as a theophany, or revelation of the divine. Set in a cosmological context, this book is a veritable redemption of the Garden of Eden story. When the lovers exit from behind a bush hand in hand, they are said to have come from the "wilderness." Thus human love is a kind of wilderness experience, and wilderness often expresses a Divine revelation. "I will call you into the wilderness and there speak to you heart to heart," says the prophet Hosea.

One day I had a conversation with a young faculty member from southern India, where they have worshiped the mother goddess for thousands of years. When the subject of sexuality came up, he said, "Well, of course, sexuality is a power within myself that I must respect." This statement struck me as very non-Western. When I was an adolescent, the instructions given me about sexuality were: "Treat your date as you would your sister." Sexuality was projected outward. Little positive was said about this "power within myself that I must learn to respect." But to recognize the sexual chakra is to take back the power of one's own sexuality and to honor it within. *Then* one is in a position to "love one's neighbor as oneself," that is, to respect the sexuality of others.

A healthy spiritual training program is sure to awaken the chakras, and the second chakra is no exception. In our program at the Institute in Culture and Creation Spirituality and now at the University of Creation Spirituality, sexuality invariably becomes a special issue around the sixth week or mid-October. One October, as I finished a lecture, a student spoke up. "I have never felt so sexual," she said. "I want to give everyone, men and women alike, my room number in the dormitory." I was a bit taken aback by the forwardness of the remark, but after thinking it over I offered the following observation. Our sexuality is one-seventh of our chakra powers. It should be put in that context. It's not a question of denigrating our sexual impulses, but neither ought we deny the other six chakras their role and power. If someone wishes to run their life on just one of their chakras, that is their business, but it may well be a one-sided life that soon runs out of gas, for all the chakras are meant to work together.

The sexual chakra is not just about sex; it is also about generativity, the power to beget, conceive, and give birth. You do not have to have an active sex life to pay attention and honor this chakra. Healthy celibates are capable of honoring this chakra. A good example is the Tibetan monks, whose deep and sonorous chants are so full of vibration and depth that they are clearly sexual as well. Aquinas taught that sexuality is a "great blessing" and that "all generativity comes from God." How different this teaching is from the ascetic injunction to repress one's sexual energy in the name of climbing up to God. Philo, for instance, said that "we must keep down our passions just as we keep down the lower classes." Meister Eckhart celebrated that we are all "meant to be mothers of God," and in doing so he honors the profound generative powers of men and women alike.[15]

The second chakra can be said to correspond to *feminist philosophy* in Creation Spirituality. For as a philosophy, feminism is committed to overcoming dualism and to living out a life of interconnectivity. But sexual dualism—separating matter from spirit, spirituality from sexuality, and male from female—lies at the heart of a patriarchal worldview. Since the second chakra integrates our sexual energies and sees them as powers to respect, giving attention to it heals the dualistic one-sidedness that we inherited from a patriarchal philosophical era, which looked on sexuality with pessimism and on other genders and sexual orientations as inferior.

This chakra is symbolized by six petals, and the color representing it is orange. The musical pitch that travels with the color orange is D.

THIRD CHAKRA: LIBERATION

The third chakra is that of the solar plexus and corresponds to the pancreas, the liver, and the adrenals (as does the first chakra). Its symbol is of ten petals. The pancreas secretes the hormone insulin, which controls our sugar metabolism. Adrenals produce adrenaline, which can move a mother to accomplish such feats as lifting a car when her baby is underneath it.

This chakra is located just below the belly button, and it is the place of chi and of centering. (Chi or qi is understood in Taoism to represent movement; it is the life essence and the energy circulating in the body.[16]) In aikido, tai chi, and other martial arts, the practitioner centers himself or herself at this center point so as not to be moved. It is a place of strength and empowerment.

Being a chakra of empowerment, the third chakra corresponds in Creation Spirituality to liberation theology, for liberation theologies are about people becoming empowered who are in touch with their own oppression. Compassion and moral outrage begin in this chakra—it is in our "guts" that we feel injustice or feel kicked by oppression. In the gospels the Greek word *splanchnizomai,* meaning "compassion," is used often about Jesus; it means, literally, "his bowels turned over." The third chakra is about those events that move us, that make our bowels turn over. Such outrage inspires prophetic movements to act. Perhaps the pancreas contributes to such action, since sugar can be a quick-action stimulant.

People who are bitter, Aquinas taught, carry anger inside them for a long time. The third chakra is about responding to that anger, rather than letting it fester, and investing it in empowering acts of liberation. Justice-making is an important expression from this chakra. Where the justice-making aspect of compassion is ignored, this chakra is underutilized. Perhaps the increase in colon cancers is in some way related to a feeling of disempowerment and inability to express one's outrage in healthy ways.[17]

Yellow is the color associated with this chakra. In its negative form the body turns jaundiced yellow when the liver is inflamed from toxins. The musical tone that travels parallel to wavelengths of yellow is E. It is a place of strength and empowerment.

FOURTH CHAKRA: COMPASSION

The fourth chakra is the heart chakra. It is located in the center of the body, midway between the three lower chakras and the three higher chakras. Meister Eckhart speaks of the heart's primacy in the following manner.

We should begin with the heart which is the noblest part of the body. It lies in the center of the body from which point it bestows life on the whole body. For the spring of life arises in the heart and has an effect like heaven.... Heaven is also in the middle of things. It is equally close to all the extremities.... The spring of life is placed in the heart.[18]

The fourth chakra's strength depends on the health and vitality of the lower chakras, which support it and send energy its way. The tone for this chakra is F-sharp, and its color is green. Significantly, the twelfth-century abbess and mystic Hildegard of Bingen built her entire theology on what she called *viriditas* or "greening power." She felt all creatures contained the greening power of the Holy Spirit, which made all things creative and nourishing. Hildegard also painted a picture of "the man in sapphire blue" whose hands are outstretched in front of his chest. This gesture is an ancient metaphor for compassion, since compassion is about taking heart energy and putting it into one's hands—that is, putting it to work in the world. In Creation Spirituality, the fourth chakra corresponds to compassion, which begins with moral outrage (chakra three) but culminates in healing energy (chakra four).

In the *Yoga Darshana Upanishads* it is said that *prana,* or the Divine energy force, "is omnipresent: in the throat, in the nose, in the navel, in the heart—there it resides permanently.[19] The heart chakra is a special energy place. It includes not only our heart, which pumps blood throughout our body, but also our respiratory system. A normal human being breathes in about five thousand gallons of air per day. In weight alone this amounts to thirty-five times the food or drink we take in daily, and while we can go weeks without food and days without water, we can only go minutes without air. Air immediately enters the bloodstream, and if oxygen is not supplied to the cells, they will die. Our circulatory and respiratory systems therefore work in tandem. Every red blood cell transports oxygen molecules from the lungs, distributing them to tissues and organs, which in turn infuse the red blood cells with carbon dioxide. This waste product is expelled from the lungs when we exhale. We breathe in order to bring oxygen and blood together.

Is it any wonder that so many spiritual traditions and meditative practices advise paying attention to the breath rather than taking it for granted? After all, our first breath constitutes our coming into the world, and our last breath constitutes our exiting this world. One creation story in the Bible says that humans were created when God breathed the divine breath into the clay. Surely this is an affirmation of the holiness of breath, which is also *ruah* or spirit. Hildegard says that there is only one spirit or breath in the universe, and it is God's. We all participate in breathing it in and out.

The truth is that most people do not breathe deeply—they do not take advantage of having lungs that work. Studies demonstrate that while our lungs can hold about two pints of air, the average person breathes in about one pint or even less per breath. In a lifetime we breathe about 75 million gallons of air.[20]

The fourth chakra is about not just the heart and lungs but also the thymus, the heart-shaped endocrine gland that is the major gland of the immune system. The thymus produces white blood cells, which constitute the immunological resistance of the body. White blood cells produce antibodies to fight viruses, and some of them even eat and digest bacteria. The thymus gland prepares the T-cells to do their work in resisting invading cells. It fights infections and cancer itself. When I had pneumonia recently, a holistic doctor told me that my thymus had shut down. Many pneumonia patients are prone to catching other diseases for this reason: their thymus closes down.

We can engage the thymus by thumping the chest gently and firmly. Interestingly, both Roman Catholics and Jews have this in their spiritual traditions. The *mea culpa* of Catholics when admitting guilt for their misdemeanors is like the beating of the chest by Jewish people in grief or on Yom Kippur, the Day of Atonement, the time of forgiveness. To thump the chest is to stimulate the thymus, and therefore the heart chakra. Forgiveness is indeed part of compassion and heart energy. It has been so often underestimated as a power in the human race. Jesus and Buddha and other spiritual teachers tried to stimulate forgiveness in all of us. It is a kind of letting go. It is not about altruism but about liberation—one's own—for until we forgive, we are still in a resentful or spiteful relationship. We are still running on anger. While anger has its place (as in the third chakra), we ought not cling to it, for if we do, we are still in a negative relationship with the source of that anger. Even if a person or situation deserves our anger, it does not serve us to remain angry forever. Freedom comes from forgiveness, from getting on with our lives, and letting go to become as young and free as our "unborn self," as Meister Eckhart put it.[21]

Aquinas said that the first effect of love is "melting."[22] The warmth of the heart melts anger and resentments. The heat generated by love enters the hands to make them healing hands. The poet William Butler Yeats sang of the fourth chakra when he wrote:

> When such as I cast out remorse
> So great a sweetness flows into the breast
> That I must dance and I must sing
> For I am blessed by everything.
> Everything I look upon is blessed.[23]

Our whole perception of reality changes when our heart changes—we see all as blessing, all as praiseworthy and good. For this to happen we must forgive; we must let go of remorse. After that forgiveness a sweetness flows "into the breast," the heart chakra. All comes alive for us.

Perhaps our neglect of the heart chakra explains some of the many heart attacks among men in our culture and breast cancer cases among women. Christiane Northrup, a physician who has spent over twenty years working with women with breast cancer, feels that the latter is indeed the case. Women who feel they are loving and are loved are less prone to that disease than other women.[24]

FIFTH CHAKRA: PROPHECY

The fifth chakra is the throat chakra. The thyroid and the parathyroid are the glands associated with it. The word *thyroid* means a "shield-shaped door"—and this metaphor of door may be as good as any for the voice area, which is also an eating area. Things go out and things come in. The thyroid produces the hormone thyroxine, which in turn produces iron-containing amino acids, which are the chief component of proteins that are essential to diet and to life itself. In this way the thyroid controls energy levels. The parathyroid secretes hormones that regulate calcium metabolism.

This chakra represents the throat and the expressing of one's truth and wisdom. The throat lies between the heart and the mind chakras. Truth comes from both heart and mind. This chakra is also the *prophetic chakra:* The throat is the trumpet that speaks our truth, as the prophets also *spoke out* (the meaning of *prophetein* in Greek) their truth. It is surely telling that a calcium shortage is common among many women today. Some people say it is because of childbearing, but women have always borne children. Perhaps it has something to do with the closing down of the parathyroid, which regulates calcium metabolism—in other words, with the "loss of voice" that many women experience.

It is my experience, in listening to stories of people over the past two decades, that many people are having dreams about their throats. This is especially true of women and of gay people, and I think the meaning is that these people are finding their voice after having had it taken away for many centuries. They are on a search for their true voice. A few years ago a diminutive Catholic sister in our spirituality program embarked on a vision quest. During the vision quest an eagle kept appearing to her and pointing at her throat. Upon graduation from our program six months later, she went to work in a large hospital that her religious community managed. A few months later I got a call from her superior: "What happened to this tiny sister we sent to Oakland?" she asked me. "She came back and is practically running the hospital. And doing a fine job of it too." What happened was that she found her voice.

The prophetic call is to speak out to interfere with what we see is obstructing what we deeply believe in. This chakra recovers the sense of the "holy word" that we are called to speak regularly in our lives. Its symbol is sixteen petals. The color for the fifth chakra is sky blue, and the musical pitch that accompanies it is G.

SIXTH CHAKRA: CREATIVITY

The sixth chakra is the brow chakra, sometimes called the third eye. It is said to house our insight, intuition, and perception. It is symbolized by two large petals, each of which contains forty-eight divisions, and it is located in the center of the forehead where the eyebrows meet. The endocrine gland associated with this chakra is the pituitary, often called the "master gland." The hormones it secretes control the thyroids, the sex organs, and the adrenal gland's blood-sugar levels; it also regulates the ovaries and testes. Sunlight arouses the sex drive by activating this gland, which in turn emits hormones that give the euphoric feeling of love. When alteration occurs to this organ, falling in love rarely occurs. The chemical produced is phenylethylamine—which is also found in chocolate.[25]

The pituitary also makes beta-endorphins, or natural opiates that help the body reduce pain, stress, and depression. The pituitary gland plays a special role in motherhood, as scientist Arne Wyller points out:

> The pituitary gland in the mother's brain releases a special chemical, the hormone oxytocin. That particular chemical will travel in the bloodstream to different parts of the body and will enter numerous nerve cells. In most cells nothing will happen as a result. Only in the nerve cells attached to those muscle cells responsible for uterine contractions will oxytocin find the right receptor molecules to initiate contractions.[26]

In Creation Spirituality the sixth chakra corresponds to the theme of creativity. Here art as meditation, which plays so prominent a role in Creation Spirituality education and training, finds a physiological base: The act of creativity actually produces hormones or beta-endorphins that reduce pain, stress, and depression and initiates birthing contractions! The somatotrophic growth hormone that the pituitary gland secretes, if stimulated by touch on a regular basis, produces calmer and less excitable behavior among rats, Deane Juhan reports. "They are more lively, more curious, more active problem solvers. They are more willing to explore new environments (ungentled animals usually withdraw fearfully from novel situations), and advance more quickly in all forms of conditioned learning exercises." Though calmer, "they tend to be more dominant in social and sexual situations."[27]

In my years of teaching art as meditation, I have found a parallel.[28] Several years ago, on the first day of class, I had the students in our program draw pictures of their souls. One student demonstrated some deep soul trouble. Her picture was full of dark lines and chaos. When I spoke to her out of class, she told me she had been an artist and had painted in the convent where she lived. Ten years previously the convent had burned down with all of her paintings in it. Instead of taking up painting again, she was assigned by her community the task of sorting the mail. She became ill and depressed and was on drugs prescribed by her psychiatrist. I called her provincial and complained that she had no right to send us a student who was on drugs. "Oh, Father," she exclaimed, "we were desperate. We tried everything and have spent hundreds of thousands of dollars on therapists and drugs."

We kept her in our program, and she went off the drugs and shed her depression. Upon graduating, she attended an art school. A gifted artist, she is now back in her community earning a living through her art. In short, she found her soul again. I find this to be a powerful story about what happens when the sixth chakra is neglected.

As we have seen, the brow chakra is the place where the opening of the third eye takes place. Meister Eckhart said that "the eye with which I see God is the same eye with which God sees me." Creativity is like that. Many people feel the spirit flow through them when they are in the act of creativity.

The brow chakra also symbolizes the midground between the left and right hemispheres of the brain. To balance this chakra, one needs *both* an intellectual life *and* an intuitive life. An artist—contrary to the caricature of our society—is decidedly *not* solely an "intuitive" personality. An artist is also a thinker, an intellectual, with ideas to share through the medium of artistic expression. The sixth chakra demands a balance of right and left hemisphere, of synthetic and analytic work.

Not long ago when I was lecturing in Ohio, a woman approached me with the following story. A judge had said to her, "I am sick and tired of sending teenage offenders to jail. But they are too tough for the schools. Can't you invent me a school where I could send them as an alternative to jail?" She was reading my works at the time on the importance of creativity in education, so she invented a school that was all about creativity.

The students came at nine A.M. and left at four P.M., and all they did was creative work: dance, drama, video-making, painting, clay, poetry, and so on. The result? First, they liked it. Second, they came every day.

Third, they worked hard. Fourth, they learned self-discipline. Creative work gave them a language and an outlet by which to express their grief and rage and sorrow, and it was fun. Many of our social problems might be relieved if we paid appropriate attention to the sixth chakra. But where educational curricula systematically exclude the opportunity to develop creativity, troubles ensue. Several charter schools I know that are successful with youth in trouble are also employing methods of learning that ignite this chakra. Many young people driven to despair and frustration at home and school need creativity more than anything else to find their way, to find their souls. This should not be so difficult for adults to figure out. But institutions that are frozen in rationalistic definitions of education put creativity in the backseat, and those experiencing a budget crunch more often than not jettison the theater, art, and music departments first.

The color for this chakra is indigo or midnight blue. Its musical tone is A.

SEVENTH CHAKRA: COMMUNITY

The seventh chakra is located at the back of the head, where a newborn baby's head is so soft and where monks shave off their hair in what is called a "tonsure." It is also where Jewish people wear a skull-cap called a yarmulkeh at sabbath services, funerals, and other sacred occasions. The purpose is to keep the crown energy harnessed and earthbound in times of grief, when it may prefer to disperse. The seventh chakra is called the crown chakra because it is located at the crown of the head. Its symbol is twelve petals, with eighty subpetals each. Sometimes the crown chakra is called the "many-petaled lotus." The number of petals associated with this chakra is a cosmic number: There are twelve months of the year and twelve signs of the zodiac; twelve is also the number of the lost tribes of Israel and the disciples of Jesus. Twelve signifies wholeness and completion; it alerts us, as does the number four (twelve is four times three), to cosmology, an experience of the whole.

In the tradition of Creation Spirituality, this chakra corresponds to connecting and relating, to ecumenism and the building of community.

In this chakra we send light out into the world to link up with other light beings, whether these be our ancestors (called the "communion of saints" in Christianity) or angels or spirits (who are light beings), or time and space, or birds or animals. The tradition of the Cosmic Christ is a tradition about the light waves in every being yearning to link up with every other being. (Science now assures us that photons or light waves exist in all beings.) The seventh chakra is like a *beacon* or searchlight that extends into the heavens and into the past (our ancestors) and the future (our descendants) to make community happen. The seventh chakra puts forth the light aroused in our being and searches for the light, *doxa,* glory, or wisdom in others. Indeed, it is light meeting light; it is going out to the Christ- or Buddha-nature in all things and in all religions and ethnic groups, without abandoning one's own tradition. It is about touching the universalism of all people under one Light, the Creator of all.

The endocrine gland corresponding to this chakra is the pineal gland, located at the base of the brain. Its function, interestingly enough, has to do with internal and external light. The pineal gland involves our sense of season, well-being, the onset of puberty, and the amount of testosterone or estrogen we produce.[29] It secretes the hormone melatonin, which we now understand stimulates the immune system and modulates endocrine gland functions while regulating the body's natural cycles. Melatonin inhibits ovulation, sperm production, and the hormones responsible for sexual desire and can increase psychic ability, visions, and hallucinogenic effects.[30] Testosterone is highest in men during the sunlight summer months and lowest in winter.[31] Apparently melatonin is secreted only at nighttime, in the dark. Thus we have in this system a metaphor about the interconnectivity of light and darkness. This chakra, which connects us to cosmic light, is dependent on cosmic darkness to do its work. With this chakra we put our light and energy into the world, it represents a culmination of all the accomplishments of the other chakras.

This chakra is about gathering one's light energy and fire from all the previous chakras and extending it into relationships with other light beings in the universe. It is eminently an energy of sharing and of community building and of reaching out.

The color for this chakra is violet, and the musical tone that corresponds to violet is B-flat.

GENERAL OBSERVATIONS AND CONCLUSIONS ABOUT THE CHAKRAS AS BLESSINGS

Reflecting on the Eastern tradition of the chakras in light of the Western tradition of Creation Spirituality allows us to appreciate more deeply the blessing that we all carry around in our bodies. It prevents us from taking our bodies and their amazing powers for granted. Below is an illustration of the parallels between chakra teachings and the teachings of Creation Spirituality, that oldest of Western spiritual traditions.

7 CHAKRAS   7 PRINCIPLES OF CREATION SPIRITUALITY

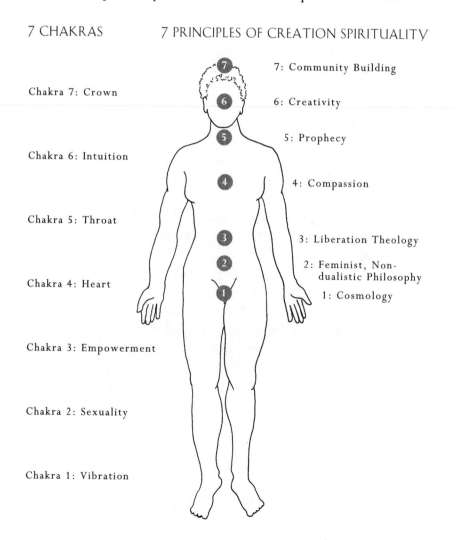

Chakra 7: Crown

Chakra 6: Intuition

Chakra 5: Throat

Chakra 4: Heart

Chakra 3: Empowerment

Chakra 2: Sexuality

Chakra 1: Vibration

7: Community Building

6: Creativity

5: Prophecy

4: Compassion

3: Liberation Theology

2: Feminist, Non-dualistic Philosophy

1: Cosmology

There is nothing hidden about the agenda of Creation Spirituality. This schema shows how the chakra tradition helps to ground Creation Spirituality in the body. Creation Spirituality helps to assure that the chakra tradition is not self-absorbed and shows how the "body" is a cosmic body, body politic, even mystical body, as in the phrase the "mystical body of Christ." The seven themes of Creation Spirituality are a fine summary of that spiritual tradition's "agenda."

It is useful to compare some of the chakras to each other for the special relationships that ensue. For example, the first and seventh chakras are both cosmological in a special way. How do they differ? The first chakra *brings in* the *sounds* of all beings, while the seventh chakra *puts out* the *light* to all beings, connecting up with the light within all beings. One takes in; the other puts out.

The second and sixth chakras also have a special relationship because both are about creativity or generativity in their own way. The sexuality of the second chakra is an obvious expression of creativity, a kind of marriage of female and male, while the sixth chakra is a marriage of right and left hemispheres of the brain, if you will, of intellect and intuition. The third and fifth chakras also share a common base, insofar as the prophet speaks out from a place of moral outrage and compassion, understood as the quest for justice. The prophetic fifth chakra is a kind of warrior chakra, and the warrior needs the centering and the empowerment that the third chakra affords. The fourth chakra remains central—it takes in air and it gives air out; it pumps blood out and it pulls blood in; it reminds us that all our powers, all our chakras, are about love and compassion, giving and receiving.

We may understand sins of the spirit as imbalances in our chakras or, as Aquinas put it in defining sins, as "misdirected love." The chakra tradition helps us ground spirit in our bodiliness and to honor our flesh, and assists in shedding light on human mistakes to which we are prone.

SPIRITUAL EXERCISES APROPOS OF THE SEVEN CHAKRAS

Having considered the seven chakras in the light of the Creation Spirituality tradition, the following exercises may help us develop a deeper awareness of these chakras or energy systems.

1. "Count Your Blessings." In this exercise, consider each of the seven chakras, and elaborate how many more blessings you can count around each of them.

     First chakra: Blessings of sounds and vibrations you have accepted in in your life.

     Second chakra: Blessings of your sensual and sexual self.

     Third chakra: Blessings of your gut reactions, your anger, your journey to empowerment for self and others.

     Fourth chakra: Blessings of your heart and immune system, your defenses, and your circulatory system.

     Fifth chakra: Blessings of your throat—the singing, speaking, praising, you have done.

     Sixth chakra: Blessing of your mind—the study, the learning, the creativity you have enjoyed and that others have enjoyed through you.

     Seventh chakra: Blessings of warmth, of light-giving and light-connecting, of community-making, of broadening diversity and reach-out or ecumenism in which you have been involved.

2. Create a litany around all seven chakras, and chant it as a group.

3. Create a litany unique to each of the seven chakras.

4. With a list of the seven chakras in front of you, draw a picture of the two chakras that you feel are the most developed in you. Share this picture with another person, who also has drawn in response to the same question. Listen to what she or he has to say about your drawing and its meaning, then speak about your own.

5. With a list of the seven chakras in front of you, draw a picture of the two chakras that you feel need the most attention in your life at this time. Share as in question 4.

6. Consider your answers to questions 4 and 5 in relation to the Creation Spirituality themes. Do your answers to these questions shed light on your awareness of this tradition? How can Creation Spirituality assist in the development of your chakras? How can the development of the chakras help you deepen the Creation Spirituality tradition in your life?

7. Meditate on each of these categories of beings, then create a ritual for each, thanking the universe for them, perhaps with paint-

ing or dancing or chanting or whatever mode of gratitude and expression you or your group feels like:

    a. All cosmic beings giving off sound.

    b. All sexual beings.

    c. All self-empowered beings.

    d. All heart beings.

    e. All speaking, expressive beings.

    f. All creative, reflective beings.

    g. All connecting and relating beings; all light beings practicing community.

Humanity is meant to be all seven. If we lack one or more, we have a problem.

8. "Gifts of the Earth." Make a circle and, with paper and crayons, create a mask that represents some creature of the Earth, such as rocks, water, microbes, soil, plants, trees, animals, fishes, or birds. Put on the mask, and speak your truth about your species' beauty. Listen to one another as you each speak on behalf of the beauty and dignity of other species.

THE EVOLUTION OF SIN:
SIN AND ITS MEANINGS

*H*aving considered the blessings of flesh, we have set the *context* for exploring the assaults we commit on blessing. Sin, like all else in our universe, evolves. As cultures evolve, we see the world differently. We develop tools with which to imprint our values, ideologies, and powers onto the world. Our perspective on sin and our awareness of it undergo gradual and sometimes radical transformations.

Context is very important. Getting the context right is about *perspective,* which some might say is everything. At least it is the way we see everything. I had a recent experience about perspective. As I write this, I am staying at a friend's summer home, which his family has lent me on three previous occasions to help me write this book. But this time around, two perspectives have changed for me. First, it is now late October, and my previous visits were in June, July, and August. The seasonal change has put me into a totally different perspective about this place. The days are shorter and much cooler; the summer vacationers have departed—the place is even quieter than it was before. The direction of the sun, its rising and its setting, is altered. Fewer deer and geese are roaming about.

When I went hiking on the opposite side of the lake for the first time, I hardly recognized the lake at all; its shape was different. I searched for the home I was staying in, now across from me, and its appearance altered drastically from the view that I was used to. The hills, the trees, the water, all these were changed. When I was among the Aboriginals of Australia for a day of art and spirituality, they explained to me that they do not put their paintings on the wall for people to look at, but on the ground. Viewers all sit around the painting, and *because each one sits in a different place, each one has his or her own story to tell about the painting.* The perspective is different, and so the painting receives many interpretations.

If these modest experiences, brought on by a change of season and a change of hiking venue, could so affect my *perspective* on a house, imagine how a new creation story, a new cosmology that gives us 15 billion years in which to view our universe, can alter our perspective on human existence, on human wonders and human sin. Imagine what a difference it can make in our awareness of the shadow side of humankind if we place the discussion in the *context and perspective* of the glorious wonders and gratuitous grace of the cosmos, the Earth, and our own flesh and spirit. This is what I mean by getting the context right. Our perspective is changing, and with it our self-understanding of both our glory and our iniquity.

To discuss the human condition in proper perspective, the blessing of flesh is not enough. We must *protect* flesh as well as celebrate it, and we must take responsibility for what we claim to cherish. Let there be no question about it: *The eco-crisis is a flesh crisis.* The diminution of fourteen of our seventeen fisheries in the oceans, the annual disappearance of 26 billion tons of topsoil, the more-than-one-acre-per-second loss of the rain forests, the extinction spasm of 26,000 species yearly, the diminished vigor of the food we eat, the pollution of the waters, the failure of immune systems—all this is about flesh in crisis, flesh disappearing, flesh losing its powers, flesh under attack. Sacred flesh is being offered anew on an altar of sacrifice.

Now we come to the second part of our study: when we ignore flesh's wonder, that ignorance leads to abuse. The traditional name for such ignorance is *sin*. Ignorance as sin is an ancient tradition of the East, and Hinduism in particular considers the basic sin of humanity to be ignorance. In the West, Thomas Aquinas, among others, writes about the serious sin that willful ignorance entails.

In Part II we will consider what the mystics say about sin, and the various meanings of the term *sin* from biologists and theologians. In Part III we will examine the seven chakras of the East and the seven capital sins of the West.

CHAPTER 6

WHAT THE MYSTICS SAY
ABOUT SIN,
INCLUDING RUMI, KABIR, JULIAN,
ECKHART, JESUS, AND PAUL

> Mystics are hungry for goodness, hungry for blessing,
> which helps explain why they spend little time talking
> about sin. They prefer to talk of God and ways to God than
> to talk of sin and human folly. Kabir, the fifteenth-century
> mystic from India, sang, "O Brother, what is good? What
> is bad? They are all reflections of the same Light!"[1]

In Psalm 104, the poet is so enraptured with God's creation that he
sings thirty-four verses about God's holy creation; only in half of the
last verse does he refer to "sinners" and "the wicked." Mysticism offers
a different *context* for dealing with sin and morality. Mystics often
encourage people to go beyond good and evil as popularly understood.
They encourage ecstasy or drunkenness, being on fire, heart excitement, oneness as opposed to dualism, silence over noise and busyness,
madness, inner purity rather than outer conformity, remembering of
our origins, connecting to the Source. One reason mystics are slow to
judge good and evil is that they are artists, artists of the soul's deep
experience. As artists, they are slow to judge, but they want to

experience first and want to encourage others to experience before judging.

During the machine era of the modern period, as Theodore Roszak points out, mysticism has been ignored and even "ridiculed." But mysticism is the awe with which we respond to existence and to creation, when we learn not to take it for granted. I believe most people are mystics, at least as children and on their deathbeds, when they begin to realize how precious every breath is.

The surest way to begin to consider sin in the context of mysticism would be to quiz some mystics, people who have lived out their lives in the context of awe and wonder. We are blessed to have many such people in our various heritages. In this chapter we shall consider six of them for their teachings about sin.

RUMI

Rumi does not speak a lot about sin. As we indicated in the Introduction, he criticizes those whose preaching about morality interferes with the pleasures of spirituality:

> Out beyond ideas of wrongdoing and rightdoing,
> there is a field. I'll meet you there.
>
> When the soul lies down in that grass,
> the world is too full to talk about.
> Ideas, languages, even the phrase *each other*
> doesn't make any sense.[2]

The nondualism that mysticism elicits does not lend itself to a lot of talk—including talk about morality. In another poem Rumi again takes up the subject of the tension between morality and spirituality when he sings:

> They say you bring the word of God
> yet all I hear is talk of good and bad—
> nothing of love and truth.[3]

Here Rumi complains that preachers are better on rules and judgments than on the bigger picture of love and truth. But he is not saying there is no room for talk about good and bad—just that it must be put in a larger context of love and truth. Morality talk can be cheap talk.

A strong case can be made that most mystics who are awakening a culture at a particularly dangerous time of change and transformation are critiquing language, including the language around good and evil, good and bad. Morality gets stale when it is cut off from everyday living. It can be outgrown. In the Victorian age a woman was not to reveal her ankle lest lustful men would find themselves swept away. Ankles hardly seem worthy of note in the late twentieth century.

Moralizing requires its own critique, as the mystics knew well; Rumi is a good example. Yet even he calls people to task for their actions when he says:

> If you hurt others, don't expect kindness in return.
> One who sows rotten seeds will get rotten fruit.
> God is great and compassionate
>> but if you plant barley,
>> don't expect a harvest of wheat.[4]

In spite of the great one-ing with the Divine One who is Compassion itself, we do still take responsibility for the seeds that we sow. They will return with either their fruit or their weeds. Rumi did not deny our capacity for sinfulness, but he put it in the context of our empowerment to do something about it.

> The winds of anger, lust, and greed
> carried off him who did not keep
> the times of prayer. I am a mountain
> and my being is His building. . . .
> but anger, once bridled, may serve.[5]

We have within us both heaven and earth, freedom and enslavement.

> An Egypt is within you,
> you are its fields of sugar cane,

yet appearances enslave you—
you're occupied with idols.
You resemble Joseph, yet cannot glimpse
your own beauty. By God,
when you see it in the mirror,
you will be the idol of yourself.[6]

Sin as idolatry; sin as failure to see one's own beauty; liberation as seeing one's own beauty. Mystics do not talk about sin as mere guilt, do not rant and rail against sin without showing ways out of sin. In a powerful poem on acedia and the lack of energy that accompanies luxury living, Rumi talked about a city where "there was a glut of wealth" and where "There were no robbers/There was no energy for crime,/or for gratitude." And there was no curiosity for spirit, for "no one wondered about the unseen world. The people of Saba felt bored with just the *mention* of prophecy. They had no desire of any kind." What is the solution? It cannot come from within that city, Rumi declared. Silence will begin to revive the soul, as will teachers who do not live in so comfortable a setting: "They can help you grow sweet again/and fragrant and wild and fresh/and thankful for any small event."[7] Gratitude *can* return—even for small events.

Rumi warned us that we will be judged by how we respond to the blessings of creation and indeed of our flesh with its senses: "On Resurrection Day/God will say,/'What did you do with the strength and the energy/that your food gave you/on Earth?/How did you use your eyes?/What did you make with your five senses/while they were dimming and playing out?/I gave you hands and feet as tools/for preparing the ground for planting./Did you, in the health I gave,/do the plowing?'"[8] Rumi did not ignore or repress what he called "the dragon" of our appetites. He said: "To change,/a person must face the dragon of his appetites/with another dragon, the life energy/of the soul." And he warned us of a "sensual life that has no spirit in it."[9] He was not putting down the dragons of appetite; nor was he running from the sensual life. He was only cautioning us to live a spirit-filled sensuality and a life-filled energy of the soul to combat the other appetites.

For the mystic, to be unaware and without fire is a state of sinfulness and sleepfulness. "Sometimes people don't see the signs/that are so close, even how their homes/are unlit! The way you're living now is like/living in a tomb! There's none of God's light,/and no openness./Remember that you're alive!/Don't stay in a narrow, choked place./Let your Joseph out of prison!/Your Jonah has cooked long enough in the whale!/Have you forgotten what praise is?"[10] Spirit means waking up. "The way you distinguish a true commentary/from a false is this: Whichever explication/makes you feel fiery and hopeful, humble/and *active,* that's the true one./If it makes you lazy, it's not right."[11]

KABIR

The great Kabir, a fifteenth-century Indian mystic, also criticized those who judge too much and live too much in a land of good and evil rather than a land of love and heart-song. His awareness of cosmology and the Cosmic Christ and the awe that accompanies it moved him to sing a song of rapturous delight. "O men!/O my brothers!/Why don't you see/that the Creator/manifests Himself/in all His Creation,/and the entire creation/is the embodiment/of the Creator?/From one Light/all has come to be!/What is *good?*/What is *bad?*/These are mere/Phantoms of your/own mind!"[12] Anticipating today's creation story from science, Kabir believed all matter came from a single light. (John's Gospel taught the same, as does Psalm 104 and Genesis 1, as we have seen.) But goodness and badness seem to be merely phantoms of our minds.

Yet Kabir was not blind to human mistakes or imprisonment or addiction, as when he sang: "Lust, anger/agitation, avarice/So long as one/is possessed by them,/O my friend/there is/little distinction/between a fool/and a scholar!"[13] Like many a mystic before him, Kabir got himself into deep trouble as a prophet who sought to interfere with hypocritical religious practices: "Look at these men,/O Kabir/How their god/is on sale,/and how in blind pursuit/and sheer imitation/of one another,/they go to places/of pilgrimage/performing/empty rituals/Lost and bewildered!"[14] He criticized text-oriented religions: "Scriptures/you have read all,/O Pandit/But like a parrot/in a cage,/you only recite them/to others,/without understanding,/with-out practice."[15] It is the inside that needs cleansing, not the outside, he insisted: "O Pandit/You sit on/the throne/telling beads/and uttering profundities,/but who is it/that you delude?/The Master knows/all the rot/that resides in/your heart!"[16] Sin as rot in the heart; sin as fail-ure to practice on oneself; sin as performing empty rituals; sin as putting one's god on sale; sin as projection onto others and fleeing from self-criticism: "Who is wicked?/Where is evil?/I searched every-where/but found none!/O dear friend/when I looked/within/I understood/that the evil/resides/in one's own heart!"[17] Sin as failure to be transformed: "For eons/you have moved/the beads/in your hand,/yet nothing/has moved/in your heart!/O my friend/leave aside/the beads/open your hands;/let the heart/turn!"[18] Sin as being asleep, sin as the failure to seek, as lack of curiosity and searching: "If a true seeker/falls asleep,/dear friend/awaken him!/But there are some/who are better/left sleeping:/A fool, a tiger/and a serpent."[19] Sin as pride even in the religious practices we undergo: "O seeker/an ascetic may be/possessed of avarice,/and a house-holder/be free/of all things!"[20] Sin as being possessed, as lacking freedom in our relation-ships. "Chanting, penance/abstinence, fasting/bathing in the holy water——/O friend, listen:/These are all useless!/There is only one way:/Open your eyes,/immerse yourself/in the devotion/of the Lord,/in His love!"[21] The rosary beads themselves talk back to the prayer, saying, "Why keep turning me,/O seeker/when you don't turn/your own heart?"[22]

JULIAN OF NORWICH

The fifteenth-century English mystic Julian of Norwich suffered with her contemporaries through the terrible bubonic plague that killed one-third of her countrymen and women, yet she did not dwell on sin or darkness. In fact, she offered some seldom-heard teachings about both. First, she celebrated the blessing that our flesh is when she wrote: "I understood that our sensuality is grounded in Nature, in Compassion and in Grace. This enables us to receive gifts that lead to everlasting life. For I saw that in our sensuality God is."[23] She insisted on the one-ing that happens between our existence and God's: "God is the means whereby our Substance and our Sensuality are kept together so as to never be apart."[24] The Cosmic Christ dwells in our very fleshiness: "Our Sensuality is the beautiful City in which our Lord Jesus sits and in which he is enclosed."[25]

Julian, like Thomas Aquinas before her, saw the antagonists of grace as not nature but sin. "Nature and Grace are in harmony with each other. For Grace is God as Nature is God. . . . Neither Nature nor Grace works without the other. They may never be separated."[26] She fully understood a theology of original blessing, exclaiming, "Nature is all good and beautiful in itself, and Grace was sent out to liberate nature and destroy sin and bring beautiful nature once again to the blessed point from whence it came: that is, God."[27]

To Julian, sin meant sickness. She underscored two kinds of sickness in particular that "cause the most pain and tempest us." They are as follows: "one is our lack of ability to endure, or sloth—for we bear our toil and our pains heavily. The other is despair, or fearful awe." Interestingly, she charged us to move ourselves beyond sloth and despair: "God wants us to forgive our sin instead of falling into a false meekness that is really a foul blindness and weakness due to fear."[28]

Julian cautioned against too much self-accusation: "God says: 'Do not accuse yourself too much, allowing your tribulation and woe to seem all your fault; for it is not my will that you be heavy or sorrowful imprudently.'"[29] It is our failure to see God in all things that leads to our despair and self-berating: "We often fail to see God and then we fall into ourselves and feel there is something wrong with us—that we are perverse and responsible for the entrance of sin into the world and all subsequent sins."[30] The solution to such despair is a rekindling of power, wisdom, and goodness on our part.[31] Because we were "loved from before the beginning" and "made for love," and love is about one-ing, sin does not have the last word, any more than it had the first word. Love is love and not wrathful.

Holy Church taught me that sinners are sometimes worthy of blame and wrath, but I could not see these in God in my showing. I saw that our Lord was never wrathful, nor ever shall be. God's lucidity and unity will not allow this. God is the goodness, that cannot be wrathful. Our soul is oned to God, unchangeable goodness, and therefore between God and our soul there is neither wrath nor forgiveness because there is no between.[32]

Self-esteem and knowing our own beauty are the cure to our weaknesses, Julian insisted: "We are not certain that God hears us because we consider ourselves worthless and as nothing. This is ridiculous and the cause of our weakness. I have felt this way myself."[33] She put sin in the larger context of blessing when she taught that "my own sin will not hinder the working of God's goodness."[34] We ought not dwell on sinfulness: "As long as we are in this life and find ourselves foolishly dwelling on sinfulness, our God tenderly touches us and joyfully calls us, saying: 'Let all your love be, my child. Turn to me, I am everything you need. Enjoy me and your liberation.'"[35] Julian wanted to move beyond sin as guilt: "God showed me that we should not feel guilty because of sin for sin is valuable."[36]

There is much to learn from sin and much to learn from being emptied by mistakes. Sin is that which causes pain, and "this pain purges us and makes us know ourselves and to ask compassion."[37] Julian said that she could not see sin but only the pain that it causes, for "it has no kind of substance nor any part of being."[38] She cautioned against too readily seeing good and evil in things: "We perceive some doings as good and some as evil, but our Lord does not perceive them so. . . . There is no doer but God."[39] God is cited by Julian as saying, "It is necessary that sin should exist. But all will be well, and all will be well and every manner of thing will be well."[40] Wellness is another word for goodness or blessing.

MEISTER ECKHART

Sin did not play a major role in Eckhart's theology; he rarely talked about it. He did say that "opposition" or dualism "has no permanency in being."[41] That is why to commit ourselves to dualism is to step outside of a relationship with the Divine. "One who sees duality or distinction does not see God," he declares. For God is in all being, indeed, "Being is God."[42] God is always near to us, though we can wander far from

God. Sin cannot truly put distance between us and God: "A person should never in any way think of himself or herself as far from God, either because of some sin or weakness, or for any other reason. If at any time your great sins drive you away, so that you cannot feel to be near God, you should nevertheless feel that God is near you.... God never goes far; he always remains standing near and if he cannot remain within he still does not go farther away than just outside the door."[43] The invitation to return home is always at the forefront, for "God is within, but we are outside. God is at home in us, but we are abroad."[44]

Eckhart did talk explicitly of sin when he counseled us to pay attention to silence: "The most beautiful thing which a person can say about God consists in that person's being silent from the wisdom of an inner wealth. So be silent and do not flap your gums about God, for to the extent that you flap your gums about God, you lie and you commit sin. If you want to be without sin and perfect then do not flap your gums about God."[45]

Eckhart raises the question of cosmology and the relativity of evil. "What is evil for one person is good for another or for the universe; and he who takes harm from it now and in the present instance will benefit from it later in other circumstances."[46] When one is undergoing suffering, Eckhart counsels holding on to memories of blessing. "When you are in pain and suffering, remember the good and the comfort that you still have and retain."[47]

Eckhart raised the question of whether the birth of God in the soul takes place in sinners as well as in the good. The excess of light from the soul's foundation, he said, overflows into the body, which then becomes full of a brightness: "Sinners, however, cannot receive any of this, nor are they worthy of it because they are filled with sin and evil which is called 'darkness.' For this reason it is said: 'The darkness receives and does not understand the light.' (John 1:5) The blame for this is that the ways along which this light is to enter are burdened and blackened with falseness and darkness. Light and darkness cannot be together, nor can God and a creature. If God enters, the creature must at the same time go out."[48]

Grace is like sunlight—it does not coexist with darkness. Sin is a kind of absence of light, or darkness. "Because this light cannot shine and give light within sinners, this birth could not possibly take place within them. This birth cannot exist along with the darkness of sin."[49] Sin comes from a lack of strength, Eckhart advised: "Sin and lack of firmness go together." And strength comes from "making one's heart firm in the Godself."[50] In another instance Eckhart defined sin as a "deprivation or falling off from the good of created nature." It is yielding to what is external or superficial. Evil "stands outside, draws and directs things outward, distracts from inner things, draws to what is other, smacks of otherness, of division, of withdrawal or falling away."[51] Sin is a "contraction of awareness"[52] that cuts us off from the magnificence of the Creator and creation. In an otherwise vast and magnanimous universe, it renders us small.

Eckhart equated sin with injustice, as in his commentary on the line "Give us this day our daily bread." He remarked, "Not only bread but all things which are necessary for sustaining this present life are given to us with others and because of others and given to others in us. Whoever does not give to another what belongs to the other, such a one does not eat his own bread but eats the bread of another along with his own. Thus when we justly eat the bread we have received, we certainly eat our bread, but when we eat evilly and with sin the bread we have received, then we are not eating our own bread but the bread of another. For everything which we have unjustly is not really ours."[53]

JESUS

Like Rumi, Kabir, Julian, and Eckhart—and unlike Paul and Augustine—the historical Jesus did not dwell incessantly on sin. What he had to say about sin had to do with social sin and with personal integrity. Like the mystics we have already considered, Jesus was keen on paying attention to the *inner* as opposed to the *outer* self.

In his excellent book *Meeting Jesus Again for the First Time,* theologian Marcus J. Borg finds a growing awareness of the spirituality of the historical Jesus. Speaking autobiographically, Borg admits that as a scholar of the Scriptures, his understanding of Jesus was transformed when he started paying attention to his own mystical experiences in nature and to a more panentheistic (my word) God. "Everything is in God," he began to realize.[54] "I now was able to see the centrality of God (or 'the

Spirit,' to say the same thing) in Jesus' own life." He began to see that Jesus was one "whose spirituality—his experiential awareness of Spirit—was foundational for his life."[55] It is a remarkable and welcome event at last to hear from theological scholars about their own mystical experiences and how they or the lack of them affects their research on Jesus. A truly postmodern happening!

Jesus learned to trust his experience of the Spirit—as Borg puts it, "He was a 'spirit person,' a 'mediator of the sacred,' one of those persons in human history to whom the Spirit was an experiential reality."[56] The result was that Jesus had both the imagination and the courage to deconstruct and to reconstruct the worlds of conventional wisdom that his culture took for granted: "He directly attacked the central values of his social world's conventional wisdom: family, wealth, honor, purity, and religiosity."[57] His image of God was not one of judge but "an invitation to see reality as characterized by a cosmic generosity and by an overflowing effulgence of life."[58] In addition to being a spirit person, Jesus was a teacher of wisdom who taught "a subversive and alternative wisdom," a social prophet who "criticized the elites (economic, political, and religious) of his time," and a movement founder "who brought into being a Jewish renewal or revitalization movement that challenged and shattered the social boundaries of his day."[59] He was a healer, a storyteller, a courageous challenger of the status quo, and a man who employed dramatic public actions, such as eating with untouchables and parodying ideas of kingship by riding a donkey.[60]

In saying that "it is easier for camels to enter the eye of a needle than for rich men to enter the Kingdom of God," Jesus is offering, according to scholar Dominic Crossan, a "biting" argument, typical of much of his teaching, in favor of the poor and critical of the wealthy. Possessions are not evil in themselves in Jesus' teaching, for he calls for their redistribution.

The *systemic* question is how the rich became rich in the first place. The indictment is not against the personal evil of any individual rich person but against the structural or systemic evil of surplus expropriation, indebtedness, land dispossession, and the slow slide from freeholding to tenant farming to day laboring to beggary, banditry, or worse.[61]

In the teaching we know as the Sermon on the Mount, Jesus says, "Blessed are the destitute," meaning that the destitute are innocent or blameless. Is he romanticizing the homeless and poorest of the poor? Crossan thinks not. "Jesus speaks to a situation of *systemic* injustice and *structural* evil, where empires live off colonies, aristocrats live off peasants, and only a large percentage of expendable people make the process possible."[62]

Jesus says, "Purity and impurity is not what goes into the mouth. Purity and impurity is what comes out."[63] Crossan believes that in such teachings Jesus is critiquing not so much his Jewish tradition as the issue of authority: Who has it? Who says what you can and cannot eat? When it comes to eating or not eating certain kinds of foods, the poor have far fewer choices than the comfortable. The "purity/impurity code maps the religious control of society on the physical control of its members' bodies. . . . Purity codes are always much easier for elites than for peasants, who must, after all, eat whatever they can get, whenever and wherever they can get it. . . . But what is absolutely at stake is who gets to decide on society's rules: aristocrats or peasants?"[64] Jesus also addresses the inner integrity of each person when he insists on inner purity: "Purity, impurity, and the outside of your cup? Purity, impurity and the inside of your heart!"[65]

In not a single recorded text does the historical Jesus denigrate the body. Rather, on several occasions he sees it as a blessing, as when he remarks: "God counts the sparrows. God counts the hairs on your heads. That makes you much more important than sparrows."[66] Here he is not denigrating sparrows either; in fact, he is lifting human esteem by comparing us to sparrows and showing how we and sparrows—and presumably all of creation—share in common the Divine caring. "If you ask your earthly father for a loaf do you get a stone? If you ask your earthy father for fish do you get a snake?"[67]

Jesus' images of the kingdom of God, the core metaphor of his preaching message, are invariably drawn from nature: a mustard seed; a vineyard; a treasure in a field; a shepherd seeking his stray sheep; leaven in baked bread; a pearl; rejection of one's literal family; a seed planted by a farmer; a fisherman throwing back small fish and keeping a large one captured in his net; grain and weeds growing together; homes where healing of the sick and sharing of the meal take place; becoming a child; what is "already here, among you, now."[68] And in a well-known text, he offers this picture of the kingdom of God:

> Look at the birds above your head
>   they neither plant nor reap
>   they neither store nor hoard
> yet day by day God gives them food
>
> Look at the flowers beneath your feet
>   they neither card nor spin
>   they neither sow nor weave
> yet King Solomon shone less brightly than they
>
> > So why worry about your life
> >   what you will get to eat
> >   what you will have to wear[69]

Jesus trusts the universe, trusts the beauty and order he has beheld in the birds and flowers, in the up and the down, in the sky and in the earth. From that beauty he urges us to trust as well. He is looking for creation as an alternative to sinful culture. He does not indulge in denigrating nature or in separating it from grace. Says Crossan: "Radical counter-culturalism turns almost inevitably to nature for models of an alternative mode of existence."[70] Indeed, as reported in the Gospel of Thomas, Jesus finds it amidst the fleshy substances of nature and cosmos: "Split a piece of wood; I am there. Lift up the stone, and you will find me there."[71] He is talking not only about his omnipresence in nature but about his omnipresence in *work*. When we work in nature, as in splitting wood or lifting stones (of which there are many to lift in Jesus' land), the memory of the Divine can be found within the work itself and within the sweat of everyday labor.

In his teachings against divorce, Jesus is critiquing the aristocrats who indulged in divorce more than the poor. He is also critiquing patriarchy, for in Jewish law only the husband could initiate divorce, and adultery could be committed only against his rights, not hers (see Deuteronomy 21:1–3). "A man could commit adultery against the rights of another man, but women had no such rights," observes Crossan. "What Jesus asserts is that women have exactly the same rights as men have in marriage. Adultery can be committed against a wife's rights just as well as against a husband's."[72]

Jesus interfered with the "purity system" of the Jewish world into which he was born. This system was quite demarcated in his day, depending on birth and also on behavior, physical appearance, economic class, gender, and whether one was a Jew or a Gentile. "Sin becomes a matter of being impure or 'dirty,'" says Borg, "and renders one 'untouchable...in first-century Judaism: *sinners* often meant 'the impure.'"[73] Jesus took it upon himself to attack the purity system. "In the message and activity of Jesus, we see an alternative social vision: a community shaped not by the ethos and politics of purity, but by the ethos and politics of compassion."[74]

Furthermore, as a wisdom teacher, Jesus was primarily a teacher not of credal beliefs or of moral behavior but "of a way or path of transformation."[75] Spirituality is a path, a way of transformation—Jesus taught spirituality in that he taught ways to be transformed. In doing so, he was subverting the dominant wisdom of his time and culture, offering his listeners an alternative way of living. His wisdom had an edge to it. What the culture took for granted, he questioned: "He directly attacked the central values of his social world's conventional wisdom: family, wealth, honor, purity, and religiosity."[76] Rejecting family, he critiqued one's literal father and mother on behalf of a larger sense of family, as when he said, "Call no man on earth your father, for you have one Father, who is in heaven," and, "Who is my mother? Everyone who hears the word of God and keeps it." His images of God replace the idea of God as Judge with that of a "gracious and compassionate" Creator. "Consider the birds of the air—they neither sow nor reap, they have neither storehouses nor barn, yet God feeds them."[77]

Borg believes that the historical Jesus today challenges Christians and others to move from "second-hand religion," based on the Bible and church doctrines, to "first-hand" religion, which is "life centered in the Spirit" and is experiential.[78] In other words, from religious faith to spiritual practice.

PAUL

Guilt can develop into a hellish journey, one that takes on all the burden of life as a burden of death. Paul, Augustine, and Luther especially traveled this path—indeed, Paul Ricoeur feels that Paul carried guilt to depths never fathomed before him. (This may be one reason that work on the historical Jesus is so valuable—it helps Christians know the difference between Jesus' teaching and Paul's—and there are vast differences.) Paul complains that sin takes him over and proposes that flesh is the problem, indeed the curse: "It is, then, I myself who by reason serve a law of God and by the flesh a law of sin" (Romans 7:25).

Flesh, as we have seen, does not mean sexuality for Paul but the self alienated from itself, opposed to itself, and projected outward. Flesh might be understood in the way that the Eastern tradition uses the term *ego*. It is the propensity to see only oneself.

But what is "most astonishing" to Ricoeur in Paul's treatment of death and guilt and law and conscience is that sin is something of the past: "Once you were dead in your sins, but now . . ." Death is in the past because "justification" happens now. Here Paul breaks with both Judaism and Hellenism. For Paul, the virtue of justice that the Greeks invoke as a sign of morality is not primary; rather, being justified is primary. Liberty is not about choosing well so much as about "being at home with oneself, in the whole, in the recapitulation of Christ."[79]

For Paul, in opposition to Judaism, a person is justified "without the works of the law" but by faith (Romans 3:21–28). Says Ricoeur, "The supreme sin consists, in the last resort, in the vain attempt to justify oneself."[80] Sin constitutes an "ambiguous threshold," for on the one hand it leads to the hell of guilt, but on the other it lays open the possibility of grace and justification by grace. Ricoeur believes that Paul reached "the farthest limit of the whole cycle of guilt."[81]

The grace of Christ relieves Paul of guilt. Now it is "not I who lives but Christ who lives within me" (Galatians 2:20). Sin, guilt, and defilement are all in the past. The power of Christ is to wash them all away. Paul's mysticism takes on new depth and clarity when he can say that "in Christ there is no distinction between Gentile and Jew, male and female, slave and master" (Galatians 3:28). Being cleansed of worldly dualisms has class, racial, and sexual implications. In addition, Paul recognizes the Cosmic Christ in all when he declares, "And we, with our unveiled faces reflecting like mirrors the glory of the Lord, all grow brighter and brighter as we are turned into the image that we reflect" (2 Corinthians 3:18). Not only are we images of Divinity, we evolve brighter and brighter into this image, and we get better at it as we go along. Here indeed the pessimism of Paul gives way to a sense of Divine *doxa* or radiance within us all—provided we can get down to our "unveiled faces," our true inner selves, beyond the superficialities of our personas and masks and self-illusions.

Mystics like Rumi, Kabir, Julian, Meister Eckhart, Jesus, Paul, and Thich Nhat Hanh agree on our housing seeds of goodness and badness in us. There seems to be a consensus that humans are born with "seeds" of peace and love, violence and hate. The former need to be cultivated and attended to if we are to do our best and to survive together. (Seeing as there is no other way to survive except together.)

CHAPTER 7

MEANINGS OF SIN FROM
THEOLOGIANS AND BIOLOGISTS

We have considered thoughts about sin from mystics representing spiritual traditions of the East and the West. In this chapter we will discuss briefly what world traditions tell us about sin and in particular what some biologists, and anthropologists are saying about sin.

DEEP ECUMENISM
AND MEANINGS OF SIN

1. *Hinduism*. Hinduism teaches that human folly comes from ignorance, from ignoring truth. It is everyone's task then to teach truth and to live it and to search for it. Those who are the worst off are those who are the furthest from truth, and these must be assisted to become more enlightened. Mahatma Gandhi cautioned how the following internal forces could destroy a nation:

Politics without principle
Wealth without work
Commerce without morality
Pleasure without conscience
Education without character
Science without humanity
Worship without sacrifice

2. *Buddhism*. Buddhist abbess Pema Chodron teaches that there are three "poisons": passion, which includes craving and addiction; aggression; and ignorance, which includes denial or the tendency to shut down and close out. Instead of avoiding these poisons, she recommends breathing them in. "We breathe it in for everybody. This poison is not just our personal misfortune, our fault, our blemish, our shame—it's part of the human condition." Instead of pushing these poisons aside, we take them in with the intention of freeing others as well as ourselves of suffering.[1] Chodron believes that a "fundamental groundlessness" lies beneath our fear that motivates "passion, aggression, ignorance, jealousy and pride." To get to its essence we need to refrain from business to enter the restlessness. This is possible because deep down we are trustworthy—"we have basic goodness, basic wisdom, basic intelligence, [therefore] we can stop harming ourselves and harming others."[2]

Vietnamese monk Thich Nhat Hanh reminds us that Buddha was called the "king of healers" and that wars inside us are fueled by wars outside us and vice versa. It is for this reason that developing mindfulness through meditation is a great healing energy. "The violence, hatred, discrimination, and fear in society water the seeds of the violence, hatred, discrimination, and fear in us." Through meditation we enter this world within and "we can calm things down, understand them, and bring harmony back to the conflicting elements inside us. If we can learn ways to touch the peace, joy, and happiness that are already there, we will become healthy and strong, and a resource for others."[3]

3. *Taoism*. "Sin" is a lack of balance, an appropriation to the human of the rhythm that is nature's kind of balance. To be overly attached and to overly insert oneself into the action of the universe that desires to work through us in a "wayless way." A refusal to follow the spontaneity of nature. When one is out of touch with one's own "quiet being," robbery results and chaos that is not in keeping with the Tao or the Godhead.

4. *Judaism*. Judaism teaches that sin is "missing the mark" and that staying true to the goal or the mark is the proper way to heal from sin. Among Hebrew words for sin, in addition to "missing the mark," another means "a tortuous road." Thus, a divergence from order, a dis-

order, a wrongful path. A third term denotes rebellion, revolt, or stiff-neckedness. "Sin is 'against' God, as existence is 'before' God."[4] Thus, refusal to listen and to hear, hardness of heart and stiffness of neck all denote sin. Going astray, becoming lost, is another image for the sinner. In this context there is a silence of God, an absence of God, even an abandonment by God. The prophet Hosea introduces a tender element of divine affection and equates sin with adultery or wandering from this loving relationship—a betrayal of the Beloved. Isaiah talks of sin in relation to the holy God of sovereignty and majesty.

Rabbi Abraham Joshua Heschel defines sin as "the refusal of humans to become who we are," and Erich Fromm writes about a "biophilic ethics" wherein "good is all that serves life; evil is all that serves death. Good is reverence for life, all that enhances life, growth, unfolding. Evil is all that stifles life, narrows it down, cuts it into pieces."[5] For Martin Buber, the question is not about sinning and not sinning but about "those who are pure in heart and those who are impure in heart." What is the difference? Sinners who are pure of heart experience God's goodness as it is revealed to him or her. "As Israel purifies its heart, it experiences that God is good to it."[6] One who

> draws near with a pure heart to the divine mystery, learns that one is continually with God. It is a revelation. It would be a misunderstanding of the whole situation to look on this as a pious feeling. From man's side there is no continuity, only from God's side. The Psalmist has learned that God and he are continually with one another.[7]

To be wicked is to persist in impurity of heart and to experience no goodness.

> The man who is pure in heart, I said, experiences that God is good to him. He does not experience it as a consequence of the purification of the heart, but because only as one who is pure in heart is he able to come to the sanctuaries. This does not mean the Temple precincts in Jerusalem, but the sphere of God's holiness, the holy mysteries of God.[8]

Ricoeur comments on the evolution of the understanding of sin in Hebraic thought and experience: "The consciousness of sin advances and becomes boundless as historical insecurity grows, as the sign of history as devastator replaces the sign of victory, and as the failure of might becomes the sacrament of holy majesty."[9] For the prophets sin was often described as adultery, infidelity, or betrayal—which is more than disobeying commandments or breaking taboos.

Sin, unlike defilement, cannot be reduced to an individual dimension—"it is at once and primarily personal *and* communal."[10] Other descriptions of sin include separation and rebellion. In addition, biblical writers discern in sin a "fascinating, binding, frenetic force. The power of a man is mysteriously taken possession of by an inclination to evil that corrupts its very source."[11] Sin is a kind of captivity and the Egyptian bondage symbolizes that state of imprisonment. "The sinner is 'in' the sin as the Hebrew was 'in' bondage, and sin is thus an evil 'in which' man is caught."[12] Liberation becomes more important than liberty in this context.

The law of the Torah "is both religious and ethical," and what was unique about the journey of Israel was its being tied to ethics from the very beginning via Moses. "The ethics itself is historical through and through; it is the ethics of a chosen people. That is why also the whole of the symbolism of sin and repentance is itself a 'historical' symbol that draws its 'types' from certain significant events" such as captivity and deliverance of Exodus.[13]

In Judaism to repent is to return. Repentance means that "'return' to God, freely chosen, [that] is always open to man; and the example of great and impious men who have 'returned' to the Eternal attest that it is always *possible* for a man to 'change his way.'"[14] This is why repentance as return is so primal to Jewish piety.

5. *Christian*. One sees this emphasis on repentance in the early preaching of the historical Jesus. Repent! Return. Start over. Metanoia. Change your heart and your ways. Jesus, like certain prophets before him, teaches that sin comes from the inside of us, from our hearts and minds, and that it is there that the healing and balancing must be effected. Sin is bad fruit.

Following are some comments on sin from diverse Christian theologians over the centuries:

- Hugh of St. Victor: Sin is an act of unrighteousness.
- Hildegard of Bingen: Sin is drying up. It is care-less-ness. Not caring. It is also "uselessness"[15] and indigestion and the lack of eros or passion.[16] It is sterility: "Those of us who do good are like an orchard full of the fruit of good works. Such persons are like the Earth, which is strengthened and adorned by rock and trees. But if we do evil works in the stubbornness of sin, we shall remain sterile in God's eyes, like the stubborn Earth that bears no fruit."[17]
- Thomas Aquinas: An action that obstructs grace, or an attitude that closes the door to grace. (It can never be closed totally.) Not so much a "falling away from grace" or "out of grace" as an obstacle to grace erected by self or society or both. A turning away of the created will from the ultimate end, i.e., God. Any act lacking due order or form or measure. A defect. (Is this a lot like the Jewish understanding of "missing the mark"?) A partial privation or a sickness of the soul, a wounding of our nature that grace can heal.[18] Death of the soul or a privation of grace by which the soul was united to God.[19] "A breach of the love of God and neighbor. This alone is the law broken in sin and none other."[20]

We must not give sin too much of our power, for "it is impossible that the good of the nature which is suitability or aptitude for grace be totally taken away by sin."[21] For "sin is not the very privation of grace, but an obstacle to grace by which grace is precluded.... Sin excludes grace but not the suitability for grace."[22] Our creation is too good and wonderful to be destroyed by our malfeasance. "The good of the nature cannot be totally eliminated by fault."[23] Indeed, "sin does not place a person entirely outside of the order of nature but outside its perfection."[24]

- Reinhold Niebuhr: Sin is "the unwillingness of man to acknowledge his creatureliness and dependence upon God and his effort to make his own life independent and secure."
- Paul Tillich: Sin is estrangement; grace is reconciliation.
- Gustavo Gutierrez: Sin is denial of love.
- Norman Pittinger: Sin is estrangement from self, others, God, and Nature[25] and the lack of agape love, which is outward-going, open-hearted, self-giving concern and care.[26] Sin is "an unwilling-

ness or incapacity to participate in the basic thrust of life toward future and better realization of love."[27]

· William May: "Sin is whatever we do that violates our life in God."[28]

· Langdon Gilkey: "Sin may be defined as an ultimate religious devotion to a finite interest; it is an overriding loyalty or concern for the self, its existence and its prestige, or for the existence and prestige of a group. From this deeper sin, that is, from this inordinate love of the self and its own, stem the moral evils of indifference, injustice, prejudice, and cruelty to one's neighbor and the other destructive patterns of action that we call 'sins.'"[29]

· Howard Thurman: Good is that which makes for peace; evil is that which makes for turbulence.[30]

· Paul Ricoeur: Evil is "the power of darkness."[31] Evil seduces— "evil, although it is something that is brought about, is already there, enticing." Humans are not evil; they are "wicked through seduction."[32] A kind of "infection" is associated with evil, an enslavement. But to be enslaved is not to give up one's being—it is to work in an alienated situation as the Hebrew people were forced to do when they were enslaved by the Egyptians. "To infect is not to destroy, to tarnish is not to ruin." Captivity is one thing, but one's very being is another.[33]

· Duncan Littlefair: Sin is when I can say: "I have fallen short." It is "any act whatsoever that interferes with the creating of life, any act that interferes with love and the opening up of our individual, family or corporate life...anything that interferes with the evolutionary process toward a greater, nobler, more joyous humanity."[34]

· M. Scott Peck: "Evil is opposition to life. It is that which opposes the life force. It has, in short, to do with killing....Evil is also that which kills the spirit....Evil is that force, residing either inside or outside of human beings, that seeks to kill life or liveliness. And goodness is its opposite. Goodness is that which promotes life and liveliness."[35] "The central defect of the evil is not the sin but the refusal to acknowledge it...their *absolute* refusal to tolerate the sense of their own sinfulness."[36]

· Angela West: "Sin is about compulsive repetition, about never being able to do a new thing or reach a new place.... The ways in which we are sinful are historically and culturally conditioned,... and sin is patterned according to race, and gender and class. Thus there are patterns of sin among the powerful and somewhat different patterns among the powerless."[37]

- Valerie Saiving Goldstein: Saiving criticizes Anders Nygren and Reinhold Niebuhr and other theologians for representing "a widespread tendency in contemporary theology to describe man's predicament as rising from separateness and the anxiety occasioned by it and to identify sin with self-assertion and love with selflessness."[38] But women suffer less from a sin of pride than from "triviality, distractibility, and diffuseness; lack of an organizing center or focus, dependence on others for one's self-definition; tolerance at the expense of standards of excellence; inability to respect the boundaries of privacy... in short, underdevelopment or negation of the self."[39]

- Susan Brooks Thistlethwaite: "The questions of innocence and guilt are complicated by questions of sex and gender as well as by color and race.... The liberal tradition [of process theology] separates the knowledge of God from the physical and material situation of human beings and locates it in an artificially distorted version of human mental process. This is as inadequate in developing a trenchant critique of the social origins of sin, and the social sources of salvation, as is the theological perspective that places God outside the world..."[40]

- Rosemary Radford Ruether: "What is appropriately called sin belongs to a more specific sphere of human freedom where we have the possibility of enhancing life or stifling it. It is the realm where competitive hate abounds, and also passive acquiescence to needless victimization.... The central issue of 'sin' as distinct from finitude is the misuse of freedom to exploit other humans and the earth and thus to violate the basic relations that sustain life.... Sin... lies in distortion of relationship, the absolutizing of the rights to life and power of one side of a relation against the other parts with which it is, in fact, interdependent. It lies further in the insistent perseverance in the resultant cycle of violence, the refusal to empathize with the victimized underside of such power, and the erection of systems of control and cultures of deceit to maintain and justify such unjust power."[41]

• Carter Heyward: "It is exceedingly dangerous for us to allow *any* structure of sin and evil to go unchecked in the society, because in the end we ourselves will be the victims. Those forces in the world (which, in the advanced capitalist quarters of the earth, take the impersonal shape of militarism and multinational interests, flying under the guise of 'free enterprise' and 'Christian blessing') are bound to act *against* women's liberation, racial equality, gay/lesbian rights, the demands of the poor, all revolutionary movements, and the integrity of the earth itself."[42]

• Clarissa Pinkola Estés: Estés talks about the "disarrays of the psyche" and a "disrupted relationship with the wildish force in the psyche" and the need to explore "what is the matter."[43] She lays out an entire list of symptoms of this state, symptoms that might well name the traditional effort to talk about the relation of sin to psyche and what is lost when the psyche is off center or unbalanced. To have partially severed or even lost entirely the relationship with the deep, instinctual psyche there are symptoms like the following:

> Feeling extraordinarily dry, fatigued, frail, depressed, confused, gagged, muzzled, unaroused. Feeling frightened, halt or weak, without inspiration, without animation, without soulfulness, without meaning, shame-bearing, chronically fuming, volatile, stuck, uncreative, compressed, crazed. Feeling powerless, chronically doubtful, shaky, blocked, unable to follow through, giving one's creative life over to others, life-sapping choices in mates, work or friendships, suffering to live outside one's own cycles, overprotective of self, inert, uncertain, faltering, inability to pace oneself or set limits. Not insistent on one's own tempo, to be self-conscious, to be away from one's God or Gods, to be separated from one's revivification, drawn far into domesticity, intellectualism, work, or inertia because that is the safest place for one who has lost her instincts.[44]

Perhaps "losing our instincts" is an important definition for sin in our time.

SIN AND PESSIMISM IN THE MODERN ERA

Unfortunately, since the term "original sin" was first conceived in the mind of St. Augustine of Hippo in the fourth century, it has been reshaped in the theological hands of empire builders so that a benign interpretation—one that acknowledges both good seeds and bad seeds in the human—has not held sway. Nastiness has prevailed under the guise that God is out to get us from the very start of our existence. It has fed continuously the engines of pessimism and despair in Western culture.

Evidence of this abounds in French historian Jean Delumeau's major study on *Sin and Fear: The Emergence of a Western Guilt Culture, 13th–18th Centuries*. The author calls his work "A Cultural History of Sin," and notes that the fourteenth century birthed a "scruple sickness" that in turn gave birth to a "new fear—the fear of one's self."[45] This and an "excessive sense of guilt and culpabilization" created a gap which advanced the "dread of God" over the "fear of God."[46] Delumeau sees Protestantism as upping the ante on despair:

In its sixteenth-century form, the doctrine of justification by faith thus represents the logical (although extreme) end of the long and desolate road through pessimism. Incessantly, repeated for more than a thousand years, the affirmation of the world's fragility, of its vice and its vanity, reached a vast audience. Man was but "dung" and "filth"—no wonder the result was despair.[47]

Calvin says: "Life in this world is full of worries and troubles. It is totally wretched. Nowhere is happiness to be found." The things of this world "are transitory, uncertain, frivolous, and mixed with infinite misery."[48] Instead of blessing in the cosmos, Calvin sees only *curse*. "No matter where we look, high or low, we can see only a curse that, spreading over all creatures and embracing the earth and the sky, ought to burden our souls with horrible despair."[49] John Calvin did not have the cosmology to believe in the beauty of humankind, and he says so explicitly:

If God had formed us of the stuff of the sun or the stars, or if he had created any other celestial matter out of which man could have been made, then we might have said that our beginning was honorable.... But when someone is made of clay, who pays any attention to him?... [So] who are we? We are all made of mud, and this mud is not just on the hem of our gown, or on the sole of our boots, or in our shoes. We are full of it, we are nothing but mud and filth both inside and outside.[50]

How telling that today's cosmology, which does indeed instruct us in our kinship with the stars, could dispel even Calvin's pessimism by his own admission! Luther was no more hopeful. He says in his Epistle to the Galatians that the world is the "son" of the devil and deserves to be called "all bad," and filled with "ignorance hate, blasphemy, contempt of God, lies and errors, not to speak of gross sins such as murder, adultery, fornication, theft, pillage, etc." He calls the world the "devil's kingdom."[51]

The modern age began with the sixteenth century's pessimistic theology. Delumeau concludes that

it was therefore in the sixteenth century, and specifically in Protestant theology, that the accusation of man and the world reached its climax in Western civilization. Never before had they been so totally condemned, and never had this condemnation reached such a large audience. Luther and his successors urged all Christians to "despair totally of themselves in order to be able to receive Christ's grace" "Having grown into a bad tree, man can only want and do evil."[52]

One wonders if the modern era, so lacking in a cosmology of awe and wonder, substituted in its place and with the help of original sin Christianity a pseudo-mysticism of guilt. Guilt might represent one of the few *subjective* experiences allowed persons in the modern age. And fundamentalist religion cashed in on this.

What about original sin? "Christian civilization placed the Fall at the center of its preoccupations and construed it as a catastrophe initiating all history." Yet neither Islam nor Judaism did so. "Although the story of Adam and Eve's crime appears in the first book of the Old Testament

(Genesis 3:1–24), ancient Judaism did not focus its theology on the first sin." Nor is original sin prominent in the Gospels or even in the Creed of Nicaea.[53]

Nor was it an issue with Paul and Jesus, as I demonstrated in my book *Original Blessing.*[54] Augustine was the key in the original sin ideology and the condemnation of unbaptized children is a logical outcome—condemnation was pronounced at the Council of Carthage in 418. "Behind this damnation of unbaptized children, one rediscovers the dramatic vision of a first crimes, so monstrous that it must have logically brought offended divine justice to throw into Hell all sinning humanity, as embodied in Adam."[55] Thomas Berry believes that the Black Death that ravaged Europe so drastically in the fifteenth century may have been the most determinative cultural factor to plant pessimism into the Western religious psyche and that sixteenth-century Protestantism inherited that sense of despair.[56]

The conception of original sin had such a profound impact that "all future theological reflection on this problem in the Christian West was geared toward it, whether to lighten it (as with Aquinas, Erasmus, or Molina), or to darken it a bit more, as especially with Luther.... Augustinian pessimism gained both its strongest coloring and widest audience during...the years 1400–1700."[57]

Moreover, Original Sin ideologies spread into the scientific and philosophical domains as well. In the modern era, Malebranche "used the doctrine of Original Sin to justify the Cartesian theory of animal-machines.... Since animals have not tasted a 'forbidden fruit,' they cry without pain."[58] Indeed, the most important single philosophical influence on Rene Descartes was Saint Augustine, and his idea of beginning philosophy with "doubt" instead of "wonder" (where Aquinas begins philosophy) parallels the idea of original sin as a starting point for theology. The modern era bought heavily into sin consciousness, and some in today's scientific community are still playing out that tune.

BIOLOGISTS ON SIN:
THE PESSIMISTIC VIEW OF NATURE

Today biologists are weighing in on the subject of good and evil. We will discuss two views of the subject, a pessimistic one and a more optimistic one. In his book *Dark Nature: A Natural History of Evil,* biologist Lyall Watson wrestles with issues of sin and evil from the perspective of today's biology and anthropological studies. He subscribes to what I call the "two seeds" view of peace and of violence in the human race when he writes that "the roots of war lie deep in nature, it seems, but then so too do the roots of peace."[59] He also cites Ralph Waldo Emerson, who said: "There is a capacity of virtue in us, and there is a capacity of vice to make your blood creep."[60] Watson ascribes the evil in us to our inherited roots: "The roots of all we now regard as evil, weak or strong, lie very firmly in the camp, and in the action, of natural selection."[61]

Watson acknowledges the blessing side to nature when he recounts the story of a team of whales that selflessly held up an aging and dying whale in shallow water—water whose shallowness could have killed the assisting whales. The whales kept their vigil for many hours and even helped the humans who came in snorkeling equipment to watch; the whales held the humans up when they perceived they were tired. "The whales were involved in an act of altruism," Watson observes.[62]

Watson also acknowledges nature's friendlier side when he remarks that "there is abundant evidence to show that something like moral behavior exists in other species. . . . The facts are simple. Societies, both human and animal, are networks of interacting individuals. . . . It is not ideology, but self-interest that keeps alliances together."[63] And again: "We were social long before we became human. And in that long social experience lies the biological origins of virtues such as compassion, empathy love, conscience and a powerful sense of justice."[64] Watson also recognizes a role for awe and wonder, as Charles Darwin himself experienced on first entering a Brazilian forest: He is said to have described his feelings of "wonder, astonishment and sublime devotion."[65]

But Watson, like patriarchal theologians before him, spends far more time describing the sinful side of humanity than the positive side, and he prefers highlighting nature's violence to its potential for peace. He is especially taken with the hypothesis of biologist Richard Dawkins that nature has a "selfish gene" and that human nature inherits that selfish gene: "Genetic evolution is the ultimate in selfishness. All three genetic laws—be nice to insiders, nasty to outsiders, and cheat a lot—require it." We've had "billions of years of selection *for* selfishness."[66] As anthropocentric as it may sound, Watson believes that genes are indeed selfish and have their own rather simplistic agenda to play out:

Genes are simple-minded and mean-spirited. They have no vision and cannot be expected to have the welfare of the whole species at heart. Which is why universal love does not exist or make evolutionary sense. Generosity and unselfishness are not part of biological nature. Where such things exist, they have had to be learned or cultured by working against the trend. The sad fact is that we are born selfish.[67]

Watson believes our genes drive us to aggression and adultery alike: "It is the genes that 'want' men to have sex with as many women as possible. Sex and power are the nuts and bolts of natural selection."[68] For most of our history, Watson believes, the better part of our nature was at work because we lived in tribes of such modest size that we knew and supported and corrected one another. The real trouble began when we expanded into larger gatherings. (This idea seems to parallel somewhat the feminist theory that the building of cities and the movement from the land that agriculture made possible was the beginning of many of our troubles.) Says Watson:

Through most of human history we lived in small groups, less than 200 strong. Most of those we lived among were relatives, our flesh more or less. What happened to them happened to us. What we did unto others, we did to ourselves. Altruism made sense, and continued to do so until we moved more and to greater lengths. Until we found ourselves amongst strangers, people who were no longer family.[69]

We have now to work at being good: "Charity doesn't come naturally to us. It is the result of deliberate choice, of a conscious decision to revolt against the tyranny of the genes."[70] This tyranny of the genes challenges us to make a great effort to be good because our genes "are essentially and necessarily selfish, with a rigid set of rules that maximize a very narrow kind of short-term advantage. . . . [They are] completely amoral, devoid of empathy and long-term concern."[71]

Venturing into theological territory, Watson proposes that original sin may actually be the equivalent of the selfish gene: "Genetic morality is the biological equivalent of original sin—something we need to overcome."[72] Our task in life is to provide some morality and to fight the good fight: "It is up to us to provide these moral qualities, to give life on Earth a conscience. We are this world's first ethical animals, at the mercy still of our biology, but capable also of rising above it."[73] Intelligence helps.

In this struggle Watson finds the dualistic division between "good" and "evil" to be, not the solution, but part of the problem. There is so much evidence of evil in nature that we cannot accept the distinction between good and evil too strictly. Rather, there is a spectrum of good and evil: "The dualism of good is good and evil is evil, is unhelpful, possibly even dangerous, encouraging violent eruptions of anger and destruction by participating in the process of evil, giving that which is negative unnecessary credibility."[74] What is the solution? "True health lies in integrating good and evil, nurture and nature, the moral with that which just happens to be genetically expedient. . . . The genes are not smart enough to get organized in that way. They have no plan, no long term goal. They need fighting, but ought not to be misjudged, given any more credit than they deserve. Or, indeed, any more blame."[75]

But what constitutes good, even if on a scale or spectrum? 'Good' is what is right for the whole; and 'bad' is what is wrong for the whole. There is a sliding scale between 'good' and 'bad,' but there appear to be three principal ways in which benign things most often deteriorate and become malign:

1. Good things get to be bad if they are displaced, taken out of context, or removed from their locus.
2. Good things get very bad if there are too few or too many of them.
3. And good things get really rotten if they cannot relate to each other properly and their degree of association is impoverished.[76]

Watson invokes Aristotle's understanding of goodness as that which is "just enough," and he compares this to Goldilocks's experience on finding just the right porridge, sitting chair, and bed.

And what is bad? Borrowing from physics, Watson distinguishes between "weak" and "strong" evil. Weak evil is hostility to outsiders; strong evil is hostility to one's own.[77] If good is what is good for the whole, then bad is what is bad for the whole.[78] Indeed, "evil can be defined as anything that upsets the ecology. Anything that works against, rather than for, equilibrium." Sinfulness means missing the mark, "something which fails to find its proper level, that position in which it is 'just right.'"[79]

Watson consciously distances himself from the worldview of Thomas Hobbes, who called nature "solitary, poor, nasty, brutish and short" and whose motives were highly political, as he was arguing for a strong central government in the seventeenth century. Yet Watson shortchanges the dimensions of awe, wonder and love of which, by his own admission, humanity has long been capable. Much of Watson's pessimism seems to come from today's culture more than yesterday's biological inheritance. Indeed, he concludes by dismissing any hope on the horizon from capitalism or government or religion. He doesn't get back to the power of awe to awaken, nor to the potential of cosmology to do the same. In the long run, then, his "original sin"–based science could take a lesson from an "original blessing"–based science as well. He needs to balance hope and despair, lest his approach be déjà vu and very much what fall/redemption theologians have been telling us for centuries.

Watson thus does not present a whole picture. While paying lip service to cosmology, his pessimistic ideology ignores the deeper meaning and appreciation of the 15 billion years that made life as we know it and and as we share it with other species. Much anthropocentrism reigns in his language—for example, that of the "selfish gene" (why not call it the "survival gene"?), so much that one has to question what kind of science is at work here. It is so male, with little mention of birth as mystery and the wonder of it. His invocation of Augustine's original sin ideology is a giveaway about his own.

Moreover, his evidence seems highly selective as he finds evil everywhere but remains silent about the heroics and courage and sacrifice of animals and humans. In short, he lacks a cosmological context. The result is more male pessimism and cynicism and even nihilism with little hope born from the power of birthing or what Charles Jencks calls "jumping." Absolutely no spirituality enters—no praise, and all is blind chance. Mysticism and creativity are absent. In Creation Spirituality terms it is all via negativa, with no via positiva and no via creativa and therefore no via transformativa. On the last page of the book, he dismisses religion in less than a sentence, and he nowhere alludes to

Martin Luther King, Jr., or Mahatma Gandhi, or Mother Teresa, or Dorothy Day or even Jesus. He expresses no belief in the grace and greatness of people. No saints, no spirit. He describes at length his courtroom visits to observe ten-year-old murderers—but he makes no mention of pilgrimages to see anyone doing good in the world.

Watson sets up a moral straw man and caricature, then shoots it down when he goes searching for the "altruistic gene" and fails to find it. Jesus does not talk about altruism. Jesus never said, "Be you altruistic," but he did say, "Be you compassionate as your Creator in heaven is compassionate." Watson would have better spent his time looking for evidence for compassion rather than altruism. Morality is not about altruism; it is about justice and compassion. And others, less biased by their secularized ideologies, have indeed found it among animals, including human ones.

BIOLOGISTS ON SIN:
THE MORE HOPEFUL VIEW

A different view of nature is put forward in Jeffrey Moussaieff Masson and Susan McCarthy's study, *When Elephants Weep: The Emotional Lives of Animals.* Consciously taking on the "scientific dogma" that dictates that animals do not feel and do not share lives of compassion and caring as well as fighting and struggling, the authors break new scientific ground regarding the depth of the inner lives of animals. The authors ask the question, "Why is it controversial to discuss the inner lives of animals, their emotional capacities, their feelings of joy, disappointment, nostalgia, and sadness?" They cite Jane Goodall, whose work on chimpanzees was at first ridiculed as anthropomorphic because she saw different "personalities" among chimpanzees.[80]

Apparently scientific dogma has it that all animals are dumb and indistinguishable and unfeeling. This view runs up against the facts, however, of those who have lived more intimately with animals than just keeping them in cages and putting them under microscopes. In her book *Ape Language,* Sue Savage-Rumbaugh, a scientist at the Yerkes Primate Center in Atlanta, wrote, "There are few feelings that apes do not share with us, except perhaps self-hatred. They certainly experience and express exuberance, joy, guilt, remorse, disdain, disbelief, awe, sadness, wonder, tenderness, loyalty, anger, distrust, and love."[81] Is the "self-hatred" that seems unique to our species encouraged by the indiscriminate dissemination of original sin ideologies?

Masson and McCarthy criticize Richard Dawkins's "selfish gene" thesis first of all for its confusion of terms: "The socio-biological debate about altruism is deeply confused by the redefinition of this everyday word. If compassion for kin exists as an emotion, rather than exclusively as an adaptive behavior, then compassion for nonkin also becomes possible."[82] I would maintain that Dawkins and Watson misdefine both altruism and selfishness. The quest for survival is not selfish; it is the basis of all other quests. Jesus never instructed people not to seek to survive; he merely advised, "Love others as you love yourself."

Evidence abounds in nature that animals other than humans go out of their way to assure the survival of others—their children, their parents, their siblings, and quite often other beings as well. Dawkins defines altruism as "self-destructive behavior performed for the benefit of others." Since when is love or compassion "self-destructive behavior"? Behind such ideologies lies a peculiar bias against true compassion.

The fact is that compassionate behavior on the part of animals to their own kin *and* sometimes to other species abounds. Just recently a Florida newspaper told of a man whose boat capsized in the evening in the Gulf of Mexico off the Florida coast. All night long the man was assisted by dolphins, who among other things held him up until help arrived in the daytime. Vampire bats share food with other bats, including strangers, we are told.[83] Many scientists of animal behavior seem to want to subscribe to the theology of original sin and leave behind all mention of original blessing—they subscribe to theses of a selfish seed or gene but not to theses of a good seed or gene. Masson and McCarthy challenge the selfish gene projection in patriarchal science when they write:

> For some humans, many of whom are scientists, there seems to be a powerful allure to the proclamation that all the world is ruled by self-interest, proving that kindness, self-sacrifice, and generosity are at best naive, at worst suicidal. Projecting this onto animals may be one of the more major hidden examples of anthropomorphism in science. . . . Proving that all behavior is ultimately selfish to the bone gives some people special pleasure.[84]

The astounding fact is that scientists have published very little about the inner life of animals. Darwin did write a book called *The Expression of the Emotions in Man and Animals,* but very little has been written on it since. Now that more and more women scientists are entering the field, however, new questions and new answers are being put forward. Masson and McCarthy have assembled previously uncollected documentation of scientific observers of animals and conclude that animals do indeed demonstrate feelings of love, loneliness, grief, depression, joy, friendship, peace, generosity. And while battles and even tribal wars continue to exist, "what is common is the overall peacefulness with which animals live together. Human history is incomparably more violent."[85]

SIN: THE TWENTIETH-CENTURY EXPERIENCE

It is ironic that the era that gave us the industrial revolution, rationalistic education, high-technology warfare, and an environmental disaster, and that put destructive weapons in the hands of Stalin, Hitler, and others like them made claims at its highest echelons—such as science and psychology—of being "value free." Otto Rank complains that one reason that psychology has little to offer the future is that it has no concept of sin: it fails to critique the status quo and is therefore conformist.

> While religion still offers the acceptance of sin, that is, human nature, as a constructive remedy, psychoanalysis, despite its naturalistic terminology, does not accept human nature, because it is based on a social ideology aiming at the individual's conformity to the prevailing standards of goodness.[86]

Though not himself a Christian, Rank believed that "Christianity signified a new interpretation, a revitalization of an outlived ideology [of deliverance] in terms of the needs of the present; whereas psychoanalysis merely offers a consolation and justification of the existent type of man."[87]

Contemporary society has lost the drama of a sense of evil and sin—angels, demons, powers, principalities. We have substituted psychology for spirituality—a psychology that, like our religion, lacks cosmology. A psychology or a religion that lacks cosmology (as much of the Protestant and modern era has) is a weak substitute for the quest for the sacred as a wrestling with cosmic powers.

Morality easily gets reduced to *moralizing*. And what there is of cosmology gets sucked into a grotesque caricature of apocalyptic projection such as the fundamentalists call "rapture," which seems to mean: Have a war so that Christ will return.

When reductionism is committed on sin itself, our species and many others pay a terrible price. While the twentieth century has been about great sins, it has, as we considered in the Introduction, been loath to hear about it. Sin by itself, as we see in Ricoeur's analysis of human fault, does not grasp the entirety of the power of evil or our human share in it.

I propose that it is this evolutionary understanding of sin that has been missing in the Theodicy dilemma (the question: How can a good God allow so much evil?). We need to remember—as process theologians and creation mystics remind us—that God's awareness of sin also evolves. "God becomes as creatures express God," says Eckhart.[88] Does Satan also become as humans express him? Did Hitler teach God something—even *regret* at sharing so much divine power of creativity with an animal capable of so much treachery?

Hitler has taught us—and God also, we might presume—things so powerful about the human species that we do not want to know them. That is why prophets like Elie Wiesel and others who keep the stories of the Holocaust alive are doing all of us a great favor. The courage of suffering and human loss in the war and of wretchedness in the gas chambers and crematoria cries out to God and Satan alike. Today's eco-carnage and the courage of indigenous peoples and others resisting it does the same. The scars are everywhere.

Just as the evolution of humanity's creativity has birthed amazing technological powers for construction and for destruction that we see at work, so, too, this technology has rendered sin more effective and more efficient and more deep. Evil abounds when humanity's capacity for creativity is the greatest. Consider how the Hitler regime "progressed" from killing victims in the back of trucks using carbon monoxide exhaust fumes to the far more efficient methods of elimination through gas showers and crematoria. One can see a parallel evolution of sin in the ecological peril of our time. In Greece back in the fifth century BC, Plato complained of the pollution of the streams and rivers. But because of modest technology, what fifth-century Greeks were able to accomplish in the destruction of the land was minor compared to the destruction we wreak today. Our "progress" in technological prowess and power has actually *increased our capacity for evil*.

Of course, today's technology offers opportunities to accomplish much good by way of cleanup and alternative, clean, and renewable fuels. Another example of the evolution of sin is a deeper understanding of the distinction between *personal* and *social* sin. One Catholic sister I know who spent years in Latin America starting base communities with grassroots organizations tells me that the biggest theological breakthrough for her was learning the distinction between personal and social sin and learning the depths of pain that social sin brings about. This experience of seeing the extreme poverty of have-not peoples has also been mine. I remember visiting a favela in Brazil where the inhabitants shared living space with their chickens and pigs, all living together in their mud-floored huts. I met a woman there who looked about seventy-five years old and I learned that she was in fact thirty-one years old and had seen three of her five children die. Gun-toting hired hands of the landowner would periodically invade the village and take away young men, many of whom were never seen again.

David Korten also tells the story of the evolution of sin. How the days of imperial nation-states conquering the world's weaker and tribal cultures may be near an end, but now transnational financiers are carrying on their own dreams of global empires with their unique brand of "corporate colonialism" in the movement known as "globalization."[89] The results are disastrous for the poor and middle class.

The very naming of eco-sin is also a sign of sin's evolution. The integration of social injustice and ecological injustice signifies an evolution in sin awareness. In considering the evolution of sin one might consider how technology has brought sin into our living room at speeds and intensity that the print media did not do. How has sin been more rapidly reported on, and more vividly so, because of the electronic media? The news of a bomb blast or the kidnapping of a child or the murder of a local citizen is all brought home live and quickly.

Before television one had some breathing room to digest the news and the sins contained therein. Television also has its own slant on the news and its own appeal to the shadows within humans, as Bill McKibben demonstrates in his important work *The Age of Missing Information*.[90]

The Internet also speeds up information that includes reportage of human folly and misbehavior. These postmodern technologies of electronic communication are creating their own influences that will contribute to the evolution of our understanding of human malice and resentments.

Of course, spiritual healing can also be elicited by certain technologies as well. In particular, the *context* of cosmology can be more forcefully and sensually laid out in the multimedia and multisensual forms of postmodern technologies and rituals than was possible previously with the text-oriented media. It is to be expected that, given the grand scheme of evolution's unfolding, as humans evolve their sin will evolve. A modern world had its sins, and a postmodern world will have its particular foibles and treachery. This too may help to explain "what happened to sin" in recent decades: The bridge generation between the modern and postmodern worlds has been very reluctant to engage in sin-talk. This is because, just as Dietrich Bonhoeffer pointed out the reality of "cheap grace," there is such a thing as *cheap guilt* and many people wisely resist it. (Indeed, many fundamentalist preachers are still invoking this distortion of religion.) Very often a fall/redemption religious ideology trivializes sin just as it trivializes creation and grace and spirit. No cosmology means no real theology of evil—only a theology of psychological guilt and an invitation to projection and scapegoating onto others.

While this may explain some of the reticence around the term sin in our time, it does not do away with the reality of sin. Sin has not and will not go away. Indeed, human sin looms larger than ever on our horizon because human creativity—in the form of technology and powerful institutions from banks to governments to universities to professions of all kinds—has the power to wreak havoc with nature as well as with human populations.

To talk to a Holocaust survivor, to visit the ovens of Auschwitz, to see a slave ship, to meditate on what biological warfare can do to a city's inhabitants, is to be struck by a kind of awe: the kind that reminds us of humanity's immense capacities for negative creativity, for choosing death over life. A violation of the sacred is indeed *part of* (not an exclusive part) the experience of the whole that is an experience of the sacred.

TEN DEADLY SINS OF OUR TIME

I propose the following meanings of sin that challenge us in our time. Their flavor will prove to be, as the reader will see, quite ecumenical.

The suffering we cause one another. The sin of wronging others is close to a Buddhist understanding of sin, and I think it is important. All beings suffer; all life is painful at times. From the continents that wrench apart to the atoms cooking in the original fireball, life is not easy. Why add to its difficulties? Why add suffering to what already suffers? That is sin: the choice to add suffering to suffering.

Sometimes our first experience of sin is not as subject but as object. We learn what sin is by what others do to us. When we are young, however, we can have guilt without sin—that is to say, we can be made to feel guilty for the wrong that others, especially adults, might do to us. Abuse is often this kind of experience, and perhaps what makes the memory of abuse so deep and haunting, and the yearning for cleansing and healing so intense, is that abuse creates guilt apart from sin on the part of the object of abuse. That sin and guilt go together, we can understand. But that there can be guilt without sin is not readily processed, and an abuser feeds on his or her prey in this way, threatening more guilt "if you tell," for example.

Ignoring. This is close to the Hindu understanding of sin, and it too is important. In the West the word *ignorance* usually means lack of knowledge. But to ignore is not just to be without knowledge, it is to choose not to look, not to see, not to hear, not to feel. Choosing to turn our back on what is, to remain ignorant, is the beginning of denial. Ignorance in the West often implies a lack of education, but in fact many, many educated persons are the most ignorant, the ones most ignoring what is; and many simple people who have not undergone education have developed their powers of hearing, listening, feeling, and connecting to a far greater degree. Thomas Berry says the greatest destruction of the Earth is being undertaken by "educated" people—people who are educated and knowledgeable but busy ignoring and hence ignorant.

Imbalance, injustice. Taoism teaches of the need to bring yin and yang together without erasing one or the other, to find the one in the other yet keep one distinct from the other. To be unbalanced is to be either/or, to insist on this and not that, to be overly committed to one's particular tribe or worldview. It is to interfere with the flow of togetherness and union that so many energies, from sexuality to art and imagination, require. The word for imbalance in the West is *injustice,* for justice is a kind of balance.

Severing relations. Indigenous prayers address "all our relations." To block our relations or to sever them is therefore serious business. If relationship is the essence of everything that exists, to cut off relations is to do something hostile to what is. It is to harm ourselves and others at a radical level, the place where relation takes place. All sin is then a kind of severing, a cutting-off from how we connect and how we find one another in the universe. Sin is that which severs relationships of justice or love.

Dualism. In this sense sin is settling into either/or relations; being segregationists, whether around race or class or sex or sexual orientation or profession; settling for the part and ignoring the whole.

Reductionism. In this sense sin means oversimplifying the depth, intensity, or complexity of our relations and of their bright *and* their painful dimensions. An example would be reducing all issues between human beings as due to sexism or racism or class. Some gender justice activists, racial activists, and Marxists tend to do this. The result is often that rhetoric replaces healing, and little gets accomplished in the accompanying politics.

Lack of passion. In today's world of urban living, television watching, unemployment, air-conditioning, car driving, distancing from nature's wildness and demands, office working, and computer gazing, lack of passion strikes me as an especially powerful issue. Clarissa Pinkola Estés speaks of it eloquently as the taming and forgetting of the Wild Woman and the Wild Man. It is the cooling of the kundalini energy, the putting-out of the fire energy.

Misdirected love. All love is about desire, and all sin is about both desire and love. So sin is ultimately a quest for love—for expressing it *and* for being embraced by it. "Every sin is ill-directed love as concerns its cause but not its essence," said Thomas Aquinas.[91] Love is behind everything in the universe—even sin. "All the passions of the irascible power begin from love, which is a passion of the concupiscible power, and terminate in joy or sorrow which are also in the concupiscible power."[92] This is very Buddhist, the notion of love/desire as basis of passions. "Every sin has its foundation in some natural appetite," said Aquinas.[93] Concupiscence is an "inordinate desire of a good."[94] And: "Deordination of the appetite constitutes the nature of sin."[95]

Dissipation of energy. The chakra tradition underscores what we should do with our energy, and it also addresses how we can avoid dissipating it. It may be appropriate to see the seven chakras as seven kinds of love. To misdirect our powers for love is to invite a loss of energy, a misspent energy, a dissipation of energy.

That which devours. Sin is that which destroys and devours. It is the dark and dangerous side of Kali and of black holes, however we imagine them in our own personal, psychic, or cultural lives. It is drowning into nothingness, disappearing into forgotten wells of sadness and loss of appetite and power. It is being swallowed whole by events or feelings or circumstances. It is becoming someone else's food—unwillingly. It is becoming an addict or a slave to that which does not beautify us. Darkness, like the eclipse of the sun, is a temporary covering-up of the light that is the source of all flesh. But sin kills the flesh and dampens the spirit.

Perhaps evil is inevitable in a universe as powerful and creative and full of eating and being eaten, living and dying as ours is. Perhaps evil is to blessing what terror is to beauty. Perhaps evil is the moral equivalent of terror, the moral counterpoint to beauty. Just as beauty and terror go together, so do goodness and evil, blessing and malice. Perhaps.

SINS OF THE SPIRIT:
THE SEVEN CHAKRAS
AND THE SEVEN CAPITAL SINS

*I*n Part III I will compare the Western notion

of the seven capital sins with the Eastern teach-

ing of the seven chakras. In doing so I will utilize

the Western understanding of sin as *misdirected*

love, and I will treat sin as misdirected love

within the chakra energy.

This methodology can be seen as an appli-

cation of one of Thomas Aquinas's definitions

of sin, as "misdirected love." The chakras are all

about love, about authentic power shared and received, about balance and therefore justice. All sin, Aquinas taught, has love and desire as its base. But our love and energy systems—our chakras—which are meant to be love centers, can be off balance or misdirected. It is this misdirection that we are pursuing when we pursue sins of the spirit— misdirected spirit on our part. In Hebrew the root word for *sin* means "missing the mark." Missing the mark is another way of talking of misdirected love. (Or is misdirected love a form of missing the mark?) In his *Divine Comedy,* Dante, whose mentor had studied at the University of Paris with Aquinas, deduced all the seven capital sins "from the principle of misdirected love."[1]

THE TRADITION OF THE SEVEN CAPITAL SINS AND ITS EVOLUTION

Since this book centers on the tradition of the seven capital sins, and how they relate to the seven chakras, it seems appropriate to consider them in their evolutionary context.

The notion of the seven capital sins emerged from the Christian monks in the Egyptian desert, whom we know as the Desert Fathers, but they antedate Christianity. As Professor Bloomfield has observed, "the conception of seven evil aerial powers [was] originally pagan and associated with the planets.... Christianity assimilated in its course certain pagan elements, among which were the seven cardinal sins."[2] Before Christian desert monks wrestled with these seven demons the Zoroastrian and Gnostic traditions wrestled with the notions of the "seven heavens" and "seven evil keepers" (the Babylonians detected eight). The soul journey had to travel through these seven dimensions and the number seven represented the cosmology of the period: Seven planets, seven parts of the body, seven colors, seven diseases, etc. "The soul journey was based on the sciences of the day," Bloomfield observes.[3] A late-fourteenth-century poem, *Templum domini,* links the seven sins to the seven planets, demonstrating a cosmic linkage to sin that we have lost for many centuries.[4]

In a time like ours when so much in culture has been reduced to the anthropocentric and psychological, it is refreshing to learn that our premodern ancestors looked upon the soul journey as a cosmic journey and put sin in the context of the relationship between microcosm (human) and macrocosm (universe). Indeed, this methodology raises important questions about how our new cosmology today might offer us insights about the understanding of sin in this postmodern time.

Evagrius of Pontus (364–399), who in the year 383 went into the desert to live a hermit's life, was the first theologian to lay out the seven capital sins. In the fifth century his theology traveled to Marseilles in southern France through the monk Cassian (c.360–435). Saint Benedict (480–c.550), the founder of Western monasticism, took up the issue in his sixth-century rule. The tradition of the capital sins found a special articulation and influence in the work of Pope Gregory the Great (c.540–604) in his commentary on Job 39:25.

Two schools were represented in the traditional thinking about capital sins: that of Gregory the Great and that of John Cassian. The Celtic church followed Cassian, who is called the "father" of the sins in the West, but Gregory the Great's adaptation proved to be the most influential. Gregory differed from Cassian in his list of sins—Cassian counted eight, while Gregory counted seven.

Gregory made reference to the seven devils driven from Mary Magdalene (Luke 7:36–50), and this reference became very popular through the centuries. Depending on the theologian, particular sins were sometimes added or subtracted, and sometimes the order of the sins varied. Some authors found pride to be number one, while in the late Middle Ages avarice was considered number one; in the modern age number one was either sloth or pride. When writers made penitential lists, the original meaning of the sins was obscured.

Those who thought and debated about these sins never fully agreed on them. "They were never standardized," as a Greek Orthodox theologian reminds us.[5] Even in the Middle Ages, "the chief sins were in flux; the authorities disagreed."[6]

Some writers offered seven, some six, some eight. The fact that there is no standardization of sins—even of the seven capital sins—is good news. It invites imagination and wit to the theological table, and it dismantles the effort to overly systematize sin. Each epoch must wrestle with its own special sins and relationships of loss.

In attempting to deconstruct and reconstruct the notion of the seven capital sins, we should remember that the seven capital sins are not necessarily the worst sins. For example, hatred is not listed as a capital sin, even though it is considered an ultimate offense against God and neighbor. It arises from the capital vice of envy, according to Thomas Aquinas.[7] The capital sins are prominent or "cardinal" or "chief" because they open the doors of our hearts (and chakras, presumably) to even worse goings-on. They represent tendencies or final causes rather than specific vices. Aquinas says they are called "capital" because other sins frequently arise from them. They constitute, said Hugh of St. Victor in the twelfth century, the "heads, beginnings, or origins of all other" vices.[8] Rabbi Solomon Schimmel, borrowing from Bloomfield's classic study, calls them "universal human tendencies from which sins result." *Baltimore Catechism* called them "the chief sources of actual sin," and Professor Daniel Maguire, working in the Roman Catholic tradition, calls them tendencies that possess "negative dynamics that pollute relationships, politics, and economics." He warns: "Neglect of them is worse than naive."[9] We might look on them as spiritual states, conditions, or attitudes that let evil spirits into our hearts and souls.

Gregory the Great talked about the seven "daughters" that accompanied each of these sins—phraseology that is unfortunately but tellingly patriarchal and sexist. The traditional treatments of these sins usually included the "daughters" (usually seven in number). In this book I too will explore the *"offspring"* in light of the cultural and personal choices that face us today.

There is no one way to treat the seven capital sins. As one scholar put it, "there is no consensus." The fact that Evagrius placed them in one order in the fourth century in Egypt; that Cassian placed them in another order in the fifth century in Marseilles and added an eighth; that in sixth-century Rome Gregory the Great placed them in another order following the list of seven; and that medieval theologians tended to split over the number eight or the number seven, over Evagrius' enumeration or Cassian's or Gregory's—all this indicates that there is latitude in our treatment of these sins today. Indeed, the more deeply I study this tradition, the more I see what it has in common with the chakra tradition in the East. Neither was fully systematized, and this leaves openings for our own lived experience today.

Another theological difference arose in the phrase "sins of the spirit" and "sins of the flesh." Cassian introduced this distinction, but it was not always accepted by subsequent thinkers. (Gregory the Great adopted it, but Isidore of Seville [c.560–636] did not.) About the distinction, Cassian had this to say:

> Although the Apostle declared that in general all vices are carnal, . . . we distinguish them by a twofold division for the purpose of considering their cure and nature more diligently. Those we call carnal . . . especially belong to carnal movement and sense, by which the flesh receives such delight and nourishment that it also excites our quiet minds and often draws them reluctantly to the consent of the will. . . . But we call those spiritual which arise from the soul alone and not only do not give the flesh any pleasure, but also affect it with a most grievous languor, while they nourish only the diseased soul with a most miserable delight.[10]

Traditionally, the vices are linked logically and psychologically to one another.[11] I am proposing such a linkage as well.

In writing about the sins of the spirit and the capital sins, in some respects I am resurrecting an old scheme of looking at human folly. They were richly developed in the medieval or premodern period, but as one scholar has observed: "Although the seven deadly sins still survive today in some catechisms, the scheme has played no important part in the analysis of human behavior since the Renaissance, when it was replaced by ethical systems based on Aristotle, by characterological analyses based on the humors, or by other thought patterns."[12] Even Gregory only spoke of the scheme in one section of his work, and Aquinas ignored it in the second part of his *Summa Theologica* (II–II).

My method in the chapters that follow will be to blend the blessings of the flesh with the sins of the spirit by combining the Eastern teachings of the seven chakras with the Western teachings of the seven deadly sins, keeping in mind how closely intertwined so-called sins of the spirit and flesh actually are. This effort brings Eastern and Western wisdom together and grounds our understanding of both spirit and sin in the flesh—that is, in our living bodies. I myself find the convergence between the seven capital sins and the seven chakras to be uncanny, and each tradition sheds light and insight onto the other. When I have completed the survey, I invite the reader to make his or her determination of the usefulness of this practice in Deep Ecumenism.

CHAPTER 8

MISDIRECTED LOVE
IN THE FIRST CHAKRA:
ACEDIA, ARROGANCE

I believe that acedia is the misdirected energy of the first chakra. It is what happens when people live without a cosmology. For Dante, who shared a strong cosmology with Aquinas, it is love that "moves the sun and the other stars."[1]

Etymologically the word *acedia* is said to have two derivatives. One is *a-kedos* in Greek, which means "not caring." The other is from the word for *sour*. There is a not-caring aspect to acedia, a lack of passion, and there is also an attitude of sourness or cynicism toward life. It is said that acedia "consists in loving a great good with less intensity than it deserves; it is 'slow love.'"[2] "Slow love" is Dante's definition for acedia. A "slow love" is presumably love that fails to connect to the cosmic love.

The first chakra, we will recall, concerns taking in the sounds of the universe. It is about cosmology and ecology. The sciatic nerve is linked to the minor chakras of the knee and foot. It is about being grounded in the sacredness of all being and all relations. (Remember that the *sacrum* means literally "holy bone.") It is about *listening*—listening to the vibrations and music of all that is, to all that is holy. Its color is the red of blood and excitement and eros.

Acedia was defined by Thomas Aquinas as the "lack of energy to begin new things." It is a kind of ennui, depression, cynicism, sadness, boredom, listlessness, couch-potato-itis, being passive, apathy, psychic exhaustion, having no energy. An ancient text from the monk Evagrius calls it the "noonday demon" that is "the most oppressive of all demons." The desert monks considered it the most dangerous of the demons, for it tempted a monk to flee from his vocation back to the comforts of "the world." Rabbi Solomon Schimmel calls acedia "the most explicitly religious" of the seven deadly sins,[3] and Hildegard of Bingen talked about the soul being "weakened by the coldness of indifference and neglect," which she contrasted to the strengthening of the soul "to all manner of good by the fire of the Holy Spirit."[4] Acedia for her included the dullness born of boredom, sloth, uselessness, and "numbness" that "postpones doing good" and lacks the vigor to fight for justice.[5] Acedia prevents one from accomplishing the greatness of one's work: "Therefore it says to itself: 'If God exists, let God be, because he does not need my work. I desire nothing more than to live fully.'"[6] True living includes working fully.

The opposite of acedia is *joy,* joy at spiritual things. A joyless culture is a culture locked in acedia. Joy is the fruit of *caritas* or love. A joyless person or culture is one starving for love, one out of touch with the real love of the universe transpiring all around.

The first chakra is the beginning of all the chakras: it is where the fire, the seed, the snake lies coiled up and ready for action. If that fire, seed, or snake is not uncoiled, no energy happens. We are listless. Acedia is the first sin of the spirit because it is where our energy dries up. The lesson learned here is that *a life without cosmology and a life without relationships is an energyless life.*

I believe that acedia is the most dominant sin of our culture today. Couch-potato-itis is a conspiracy (conscious or unconscious) of an economic system that is geared to rendering consumerism a daily addiction. Our economic system creates a kind of spiritual enslavement. Just recently an African-American pastor in a city church told me how sad she is at how little energy the young people she knows have. "They are so tired. I am much more energetic than they are!" she exclaimed. Another adult I spoke with lately said: "This generation of young people seems to wake up tired. Why is that?" Where has all the energy gone? That is the question of acedia.

DESPAIR AND ACEDIA

Acedia feeds on *despair,* and despair feeds on acedia. Aquinas says that despair "tears charity out by its roots" and that when we are in despair, we can do the most wicked things because nothing seems valuable to us anymore.[7] Saint John Chrysostom wrote, "It is not so much sin as despair that casts us into hell."[8] Despair gives up; hope is lost. Hope is about the possible; despair is about the impossible. When possibility is lost, despair sets in—and with it still more acedia. Despair and acedia are rampant among young persons today.

Until the early 1970s black Americans had the lowest suicide rate in the United States, but now young black people lead the nation in the rate of increase in suicide. In his book *Race Matters,* theologian Cornel West calls despair or nihilism the number-one issue in black America:

> The proper starting point for the crucial debate about the prospects for black America is an examination of the nihilism that increasingly pervades black communities. *Nihilism is...the lived experience of coping with a life of horrifying meaninglessness, hopelessness, and (most important) lovelessness.* The frightening result is a numbing detachment from others and a self-destructive disposition toward the world. Life without meaning, hope and love breeds a cold-hearted, mean-spirited outlook that destroys both the individual and others.... The major enemy of black survival in America has been and is neither oppression nor exploitation but rather the nihilistic threat— that is, loss of hope and absence of meaning. For as long as hope remains and meaning is preserved, the possibility of overcoming oppression stays alive.[9]

Despair and nihilism often plagued the slaves and descendants of slaves, but the very "genius of our black foremothers and forefathers was to create powerful buffers to ward off the nihilistic threat."[10] Among these buffers were cultural structures of meaning and feeling that created and sustained communities and embodied values of service and sacrifice, love, discipline, and excellence. West believes that market forces and market moralities in black life have shattered black civil society—families, neighborhoods, schools, churches, mosques—leaving more and more black people vulnerable to despair. West sees this nihilism as a sin of the spirit:

> Like alcoholism and drug addiction, nihilism is a disease of the soul. . . . Any disease of the soul must be conquered by a turning of one's soul. This turning is done through one's own affirmation of one's worth—an affirmation fueled by the concern of others. A love ethic must be at the center of a politics of conversion. . . . One must talk about some kind of *politics of conversion*. New models of collective black leadership must promote a version of this politics.[11]

One can only imagine how a renewed cosmology could assist this conversion process, which must indeed be a transformation process—a transformation of regained self-esteem that only a creation story can bring. Indeed, West believes that any strategy for combating nihilism must include "a direct attack on the sense of worthlessness and self-loathing in black America."[12]

Knowing that acedia and despair are first-chakra issues helps us to offer *ways out of despair*. Thomas Aquinas offered a way out when he observed that *zeal* (or heightened energy, clearly the opposite of acedia) comes "from an intense experience of the beauty of things." This is why, he taught, we call God "zealous"—because God knows the intense beauty of every being in the universe. "Love and also zeal are caused in us from beauty and goodness," Aquinas said, "for a thing is not beautiful because we love it, but we love it because it is beautiful and good. . . . God is called a zealot because through God things become objects of zeal, that is, intensely lovable."[13]

The primary way out of acedia is an awakened cosmology, a cosmology that does not pretend to be value free or beauty free but indeed is all about beauty. *All our relations* are graced relations, are relations of beauty to beauty. No one can look at the photographs of the edge of the universe being sent to us from the Hubble telescope and remain indifferent to the beauty and awe and wonder that brought us here. Who can hear the news of the 15 billion years of the unfolding of the universe and remain indifferent to its beauty? Who can hear about the wonders of this planet and its creativity or the wonders of our bodies without being star-struck, awestruck, mystically awakened?

Yes, cosmology is the solution to the misdirected love of the first chakra. To tell the story of how we got here is to reawaken this chakra and drive out despair and acedia. This could be what the historical Jesus was about when he insisted that the domain of God is here. "Do not look here or there, he said; it is among you already." (The great theologian Krister Stendhahl taught that every time the gospels use the word *basileia*—usually translated as "kingdom" or "domain"—we have a right to translate it as "creation.") God's grace is everywhere. It is the primary task of elders to teach the young a creation story. They should do so through whatever creative means are available and interesting in their society. We used to call this storytelling "ritual" or "worship." Today, however, elders are failing to tell the creation story or pass on a cosmology. Indeed, many elders cannot tell the story because they are themselves ignorant or are busy exploiting creation or have themselves succumbed to acedia and depression. So the young remain stuck. The most creative among them are striking out to create their own rituals—which often depend on drugs, alcohol, unsafe sex, gangs, or suicide—just to work out their despair.

It is important to consider each of the sins of the spirit from a socio-political-economic point of view, for "missing the mark" is an act not merely of individuals but of society as a whole. Acedia, the lack of a lit fire, is more of an issue with the lower and middle classes than with the more economically powerful classes. The latter, after all, have the most to benefit from the prolonged dependencies of large numbers of television and entertainment addicts. The owners of the media and the corporations that sponsor sports stars are not poor people.

In their quest for still more power, the powerful often find a kind of quasi-cosmology. The desire for success or riches or fame or power often lights a certain kind of fire in the first chakra. Those on welfare, out of work, bored with their boring work, subjected to menial drudgery at work, or paid minimum wages are most subject to the ravages of couch-potato-itis. Those at the top can buy many distractions, ranging from vacations to business trips to grand homes, art collections, and parties that glitter. They can buy better food, health care, healthier air to breathe, quieter places to live. Those at the bottom, however, are confined to modest distractions that they seldom choose for themselves. Video games and movies and 150 channels of television widen the scope of their choices only modestly, and the Internet allows them to become players on the Web. But for the most part they remain consumers. Oddly, it is they who become financial supporters of the already well heeled. In this way capitalism condemns the nonplayers at the middle and the bottom to acedia.

In the fourteenth century Petrarch, who has been called the "first modern man of letters," wrote a partially autobiographical work called *Secretum* or *Discourses on the Contempt of the World*. In it he is said to have anticipated humanism and the Renaissance and the "bitter-sweet disgust with the world and with life which the Elizabethans [would call] melancholy and the Romantics, *ennui* or *Weltschmerz*."[14] A character named Franciscus is examining his soul and finds there a depression and a general "hatred and contempt for the human condition."[15] Everything gives him displeasure, not just one thing: his failure to reach even his modest goals in life; his need to live for others and not for himself; the weaknesses of his body; his bad luck; the city where he lives, with its stinking streets full of dirty pigs and wild dogs and clanging wheels. It is a kind of hell. Interestingly, these late-medieval people, not unlike the humanists and modernists who followed, lacked a cosmology. In the context of the strictly human, depression and acedia do indeed take over. "Grief, tedium, joylessness and hatred of life and a constant inclination to despair" do indeed take over.[16]

These late-medieval writers show no hint of the "love that moves sun and moon" of Dante's worldview: more evidence that acedia and the first chakra, the cosmological chakra, belong together. Perhaps acedia passed from being a sin of the spirit to a sin of the flesh because at the same time the cosmic flesh was being lost. Thus all flesh was not becoming sinful. Idleness happens when the cosmos is ignored. Who can deny that grief, tedium, joylessness, and hatred of life are leading to despair in our day as well?

ACEDIA AND BOREDOM

Psychologist Erich Fromm believes that boredom has grown exponentially with contemporary culture. Chronic boredom "constitutes one of the major psychopathological phenomena in contemporary technotronic society, although it is only recently that it has found some recognition."[17] Bored people are "affectively frozen, feel no joy—but also no sorrow or pain. They feel nothing. The world is gray, the sky is not blue; they have no appetite for life and often would rather be dead than alive."[18] Today it is not only work that bores but free time as well. "Leisure time itself is manipulated by the consumption industry and is fundamentally as boring as work, only less consciously so."[19] Theologian Sam Keen has written about what he calls the "boredom epidemic" of our culture. He distinguishes four levels of boredom: simple boredom; chronic boredom; depression; and apathy.

> All these states share a feeling of disengagement, alienation, slow passage of time, paralysis of will, reluctance to act and take risks, feelings of helplessness and passive waiting, repression of some or all feeling, loneliness, slowing down of psychic and motor responses, dulling of sex drive, loss of sense of meaning and value.[20]

Wisely Keen observes that "the epidemic of boredom and depression is a symptom of cultural rather than individual failure."[21] As medicine, he calls for voluntary simplicity and a deeper grounding of all our relationships. "To suggest that we make massive changes in the way we construct our relationships, communities, work, and warfare may seem naive and utopian at best. But what is the alternative? More boredom. More depression. More consumption. More violence."[22] We need first to admit how all-pervasive acedia is today in our cultural structures. "In politics, as in psychotherapy, the cure begins with accepting the disease, admitting that our boredom and depression are signals of a deep crisis in value and imagination."[23] From that cutting-through of denial we can enter into the depths of what acedia, in its many manifestations, can teach us. Keen offers a "litany of the bored" that reads as follows:

> It doesn't matter.
> It's not worth getting excited about.
> I'd rather not risk it.
> Why fight the system?
> Find out what they want and give it to them.

Why should I care?
I don't let anything bother me.[24]

In addition, we might add the following to this litany:

I've seen it all before.
Who does she (or he) think she (or he) is?
Know your place.

The negative *senex,* the tired old sheep who is cynical and resents the curiosity of the young or *puer* or *puella,* is born of acedia. Tired of life, the negative *senex* resents enthusiasm in others and sets up rules to prevent the red blood from flowing. Hildegard of Bingen cries out: "O human being, why do you sleep? Why do you have no taste for the good works that sound in God's ears like a symphony? Why do you not search out the house of your heart?"[25] Hildegard links tiredness with ignoring the *sounds* of the first chakra, which resound like a symphony. Ultimately the cure is to explore the house of our hearts.

ACEDIA INVITES A COSMIC LONELINESS

Stripped of our relations to the whole, we become cosmically lonely. Indeed, loneliness often accompanies acedia. "Boredom is lonely. . . . The chronically bored are unreachable. The door of the prison must be unlocked from the inside," says Keen.[26] Of course acedia is lonely—it is about being cut off from *all* our relations, after all! The "epidemic of loneliness" in our world today (Dr. Dean Ornish's phrase) is another sign of the omnipresence of acedia. Loneliness accompanies the loss of cosmology, the loss of our place in the universe, of our touching the universe and its touching us. Isolation is built into a culture that teaches that the universe is a (cold) machine and uncaring and exists only by chance. Such isolation can easily lead to violence. For we have within us powers that yearn to be expressed, but an uncaring universe provides no gentle or appropriate or disciplined way to express those powers. They may have to force themselves to the surface.

Howard Thurman speaks eloquently of this loneliness and the consequences of cutting off the psyche from the rest of nature.

Man cannot long separate himself from nature without withering as a cut rose in a vase. . . . It is but a single leap thus to regard nature as being so completely other than himself that he may exploit it, plunder it, and rape it with impunity.

This we see all around us in the modern world. Our atmosphere is polluted, our streams are poisoned, our hills are denuded, wildlife is increasingly exterminated, while more and more man becomes an alien on the earth and a fouler of his own nest. The price that is being exacted for this is a deep sense of loneliness, of being rootless and a vagabond. Often I have surmised that this condition is more responsible for what seems to be the phenomenal increase in mental and emotional disturbances in modern life than the pressures—economic, social and political—that abound on every hand. The collective psyche shrieks with the agony that it feels as a part of the death cry of a pillaged nature.[27]

Grief is the price we are paying for ignoring the first chakra.

RESTLESSNESS OF SPIRIT

The cure for acedia is not *busyness* and the constant distractions of pseudo-relationships, pseudo-friendships, pseudo-work, or pseudo-sound (the noisiness of television and radio, for example). Indeed, theologians of old noted that a certain *restlessness of spirit* accompanies the sin of acedia. Our driven pursuit of distractions is part of our flight from what acedia has to teach us, especially its demand that we ground ourselves in the earth and in the mother of the earth, the cosmos. Many people today are channeling their restlessness of spirit into consuming the variety of goodies that our consumer culture promises, making uncountable visits to shopping malls and watching uncountable television programs. The real solution to boredom and acedia is *finding the fire,* the *red* fire that is still flickering within us, the *ancilla animae,* that spark of the soul that yearns to become a fire and then a conflagration.

THE GOOD SIDE TO PRIDE

For centuries Christians and Jews have been told that the primary sin is the sin of pride, which gives rise to the sin of disobedience. The story about Adam and Eve in the Garden of Eden has often been preached as a story about pride and disobedience. Thomas Aquinas, following an ancient tradition, called pride the "mother of all vices."[28] However, pride is by no means entirely sinful or a sign of imbalance. In fact, to lack pride is to invite imbalance and is thus a sin, as Aquinas pointed out when he said: "Self-love is the form and root of all friendship. Well-ordered self-love is right and natural—so much so that the person who hates himself or herself sins against nature. To know and to appreciate your own worth is no sin."[29]

Self-love is the basis of all other loves. Cornel West makes this point most strongly when he writes that a strategy for combating nihilism and despair must include "a direct attack on the sense of worthlessness and self-loathing in black America."[30] Self-esteem is healthy and necessary. Healthy pride is not a problem; it contains answers. Unhealthy pride or *arrogance* (what Eastern spirituality often calls *ego)* is the problem, as we shall see presently. Ken Wilbur points out that *dreaded pride,* the "attempt to rise above one's station," was the "arch-sin" of the modern age.[31] In the industrial age everyone was to know their station and stay there. This mechanical obedience served well the powers of that time and played itself out in wars, when young men were indoctrinated to march to war obediently. What does such instruction do to healthy pride? What about the good and necessary dimension to pride? Where would we be without proper self-esteem? Jesus said to love others *as we love ourselves.* This presumes that self-love is goodness and a necessity and indeed a starting point. Pride is not bad; distorted pride is the problem.

THE BAD SIDE TO OBEDIENCE AND DISOBEDIENCE AS NOT LISTENING

A strong argument can be made that the primal story of our first parents' sin is about acedia. Why do I say this? First, because the very word *disobedience* means, etymologically, "failure to listen." *(Obedire* in Latin means "to listen.") A failure to listen is clearly an imbalance of the first chakra, whose task it is to take in the sounds of the universe. The first chakra critique of true disobedience—failure to listen—lays open the sick and sinful kinds of obedience that have been very evident through history. In the modern era, I propose, *obedience has proven to be a far more serious sin than disobedience.* Consider, for example, the obedience of the mass murderers under Hitler—"I was just following orders," they declared. Yes, they were following orders and obeying. But they were not *listening* to the cries of their victims or to teachings of justice and compassion that society and religion are supposed to pay heed to. Such sinful disobedience is the opposite of listening.

German theologian Dorothee Soelle, in *Beyond Mere Obedience,* analyzes the dark side of obedience and points out that "obedience presupposes duality: one who speaks and one who listens; one who knows and one who is ignorant; a ruler and ruled ones."[32] The commandant of the death camp of Auschwitz, she observes, was raised an obedient Christian, and as late as the 1950s a theological lexicon praised obedience as the "central point and key thought of the entire Christian message."[33]

Reflecting on a Nazi state steeped in obedience, Soelle writes: "Surely it is no longer possible to speak of obedience, as it is here used, with a sense of theological innocence....I suspect that we Christians today have the duty to criticize the entire concept of obedience and that this criticism must be radical, simply because we do not know exactly who God is and what God, at any given moment, wills."[34]

Soelle warns that "obedience operates in the barbaric ethos of fascism, but also in that of technocracy as well."[35] The errors of religious obedience, she feels, need to be cured by the mystical approach, wherein "our relationship to God is not one of obedience but of union...of being at one with what is alive. This then becomes what religion is about. When this happens solidarity will replace obedience as the dominant virtue."[36]

Solidarity is what the first chakra is all about: being solidly connected to the solid earth and the earth's home, which is the universe, and being in solidarity with all the sounds of the universe and its yearnings for life. To be in solidarity requires listening with and to one another. Thus obedience may prove to be a far greater sin than disobedience.

TRIVIA, AUTISM, AND THE REFUSAL TO LISTEN

Our age has been called the "information age" because a great deal of hearing is going on—but how much listening? In his amazing book *The Age of Missing Information,* Bill McKibben suggests that we are hearing a lot of noise from the media about an incessant amount of trivia—but we are listening less and less to the deep words of nature. One example would be how we treat the reality of growing old. "On television, 'coming to terms' with aging inevitably means salting away cash, not wondering about death."[37] In nature, on the other hand,

> death surrounds you always. Dead trees, the insects and the birds excavating their guts; dead leaves under your feet beginning to disintegrate with a year of rain and snow; dead bones in the woods where the coyotes hauled down a deer; dead shrubs where the beavers revised the level of the pond and flooded them out; the soil under your feet an enormous crypt holding the death of all the years since the Ice Age ended.[38]

McKibben feels that the information we are receiving in our culture is mostly *mis*information. We need to return to nature—to our first chakra's relationships to earth and cosmos—to bring what he calls *"fundamental* information" into our senses again. One piece of fundamental information would be what the farmer knows about *limits:* "You can't harvest crops successfully until you understand how much can be grown without exhausting the soil, how much rest the land requires, which field can be safely plowed and which are so erosion-prone they're best left to some other purpose. This sense of the limits of one particular place grants you some sense that the world as a whole has limits, a piece of information we've largely forgotten."[39]

The media edit our information and our listening for us. But to be alive is to do our own listening, the work of the first chakra. One cannot listen vicariously any more than one can live vicariously.

Thomas Berry, who is today in his eighties, says that his generation was *autistic:* It failed to listen to the cries and anguish of a dying planet and the dying of species that was happening all around it at the hands of Western industrial civilization. A willful autism derives from the sin of acedia, a failure to pay heed to the first chakra's yearning for connection and cosmology. Such failure to listen is indeed a kind of preoccupation with self or with one's petty world, however defined by culture or parents or school or religion or government.

ARROGANCE

Arrogance is a better word than pride for naming misdirected love in the first chakra. The word "arrogance" comes from the Latin word *arrogo* which means "to appropriate to oneself something to which one has no claim." Racism and sexism (one sex superior to another), colonialism and heterosexism, adultism (the older superior to the younger), and ageism (one age superior to another) are all species of arrogance and are all connected to the first chakra. It is this unhealthy pride or *arrogance* (what Eastern spirituality calls "ego") that is the problem, as we shall see below when we explore racism, anthropocentrism, ecocide, and denominationalism. In this sense, acedia and pride in its negative sense—better *arrogance*—go together. Acedia's indifference and coldness and uncaring—what Hildegard of Bingen called "drying up" and "carelessness" or lack of care and passion—flows from a rejection of the sounds of others, the cries of others for help. Ignoring their dreams, their despair, their rage, their hopes—all this settles in when humans succumb to acedia. "O human," Hildegard asked, "Where is your passion, where is your blood?" Again, a call for the red stuff—for blood. First chakra.

RACISM AS ARROGANCE

The arrogance that comes when humans isolate themselves by nationality or religion or race or class or sex or sexual orientation is evident everywhere in our world. Racism would be one example of this son or daughter of acedia. Wendell Berry writes about racism's roots in an essay called "The Hidden Wound" when he says:

> The root of our racial problem in America is not racism. The root is in our inordinate desire to be superior—not to some inferior or

subject people, though this desire leads to the subjection of people—but to our condition. We wish to rise above the sweat and bother of taking care of anything—of ourselves, of each other, or of our country. We did not enslave African blacks because they were black, but because their labor promised to free us of the obligations of stewardship, and because they were unable to prevent us from enslaving them. They were economically valuable and militarily weak.[40]

Berry is saying that our arrogance or feelings of superiority stem from our lack of groundedness in the earth and in the ways of earth and universe. First we made the earth a slave, and *then* we justified the enslavement of other races to work the earth that we had already learned to hate and put down. Dispossession occurred in particular when African-Americans migrated to the cities and lost their family farms (as did many white families). In 1920 black farmers owned 916,000 farms in this country, totaling 15 million acres. By 1988 blacks owned only 30,000 farms, totaling 3 million acres. Small farms were sucked into the industrial agricultural machine, which made a few people very rich but the land and the waters and small families very poor and dispossessed.

"The willingness to profit from a destructive economy at the top results in economic nonentity at the bottom," warns Berry.[41] The existence of economic nonentities or nonplayers is a recipe for conflagration. On a farm one can still *create* things; but in the city one *buys* things. The satisfaction derived from the two kinds of work is not equal.

Growing up in the Midwest, my knowledge of racism was restricted to that experienced by Native Americans and African-Americans. Only recently, living now in California, have I learned the realities of what Asians have endured. Nineteenth-century American newspapers proclaimed that the Chinese were "heathens and barbarians—savage, lustful, impure, diseased." They were "idol-worshipers" because they "worshiped" their ancestors. A speaker at the California constitutional convention declared that, were Chinese to intermarry with Caucasians, "it would be with the lowest most vile and degraded of our race, and the result of that amalgamation would be a hybrid of the most despicable, a mongrel of the most detestable that has ever afflicted the earth."

Numerous state laws prohibited issuing marriage licenses between a white person and a "Negro, mulatto or Mongolian."[42] Taxes were directed specifically against the Chinese—for example, a fifteen-dollar tax for a laundryman who carried his livelihood on poles (two dollars for one who owned a horse and wagon). The Chinese were forbidden to buy land or to attend schools with white children, and white businesses who hired Chinese were fined. In the 1876 presidential campaign the winner, Rutherford Hayes, endorsed the exclusion of Chinese from the United States by declaring the "present Chinese invasion [was] pernicious and should be discouraged. Our experience in dealing with weaker races—the Negroes and Indians...is not encouraging."[43]

James Garfield, who followed as president, also campaigned against the Chinese. In Los Angeles on October 23, 1871, the "night of horrors," mobs of vigilantes attacked the Chinatown area, and by the end of the night seventeen bodies of Chinese men and boys hung from crossbeams in the neighborhood; most of them had been kicked, pummeled, and shot before they were hanged. At least five hundred Angelenos, or 8 percent of the city's population, had participated in this race riot.[44]

In 1882 the Exclusion Act was passed. This law forbade Chinese laborers to enter the country for ten years and barred wives of current resident laborers from entry. Chinese who did not carry registration papers with them at all times could be jailed for a year and then deported. Chinese were declared totally ineligible for citizenship. "This clause alone allowed the United States to join Nazi Germany and South Africa as the only nations eager to withhold naturalization on purely racial grounds."[45] In 1886, the entire Chinese population was driven out of Seattle and told to go to San Francisco.

In 1892 the Geary Act toughened the Exclusion Act. What followed was a lawless outpouring of racial violence. In Denver and Tacoma; in Tombstone, Arizona; Rock Springs, Wyoming; and Redlands, California, Chinese were hunted down, driven out of town, shot, beaten, tortured, and burned alive in their homes. In Alaska Chinese miners were crowded onto small boats and set adrift; in Tucson a Chinese man was tied to a steer and sent into the desert; in Tacoma seven hundred laborers were herded into railroad cars and driven out of town.

The racism persisted. In 1907 union leader Samuel Gompers declared that "the Caucasians are not going to let their standard of living be destroyed by Negroes, Chinese, Japs, or any others" and that "the offspring of miscegenation between Americans and Asiatics are invariably degenerate."[46] The following states passed laws forbidding intermarriage between Chinese and Caucasians: Arizona, California, Georgia, Idaho, Louisiana, Mississippi, Missouri, Nebraska, Nevada, South Dakota, Virginia, Utah, and Wyoming. The Exclusion Law remained in effect until 1943.

Recently I saw the Ken Burns series on Thomas Jefferson on PBS. Commentator George Will, so earnest, so knowledgeable about isolated facts, praised Jefferson as the perfect American, a quintessential American. Sorry to say, he may have been just that. Lofty in rhetoric that "all men are created equal," he nevertheless kept slaves to the very end of his life. Indeed, evidence is strong that for thirty-eight years following his wife's death he had a mulatto lover. As a young man he spoke and wrote against slavery, but he lost the vote in his Virginia legislature by one vote and never divested himself of his own slaves.

The apartheid of South Africa was the most totalitarian and racially based system of oppression since Nazi Germany. A person's whole life was determined by their race—where and how you were born, the school you attended (if any), the work you did, and the access or lack of access to basic health care. Apartheid was actually legitimized by a pseudo-religion that called it "God's will." It was supposedly God's will, then, that black homelands existed like concentration camps. Church, media, and schools spread this religion. In a nonviolent march in 1960, sixty-eight people were killed and a hundred injured, the majority shot in the back by police. The World Council of Churches called apartheid a sin and heresy and blasphemy and idolatry in 1960 and declared the suspension of members who did not agree. In the 1980s the strategy of boycotts and sanctions got the world's attention and succeeded, but only after thousands died or went to jail between 1985 and 1987. Forty percent of the eighty thousand incarcerated were under eighteen years of age. Forty-two children were killed by police. One officer said to a grieving mother, "We killed your four-year-old girl because we thought she was a dog."[47]

These stories, like those of the Holocaust and parallel stories of races and ethnic groups suffering in America, are reminders of the power of people to endure oppression; and therefore of the power of the spirit.

These stories call out for a sense of cosmology, a sense of welcoming the whole, a sense of accepting, honoring, and celebrating diversity, a sense of resisting a parts-oriented mentality.

ANTHROPOCENTRISM AS ARROGANCE

Clearly, pride understood as arrogance results from acedia. When we shut our ears to other groups, we are setting ourselves above them. Thus anthropocentrism—setting our species and its needs above other species—is an outgrowth of acedia. Is anthropocentrism not a form of collective human egoism? Has humanity not been on a collective ego trip, wherever it has cut itself off from its roots in the rest of nature? I do not disparage the great accomplishment of developing a healthier ego in adolescence. But the *collective ego*—now, that is something to be scared of. And in the individual ego that refuses to let go or connect to all its relations lies folly and danger as well. These kinds of egoism kill, destroy, make ugliness, and leave that ugliness for other generations to deal with.

Our species at this time in history is afflicted by an inflated ego. Our lack of cosmology and a sense of our interdependence with other beings sets us up for a collective inflated ego. Too many of us think we are the only inhabitants of this planet and that all other species exist to serve our needs and wants.

Anthropocentrism may have reached a whole new low in the United States in the last century, when European Americans slaughtered the buffalo. Two years after the transcontinental railroad was built, 99 percent of the huge buffalo herds of the Great Plains were wiped out. A television program on this subject interviewed an Indian who was trying to conjure up what his people must have felt when the buffalo, a sacred animal for them, was slaughtered wholesale. The buffalo's flesh had provided food, shelter, utensils, and other tools for the Indians, and suddenly the white man was killing it indiscriminately. "We killed buffalo, but we killed them with reverence, we killed them in a sacred act. These people were killing them for no reason at all." Buffalo lay rotting all over the plains; a stench went up clear across Kansas and Nebraska. It was doubtless a moral as well as a physical stench. This kind of thing happens when the sense of the sacred and its connection to other beings is swallowed up by the enticements of anthropocentrism.

DENOMINATIONALISM AS ARROGANCE

Denominationalism also carries an attitude of superiority: "My religion is better than yours because…" and "My God allows me to beat up on you because…" Someone I know tells me he looks on the various religions pretty much as he looks on baseball teams: Each competes with the other for very little reason.

How many people have been condemned to death and suffering, to hell in this life and the next, in the name of denominationalism? Not only violence but ignorance and isolation are perpetuated by this narrowness. To fail to recognize other groups as possessing wisdom is to exclude oneself from growing and learning. It fosters one's own ignorance. It is interesting how far *beyond denominationalism* Jesus was when he honored the Samaritan woman and others who were not within his own strict heritage. Wisdom in Israel is always *universal,* not sectarian. She rules over "all nations and all peoples" (Ecclesiastes 24:6). The first writers of the Christian Bible understood Jesus to have been such a wisdom figure.

It is striking, too, how ecumenical and beyond denominationalism other mystics were. Kabir, for example, exclaims: "Now beyond caste or creed am I/O brother what am I to be called?"[48] And on another occasion: "Neither a Hindu/Nor a Muslim am I!/A mere ensemble/of five elements is/This body,/Where the spirit/Plays its drama/of joy and suffering."[49] It is his cosmology and his sense of relation to the other elements that teaches him to go beyond sectarianism: We all share common elements of the universe that make up our bodies and our souls, made up of joy and sorrow. Kabir taught: "O seeker, follow your own path,/Forget the mosque, forget the temple,/Be your own light;/Open your eyes and see/That Rama and Allah are One!"[50] Kabir fought against those who demanded only one expression of faith when he said: "God was neither in Kailash nor in Kaaba…neither in the Puranas nor in the Koran…I say He is everywhere, But, O pandit, you keep hiding him in the Book."[51]

It was his cosmology that gave Kabir the courage to go beyond the book. "I am engaged in the whole creation,/but I am possessed by nothing."[52] Rumi too went beyond denominationalism when he said: "For those in love,/Moslem, Christian, and Jew do not exist./For those in love,/faith and infidelity do not exist,/For those in love,/body, mind, heart, and soul do not exist./Why listen to those who see it another way?/If they're not in love/their eyes do not exist."[53] Meister Eckhart wrote that "God is on all paths for the person who knows."[54]

For some people denomination plays a great role in their identity, and suggesting that the skin of denominations might be permeable threatens them profoundly. I have experienced this firsthand with former coworkers who were Roman Catholic; upon my joining the Episcopal Church, they simply could not deal with this threat to their identity. For a certain older generation, tribal allegiances and denominationalism die hard. But for young people today, I find it to be a total nonissue.

If expressions of misdirected love come from an unbalanced first chakra, then their cure is also found in a reawakened first chakra. When people of different races, sexes, ages, classes, sexual orientations, religions, and ethnic origins rediscover their common ancestry in a common creation story, then our fires will intermingle instead of being used for destruction, rage, and violence, whether this takes the form of guns, armaments, inquisitions, attacks, wars, trials, proselytizing, forced conversions, or torture.

IDOLATRY AND ACEDIA

When denominationalism gets out of hand and tradition gets spelled with a large T, idolatry happens. Idolatry is a uniquely religious sin of confusing the part with the whole. Is all racism not a confusion of the part with the whole? And all sexism? And all heterosexism? And all classism? And all excessive nationalism? If so, then these movements are idolatrous. What Michael Lerner calls the "politics of identity" (as distinct from the politics of meaning) similarly overemphasizes the part at the expense of the whole. The first chakra, which is occupied with the whole of things and with cosmology, is an antidote for parts-idolatry. Thomas Aquinas warns that idolatry is a kind of tyranny, and all tyranny involves idolatry.[55]

Might Aquinas's insight apply to addictions of any kind? After all, the word *addict* shares a common root with the word *dictator*. Do all addictions have something tyrannical and idolatrous about them: a settling for the part instead of experiencing the whole? Honoring a false god, be it in a bottle or a pill, a relationship or a shopping spree, or a religion that is literalist and addicted to a book, is all about settling for someone, something, or some relationship that is less than worthy of the greatness of one's soul and beauty. These false gods might be washed away by a Creator God—the Source without a Source who sends us all the sounds of cosmic creation, all the "words" and the revelations that the first chakra is meant to pick up on.

Aquinas warns that idolatry is among the gravest of all sins.[56] False gods are not those that reveal themselves to us in the word from the universe's mysteries but instead are invariably manufactured and indeed projected from within our own fear and control. Idolatry is a perverse religion, and it always rejects a cosmology, a creation that is bigger than ourselves and that we do not control. Indeed, any ism is capable of becoming an idol and a pseudo-religion, be it fascism or nationalism, racism or sexism, denominationalism or colonialism. So powerful are these forces that they can smother and even co-opt other belief systems. You can tell an idol by what it demands of you: complete surrender of your conscience—that is to say, total obedience.

PUSILLANIMITY AS OFFSPRING OF ACEDIA

Philosopher Josef Pieper calls acedia "the dreary sadness of a heart unwilling to accept the greatness to which man is called by God."[57] In the early thirteenth century the theologian Peraldus equated acedia with tepidity; both are *"parvus amor boni"*—a puny love of the good. "Tepidity is small love of good," he wrote, "and it seems to be the first root in the sin of *acedia*."[58]

When we lack courage and bigness of heart, when we favor pusillanimity over magnanimity, acedia is accomplishing its task. Big heart and big soul do not grow from acedia. Despair and fearfulness or pusillanimity do. The Western monk John Cassian taught that acedia leads to growing listlessness, to giving up, sleeping, and quitting. The opposite of acedia, he says, is *fortitude*. A medieval theologian, Jordan of Quedlinburg, wrote that "everything that is caused by a lack of fortitude, such as fear, pusillanimity," can be attributed to acedia.[59]

A kind of warrior energy is needed to combat acedia, as Cassian saw it: "It is proved by experience that the attack of acedia must not be eschewed by flight, but fought by resistance."[60] Aquinas called withdrawal from doing good things and even great things a "very great evil."[61] This withdrawal, this excessive pride and fear of making a mistake, comes from acedia and therefore from a lack of cosmology. How fearful and puny-souled has our culture become?

INJUSTICE AS AN OFFSPRING OF ACEDIA

Injustice, because it is about imbalance, affects *all* the chakras. But it begins in the first chakra, where it sets a certain pace. The injustice of arrogance and feelings of superiority over other species, religions, races, and classes all begins here with the refusal to listen to others, the refusal therefore to "obey" those different from ourselves. In addition, injustice follows from acedia, because without zeal we have no energy for the struggle, and without fortitude we have no courage to persevere in the struggle. Hildegard of Bingen teaches that the real sin in life is "drying up" and that from this drying up (her definition of acedia?) there results care-less-ness, the lack of passion for justice or indeed for caring about anything at all.

Since acedia occurs when joy and charity dry up, it is also what most interferes with justice, for justice is the struggle to ensure that love is possible because powers are in balance. If we are living in times when justice is too rare and divisions are growing between races and classes and religions and sexes, then maybe acedia is rampant. We can begin to find solutions to injustice in the solutions to acedia. Justice, after all, is cosmological—the Bible teaches that the earth sits on pillars of justice and righteousness, and that injustice toward widows or orphans or others without power throws the whole universe off balance. The balance in the universe is ongoing and process-oriented. Therefore we need to seek out others of like mind and join forces in this quest for balance.

OVERCOMING ACEDIA WITH HEALTHY COMMUNITY AMBITION

The first chakra is about community—about waking up and stretching out to the larger world and taking in its holy sounds and revelations, then returning to one's local community with vision. The Western scientific era, instructing that the universe is a machine, has effectively blocked up the first chakra because it has cut us off from our cosmic relations. That is changing today, as the new cosmology emerges from science. As Howard Thurman explains, deeply embedded in each of us is a desire for community: "Community cannot feed for long on itself; it can only flourish where always the boundaries are giving way to the coming of others from beyond them—unknown and undiscovered brothers. . . . For this is why we were born: Men, all men belong to each other, and he who shuts himself away diminishes himself, and he who shuts another away from him destroys himself."[62] When our community enlarges, so does our perspective on things. Our work also takes on new dimensions. Cosmology brings something large back into our imaginations and our work. The modern age has so isolated us and rendered us so ruggedly individualistic that many of life's experiences—such as *ambition,* for example—have become suspect or reduced merely to the individual ego. But what if a whole society woke up and became "ambitious"? The United States may have done that in the Second World War and later, when we instigated the Marshall Plan, a huge financial and moral commitment to help Europe rebuild after the war.

From premodern cultures we can learn that when a whole society responds to cosmology together, beautiful and powerful works get done. One example of this is Chartres Cathedral. In the twelfth century artists and artisans, bankers and bishops, bakers and stone gatherers, engineers and theologians gathered together to create a cosmic temple, a temple in honor of Mary—the seat of wisdom and throne of compassion and mystical rose and bearer of compassion—in short, in honor of the goddess. After eight centuries that accomplishment still stands and still speaks to hearts and souls of beauty and grace and space and sacred times and the selfless coming-together of many for a greater good. Over a 125-year time period, five hundred other cathedrals the size of Chartres were created, each of them dedicated to the goddess. These temples were great works inspired by a new cosmology and a new presence of the Divine in feminine form.

Another example of great collective work is the giant megaliths, like Stonehenge. They were constructed over a four-thousand-year period (5000–1000 B.C.) in many countries in Europe, including areas we know today as the British Isles, Holland, Denmark, Belgium, Germany, Italy, France, Spain, Portugal, Malta, Sardinia, and Corsica. In the British Isles alone there were more than nine hundred stone circles. These huge monuments, built by often modest-size populations, were invariably constructed on a cosmological basis. The early dolmens in Portugal faced toward the midwinter sunrise, and the great Newgrange monument in Ireland was aimed at the winter solstice sunrise so that on that special day the rising sun shone through the narrow passageway all the way to the innermost chamber of the monument. The rebirth of the sun inspired the rebirthing ceremonies carried on therein with the living and the dead. Stonehenge was rearranged in 2100 B.C. so that it faced the midsummer sunrise. Moon cycles often were a basis for the geometry of these sites. Megaliths were recognized as "places of interchange between the cosmic forces of sky and earth."[63]

At these sacred sites macrocosm and microcosm are integrated so that "the matrix is formed for the whole physical universe. Human beings celebrate and re-enact this fixing of the mound to affirm and ensure the order of things, to keep the pillar, the *axis mundi,* in its place."[64] This act is embodied in sacred structures all over the world. Scholars attribute this intense activity—creating monuments that tell cosmic relationships—to the invention of agriculture. When humans settled down to farm, they were less connected to the ebb and flow of Gaia, and so a consciousness was created that made present that ebb and flow—estivals, rituals, sacred spaces: "The nature connection between sky and earth was broken; and complex observations and rituals were needed to find the moments when this contact could be re-established."[65]

The avenues and alignments at Avebury, Stonehenge, Carnac, Weris, and Callanish suggest "great processions." Clearly the primary and most primal activity going on in the enclosures was dance, which

> seems to have been men and women's earliest way of worshipping and celebrating and of restoring themselves to harmony with the rhythms of life. The dance plays a crucial role, as expression of the natural seizure of early man. Originally all ritual was a dance, in which the whole of the corporeal psyche was literally "set in motion."[66]

Many works of art, from statuettes in Cyprus to paintings on rocks in Sicily and Spain, celebrate these ritual dances.

The religion of the late Stone Age invoked the natural forces of the earth and the skies, the passage of the seasons, the shape of the land-scape, and the order of the cosmos and humanity coming into harmony with it.[67] Therein lies its power to excite and motivate a people. Carnac, on the southern coast of Brittany, is home to the greatest center of megaliths in the world. A Great Menhir was erected there that weighed about *340 tons* and must have been dragged at least eighty kilometers from the nearest known quarry. This dragging was achieved without wheeled vehicles. Imagine what desire inspired this ambition to connect the human to the cosmic! Such ambition did not allow for many couch potatoes among the citizens. A great fire in their bellies must have contributed to the whole community. Interestingly, scholars tell us that excavators at Carnac have found no "weapons suitable for making war, so perhaps here those human energies were directed into very different achievements."[68]

It is true that war often gets people off their couches and into spaces of danger and generosity. But maybe our ancestors of seven thousand years ago knew something we have long since forgotten: that the wonders of the universe also move people to wake up. The community effort to connect to these wonders by way of ritual provided a profound opportunity to share a common task together (the etymological basis for the word *community*) and to awaken a people. Consider that it was a combination of cosmology and ritual that did the awakening. Is this not a clue for engaging the tired first chakra of a weary civilization?

In our culture we have so much ambition to go to the moon or to Mars—but *not* to solve problems of poverty, loneliness, joblessness, disease, and ecological mayhem. Maybe the reason is that we have left the sacred out of our earthly tasks and are more willing to see it afar in other planets and galaxies, for which our awe is still alive. Maybe we no longer believe in the holy flesh of this earth. Maybe we don't bring enough ritual and mystery and cosmos—all of which incite the sacred—into our work, politics, health care, education, economics, religion, and worldview. Religions themselves have failed us here. The old religions seem to have gotten people off their couches; they ignited the first chakra. In earlier times spiritual dryness did not seem to be the issue that it is today.

SINS OF OMISSION, IGNORANCE, AND LACK OF CURIOSITY

Because the first chakra relates to the earth and to the cosmos, ecocide seems to begin with it. The fact that our civilization is destroying the forests, the waters, the soil, the fisheries, the ozone, the other species at unprecedented rates is a sign that our first chakra is out of balance. Acedia is not neutral: dropping out is itself a sin—a *sin of omission,* the tradition calls it. What we fail to do is often more serious than what we choose to do. To choose *not* to do something important is itself a choice that carries moral weight. The German citizens who did not speak out against Nazism and anti-Semitism share part of the moral guilt of that movement.

Aquinas taught that omission of a good that needs to be done— especially in the area of justice-making—is a moral action. "Nonaction is a kind of action. Omission is directly opposed to justice."[69] We omit the justice-making that we ought to be about doing. Aquinas's study *On Evil* treats sins of omission first. Omission flows from ignorance, understood as *ignoring* what we ought to know: "The cause of ignorance is the failure to apply the mind to knowing, and this very failure to apply the mind to knowing what one is obliged to know is a sin of omission."[70] If we lack holy curiosity, how can we help but remain in ignorance? If we do not care what happens to future generations, who will inherit a planet bereft of healthy soil, water, air, and people, how will we ever look for solutions?

I have met many people in my life who are *complacent* and living lives of comfort that in no way spark protest or prophetic work. They are utterly lacking in curiosity. Clarissa Pinkola Estés, like Aquinas, underscores the spiritual necessity of curiosity when she writes:

> The most valued lover, the most valuable parent, the most valued friend, the most valuable "wilderman," is the one who wishes to learn. Those who are not delighted by learning, those who cannot be enticed into new ideas or experiences cannot develop past the roadpost they rest at now. If there is but one force which feeds the root of pain, it is the refusal to learn beyond this moment.[71]

Notice that Estés talks of the "refusal to learn." That refusal is the sin of ignorance, the willful choice to remain stuck in our ignorance, that blocks our energy and limits our aliveness. Lack of curiosity actually "feeds the root of pain." It is one of the causes of suffering in the world.

VAINGLORY, ANTHROPOCENTRISM, DOMESTICATING THE WILD, AND ECOCIDE

Seeking eco-justice is part of our healing; the lack of eco-justice is part of the soul-rupture in our psyches and the despair that we are passing on to our children and grandchildren. As Theodore Roszak has put it in his study on eco-psychology, *The Voice of the Earth,* "our sense of being split off from an 'outer' world where we find no companionable response has everything to do with our obsessive need to conquer and subjugate."[72] Sanity depends, he believes, on a "balance and reciprocity between the human and the not-human." Traditional peoples knew this well. Our anthropocentrism is a deep disease that is producing a diseased planet. The idea that the human can separate itself from other beings and be self-contained

> would be the very height of madness for a traditional psychiatry. The connection between the two is not simply a matter of survival

but of moral and spiritual well-being. Relations with the environment are understood to be ethical, as much as one's relations with a fellow human. Or even more so, because the natural realm is infused with divinity; to break faith with it is not only crazy but sacrilegious.[73]

Gregory the Great, in his delineation of the capital sins, talks not about pride but about "vainglory." Vainglory is an inordinate desire to announce one's own excellence. It includes egotism, conceit, vanity, self-centeredness, self-importance, narcissism, self-complacency, pretension, and self-adulation. Perhaps *anthropocentrism* is a kind of vainglory of our species, an inordinate desire to announce that we are here and that we intend to partake of all the pleasures we can, no matter what happens to other living things that are in our way.

The irony, however, is that injustice toward the rest of nature is injustice toward our own. This is what it means to say we are interdependent with all other beings. Jose Hobday, a Seneca woman, tells me that the native people of this country consciously refused to domesticate any animal because they knew that that would kill the spirit of that animal. If they were tempted to do so, the buffalo would have been an obvious choice. But to have subdued the buffalo would have been to destroy its spirit and beauty.

Is the compulsion to domesticate not part of the attitude of acedia, to render other beings as passive and wild-less as ourselves? This killing of the wild can be found in our own spirits today, as a result of acedia. For example, we often denigrate even our negative feelings. We domesticate our wildness and become a cynical lot. We domesticate our despair and take Valium and Prozac. We domesticate our lust but watch pornography. We domesticate our anger but eat a lot. We domesticate our fear but watch horror movies. We domesticate our envy but make stars of entertainers and pay them to live our lives vicariously for us.

In the Garden of Eden story the picking of fruit—so different from the hunting and gathering of food—brings on a certain fall in our consciousness. Does it contain a memory of the early domestication of agriculture? Might the original sin have been the sin of domestication? A decision that more and more resulted in cutting us off from all our more-than-human relations? Are not the pride and arrogance that accompany acedia balanced by true humility, which means "relating to the earth"? *(Humus* means "earth" in Latin.) Ecology is about our local home, and cosmology is about our vast home. "Ecology is functional cosmology," says Thomas Berry. The earth—humus—is indeed our home, and we are part of it even when we ignore it. The nurturing planet seeks our friendship. It is a grievous act of omission to take it for granted or ignore its calls.

Looking about the globe today, it is clear that we have gone as far as we can go with our anthropocentrism. Beauty is rapidly dying, and health as well. The Philippine Islands once boasted the largest amount of coral reef anywhere in the world. Today 98 percent of that coral is dead. When I worked in the Philippines a year ago, I took a day off and went swimming. Descending to the coral reef, I saw a gray ashen mound: a coral reef cemetery. The denuding of the Philippine forests is producing floods and warming temperatures in what is already a very hot island. The land is dying along with the indigenous peoples.

So, too, the fisheries are dying in the oceans. New Bedford, Massachusetts, has 40 percent unemployment today because the fisher-families have been put out of work because the ocean is effectively fished clean. These stories are repeated all over the globe. In Costa Rica, once a model of egalitarianism, small farmers are being more and more displaced by large estates growing crops for export. The result? Foreign debt has doubled; crime and violence are on the increase; and the income gap between rich and poor is coming to resemble the situation so familiar in the rest of Latin America.

In Thailand 10 million rural people are being evicted from their lands to make way for commercial tree farms, and groundwater is being depleted to raise shrimp for export. The cultures of indigenous peoples are being destroyed, and the young are abandoning the villages and flocking to the cities, where AIDS is rampant and prostitution is a principal source of employment. A Thai monk told me that a certain beetle is the principal source of protein for villagers, but with the eco-destruction going on in the countryside, the beetle is getting rarer and rarer. Thus, even as the young are leaving the villages for the large cities, the villages, where traditions have been kept alive for generations, are dying.

Our planet is becoming a hospital, and our human hospitals will swell with victims of asthma, diabetes, cancer, malnutrition, AIDS, and more. As the earth flesh goes, so goes our own flesh. Acedia and the not-caring attitude that anthropocentrism generates is greatly responsible for the sins of omission that follow. One wonders whether, given today's eco-crisis, the sin of acedia might not be for us what it was for the desert monks: "the most dangerous" of the vices.[74]

If education or religion or the media fail to teach creation stories that move the young; if they fail to pass on a cosmology and revive a first chakra that overflows in praise; then they are participants in the grave sin of omission. As we have seen, Aquinas warned that our sins of omission are invariably greater than those we commit. Sins of omission are based on avoiding the positive precepts to love self, neighbor, and God. They number far more than the Decalogue's ten negative precepts. And they seem to get far less attention in the press.

TELEVISION'S TRIVIALIZING AND COLONIZING

American youths spend more hours per week watching television than in any other activity save sleeping. Yet TV may be intrinsically incapable of providing what needs to be included in our lives. When we go into nature, we feel and sense hundreds of sensations. McKibben recalls the simple activity of swimming:

> I can feel the water rushing past my head, smoothing back my hair. . . . I haul myself out onto a rock in the middle of the pond, and sit there dripping. A breeze comes up, and lifts the hairs on my back, each one giving a nearly imperceptible tug at my skin. Under hand and thigh I can feel the roughness and the hardness of the rock. If I listen, I can hear the birds singing from several trees around the shore, and a frog now and again. . . . I can see a hundred things—the sun reflects off the ripples. . . . I can smell the water.

One can feel in this passage an experience of cosmology, of the blessing that flesh is, of relationship with all that is. By contrast, television engages very few senses.

TV restricts the use of our senses—that's one of the ways it robs us of information. It asks us to use our eyes and ears, and only our eyes and ears. If it is doing its job "correctly," you lose consciousness of your body, at least until a sort of achy torpor begins to assert itself, and maybe after some hours a dull headache, and of course the insatiable hunger that you never really notice but that somehow demands a constant stream of chips and soda.[75]

It is significant how much *flesh* is left out of the television experience. Are the media capable of including the flesh? If not, then the media may be a continuation of the antiflesh bias that goes back to the Neoplatonists and the Augustinian Christians. When TV does attempt to treat nature, a caricature often results. TV wants action and turns nature into a "car-chase flick with animals." Nature films are like "the highlight clips they show on the evening sportscast, all rim-bending slam dunks and bleachers-clearing home runs. . . . The highlights films erode appreciation for the various beauties of the game, some of which are small and patient."[76] Animals are shown as activists, seldom as the contemplatives that they also are.

A lot of animals are remarkably good at sitting still (especially when they suspect they're under surveillance), and this is something TV never captures. The nature documentaries are as absurdly action-packed as the soap operas, where a life's worth of divorce, adultery, and sudden death are crammed into a week's worth of watching— trying to understand "nature" from watching *Wild Kingdom* is as tough as trying to understand "life" from watching *Dynasty.*[77]

Is the manipulation of animals to fit them into our human world that much different from the colonizing of peoples to fit them into our world in previous generations? Has animal colonialism replaced human colonialism? Is this issue today not the same as the issue in colonial times of old: the spiritual integrity of other beings—beings that do not exist merely to serve our purposes but that have their own reasons for existence and their own holy history of existence?

TITILLATION, THE MEDIA, AND ACEDIA

McKibben suggests that one reason we may be destroying the earth at the same time that we are watching so many nature programs on television is that the latter does not engage us for battle or indeed for much of anything. It demands bigger and bigger "hits" of cuteness or grotesqueness on the part of the animal world. When we watch television, after all, we are only voyeurs. No relationship is formed there, for we are not being watched. Television is the ultimate in subject-object relations. It freezes the subject and the object in their respective roles. But the subject, being readily bored, needs more and more titillation. TV is only too happy to oblige. Interestingly, the titillation of the media was predicted by Thomas Aquinas when he warned that acedia gives birth to sadness about Divine things, an uneasiness of the mind, restlessness of the body, instability, and "a roaming unrest of the spirit, an unbridled desire to break out of the citadel of the spirit into diversity."[78] This addiction to the ever-new is one of the sons or daughters of acedia.

Acedia is understood classically as boredom with spiritual things and a rejection of the joy that Divine love offers us. Today this boredom is played out as a boredom with creation, an indifference to its grace and its joy. Somehow it seems that television land is acedia land. And television seeks its own substitution for the cosmos when, for example, Jack Perkins on A&E says that his channel shows "the entire scope of television, which is of course the entire scope of life."[79]

The reality of the pseudo-relationship that TV fosters is all the more frightening given the fact that two-thirds of Americans say they get "most of their information" about the world from television, that the average American home has TV on seven hours per day, and that children spend endless hours imbibing it. Indeed, 12 percent of American adults say they are physically addicted to television. "The industry works hard to make this absorption seem glamorous," notes McKibben.[80] Ultimately, television by its nature is restrictive and reductionistic: It is a machine and an industry committed to omission and titillation: "Like urban living, TV cuts us off from context—stops us from understanding plants and animals as parts of systems, from grounding

them in ideas larger than 'fresh' or fierce or cute."[81] We so easily miss
the lesson learned in nature itself and beyond our living rooms: that the
world does not exist for us. Other creatures "are there because the
world belongs to them too."[82]

Omission is coming live and in living color into our living rooms
and bedrooms, and we are exporting this medium around the world to
other cultures, where once people learned lessons of survival from the
rest of nature, not from machines. Does the media perpetuate ignorance? When we once lived in nature, the first chakra was vulnerable to
being awakened and educated.

Centuries ago the monk John Cassian taught his monks that the
best cure for acedia is manual labor. Manual labor is a kind of *grounding*
in our work—a return to the ground, to the earthy, to earth flesh by
way of our own hands and bodies. Saint Anthony prayed to be delivered
from acedia and had a vision of an angel praying and weaving a rope
with his hands. Anthony responded to his vision by making creative use
of his hands and was saved. Idleness is a temptation for acedia to take
over. This return to the soil and to working the soil was recognized even
then for the health effects that it rendered the farmer. A first chakra
connection for a first chakra mistake.

DENIAL AND ACEDIA

The Travel television channel advertised a trip to Nuremberg with the
following come-on: "Three things make Nuremberg famous—its
Christmas market, the Nuremberg gingerbread, and the Nuremberg
sausage."[83] Is denial a willful or feigned ignorance? A repression of
something we know or ought to know? A deliberate *ignoring* of what is
or was? If so, then denial falls under the first chakra, for it cuts us off
from the sounds, revelations, and insights of our deeper memories and
experiences and those of others. Denial places us out of touch with our
deepest feelings of joy, anger, pain, hope, and grief. Denial is a mechanism that we employ to keep our addictions, idolatries, and relationships to dictators out of sight and out of mind. No addiction can survive
without denial.

The first chakra cuts through denial because it is about letting the whole in—not keeping it out. It is where honesty begins, as well as energy. Maybe this is why Meister Eckhart said that "God is the denial of denial." To deny denial is to let God in; to listen to God's infinite "words" or revelatory acts of creation, which all beings from hydrogen atoms to mammoth galaxies share in common—the act of vibrating and therefore of making sound.

INGRATITUDE AND ACEDIA

Gratitude flows from an awareness of a gift. Acedia sees no gifts; acedia sleeps through the gift-giving. A medieval monk, Isaac of l'Étoile, says that in the person who has succumbed to acedia, Christ sleeps; the cure is to "be vigilant."[84] This language sounds a lot like Eastern mysticism, which also speaks of the importance of waking up. Acedia takes for granted and eschews even looking at our giftedness, our blessings. Aquinas went even further in talking about acedia and ingratitude. He attributed acedia's very origin to the "contempt" of ingratitude. Ingratitude causes acedia and sorrow in our hearts. He put it this way: "If anyone despises the good things they have received from God, this— far from being a proof of humility—shows them to be ungrateful. And from this contempt acedia results, because we sorrow for things that we reckon are evil and worthless."[85]

Cosmology, on the other hand, awakens gratitude, awe, and reverence. Creation stories are the first stories taught to children, to tell them where they come from, how wonderful it is to be here, and how wonderful they are. As sure as warmth follows the sunlight, gratitude will follow.

Arrogance also breeds ingratitude, as does our refusal to acknowledge blessing or goodness and its source. This refusal derives from a certain arrogance, as Aquinas observed when he said that what strictly pertains to the sin of pride is "that a person does not acknowledge his good as coming from another."[86] Notice he is speaking first of acknowledging the presence of blessing or goodness and second of acknowledging its authentic source or giver.

Gratitude makes the heart grow and the imagination come alive. To feel grateful is to feel the desire to praise. Praise is at the heart of all ritual; praise is at the heart of healing ourselves of acedia. To be grateful is to remember the many gifts that the cosmos has bestowed on us. One form of remembering is meditation. Vietnamese monk Thich Nhat Hanh recommends that we do the following meditation and repeat it often: Breathe in gratitude, breathe out a smile. Forgetting is the very opposite of mindfulness, according to Thich Nhat Hanh.

So important to our hearts and energy is gratitude that the mystic Meister Eckhart said: "If the only prayer you say in your whole life is 'thank you,' that would suffice." There is a spontaneity to true grateful-ness, and Aquinas taught that thankfulness lies at the very core of true religion. Indeed, for him religion is "excelling thankfulness or grati-tude."[87] Praise is the noise that joy makes; gratitude is our response to a gift. From time to time it is necessary that we go out of our way to experience gift awareness and the sense of blessing. Part I, "Blessings of the Flesh," lays open entire litanies of blessings of which we all partake: blessings from the cosmos, from the earth, from our own bodies. Any one of these blessings can move us to gratitude, and we have many more in our lives. But we must go blessing-hunting, because our culture is so steeped in cynicism and despair—offspring of acedia—that we have lost our awareness and even *curiosity* about what is good. To the extent that the Christian church has failed to be curious about the wonders of the human body and about flesh everywhere, the sin of acedia has haunted it as well. This failure in curiosity has led to a failure in teach-ing reverence and wonder and gratitude and has a lot to do with the exhaustion of Christianity in so many of its forms. In some Christian circles a kind of cynicism about the flesh can be sensed.

SADNESS AND ACEDIA

Aquinas described acedia as sadness about a Divine good; centuries before Aquinas, John Cassian considered sadness to be a synonym for acedia. Gregory the Great, who created his own list of the seven capi-tal sins, actually replaced the word *acedia* with *sadness*.

Acedia is not only a refusal to be grateful and a flight from blessing and goodness; it is also a takeover by sadness and despair. Meister Eckhart warned that sadness "is the root of all evil,"[88] and in this sense

acedia is the first of the sins of the spirit, the basis of so much miscon-
duct on our part, the root of all evil. Where sadness takes over, all kinds
of shadow projections occur. Both as individuals and as groups, we
become overrun with our pessimism, and the next step is projection
and violence against others whom we imagine to be our enemies. When
despair sets in, violence is often just around the corner.

Thich Nhat Hanh talks about "negative seeds" that are in all of us,
as well as seeds of beauty and peace. We need to cultivate the latter over
the former; we must water and nourish these seeds if something beautiful is to flourish. That is why meditations of gratitude and blessing are
important to ground ourselves and to release healthy energy into the
world. "One flower is made of the whole cosmos," he declares, and
given today's cosmology, he is right both mystically and scientifically.[89]
But one must yield to cosmology, one must do one's spiritual practice
and *cosmological listening* to let this truth into the heart and to nourish it
there. This entrance into the heart begins with the first chakra itself.

ACEDIA AS SLOTH

During the Middle Ages a movement began in which confessors to
laypersons took up the sins of the spirit from the eremitical and monastic tradition. In the process the sin of acedia often became translated as
sloth. In the fourteenth-century English poet William Langland developed this notion in *Piers Plowman,* a poem that, it is said, elevated the
seven sins "into a powerful instrument of satire on the human race."[90]
Langland allegorized and psychologized the sins—they were no longer
issues of relating to the cosmos, as they had been with Dante and
Aquinas. In Europe at this time a sense of cosmology was rapidly disin-
tegrating, and the human was becoming ever more preoccupied with
the human. Petrarch, it is said, excised the *bonum divinum* dimension
from his writings and "secularized the vice . . . reducing the concept to a
psychological phenomenon per se *(tristitia).*"[91]

Now acedia was called *Sleuthe* or *sloth* and appeared as the last of the
seven sins. Sloth was identified first as a failure to carry out one's religious duties and second as a failure to carry out one's social obligations.
Sleuthe forgets to return goods he has borrowed and forgets favors

done him; idleness prevents him from learning a craft as a youth, so that now he turns to begging. In late medieval literature sloth became identified with a sin of the flesh—that is, with physical laziness—and *Piers Plowman* followed suit when it connected sloth with gluttony.[92] In Langland's poem sloth means "negligence both in man's relations with God and in his dealings with his fellow man and society, particularly in the common laborer's attitude toward his work and his duty of providing the necessities of life."[93] The modern industrial age picked up on this notion of sloth, as capitalist owners urged laborers not to be idle and to commit to the machine labor force.

Sloth is also connected to the waste of worldly goods. This understanding of the sin of acedia may seem especially pertinent to our times, when waste is such a momentous obstacle to justice and to keeping the earth healthy. In America alone the average citizen will throw away fifty-five tons of garbage in a lifetime. How much does this have to do with an indifference to and carelessness about our relationship to the environment and to generations to come? How much does it have to do with corporations that are indifferent to the environment and to generations to come?

WASTING WASTE OR MAKING FOOD FOR OTHERS?

The first chakra seems the appropriate chakra for raising questions about waste and our attitudes toward it, since this chakra includes the anal regions of our anatomy. Our attitudes toward the waste products of our bodies may well dictate our attitudes toward waste and the earth. We treat earth flesh as we treat our own flesh. The particular trait of anal retentiveness that so characterizes capitalist misers may also lend a clue as to the cultural issue of waste and the first chakra. Interestingly, the fifteenth-century mystic Julian of Norwich did not disdain her bodily processes in the least, as in this passage, where she praised the natural function of recycling:

> Food is shut in within our bodies as in a very beautiful purse. When necessity calls, the purse opens and then shuts again, in the most fitting way. And it is God who does this because I was shown that

the Goodness of God permeates us even in our humblest needs. God does not despise creation, nor does God disdain to serve us in the simplest function that belongs to our bodies in nature.[94]

Today eco-scientists and architects like Stuart Cowan and Sim Van der Ryn are encouraging us to think and act differently about waste. "Every process of growth is linked to a process of decay," they point out. "In nature, waste equals food. Plants transform water, carbon dioxide, and sunlight into sugars, and these sugars are broken back down by other species.... Waste, *by design,* equals food."[95] Julian of Norwich would no doubt be proud of the compost privy designed by Sim. Using concrete-block walls and a slab, he built a toilet on the model of a compost bin. It saves ten to fifteen thousand gallons of water yearly. The idea has caught on in rural places, and government inspections have found that they pose no health risks. Today they are in place around the world. "When garbage becomes compost," he says, "an essential structure within nature is revealed. In nature, materials are continuously broken into their basic components and rebuilt into new living forms."[96]

Working out of today's cosmology, and paying attention to how earth flesh and human flesh behave in recycling wastes, people have found solutions to waste issues and developed creative ways to promote sustainable living. Looking at our common creation story today, Sims and Cowan point out that we can see the wisdom and imagination in the recycling capacity of the earth. Respiration itself is an act of recycling oxygen—oxygen that was dangerous to anaerobes and a waste product until they befriended it by learning to breathe it. All organisms turn food into energy and convert energy and food into waste products. This waste matter in turn feeds other organisms, from beetles to fungi to bacteria. We have to learn how to do the same thing with the industrial wastes that our species produces. One scientist observes: "Perhaps the key to creating industrial ecosystems is to reconceptualize waste as products."[97]

Many countries around the world have undertaken successful efforts to reprocess industrial wastes using plants or "living filters." In a film studio in China, wastewater is passed through ponds of water hyacinths, which can trap silver up to 35,000 times its level. When the roots are burned, silver is retrieved at a rate of 95 to 99 percent: "This ecological wastewater treatment system produces clean water and allows silver to be recycled in an effective way. The water hyacinths ingeniously turn waste into 'food.'"[98] A technique called bioremediation relies on bacteria, algae, fungi, and plants to break down pesticides. Cheaper than conventional treatments, it actually reclaims sites. Spider plants can remove carbon monoxide, aloe veras can remove formaldehyde, and chrysanthemums can remove benzene.

The wisdom that is emerging from studying eco-flesh parallels what we can learn from our own flesh processes. "Our own blood-streams constantly exchange oxygen-rich red blood and waste-laden blue blood. There is much to learn by observing the transition from blue blood to red blood, from waste to nutrients." What we are used to calling "waste" may in fact, for a friend, be food. But to go out to explore this truth, we must have a cosmology, an ecology, an engaged first chakra. "'Waste' must always be understood as material of no value only to the process at hand, and not as material of no conceivable value to any process at any time."[99] The biggest problem that faces us, according to these authors, is that our industrial system is growing so large that it threatens the natural environment out of sheer volume.

ACEDIA AND OUR FUTURE

It is true that, as scholar Siegfried Wenzel puts it, "the growth of the concept [of acedia] makes a fascinating story, from the noonday demon of the desert monks to the whisperings of Titivillus, from Evagrius' and Cassian's combat with spiritual dejection to the confession of sleuthe."[100] Where does the vice of acedia stand in today's thought?

With cosmology absent and reality psychologized, a great anthropocentrism has taken over, and with it a sadness and lack of energy. With cosmology absent, the experience of the *Divine good* is missing—and blessing is missing. God is no longer great, no longer Creator of a vast and marvelous world, but is reduced to a comforter of our tiny and puny human souls, which in turn shrink to become even punier and tinier. At such a time the blessing that all flesh is, is missing. The first chakra is practically shut down. Only war or the quest for money seems able to open it up again. Violence and avarice alone appear capable of waking people up. Nationalism and capitalism fan the flames of the snuffed-out first chakra. Pseudo-religions are born. The alternative way to reopen the first chakra is to restore the experience of blessing. Aquinas's insight about acedia applies when he wrote: "Acedia is a shrinking of mind, not from any spiritual good, but from . . . the goodness of God."[101]

Acedia, as lack of energy, is so omnipresent today that it may well be the "original sin" of our time. After all, the first chakra is the *original* chakra in the sense of housing the *origin* of the fire for all the other chakras. If it is weak, all the other chakras will be underfed and undernourished. To cure ourselves of acedia would bring great hope to our species today because it would mean our hearts and minds are opening up and expanding.

OFFSPRING OF THE SIN AGAINST THE FIRST CHAKRA: A SUMMARY

Traditionally, the following sins were listed as "daughters" of the sin of acedia: malice, rancor, pusillanimity, despair, sluggishness, wandering of the mind, sadness, and ignorance.[102] And the following were understood to be "daughters" of vainglory: disobedience, boasting, hypocrisy, contention, obstinacy, discord, and love of novelties.[103]

In my rendering I propose the following offspring to the sin of the first chakra: couch-potato-itis, despair, boredom, cosmic loneliness, restlessness of spirit, disobedience understood as not listening, autism and the refusal to listen, trivia, arrogance, racism, anthropocentrism, denominationalism, idolatry, pusillanimity, injustice, lack of healthy curiosity and ambition, ecocide, sins of omission, ignorance, vainglory, domesticating the wild, television's trivializing and colonizing, media titillation, denial, ingratitude, sadness, sloth, wasting waste.

BAPTISM, THE SACRAMENT OF THE FIRST CHAKRA

After reading my book *Original Blessing*, people have frequently asked me, "If original sin is not as important as the church has made it, then what is baptism for? Why get baptized?" Baptism is a new beginning, it is a welcoming into this universe, into this particular time and place, into this particular community and family. It is about taking it all in, all this love and care and possibility, as well as all the potential dangers and pitfalls and mishaps. It is a welcoming in the context of love and care from elders and others who have been through a lot themselves and *still and in spite of it all* desire your presence in the world and so have been instruments of your arrival and are committed to educating and training you into skills of survival and graceful living.

Baptism is a sacrament of *beginnings*. It uses the symbol of beginnings—water—for its work of empowerment. Just as the fetus lived for nine months in the fetal waters and our ancestors *all* lived for millions of years in the primeval seas, so the newborn baby gets welcomed into this universe by a sprinkling or immersion in water in the name of the Creator God. Clarissa Pinkola Estés points out, "To wash something is a timeless purification ritual. It not only means to purify, it also means—like baptism from the Latin *baptiza*—to drench, to permeate with a spiritual numen and mystery.... The renewal, the revivifying, takes place in the water, in the re-discovering of what we really hold to be truth, what we really hold sacred." [104]

Clearly, then, the sacrament of baptism corresponds to the first chakra, which is also a chakra of beginnings, the taking-in of all the wonders of the world. There is no way to undertake the spiritual journey of the chakras or any other tradition without a kind of return to the womb, a starting-over, a becoming a child. Jesus knew this. "Unless you become like a child you will never enter the kingdom." Baptism reminds all of us of our humble beginnings. And water is something we hold in common with all living things. Because it relates us to the whole of nature, it is cosmic. It is yin energy, and the meditation necessary in the first chakra to develop skills to pay attention to the sounds of the universe is also a yin kind of energy. It balances the yang energy of the fire rising up in us, beginning in the first chakra. As water wakes us up in the morning, so the first chakra is the release of energy that wakes us up, inspires us, gets us moving.

SPIRITUAL EXERCISES APROPOS OF THE FIRST CHAKRA

It seems appropriate to apply ourselves to spiritual practices that can assist our understanding of and wrestling with acedia.

1. Thich Nhat Hanh suggests the following meditation: Breathe in gratitude on your in-take breath; breathe out a smile. In, gratitude; out, smile. How does this affect your day?

2. Make a list of the sins of omission that you feel are going on in our culture. Which harbor the most serious consequences? Discuss what you can do about it. How do they relate to acedia?

3. Make a list of the blessings and gifts for which you feel gratitude. How do you show your gratitude? Create rituals that do this effectively.

4. What have you taken for granted lately or even in your lifetime? How can you make up for this lack now?

5. What television do you watch? When you do so, do you experience a roaming unrest of the spirit or pusillanimity? Do you notice this in your children? How can you and your family cut back on television watching?

6. Do you sense the difference between swimming in a pond, as McKibben describes the experience, and watching TV? Have you swum in a pond lately? What other comparable activity can you do that engages all the senses? Do it!

7. Do you agree that acedia is the number-one mistaken state in our time? What can we do to cleanse ourselves of it?

8. Take the "Blessings of the Flesh" litanies—the areas of wonder around cosmos, earth, and human body—and share them with others. Does acedia leave the room when you do this?

9. Since the first chakra is about *listening* (the true meaning of obedience), practice listening for:
    a. a sound you have not heard before
    b. birds
    c. a new kind of music
    d. a story from a new acquaintance who is different from you in age, race, sexual orientation, or ethnic origin.

10. Practice the new creation story, and tell it to young people, to older people, and/or to your children. Have others tell it. Does it drive out ennui and listlessness and other expressions of acedia?

11. Create a skit about acedia. Put it on. Video it. Discuss it with others.

12. Watch the television news with a pad and pencil in hand. Write down all references to cynicism, despair, anthropocentrism, and sadness. Now try to retell the news with less cynicism in mind. How do you do this?

13. Create rituals that heal despair. Include cosmic wonder and awe of the earth and human flesh. Report on how these work in driving out despair and ushering in hope.

14. Consider the following reflection on boredom and meditation by the Tibetan Buddhist Chogyam Trungpa: "The practice of meditation could be described as relating with cool boredom, refreshing boredom, boredom like a mountain stream. It refreshes because we do not have to do anything or expect anything. But there must be some sense of discipline if we are to get beyond the frivolity of trying to replace boredom. That is why we work with the breath as our practice of meditation. Simply relating with the breath is very monotonous and unadventurous....Nothing, absolutely nothing, happens. As we realize that nothing is happening, strangely, we begin to realize that something dignified is happening."[105] Do you dare to meditate to penetrate boredom? When was the last time you allowed yourself to experience nothing? What happened to you as a result?

CHAPTER 9

MISDIRECTED LOVE
IN THE SECOND CHAKRA:
CONTROL, ADDICTION, AND LUST

The second chakra is about sexuality and feminism. It is about feminism because it is about finding a balance between matter and spirit, the sensual and the spiritual, the sexual and the mystical. It is about finding an ongoing balance between giving and receiving, yang and yin, flowing and ordering, yielding and urging. It is about rejecting dualisms. Traditionally, the sin corresponding to this chakra was called lust. Lust has a negative side: that is to say, it can be a situation of creating power over another (or power-under) instead of expressing union and equality or searching for union and equality. But lust can also be a virtue.

THE GOOD SIDE TO LUST

Without lust, none of us would be here. Our parents' lust is what brought us into this world. Lust in itself, then, is holy and sacred. It is sacred desire wanting to penetrate and connect to another. It is a driving force that can be a happy expression of love and caring, of hope and promise insofar as it includes the dynamics for bringing another being into the world. It is not just the lust of our human parents that has brought us to this place but the lust of their parents and others before them. We can thank the holy lust of all our ancient ancestors for our being here.

Instead of seeing our sexuality as a *problem* of lust, we can experience our sexuality as an avenue and a path to the Divine. Tantric sexual practices and the Song of Songs in the Western Scriptures are examples of the praxis of sexual pleasure as a theophany or sacramental experience. Sexuality, like any rich experience, can be turned into an addiction and therefore a problem. But when we have developed skills of letting go and letting be and becoming emptied, sexuality does not overtake us as an obsession will.

It is not just the lust of our human ancestors that brought us here. The lust of animals that have blessed us with their company, their beauty, their shelter, their companionship, their meat, their wonder— we owe them and their lust a debt of gratitude as well. Also, the lust of flowers that bear fruits and grains that strive so hard to spread their pollen amidst the winds blowing and the insects flying—all the lust of the world makes us be and live and ourselves be lusty. We have so many to thank for our lust. Hildegard of Bingen, who possessed a powerful cosmology, understood the deep connection between the sexual and the earthy when she wrote:

> The fertile Earth is symbolized by the sex organs, which display the power of generation as well as an indecent boldness. Just as unruly forces at times rise from these organs, the recurring fertility of the Earth brings about a luxuriant growth and an immense overabundance of fruits. . . . Just as the power of correct procreation and infirmity, of happiness and misfortune, lie hidden within the sex organs, and just as the Earth causes both useful and useless things as well as everything needed for human existence to germinate through the sun, moon, and air, there exists a mighty power within the soul. By this capacity we are able to bring to fulfillment both good and evil, both useful and useless things.[1]

All this generativity is part of what we honor in the second chakra. All our interconnectivity reveals itself in sexuality as an *intimate* interconnectivity. Interconnectivity is not neutral or distant or abstract. It is as close as touch, as close as smell, as close as two bodies can be. Eros is profoundly near, intimate, reciprocal. When lust is this way, it is part of the blessings of life. "True love between persons is enhanced and reinforced by the sexual act," as Rabbi Solomon Schimmel puts it.[2] The gentle side to our sexuality, we call intimacy. In intimacy we practice closeness and caring, regard and respect, affection and deepening of friendship. Intimacy teaches us warmth and caring, even fondness and tenderness on a one-to-one basis. These are not minor lessons to carry through life or into the other chakras. The opposite of intimacy may be objectifying the other. The second chakra ought to teach us the important lessons of intimacy, not its opposite.

LUST'S NEGATIVE SIDE: OBJECTIFYING THE OTHER

Sometimes the way we deal with our lust is neither a blessing nor healthy. In fact, I think it deserves a different name: Violence. Or addiction. Or force that bears us away. Or obsession. Or control. Or dualism. Or rape. Or objectifying. Or sexism. Or homophobia. Our language is rich in names for second-chakra reality when it is off balance: abuse, violation, molestation, dissolution, depravity, lechery, debauchery, licentiousness, lewdness, dissipation, carousal. Would we have so many words if we did not also have the experiences to back them up? When lust becomes a vehicle for objectifying, it is no longer an intimate expression or a generative one, it is a power that needs checking, a stallion that needs bridling, a force that needs tempering.

Rabbi Schimmel teaches that lust is more powerful than shame, guilt, fear, prudence, or gratitude.[3] It does indeed need bridling at times. Lust despises after it enjoys, and when lust is interested in the other "as an object rather than as a person, [it] finds no use for the object once the gratification it afforded has been attained."[4] He offers the example of King David's murder of the husband of his lover as evidence that "lust will commit the most savage crimes to satisfy itself."[5] David's lust set a bad moral example—David's crime led to his son's raping his half sister, Amar. "Not only does a sinful father lose his moral authority over his children, but they also learn to imitate him."[6]

Schimmel defines lust as the "divorcing of sex from ethics and charity,"[7] and he calls for self-control regarding our sexual powers. Where "the sexual act is unethical it should not be performed. If we are unfaithful, dishonest, violent, exploitative, or in some other way harm others or ourselves, we are morally guilty of lust."[8]

Biologist Lyall Watson attributes most of humanity's violence to sex, for he believes that our genetic code demands that we reproduce no matter what the cost. "The subject which most occupies the big brain of the naked ape," he says, "filling more of its mind and time, flowing over into almost all of its other endeavors, is sex." The reason is that "evolution seems to work, almost exclusively at its more complex levels, by competitive reproduction."[9] And competition abounds. Men against women and men against men and tribe against tribe—seemingly it is all about whose genes will carry forward into future generations. We have inherited our genetic urges from our animal forebears, and we cannot deny their strength and assertiveness.

> Our sense of beauty, our capacity for love, our widespread tendency to be jealous and aggressive, even our vaunted intelligence— all the things which seem to make our species so special are natural consequences of our preoccupation with sex. . . . We are the sexiest of all the primates and though this may sometimes seem like a recent, decadent development, it is worth remembering that it has been this way for millions of years.[10]

Because men can become biological parents in a few seconds and women take about 266 days, with a being that dwells within them, while becoming mothers, the two sexes have somewhat different agendas and different modi operandi: "Men are a little like selfish genes, looking for convenient vehicles to carry their inheritance into the next generation. Women are more cautious, like canny investors or developers, seeing men as inconvenient sources of a seminal substance that is nevertheless necessary to realize the potential of their precious nest eggs."[11] Developing his rather unromantic view of sex, Watson, along with his colleague William Hamilton, proposes that much of our sexual drive is an effort to stave off disease. Because sexuality so shakes up our DNA, it provides a kind of vaccination, keeping our offspring one step ahead of parasites. "We are in a perpetual battle with parasites," he says, "and keeping them out means changing locks a little faster than they can change keys."[12] Competition enters the picture from both sides: Women want the best genes possible and so they may want the conquerer over the conquered, and men who conquer other males "leave more off-spring than those conquered."[13]

Watson does not discuss, however, the most overriding issue around sexuality and progeny today, and that is the population explosion. Indeed, the idea that sexuality is the cause of so much competition and strutting is put into question in a time when *there are enough of us or maybe even too many of us.* How will this reality change our sexual drives? Does artificial insemination eliminate the male's number-one raison d'être? If the masculine gender is not necessary for the sexual process, which indeed needs to be slowed down anyway, how will it pass its time? Biology can tell us of our past inheritances but perhaps not much about the future. For that we may have to look to the spiritual side of sexuality and, during this period of sex-for-immortality's-sake, more deeply than we are accustomed.

Our energy of desire seeks union and generativity in one form or another. When it is thwarted, a kind of seething occurs, and violence can naturally result. Because desire wants an outlet, the second chakra, with its emphasis on intimacy with another, has much to teach us. Theologian Cornel West believes that the violence of insatiable desire is built into the very economic structures of our culture and that the "market moral-ity" of our day is destroying healthy lust and sexuality. The result is that we get distracted from the true values of life, such as love, care, and ser-vice to others. This market morality "stigmatizes others as objects for personal pleasure or bodily stimulation. . . . The reduction of individuals to objects of pleasure is especially evident in the culture industries—television, radio, video, music—in which gestures of sexual foreplay and orgiastic pleasure flood the marketplace."[14] The powerful engines of the marketplace, especially advertising, "promote addictions to stimula-tion and obsessions with comfort and convenience. Addictions and obsessions—centered primarily around bodily pleasures and status rankings—constitute market moralities of various sorts."[15]

To make another, who is always a *subject,* into an object is asking for imbalance in our chakras and in our relationships. A subject has his or her integrity and has a right to say no as well as yes. This respect for the integrity of another applies not just to sexual actions but to the very process of our relating in friendship and justice. The fact that intense passions accompany the sexual act, passions upon which our very species has long relied for its survival, intensifies the lessons to be learned in this chakra: lessons of mutuality and reciprocity and give-and-take and equality and fairness. Lessons and energies that will flood the other chakras from this one.

How can we be violent to another when we truly look them in the eye and truly see ourselves in them and they in us? Once we can set others up as objects and not subjects, violence is possible. Violence almost demands one-sidedness. Inequity, cruelty, injustice, oppression, injury, unkindness, atrocity, and savagery follow from our not having taken in the lessons of intimacy that the second chakra has to teach us.

Our generative powers are so amazing and so powerful—what parents who undergo natural childbirth do not experience bringing a new being into the world as one of the great mystical experiences of their lives? At that time they feel the *intimate* connection between ancestors of the past and those to come. From this experience of awe and reverence, a commitment to generosity often follows.

PHILOSOPHIES OF FEMINISM AS DISTINCT FROM PATRIARCHAL PHILOSOPHY

When we discussed the chakras in Chapter 5, I proposed that feminist philosophy is part of the second chakra. Why did I say that? Violence is part of a patriarchal way of being in the world, as recorded by Dorothee Soelle: "Male power, for me, is something to do with roaring, shooting and giving orders. I do not think that this patriarchal culture has done me any more damage than it has done other women. It only became constantly more obvious to me that any identification with the aggressor, the ruler, the violator, is the worst thing that can happen to a woman."[16] One-sided obedience, based on an authoritarian model of relating, she sees as "pure submission," even though it has often been preached as the Christian gospel.[17] Yet she does not find Jesus himself teaching or living that kind of submission. Rather, any obedience he calls for is that of a "liberated spontaneity."[18] Generativity and creativity offer a kind of "liberated spontaneity" that is an alternative to violence. Through their language we may express our deepest feelings of outrage and what most deeply affects us. Soelle finds in the mystics a God-talk that encourages a "union" that leads to "solidarity" and that represents the deepest yearnings of healthy religion. Her dream is that "solidarity will replace obedience as the dominant virtue."[19]

Feminist philosophy is defined differently by various thinkers. In the year 1913 Rebecca West was asked, "What is feminism?" and her answer was: "I don't know what 'feminism' means when people want me to define it. I only know that I am called a feminist whenever I refuse to be treated like a doormat." This would seem to imply that feminism—or what I am proposing as the second chakra—is about refusing to be a doormat. It is about refusing to be passive or used or masochistically treated. It is about being a *subject,* one's own thinking, feeling person in community with other thinking, feeling beings. Writer Madeleine L'Engle has written about feminism: "It is simplistic to say that when women guide the way of life society is peaceable, and there is time for music and beauty and things of the spirit; and that when men are in charge there is war, and the tribal dances become war dances—simplistic or not, that is the basic pattern throughout history." This is feminism as peace-making, not war-making, as putting birthing and creativity forward for the sake of the tribe. It is respect for our creative powers.

In *States of Grace* Charlene Spretnak writes about the goddess spirituality. The Divine, she says, is immanent and all around us, not concentrated in a "distant seat of powers, a transcendent sky-god." A second aspect to the goddess is the empowerment that people undergo as they participate in "terms of their cosmological self." It is an empowerment "far different from a dominating 'power-over,' the binding force of social constructions in a patriarchal culture." A third aspect is a life-based rather than a death-based way of seeing the world. Goddess spirituality "celebrates the erotic as the sparking of cosmic potential" and the sensuous as expressed through the aesthetic. Eros is not ignored but celebrated.[20]

Rosemary Reuther describes feminism as the quest for wholeness as distinct from dualism. It is the way of living a nondualistic life in the world. Dualism of humans and God, of self and the world, of humanity and nature, she writes—"all these relationships have been modeled on sexual dualism.... The male ideology of the 'feminine' that we have inherited in the West seems to be rooted in a self-alienated experience of the body and the world, projecting upon the sexual other the lower half of these dualisms.... It is always woman who is the 'other,' the antithesis over against which one defines 'authentic' (male) selfhood."[21] Adrienne Rich defines feminism as "developing the nurturing capacities of women and of men" and advocates the ongoing passion of creativity.[22] Feminism as compassion, as passion-with, as nurturing and healing.

Suzi Gablik speaks of feminism as the principle of interdependence: "To see our interdependence and interconnectedness is the feminine perspective that has been missing, not only in our scientific thinking and policy-making, but in our aesthetic philosophy as well."[23] For her, patriarchal philosophy sought to be (or claimed to be) "value-free." In contrast, she believes, the value of *healing* is a value to which artists and others can commit themselves.

Another writer, Mary Giles, equates feminism with mysticism itself.[24] bell hooks speaks out on behalf of an antidomination model of family that posits "love as the central guiding principle," love which emphasizes "mutual cooperation, the value of negotiation, processing, and the sharing of resources."[25] She calls for men who do not value the assertion of manhood over the love of justice.[26] She calls on men and women alike to reject patriarchy's assumptions about power: "Manhood was not providing and protecting; it was proved by one's capacity to coerce, control, dominate."[27]

Rabbi Schimmel believes that sex is being exploited to serve interests of greed and lust—and that feminism is critiquing such exaggerations. "Feminist critiques of the advertising and media industries' depiction of women as primarily sexual objects, converge with the objections of conservative religious groups to the sexual suggestiveness of advertising and films."[28] He believes that our culture exaggerates the importance of sex. "The truth is that sex is far less important than many in our culture would have us believe. The amount of time most of us spend directly or indirectly on sexual activity is small compared to the time we spend working, eating, rearing children, studying, caring for our health, and engaging in leisure activities."[29]

Clarissa Pinkola Estés, while not using the term *feminism,* certainly addresses herself to the large issue of womanhood, what it means, and what a psychology of women means. "The wildish nature," she writes, is that "which animates and informs a woman's deepest life."When that depth is addressed, women can "begin to develop in ways never thought possible."To ignore the "innate spiritual being at the center of feminine psychology" which is the wild in women, is to fail women and to fail "their daughters and their daughters' daughters far into all future matrilineal lines." [30]

From this brief summary of certain writers' definitions of feminism, it would flow that they are saying that a one-sided way of living and being in the world that is not healthy is also sinful. These definitions or descriptions of feminism are applicable to the energy of our second chakra. When they are missing, we are off-balance, unhealthy or in a state of sin. Again, they are as follows:

- Being one's own subject, not a doormat
- Being a subject, not an object
- Creating peace, not war
- Experiencing Divinity's immanence, not distance or transcendence exclusively
- Empowerment and participation in a Divine presence in the cosmos, not in a distant being called God
- Being life-oriented (eros), not death-oriented (thanatos)
- Being whole, not dualistic
- Being creative and birth-oriented, not stagnant
- Being nurturing, not noncaring
- Being compassionate, not passionless or living power-over
- Valuing healing, not pretending to be "value-free"
- Being mystical, not just rational or antimystical
- Having solidarity as a goal, not obedience
- Seeing love as mutual cooperation and sharing, not as coercion
- Being wild and innately spiritual at the center, not powerless

The latter in each pair might serve as a list of the sins against the second chakra. But there are more.

ADDICTION

The passions of sexuality are so powerful that of all our desires, lust (or the lack of lust) can lead readily to addiction and one-sidedness—so much so that for many people in our culture today, addiction is the disease (or sin) that names the second chakra better than does lust. Lust is part of that energy that a healthy first chakra elicits but that is so often lacking in our times. "I would that you were hot or cold, but because you are neither, I will vomit you from my mouth" is a hard saying from the Western Scriptures. At least with lust there is some fire, some heat. But with addiction our fire and heat take us over—a kind of tail-wagging-the-dog syndrome. When the heat wanders from our spine and becomes all-engrossing, the second chakra is becoming unbalanced. "Misdirected love" takes over. Instead of responding to our own powers of generativity, attraction and desire, desire itself begins to dictate to us. In this dictatorship we actually surrender our subjectivity, our rights, and our responsibilities as thinking, choosing subjects, and we become slaves in the presence of the dictator, the addiction.

Addictions in our culture are by no means restricted to the sexual. We succumb to addictions of food and drink, of shopping and entertainment, of work and making money, of relationships and television—and more. But the second chakra offers clues about what is at stake and ways out of addictive habits. It contains lessons about *balance,* about not being either a victim or a controller, about giving *and* receiving and about developing an inner life. Addiction, says psychologist Anne Wilson Schaeff, is always about an *external* reference. If we can develop an interiority, we can defend ourselves against addiction.

This is where a mystical life is a big help in fighting off addiction. Meister Eckhart assures us that we all have an interior life when he says: "Become aware of what is in you." In the "innermost" part of us there is not two but only one, where things come together and unite. In the inward person God arises and speaks, and there "Christ is all in all."[31] It is through this inner person that gratitude and wonder come alive and that we learn to behold all creation as a gift.[32] Instead of gift-consciousness and gratitude, an addict accepts a dictator in his or her life. That is less than what we are here for. Better to accept a cosmos, a cosmic presence, a cosmic joy—all of which presume that our first chakra is in gear and healthily engaged in connecting to all our relations. Such connecting is very mystical and interconnected and indeed feminist, after all. It also takes strength and courage to find a balance and flow in our lives between the hot and the cold, the eros and the cooling of eros. This strength, too, needs to come from the first chakra.

Is it not true that most addictions are offensive to the flesh? We might even say that they are sins against the flesh. Alcoholism, drug addiction, watching too much television, excessive eating—these are all exercises in failing to love the flesh. Tradition has called lust and gluttony "sins of the flesh," but I would call them *sins against the flesh*. If we lived in a society that truly honored and celebrated the flesh, we would have fewer addictions. I remember leading a ritual in honor of "the Sacredness of Our Bodies" using photos of the bodily organs, and afterward a woman responded by saying, "I have been a drug addict and an alcoholic, and if anyone had led me through this ritual when I was a teenager, I never would have abused my body." Body abuse and addiction invariably go together. Just as in the first chakra environmental sin is a sin against the eco-flesh, here in the second chakra our responsibility is to honor our own sexual powers and our holy flesh.

Twentieth-century psychology and biology help us to connect *sins of the spirit* with the traditional *sins of the flesh*. In other words, what we called sins of the flesh—lust, gluttony, and sometimes sloth—are in fact also spirit-based because they are quests for the infinite. What we thought of as spirit-based is deeply influenced by endocrine glands and hormonal secretions in the brain and other organs. Gluttony and lust (and sometimes "sloth") were "sins of the flesh" to medievals, but we have found a way to make them "sins of the spirit" as well. We call the way *addiction*.

Gerald May believes that both repression and addiction kill love but that addiction is more dangerous than repression because it enslaves us: "While repression stifles desire, addiction *attaches* desire, bonds and enslaves the energy of desire to certain specific behaviors, things or people. These objects of attachment then become preoccupations and obsessions; they come to rule our lives."[33] He concludes that only grace can liberate us.

Addictions are spirit-issues, arising from needs of the soul that are not being fulfilled. Addiction is a spiritual disease because it is a search for *more* and *never having enough:* "I am sated...until the next time." Perhaps this is a middle-class and upper-class problem that medievals did not have to face: namely, the possibility that you could eat yourself to death (or drink or do drugs) merely by having enough money in hand to get you to a corner market. Perhaps this strange reality (strange in terms of the history of our species) is what prompts Bill McKibben to say that what most distinguishes wilderness from our daily lives today is not the dangers or the animals that lurk there but the fact that in the wilderness *you cannot shop.* Your Visa card and cash mean nothing when you are in the wilderness. How much has consumerism linked up with our "concupiscence," or appetites for food, drink, drugs, or sex, to create spiritually starved monsters questing for the infinite in bottled, packaged, needled, or otherwise pseudo-transcendent forms?

In a capitalist consumer society, the eagerness and availability of the *more* is built in, bred in, woven into the very fabric of our economic system. The pseudo-allurements of the daily siren calls from advertising do not cease from the time we hear the morning news to the time we retire at night. Consumerism forms the very *context* (from the Latin word *contextere,* "to weave") and fabric of our culture. Sex seems to have been made into a quasi-necessary part of our advertising lore and industry.

To connect sins of the spirit and sins of the flesh to each other and to recognize how *all* are sins of the spirit is also to offer us a *way out,* a way beyond, addiction and dictatorship. This way out involves paying attention to the graces inherent in each of our chakras and finding the appropriate balance for these powers and energies in our lives.

ONE-SIDEDNESS AS AN OFFSPRING OF THE SECOND CHAKRA

Addiction is a prime example of what I call *one-sidedness.* Addicts must have one thing and nothing else, whether it is a cigarette now, a fix now, a drink now, a sexual act now. This one-sidedness seems to be the antithesis of mutuality, intimacy, and sexual union, or any union. It is a grabbing syndrome, a having syndrome, not an expression of our primal yearning for union. Taking, using, getting, seizing, grasping, capturing, snatching, clutching, and mastering are not about relating on the basis of friendship and equality. Proof that they are not about union is that in our efforts to achieve a singular goal, others often get trampled. The goal at hand is not respected as a subject in itself but is used and used up, as objects are. Then one needs more and usually increased quantities of the same, a bigger and bigger hit. Addiction is always an objectifying of another as object. Little humor is displayed in our journey to get "it," whatever "it" or whichever "it" is intended.

The second chakra is meant to go beyond one-sidedness. It is about union with another, mutuality, a two-sidedness that, in the experience of lovemaking, can also result in a three-sided relationship. Mystics often employ this chakra as a metaphor for love of all kinds, including the Divine love: It is not only about the union of two but about the birthing of a third. The lesson here for all our love acts, all our love relationships, is not to underestimate how many lovers are really in the room when we respond faithfully to our passion for union: "Where two or three are gathered in my name there am I in the midst of them." The gathering of human lovers is always a generative activity. But the lovers must be equal partners for the real birthing to emerge.

In the Christian tradition Divinity itself was not content with self-love or even dual love. Its own love created a third love, a Holy Spirit. The Trinitarian motif carries over into the second chakra. For if we can learn to make love there, with the Divine and with the polar contrasts within ourselves, whether we call them yin/yang, masculine/feminine, animus/anima, young/old, contemplative/active, being/doing, or by any other name—then we will birth the fiery energy that the other chakras require to come alive and to energize us. To settle for dualism is to interfere with these lovers, these complementary parts of our psyches and beings. It creates coitus interruptus. Nothing can be born from such a breach.

DUALISM, IMBALANCE, BARRENNESS, AND THE SECOND CHAKRA

Is dualism the refusal to make connections? Is it tantamount to refusing to give birth, refusing to engage our gift of generativity, which is a gift not only of producing children in the literal sense but of mothering and fathering one another, befriending one another in relationship? Dualism destroys by refusing to bring together and refusing to make love. It lacks the courage to embrace the enemy and leaves the enemy objectified.

Dualism is about imbalance. It is one-sided, not two-or-more-sided. "All the species of lust pertain to the genus of intemperance," said Aquinas.[34] Might *imbalance* be another word for "intemperance," temperance being the virtue that regulates our balanced relationship to things? When we are dualistic, we only have one leg to stand on. Like a plane with one wing, we are destined for failure.

Dualism also separates, keeps people apart. It is not about love-making in any form. Refusing to give birth, it is barren—it repeats what is, but it does not bring something new into the universe. Addicts as addicts are not generative; they repeat old, familiar routines. Little new is born of that repetitive process; little is given birth to.

The second chakra, on the other hand, is all about birth: the birth of knowledge of another, the birthing and development of a relationship, the birth of the sexual adult, the birth of a child. True spirit-hood, as Clarissa Pinkola Estés remarks, has generativity as its base. The archetype of the wild woman, for example, is a "patroness to all painters, writers, sculptors, dancers, thinkers, prayermakers, seekers, finders—for they are all busy with the work of invention, and that is the Wild Woman's main occupation. As in all art, she resides in the guts, not in the head."[35] She is "multilingual" in the sense of being "fluent in the languages of dreams, passion, and poetry."[36] She refuses to be sanitized. She is a sexual being. She gives birth.

SENTIMENTALISM AND THE SECOND CHAKRA

Another example of one-sidedness is sentimentalism. Sentimentalism, or what sociologist Ann Douglas calls "feminization of culture," is the denigration of our natural instincts for contributing to the community. Douglas calls it "rancid political consciousness."[37] Sentimentalism stifles the inherent power that we all possess to speak out and contribute to the community—often in the name of a one-sided understanding of who we are supposed to be. "Proper ladies" don't show anger; clergy don't show moral outrage; academicians don't show feelings; men don't cry; and so on. One issue of *Ladies Magazine* in the nineteenth century described the proper female in the following terms:

> See, she sits, she walks, she speaks, she looks—unutterable things! Inspiration springs up in her very paths—it follow her foot-steps. A halo of glory encircles her, and illumines her whole orbit. With her, man not only feels safe but is actually renovated. For he approaches her with an awe, a reverence, and an affection which before he knew not he possessed.[38]

Masochism follows from this distortion of our bodily nature. Victimization and even immolation play important roles in a society of sentimentalism.

Sentimentalism distorts the angry side of the individual and of society itself to such a degree that, as psychologist Carl Jung warned, the guaranteed result is *violence*. Scratch a sentimentalist, and you get violence. Much of fundamentalist religiosity is sentimental, and the shadow side that comes out is violence: "Kill abortionists! Kill homosexuals! Kill a commie for Christ!" Part of a healthy second chakra is to resist and indeed throw off the internalized oppression and one-sidedness that sentimentalism fosters.

In *Women Who Run With the Wolves,* Estés by the title alone demonstrates the dangers of one-sidedness. Her call to embrace the wild woman within every woman and every relationship with woman is a direct affront against the sentimentalism of our culture. "To love a woman," she writes, "the mate must also love her wildish nature. If she takes a mate who cannot or will not love this other side, she shall surely in some way be dismantled and be left to limp about unrepaired."[39] But she warns that men too "must name their dual natures." A true man is not put off by the true—that is, wild—womanly soul: "Afeared or not, it is an act of deepest love to allow oneself to be stirred by the wildish souls of another." Instead of settling for the boredom that is intrinsic to a one-sided personhood, true lovers seek out and indeed bring out the wild in each other. In this love lies real transformation.

While one side of a woman's dual nature might be called Life, Life's "twin" sister is a force named Death. The force called Death is one of the two magnetic forks of the wild nature. If one learns to name the dualities, one will eventually bump right up against the bald skull of the Death nature. They say only heroes can stand it. Certainly the wildish man can stand it. Absolutely, the wildish woman can stand it. They are in fact wholly transformed by it.[40]

Estés encourages women (and men) to cultivate both dimensions to soul: that of wildness *and* that of the more "civilized" aspect. The latter by itself is lonely, and the wildish by itself is "wistful for relationship with the other." The stakes are high as to whether the individual marries both aspects. Estés believes that "the loss of women's psychological, emotional, and spiritual powers comes from separating these two natures from one another and pretending one or the other no longer exists."[41] Surely sentimentalism does that: it deals in pretense.

HUMORLESSNESS

Before empires took their progeny so seriously, humanity usually looked on sexuality with a great deal of humor. The Inuit people to this day call the sex act "making laughter together," and the psychologist Otto Rank writes about earlier times when sexuality was not about who will inherit the kingdom or qualify for the inheritance but essentially about play. Perhaps vestiges of sexuality as play reside in the jokes that we still like to tell one another about the subject. Sex, after all, always has the last laugh. It is not one of those experiences that lend themselves readily to control. That is one reason we are vigilant to learn about it, as if the last object of curiosity that goes cold in us is sex. Sexuality is a kind of *trickster,* and maybe we should see it anew in that light. The trickster tries to get the community to laugh at itself and not to take itself overly seriously. Maybe the second chakra is also about developing a sense of humor—even about performing the necessities of life such as begetting a new generation and passing on our family name, traits, aspirations, and all those projections we are tempted to lay upon our children.

Laughter, after all, is a fine way to create mutuality. It saves us from our solipsism and isolation. It lightens our burdens and the gravity of our existence. It welcomes paradox and learns to be at home with it. Laughter appropriately fits the second chakra, where two who are different but yearning to complement one another come together, and where what happens between them is both secret but universal. Lovers do indeed make laughter together—and not just sexual lovers, but all lovers, all beings.

The second chakra is that chakra where difference and togetherness begin to merge into a world of union and intimacy. The first chakra is about us and all things, but the second chakra is about oneself and another and still others. We move from the one-ing of the first chakra to the making-one-from-two of the second chakra, with the potential of making three. There is fun and laughter in this activity, surely, for who could predict the outcome? Surprise is built into our actions in the second chakra. To insist on one-sidedness is to abort the surprise and possibilities, the humor and the fun, that the second chakra promises. It is sure to limit the energy available to the rest of our spirit life.

Laughter is an affront to control. When we recognize the incongruities of life and relationships, we break into laughter. Much laughter is at the expense of the controlling classes, like a joke I recently heard from an Episcopalian bishop. It seems that a couple died and arrived at the pearly gates of heaven. They asked Saint Peter if they could get married in heaven because they had not been married on earth. "Well, if you must," said Peter. "But come back in five years." They returned in five years and said, "We are ready to get married now." "I'm sorry," Peter said. "Please come back in five more years." They were deeply disappointed but came back five years later and got married. After three years, however, the marriage was not going so well, and they came to Saint Peter and said, "We are sorry, but the marriage isn't working. We really think, since eternity is so long, that we should get a divorce." "Oh, no!" Peter said, throwing up his hands. "It took me ten years to find a priest up here, and now you expect me to find a lawyer!" Such humor gets back at what we perceive as the controlling classes.

CONTROL: *THE* ISSUE IN THE SECOND CHAKRA

Control plays a great role in this chakra, or the temptation to control, to refuse to let desire either flow or take over. A dance has to be learned, in the sexual chakra, between control and let-go or flow. Augustine, who had such an influence on Christian theology, confessed that he mistrusted his sexuality because in the process of lovemaking he "lost control." He was not well balanced in his second chakra, and the church inherited his suspicion.

But Jesus' teaching on sexuality, scant as it is, talks of paying attention to one's motives and to one's inner life. He does not put down the sexual. Control is not his agenda, either personally or politically. Freedom is—responsible, justice-oriented, freedom. He seems to trust desire because he trusts nature in general, much more than he trusts human institutions and ethical preaching. The alternative to sexual rapacity is not severe control but trust. Do we learn to trust in the second chakra? Trust process, trust the new, trust the other? If we are betrayed or trust is broken between us and another, what do we do then? Do we give up and return to a lethargic, pre–first chakra state? I know someone who, when her husband left her, simply ate and ate and ate. All her conversation ever since has been about food and restaurants and meals. She has not regained the resiliency to trust and therefore live again. Addiction has taken over. Eating is easier and, superficially at least, friendlier than a rapacious world, and it feeds the hunger inside— for a while.

Is addiction itself a kind of control syndrome? True, it is also about being controlled, but it is about being controlled by something apparently controllable. Perhaps this is one reason the breakthrough regarding addiction often happens when there is a breakdown of control. It is as if addiction is healed only if control gets reshuffled and redefined. Addiction might even be a sign of a *crisis of control*. Psychologist Anne Wilson Schaeff says that the God of the Addictive System "is God the Controller,"[42] and scientist Gregory Bateson makes a provocative suggestion when he proposes that the issue in healing the alcoholic has to do with moving from a *dualistic* worldview to a *complementary* one. He writes:

> The religious conversion of the alcoholic when saved by AA can be described as a dramatic shift from this symmetrical (conflictual) habit, or epistemology, to an almost purely complementary view of his relationship to others and to the universe or God. . . . The

"sobriety" of the alcoholic is characterized by an unusually disastrous variant of the Cartesian dualism, the division between Mind
and Matter, or, in this case, between conscious will, or "self," and
the remainder of the personality. Bill W's stroke of genius was to
break up with the first "step" the structure of this dualism.[43]

That alcoholism entails control issues is also supported by Bateson, who
writes that "the panic of the alcoholic who has hit bottom is the panic
of the man who thought he had control over a vehicle but suddenly finds
that the vehicle can run away with him."[44] AA succeeds because it offers
a "noncompetitive relationship to the larger world [that] is of the nature
of 'service' rather than dominance."[45] The second chakra requires that
we let go of dominating habits and gather our sexual energies, along
with our other energies, into the work of compassion and service.

CONTROL AS SADISM DERIVING FROM IMPOTENCE

According to psychologist Erich Fromm, the essence of sadism is the
compulsion to control. "The core of sadism, common to all its manifestations, is the passion to have absolute and unrestricted control over
a living being, whether an animal, a child, a man, or a woman."[46] This
need for control has profound social as well as personal implications—
the "authoritarian character" who is a sadomasochist exhibits "control of
those below and submission to those above."[47] Who is affected by this
control compulsion? "Even those on lower social levels can have control
over somebody who is subject to their power. There are always children, wives, or dogs available; or there are helpless people, such as
inmates of prisons, patients in hospitals...pupils in schools." Racism
and religious bigotry flow from this kind of sadism. "Religious and
racial minorities, as far as they are powerless, offer a vast opportunity
for sadistic satisfaction for even the poorest members of the majority."[48]
    Fromm understands sadism to be a misuse of our generative pow-
ers when he observes that the sadist is afraid of creativity.

The sadistic character is afraid of everything that is not certain and
predictable, that offers surprises which would force him to sponta-

neous and original reactions. For this reason, he is afraid of life. Life frightens him precisely because it is by its very nature unpredictable and uncertain. It is structured but it is not orderly.[49]

This explains much of the dynamic among Inquisitorial figures in our day and previous times. The second chakra is the issue as well because sadism derives from impotence. Sadism is "the transformation of impotence into the experience of omnipotence; it is the religion of psychical cripples."[50]

HOMOPHOBIA AS AN OFFSPRING OF
THE SECOND CHAKRA

Homophobia is another kind of control, as well as an affront against the second chakra. It creates a dualism of us versus them and of us (the majority heterosexual world) controlling them (the minority homosexual world). Surely the human species today can relearn what it knew in premodern times: that diversity is present in all aspects of creation, including sexual attraction, and that homosexuals have as much right to exist and be themselves as the rest of the human race. In fact, homosexuals have special gifts of spirituality to bring to the larger community. As the dominant heterosexual community lives with these facts, the homosexual community itself can undertake its own self-discovery and healing process more effectively. This healing process must surely include the integration of spirituality and all parts of one's existence, including one's sexuality.

INSTITUTIONAL FAULT-FINDING AROUND
LUST, PRIDE, AND DISOBEDIENCE:
A PROGRAM FOR CONTROLLING OTHERS

The classical teaching about sin in the Garden of Eden is that we must resist the evil trinity of lust, pride, and disobedience. Desire gets a hit, pride takes a wallop, and disobedience gets you a ticket to hell itself. But there may be genuine overkill here: What about the need for desire, for passion, for knowing what calls us and allures us, sirenlike, from our slumber? Fire is not the problem—in fact, acedia is *lack of fire,* and there lies the problem. Knowing and responding generously to what motivates us is an essential part of being alive in the world. Teresa of Ávila said that prayer is 95 percent desire! "Where your heart is, there your treasure will be also," said Jesus. Purification of desire? Yes! Squelching and denigration of desire itself? No way!

To me, this false trinity of bad-mouthing desire, pride, and initiative (the opposite of obedience?) smells fishily like a class thing. Those in power would love it if those out of power would (1) squelch their desires and forget them, (2) hate themselves in the name of humility and flee authentic pride, and (3) surrender their conscience to obey orders from above. The one-sided teaching against desire, pride, and initiative has played a prominent part in Christian theology ever since Christians escaped the catacombs and took over the reign of the empire. The industrial age invested itself in the same kind of domination ethic. Does this help to explain how Christian theologians have often given a bad name to the word *sin?* Who is calling what sin will more often than not have a political meaning.

We should take a hard look at how this trinity of sinfulness takes us beyond individual guilt to the guilt and responsibility of our institutions and cultural structures. Institutions can exhibit an unbridled desire, a greed that can actually swallow up the earth and its health and the future of its children and that knows no national, ethical, or legal boundaries. Their lust for gain may think nothing of destroying trees that are thousands of years old or the soil or the fisheries or the ozone layer itself in the name of "profits" or of destroying cultures and peoples for the same reasons. As one writer, who has lived in both northern and southern countries, has put it, "Development as we understood it thirty years ago, and as it is to this day vigorously promoted by the World Bank, the IMF [International Monetary Fund], the Bush administration, and most of the world's powerful economic institutions, isn't working for the majority of humanity. And the roots of the problem are not found among the poor of the 'underdeveloped' world. They are found in the countries that set global standards for wasteful extravagance and dominate the global polices that are leading our world to social and ecological self-destruction."[51]

Institutional arrogance and egoism can prove far more destructive than those of individuals alone. And because they are not fleshy, institutions can live (legally speaking) in perpetuity! As David Korten points out, the Supreme Court ruling of 1886 in *Santa Clara County v. Southern Pacific Railroad* established a unique situation for corporations in America, claiming that they were natural persons under the constitution and were thereby entitled to the protections of the Bill of Rights that individual citizens enjoy. (Strange to say, the constitution does not mention corporations anyplace.) Korten comments:

> Thus corporations finally claimed the full rights enjoyed by individual citizens while being exempted from many of the responsibilities and liabilities of citizenship. . . . The subsequent claim by corporations that they have the same right as any individual to influence the government in their own interest pits the individual citizen against the vast financial and communications resources of the corporation and mocks the constitutional intent that all citizens have an equal voice in the political debates surrounding important issues.[52]

With its newfound political power and backed by its growing economic power, which translated into whole new industries of advertising, "American business, after 1890 . . . began the transformation of American society into a society preoccupied with consumption, with comfort and bodily well-being, with luxury, spending, and acquisition, with more goods this year than last, more next year than this."[53] It is interesting to see to what lengths corporate power will extend itself and how distant it all is from the flesh. Corporations are not by definition fleshy—they have no second chakra and cannot make love. They have a legal or rational existence but not a carnal one. They are not made of atoms and photons like the rest of us. This is why they are eternal. As Korten puts it, "Behind its carefully crafted public-relations image and the many fine and ethical people it may employ, the body of a corporation is its corporate charter, a legal document, and money is its blood. It is at its core an alien entity with one goal: to reproduce money to nourish and replicate itself. Individuals are dispensable."[54]

SADOMASOCHISM AND CORPORATE VIOLENCE

The decisions these fleshless beings make can be very hard on creatures that are incarnated and of the flesh. An example is the way transnational cigarette manufacturers put pressure, through the U.S. trade representative, on the Taiwanese government when it was preparing an antismoking campaign for its citizens. When similar pressure was applied by American tobacco companies in Korea, the percentage of smokers increased from 1.6 to 8.7 percent among the male teenage population.[55] On the average, those who smoke die seven years before those who do not. Are American corporations killing citizens of poorer countries seven years before their time? What right do they have to do that? After the silicone breast scandal and the American government's efforts to stop their manufacture, major ads appeared in Guatemalan newspapers for silicone breasts—the companies doing the advertising had American names. Clearly institutions demonstrate disobedience—that is, they refuse to listen to groups and persons and the poor and those not yet born. Far greater evil results than when individuals refuse to listen.

Corporations that "downsize"—fire as many workers as possible—are demonstrating an *ignoring of flesh*. William Dugger, a management analyst, predicts the following fleshless scenario for corporations:

> Taken to the logical conclusion, when 100 percent of the stock is treasury stock the corporation will own itself. It will have dispensed entirely with shareholders from the species Homo sapiens. To whom or to what would it then be responsible?... Could a corporation entirely dispense with not only human ownership but also human workers and managers?... What would it be then?... It would exist physically as a network of machines that buy, process, and sell commodities, monitored by a network of computers.... It would be responsible to no one but itself in its mechanical drive for power and profit.[56]

The flesh-and-blood issue of people losing their jobs may not be felt by money monitors at computer terminals, but they are felt by the managers who do the firing. As one CEO put it to *Fortune* magazine, "You get through firing people the first time around, accepting it as part of business. The second time I began wondering, 'How many miscarriages is this causing? How many divorces, how many suicides?' I worked harder so that I wouldn't have to think about it.'"[57] A corporation distances itself from the second chakra—it has no genitals and no sex life.

In doing so, it falls out of touch with the moral issues of flesh and blood, eating and starving, breathing and dying.

The growing gap between the haves and the have-nots reveals a failure of the second chakra: a failure in equality and justice and friendship and loving. It exhibits a power-over/power-under dynamic—that is, a sadomasochistic dynamic that is not the appropriate use of our energies, either personal or collective. It underscores the origins of violence—which are more often than not injustice—and it lays bare the dynamics of violence actually operating in our world today. Violence, as we have seen, is the opposite of union-making, lovemaking, generativity of something new. If violence tends to generate anything, it is more violence and suffering. How much of the *excess* that so characterizes the misdirected energies of our economic system goes to feed the addictions of those living lives of excess: addictions to new materialistic fashions, new gadgets, new trinkets, new shopping sprees, new (or familiar) drinking, drugging, spending, and power sprees?

OFFSPRING OF MISDIRECTED LOVE IN THE SECOND CHAKRA: A SUMMARY

Traditionally, the "daughters of lust" were designated as: blindness of the mind, thoughtlessness, inconstancy, temerity or audacity, self-love, hatred of God, love of the present world, and despair of a future world.[58] In contrast, I am proposing the following *offspring* of misdirected love in the second chakra: control, objectifying the other, patriarchy, addiction, one-sidedness, dualism, imbalance, barrenness, sentimentalism, humorlessness, homophobia, institutional desire, pride and disobedience, sadomasochism and corporate violence.

RECONCILIATION, THE SACRAMENT OF THE SECOND CHAKRA

The second chakra, our sexual chakra, is about reconciling matter and spirit, sexuality and mysticism, self and other. It is the union sacrament that overcomes dualism and separation. It reconciles opposites, male and female, yin and yang, in a common act of lovemaking. It is about finding the beloved instead of a cold, distant other. And it is about union, uniting with the beloved. And for that reconciliation is necessary. Thus the second chakra corresponds to the sacrament of reconciliation. From reconciliation new energy flows, new life, new possibilities. It is a kind of born-again experience except that it happens again and again and again.

SPIRITUAL EXERCISES FOR THE SECOND CHAKRA

1. What wisdom have you learned from your sexuality?
2. Draw a picture of some thing or relationship that tempts you to addiction. Draw another picture of how you can resist that addictiveness. Discuss both pictures with another person doing the same exercise.
3. Give examples of control issues that you see every day (a) at work, (b) at home, (c) in the civic arena, (d) in the economic arena. What imaginative steps can you take to blow the whistle on these issues?
4. What sentimental fare do you see on television? What can you do about it?
5. Draw pictures, or dance a dance, or write a poem about:
    a. the positive side of lust
    b. the positive side of pride
    c. the positive side of disobedience
6. Keeping in mind the corporate issues around the proverbial trinity of desire, pride, and disobedience, create a play or skit around:
    a. the negative side of lust
    b. the negative side of pride
    c. the positive side of obedience
    d. what persons have going for them that corporations do not
7. Create union from a dualism. Do this in words or writing or in paint, clay, dance, or music
8. Share stories about the following:
    a. one-sidedness
    b. homophobia
    c. imbalance
    d. barrenness
9. Read the Song of Songs. How does it speak to you of cosmology, sexuality, and mysticism?

CHAPTER 10

MISDIRECTED LOVE IN THE THIRD CHAKRA: VICTIMIZATION, ANGER, AND VIOLENCE

The third chakra concerns empowerment and centering. Our failures around the third chakra are invariably those of not coming into our strength, of yielding our strength to others, of lacking authentic outrage. On the other hand, we misuse our strength in brutality, rage, fury, vehemence, hostility, frenzy, or ire. This misuse corresponds to the traditional sin of anger. Rather than a sin, anger in this chakra is first of all a blessing and a source of our strength. Just as smoke indicates fire, so anger indicates love. Anger has a necessary and important role to play in response to our pain or abuse. Indeed, anger is the first level of grief. Anger, motivated by love, moves us to act heartily and to persevere in our intentions.

BITTERNESS AND PASSIVE-AGGRESSIVE BEHAVIOR: FRUITS OF NEGLECTING OUR ANGER

So important is healthy anger that to fail to pay attention to it is to invite severe emotional and spiritual repercussions. Consider bitterness, for example—which Aquinas observed "comes from holding anger in a long time." Bitterness, a woman once told me, is a special issue with women. That would follow naturally from what we saw in the previous chapter about sentimentalism: If women are taught they must always be "ladylike" and not exhibit strong feelings such as anger, then their anger merely festers. This helps to explain why sentimental-ists often end up being violent—the first ones in line at a lynching or to sign up for a war. Anger seeks an outlet.

Another common response to holding anger in is one I have ob-served among many pious Christians: passive-aggression. Responding to the teaching that "a good Christian is never angry but smiles under adversity," this kind of anger gets lodged in the gut chakra so deeply that it turns into knife-stabbing. While speaking face-to-face, one finds smiles; when one turns one's back, a knife is launched into it. If passive-aggressive types and embittered people had an outlet for their anger, their relationships would be more direct and honest. They would *feel less disempowered* and indeed would *be* less disempowered. Their anger would turn to creativity and perseverance and getting the job done. By tending the fire of anger deep in the gut, where both passion and com-passion stir, empowerment might result.

Over the centuries, unfortunately, beginning with Augustine, embittered persons (often but not always women) as well as carriers of passive-aggressivity have been instructed by theologians *not to trust their anger*. "Anger is a sin," they are told; that is, strong feelings and passions are a sin. But the opposite is actually the case: Milk-toast-ness is a sin. Neutrality in the heat of injustice is a sin. Passionlessness is a sin, a mis-use of our love-energy. Rabbi Abraham Heschel says that "ours is a gen-eration that has lost its capacity for moral outrage." Hopefully, we can prove him wrong. But his teaching—deriving from the Jewish spiritual tradition, which was that of Jesus also—is that the Godhead itself is not without passion and pathos. Deep feelings accompany the Godhead, feelings for justice and care and love. Deep feelings ought to accompany our presence in the universe as well, as we saw when we considered acedia and the first chakra.

One thing about which boredom teaches us, if we go more deeply into its presence, is the anger and rage that we carry inside when we cannot relate *to the whole* or to the nontrivial. As we have seen, Aquinas taught that every soul is *"capax universi,"* capable of the universe. If our soul-lives are truncated because we are not introduced to the universe or shown our way into it or invited to celebrate it, surely our big soul will respond with big anger. If there is no universe to attract our bigness, at least our anger will do so. Sam Keen recognizes the presence of anger behind apathy: "Just half an inch beneath the blasé surface of boredom is a cauldron of seething resentment and of rage.... The chronically bored, however, are afraid of feeling and do not let their anger surface."[1] It is important to keep anger alive, to keep the red of the first chakra wet and truly red, so as not to succumb to cultural acedia. The prophets, after all, were in touch with their anger and with the larger relationships of justice and injustice that other people so often wanted to ignore. "Only those who kept a sense of outrage and rebellion alive within themselves escape the plague of mass conformity, anomie, and ennui that settles over every regimented society," Keen observes.[2]

What is anger but the effort to defend what we cherish? What is the third chakra but our taking responsibility for defending what we cherish? How we do this without anger? Anger, as Aquinas taught, is called an "irascible" passion, coming from and leading to the "concupisciple" passion of desire and love. At its best, then, anger is a means to a loving end. To ignore it or not employ it well is to limit our capacity for love. It is to love badly, to miss the mark, to misdirect our powers for love and relating.

The chakras seem to follow a certain pattern of moving from inner to outer. Their images appear to emerge from a solitary meditation that listens to the world's revelatory sounds (first chakra), to union with another being (second chakra), to movement into the world (third chakra). A well-developed third chakra is necessary for arming ourselves for struggles of power and empowerment. It is an essential part of becoming a spiritual warrior. In the previous chakras we were trained in being a lover with another, one on one. And in subsequent chakras we will expand our relationships to the whole of society.

RESISTANCE TO BEING A SPIRITUAL WARRIOR

Part of sentimentalism is that there is nothing virile worth fighting for—and that true women (and others) don't fight. But in the third chakra struggle gets grounded and compassion begins to awaken. For compassion is often born from the gut response of being kicked by injustice, being moved by suffering or by the joy of others. Paying attention to this chakra is paying attention to the birthplace of compassion. This is why the word used so often of Jesus in the gospels means literally "His bowels turned over." But we translate it as "He felt compassion."

The movement from the second to the third chakra might be pictured as moving from the mystic lover to the warrior prophet. We cannot remain with the beloved in the second chakra. Making love is not all that life is about. Making justice is equally important, and taking responsibility for the offspring of our lovemaking means becoming a warrior in some way. But that is not possible without paying attention to our power called anger.

VICTIMHOOD VERSUS FINDING ONE'S CENTER

If we do not give our anger the appropriate and creative outlet it needs, we fall into victimization. We come to define ourselves as victims and then fulfill this self-defeating prophecy by acting like victims. A victim is one who is already served up as dead. A victim is not living. One who chooses victimhood is choosing not to live fully. When we are out of touch with our anger, we often give up. Our anger allows us to live fully even under the most trying of circumstances. It puts living before languishing, victory before victimhood.

Howard Thurman, who grew up with his grandmother who had been a slave, often speaks of her powerful influence on his attitudes. She instilled in him a vision that was much greater than victimization. She used to say, "You are not a nigger. You are a child of God." This affirmation is what kept Thurman *centered* throughout his life, no matter what hostilities came his way as a black man in a racist society. "Being a child of God" became his center, his grounding, his strength. It grew stronger throughout his life. Whatever obstacles he faced, he did not succumb to an attitude of victimization. He refused to surrender what he called his "inner life." He felt this was at the heart of the teaching of Jesus: "Jesus recognized with authentic realism that anyone who permits another to determine the quality of his inner life gives into the hands of the other the keys to his destiny."[3]

The shadow side to an increased awareness of sin-against-us is a certain victimization addiction that has spawned whole industries of victimization. Groups that have been sinned against—whether women or gays or blacks or native peoples or Jewish people or Celtic people or young people or old people, indeed perhaps almost all people—can fall into the trap of victimhood and define all their woes as coming exclusively from this place. Lacking a cosmology (which, among other things, teaches of the universality of suffering and struggle), such a morality imagines that life itself is not tragic and woeful and full of pain and suffering for everyone. I have known Irish, for example, who drank a lot because they saw no end to their centuries of victimization. Some gay people wallow in victimhood with the result that they become cynical, full of self-pity, and masochistic, developing an attitude of "I can't." This defeatist attitude is the opposite of the warrior, the opposite of what the third chakra is about. "I can't because *they* have hurt me" is a mentality that self-pity embraces deeply.

The deeper response to experiences of victimization (and they are real, of course) is *creativity.* It is getting on with living by growing wings of imagination. As a child, Otto Rank was sexually abused by an uncle, but he learned as a teenager to "give birth every day" because otherwise he would indeed fall into victimhood and even suicide. His creativity saved him, as the Jewish Scriptures say: "I put before you life and death. Choose life." Victimhood is a choice for death. To soar beyond the pain and beyond the relationship that fostered such pain and broke our hearts—this is possible. Creativity is our responsibility. Without it we die, we succumb to victimhood, and we surrender our uniqueness as an image of God to those abusers who victimized us in the first place.

A cosmology also helps us to move beyond victimization—for an awareness of the *history of flesh* puts our existence in perspective and takes back the miracle of our being here *from those who are claiming it in their name.* With a cosmology we can forgive our victimizers in the sense of letting go so that we can move on with our lives and with our work in the universe.

The finest responses I know to *temptations to victimhood* come from a black man and a lesbian feminist poet, namely Howard Thurman and Adrienne Rich. Thurman warns all of us of the dangers of victimization: "Hostility tends to keep up the illusion of self-importance and pride. There are many people who would feel cheated if suddenly they were deprived of their ego definition that their suffering gives them."[4] There is great wisdom in this observation: that victimization and suffering can create an ego trip and even an identity. Working at our true identity is part of the warrior's work: to be strong in who we are, who we are becoming, what we stand for, and the values that call us forward into new places and new roles. In short, to find our true center.

Otherwise, we settle for what others want to make of us and internalize their opinion of us. Sometimes others would like nothing more than to see us as victims. We oblige them if we yield our identity to victimhood. We need to throw off any attractions this holds for us, or we will never be ourselves or make our unique contribution to the community. Victimhood is a kind of sadomasochistic relationship, of the kind we saw in the second chakra. It encourages the victim-maker to keep up his or her work. But in the third chakra one rises up and says, "No more! Take back your making me a victim! I am my own person, destined to give to the community in my own way." Rich talks about *refusing* to be a victim.[5] For her it takes a decision, a *refusal,* to cease victimhood.[6]

Cynthia Tucker, in an article entitled "Racism Rages On, Without Apology," observes that

> relations between blacks and whites—at the core of the color problem in America—remain confounded by issues of class, hampered by stereotypes and strafed by resentments. Give racism its due. It is a powerful force that fuels its own regeneration.
>
> Here's an example: Those blacks who use racism as an excuse for their failure have helped to create a callousness toward racism's real victims. Their paranoia and refusal to take responsibility for their own shortcomings aid and abet racism. Yet their claims of discrimination are validated.[7]

SURRENDERING OUR ECONOMIC AND POLITICAL POWER—OR TAKING IT BACK

Choosing not to be a victim means resisting those powers that would be happy to take our power from us. The sentimentalism that is born of one-sidedness sets us up for surrendering our power. If sentimentalism is truly political energy turned inside and rancid, as Ann Douglas analyzes it, then this energy-turned-rancid needs to be purified and redirected toward society as a whole. All that is part of the work of the third chakra, which is not about surrender but commitment.

In the face of the "new world order," which is in so many ways a corporation-dominated order, many persons in the world today are increasingly powerless. David Korten underscores that the only solution is for persons and grassroots organizations to struggle to take back their power. The "Ecological Revolution" that he calls for is nonviolent but is determined to take political, economic, and business power back to its local roots. We all have rights as well as the responsibility "to create caring, sustainable communities and to control [our] resources, economies and means of livelihood."[8] This kind of generativity is of a political, economic, and social kind. We all need to be responsible in our collective parenting of these grassroots movements.

As for reclaiming our political power, Korten observes that "political rights belong to people, not to artificial legal entities. As instruments of public policy, corporations should obey the laws decided by the citizenry, not write those laws."[9] In reclaiming our economic spaces, Korten believes that today's capitalism has transferred property rights to giant corporations and financial institutions that are largely unaccountable "even to their owners." We could be doing this differently. "There is an important structural alternative: a market economy composed primarily, though not exclusively, of family enterprises, small-scale co-ops, worker-owned firms, and neighborhood and municipal corporations."[10] The key to co-ops, credit unions, cooperative banks and insurance companies, housing co-ops, media co-ops, and worker-owned businesses is that "they establish local control of productive assets through institutions that are anchored in and accountable to the community."[11] These efforts at *local control* are third chakra efforts in the sense that returning power to its local source, to its true center in the body politic, as well as in one's own body, constitutes the important work of the third chakra. An unbalanced distribution of power is not the avenue to health or happiness; centering is.

SELF-DESTRUCTION VERSUS HEALTHY POWER

Our times have seen a vast surrender of power to others. Whether these others be bankers or lawyers, doctors or professors, priests or journalists, politicians or entertainers, scientists or advertisers, a third chakra crisis is evident. The third chakra is about *retrieving one's power*, getting it back, finding it within. Hildegard of Bingen in the twelfth century said, "What you need for working is within you."[12] The third chakra is about finding the power within, taking it back.

But notice: It is a power *within*. What we take back is not a definition of power or the trappings and entrapments of power, as it is defined for us by the very politicians and others wallowing in the sleaze of power that money brings. What we take back needs to be not pseudo-power but authentic power. It is sad to watch those without power, or with very little, trying to imitate those who have it. Maybe authentic power is that which we are able to share with others, even to give away. A truly powerful person lives simply because he or she finds resources inside, with the help of imagination and resourcefulness. Finding our power inside is what the third chakra is all about.

The destruction that emerges from violence or misdirected anger in the third chakra begins with self-destruction. To settle for experiences of power that are inadequate to satisfy the needs of our heart and soul is to begin to destroy our own inner power. Violence to the outer world follows on violence toward ourselves. We violate ourselves when we don't purify our power needs. Third chakra work is to purify our power.

VIOLENCE AND DESTRUCTION: THE NEGATIVE SIDE TO ANGER

The negative side to anger can lead us into violence and destruction. Anger becomes, in Hildegard's words, a "weapon of violence."[13] We may lash out because we have felt we were victims for a long time; we may lash out from our positions of bitterness, passive-aggressivity, or grief. Since anger is the first level of grief, not to find ways to express it can bottle up anger, and it can fester for many, many years, then ultimately lash out. Many suicides are born of an intense anger at one's own condition or at one's supposed guilt for that position. As a last resort, it is the ultimate act of violence toward the self, born of feelings of anger and self-hatred and entrapment.

When we feel like there is "no way out," we may be signaling that our third chakra is underdeveloped, for the true "warrior" is resourceful. His or her generativity is ordered toward others and toward society as a whole (as part of the act of compassion) and to oneself as well. Meister Eckhart warned that "God wants us to be compassionate even to our own body and soul."[14] Our deep loves and angers need to be steered to fulfill our own needs as well as those of others. It takes imagination and resourcefulness to rise above our predicament and stay the course, to "fight the good fight" and carry on. The third chakra needs to be strong. But the third chakra is about finding our authentic strength, as Hildegard of Bingen put it: "God, who has created me . . . is also my own power."[15]

Anger that expresses itself as fury, wrath, rage, and vengeance can overtake us and make us do things that we would not otherwise do. Hildegard observed how anger overtakes us:

> When a person is angry, he does not think about himself or others, but turning away from justice as if he were blind, he sends out storms of rage. . . . Man, however, uses the wickedness of his anger to attack his friends as well as his enemies. He brings evil to another person in proportion to the amount of good that person does. . . . His anger does not allow him to think about what is good and just.[16]

How much of our unchecked anger causes abuse to those we love or try to love? Rabbi Schimmel, speaking from his work as a therapist, says that he spends "more time helping clients deal with their anger than with any other emotion."[17] He believes that "of the seven deadly sins, anger is the most pervasive, injurious to self and others, and most responsible for unhappiness and psychopathological behavior."[18] It also links up to other sins such as pride, envy, hatred, greed, and lust. Anger is not just a personal issue—our society is filled with it, as our very high violent crime rate indicates.[19]

The power of imagination and generativity, which is practiced in the sexual chakra one-on-one, takes on a new form in the third chakra, which is a more societal chakra. It is our grounding for the manner in which we make our way in the world. Will our way be violent? Will it be creative? Will it be destructive and self-defeating (as in victimization)? So deep in us is our creativity that we cannot escape it. It is with us always, to be used either to make or to destroy. Indeed, creativity is power.

For people who feel totally marginalized and powerless in a ruthless system, some violence seems to be the only way out. The fault lies not with the anger they manifest but with the structures that keep them downtrodden. As Helder Camera once wrote, the first level of violence is often injustice itself. Anger seeks an outlet. As Korten puts it,

> Organized violence fills a void by creating an opportunity to be part of a larger human whole, to find companions who provide social support and legitimacy for the venting of one's rage at an otherwise uncaring world. Violence can be for some an almost religious experience, heightening a sense of consciousness and being by focusing the senses on the here and now and freeing the mind of the distractions of deprivation. So long as forced physical, social, and spiritual deprivation exists among us, violence will be an almost inevitable consequence.[20]

PURSUIT OF UNHEALTHY POWER

All the chakras are about developing healthy power—not power-over or power-under but power-with.[21] Compassion is about power-with, passion-with, and healing-with. But something primal to our experience of power arises in the third chakra, where our guts turn over with moral outrage and where we stand strong against adversity. Taoism calls this energy chi, and it is the basis of tai chi exercises (which locate our power in our centers and extend it to our outer muscles and limbs and into our spiritual attitudes). Thomas Aquinas called power our "aptitude or suitability for the good of grace."[22] Our capacity for blessing, then, is our power, and vice versa. The third chakra finds the *middle way* between surrendering our power to others (victimization) and lording our power over others. Victims require victimizers, and our culture seems to graduate both kinds of power failure in significant numbers. What do we do with our power? Do we use it to get *more* power? Surely capitalism teaches us to do so. Those who have more, often get more. (And those who have less see their modest sums diminished.)

My experience in starting a new university in downtown Oakland taught me this lesson still one more time. I had little money, but Oakland has great needs, and I was sure that both education and spirituality—including techno rituals and other youth-led ceremonies— would bring lively people to downtown Oakland and bring life alive in people. And so we opened our doors and good things happened—eager students and teachers did indeed show up. But eager bankers were few and far between. We couldn't even get a Visa card for the university! Or a second mortgage, once we managed to purchase our building (thanks to a Dutch philanthropist). Bankers sat on the sidelines and watched as Oakland's downtown continued to deteriorate, watched as the young grew more and more despairing. Fortunately, thanks to the Vatican attacks on me, I was notorious enough that some people with means took a risk on us and contributed to our work. Now it seems to be rolling along, and I am assured that bankers will lend us money in a year or so. I suppose I should say "better late than never," but I am tempted to say: "Keep your money. Where were you when we needed you? Where were you when the young needed you and the city of Oakland needed you?" But perhaps I will be quiet and polite and ask for money when the timing is right.

The lesson is a sobering one. It doesn't take a Ph.D. in banking to realize that a system like this makes the rich richer and the poor poorer. Despair follows. Victims follow, and the victim-makers get rich.

Meanwhile, what do the rich do with their money and their power? They can use it for good, but often they put it to use to make more money and acquire more power. When I was working in the Philippines, I learned that the government was ravaging the rain forest to sell the trees to Japan and China, and, in the process, killing its indigenous rainforest Indians. What did the government do with the money it acquired from this violence? It put it into developing the army, so that more soldiers could carry on still more violence and tree-cutting and killing of indigenous people. Yes, power makes for more power. A third chakra issue: What to do with our power?

The work of the third chakra confronts this *lust for riches and power* by localizing power *within*. It teaches us to keep our power grounded in our bodies and to honor our bodies and their capacities. It teaches us balance instead of power-grabbing, which is what the "infinite quest" of avarice is all about. And it alerts us to the beauty and potential in other bodies, especially those of the poor. Let go of the quest for the pseudo-powers of fame and wealth, and the real blessing—power—will accrue to you. These lessons ought to be learned in the third chakra, lessons of real versus bogus power. Lessons of power-within rather than power-outside. Lessons of power-with rather than power-over or power-under. Sin is not just misdirected love; it is also misdirected *power*. Love, after all, is power, but power of a noncontrolling, nonisolating, nonviolent kind. Each of the chakras, we are learning, helps us to reexamine love and refine it and reintegrate it into our bodies, psyches, and spirits.

ADULTISM AND THE THIRD CHAKRA

Adultism is the denigration of the young by older people. I believe our culture and our times are rife with adultism. Adults are busy making so many decisions about the future and therefore about young people, but how many are taking the needs of the young into consideration when making these decisions? I am talking about decisions that determine education and worship and politics and economics and farming and art that we promote. The very fact that so few adult institutions are alive with spirituality makes me shudder at how they are going to reach the hearts and souls of young people and make them feel welcomed where they truly live or want to live. The truth is that too few adults are offering the young the help they need.

Rites of passage, for example, should be third chakra work. But the forms in which we do confirmation in Christianity and bar mitzvah in Judaism are inadequate to today's needs. Adolescence is a time for young people to *come into their power* as they emerge from childhood to adulthood. Rites of passage ought to mirror that new reality. When they fail, they are feeble indeed, and young people trying to grow into adulthood will have to seek their own rites of passage. Too many adults are busy playing games of power and money and control to recognize some of the amazing spiritual leadership that is emerging from today's

younger generation, a generation that is being awakened by Gaia in special ways and has a mission to contribute to save Gaia.

How can adults assist the spiritual awakening of the young if they
themselves are still asleep? If adults have little or no spiritual life and are
not engaging their first, second, and third chakras in deep ways, what
could they possibly teach the young? If they have no cosmology and no
history of intimacy and tenderness, what do they have to pass on to the
young? Spirituality cannot be learned vicariously. Nor can it be faked.
Adults who neglect their own spiritual lives are in no position to assist
the emergence of spirit from the young. Today's young people don't
need an excessive amount of direction from their elders, but they do
need presence and support and a spirit of working together to face the
issues of our time. And of praying together. A key to working with
young people today, in my opinion, is to encourage them to take leadership and to help them along the way—there is no need to *do it for
them*. Indeed, therein lies patronizing adultism—the notion that the
young are too inexperienced or too immature to lead in spirit-actions.

Another palpable way in which adultism shows is the unfair treatment of the young. In the Bay Area this past year, there was a murder in
front of a youth center, and the civic response was to close down the
center. But there was also a murder in front of a Kentucky Fried
Chicken, yet they did not close down the Kentucky Fried Chicken.

How we define the word *power* and who does the defining is critical. Elders ought to help define the power of the young in healthy ways
and help them achieve that kind of power. When this is lacking the
young will make up their own definitions, including gang power and
killing power and vengeance power. The anger of the young *is* powerful, for their emotions are developing into adult capacity and yet their
experience in bridling these emotions is often limited. Thus, anger, at
the coming-of-age time in a person's life, is an energy that needs to be
dealt with wisely. It should be harnessed for the greater good.

INSECURITY AND THE THIRD CHAKRA

Our culture is deeply afraid at many levels. Downsizing has instilled the
fear of God (or at least of employer) into the hearts of blue collar and
white collar alike. The poor are afraid of becoming homeless or sick,

and the middle class are afraid of becoming like the poor. The haves are afraid of sharing with others, or even worse, of losing what they have. Those without health insurance (40 million Americans) are afraid of getting sick and of being wiped out financially, while many parents fear the immense costs of higher education.

Insecurity appears to be a logical outcome of our economic and political system, which in great part is run no longer by the many but by the few, especially the corporate few. Insecurity is an outcome of cosmic loneliness and isolation and lack of grounding in our own power, that is, of undernourishment in the first, second, and third chakras respectively. To pay attention to our power and give it the attention it deserves, to develop the gifts within us and especially those that center on our passions and our capacity for compassion—this offers healing to the insecure. Security cannot be bought by ever more external goodies, be they weapons or insurance policies or the perfect job. We need to relearn trust, beginning at home with ourselves and our relationships, and find our true security there. Trust in the Source of all things that has brought us this far—that would be a good way to find the security inside us and inside all our authentic relations and balance insecurity with security.

OFFSPRING OF THE SIN AGAINST THE THIRD CHAKRA: A SUMMARY

Traditionally the "daughters" of the sin of anger are quarreling, swelling of the mind, haughtiness, clamor, indignation, and blasphemy. According to Aquinas, anger is opposed to charity, true justice (if the issues raised are not authentic justice), and to good-temperedness.

The offspring I would list for the destructiveness of the third chakra are bitterness and passive-aggressive behavior; resistance to spiritual warriorhood; victimhood; surrender of power; self-destruction; violence and destruction; pursuit of unhealthy power; adultism; insecurity.

CONFIRMATION, THE SACRAMENT OF THE THIRD CHAKRA

The traditional teaching on the sacrament of confirmation employs imagery of warriorhood, "being a soldier for Christ." While many of us shrink from that language today and its implied meanings (not pretty, given the number of Christian warriors who killed indigenous peoples and enslaved others and hunted down heretics—Jews, witches, gays, and infidels in Jesus' name), it corresponds archetypally with the reality of growing up and becoming an adult. A rite of passage is meant to prepare one for working in the world as an adult, for engaging in strenuous tasks that are deep in spiritual commitment and possibility, and for becoming a spiritual warrior. All this underlies the tradition of the sacrament of confirmation. It is a confirming, strengthening sacrament—oil is still used, as it was used of old to anoint knights and strengthen warriors before battle. Clearly it corresponds to the third chakra and its focus on the development of social power. Confirmation is meant to be a rite of passage that encourages children in their efforts to become adult. Rarely does it do so anymore, given the *forms* of the sacrament today, which for many has become quite impotent.

SPIRITUAL EXERCISES APROPOS OF THE THIRD CHAKRA

1. Breathing meditations are very good for strengthening the diaphragm and the third chakra. Practice a breathing exercise each day. For example, on your inward breath inhale *strength,* and on your outward breath exhale *power-with-others.* Or breathe in *breath* and breathe out *spirit.* Notice changes in your feelings afterward.

2. Chanting is also good for strengthening the third chakra. Find a chanting record that you can accompany (like Jill Pierce's tapes), and chant for fifteen minutes daily. Notice changes in your feelings afterward. Or just choose your own sound and your own note, and chant deeply for fifteen minutes.

3. Write a poem about some violence that has been done to you. Read the poem out loud. Share it with another or others.

4. Write a poem about some violent or destructive behavior you have exhibited toward yourself. Read that poem to yourself daily for a week. How does it move you to change your ways?

5. Write a poem or a letter about some destructive behavior you have exhibited toward another. Reflect on what you learned from that experience.

6. Did you undergo a rite of passage from childhood to adulthood? If so, describe it and how it is still affecting you. If not, create a rite of passage with others of your generation for yourselves. Try to find elders to assist you.

7. Have your children undergone a rite of passage? If not, gather other parents and other children, and create such a ritual together.

8. Get involved in your church or synagogue to create a confirmation or a bar mitzvah rite of passage that is effective and strong.

9. How are you learning to be a spiritual warrior? Share stories of your own coming to grips with your warriorhood. How are you demonstrating this aspect of your spirituality today?

10. Practice or take lessons in tai chi or aikido. What do you learn about centering yourself and grounding yourself from these practices?

11. What experiences do you have of the institutional ego and the collective human ego? Share these experiences in storytelling in a group. What lessons do you learn from this sharing? What kind of resistance can you offer?

12. Reflect on the themes of pride, lust, and disobedience and why institutional forces, which themselves employ these means, denigrate them in individuals. Discuss this reality as a group.

CHAPTER 11

MISDIRECTED LOVE
IN THE FOURTH CHAKRA:
FEAR, AVARICE, AND RESENTMENT

In the previous three chapters we have discussed issues of
misdirected love in the three lower chakras. In the middle
chakra, the fourth chakra, the energies of the other
chakras converge, and if imbalance has reigned, it comes
together here in a kind of culminating expression.
Clarissa Pinkola Estés reminds us that "the heart symbolizes essence," for without it we cannot live. When the
heart is wounded or broken, life itself is in jeopardy. It is
in the heart that our energies coalesce, for it is the heart
"that thinks and calls the molecules, atoms, feelings,
yearnings; and whatever else need be, into one place to
create the matter" that fulfills creation.[1]

When the energy of the heart chakra is unbalanced or squandered or
misdirected, imagine what is lost. In the Hindu tradition, the heart is
"the nerve center that encompasses feeling for another human, feeling
for oneself, feeling for the earth, and feeling for God. It is the heart that
enables us to love as a child loves: fully, without reservation, and with
no hull of sarcasm, depreciation, or protectionism."[2]

Sometimes hearts break down, and sometimes they break open.

The latter is a gift, albeit a painful and expensive one, but it allows compassion to happen. Compassion is about feeling not pity for another but identification *with* another, and the identification that suffering and tears bring can be grasped only if one has faced one's own pain too. When this breaking-open happens in an individual, a new kind of love flows—it is not outer-directed; it flows from the inside. It is no longer the love of the breast of the mother nor of money nor of power or fame or sexuality: "It is a love that comes upon him, a love he has always carried within him but has never acknowledged before." It is the love of "a vast and oceanic heart."[3] Heartbreak is an important event in life, for it is a sign that the heart has connected, it has loved. The worst thing would be never having loved and therefore not knowing a heartbreak at all.

SELF-PITY VERSUS REAL SELF-COMPASSION

In my experience men are especially prone to self-pity. The reason is that authentic compassion is a motherly thing—if men do not realize the mother in themselves (in Hebrew the word for *compassion* is the same as the word for *womb*), then they are condemned to looking outside for the mother.

Men wrapped up in a patriarchal world are very prone to self-pity. The Vatican, for example, wallows in self-pity, yet asks no deep questions about itself or the state of its own soul. When the mother-principle of compassion is repressed or driven underground, self-pity is sure to come. For if that energy is eliminated, where will one find authentic compassion? Where the mother is absent, there is no one around to comfort or to care, and a kind of orphan feeling takes over. If she is not forthcoming, then the male falls into a "woe is me" motif, a motherless child motif, a self-pitying stance. Victimization takes over.

The solution is to learn some authentic compassion for oneself: to explore one's feelings and needs, to learn anew what solitude means, and to pay attention to one's wounds. Thus most men have work to do on their heart chakras. Their self-pity is not true compassion toward the self; rather, it is feeling sorry for themselves and blaming others and seeking a surrogate mother who will offer unconditional love. Self-pity becomes one more search for an external fix.

But adults ought to have learned a lot about unconditional love. The love we encounter in the first chakra is all gratuitous and unconditional; and the intimate love we share in the second chakra ought to be in some respects unconditional; and the grounding we undergo in the third chakra is a grounding without judgment and therefore unconditional. But pity is always conditional in some way, and sentimental. It brings tears but no cleansing. It looks outside and elsewhere for the mother-principle of compassion instead of finding it within. For this reason it gives birth to nothing great and practically nothing at all save feeling sorry for oneself. It is not generative.

Ironically, the cure for self-pity is authentic empowerment, which for men means recovering the true power of compassion. A patriarchal mind-set actually prevents men from curing themselves of self-pity, but they need to rediscover their maternal powers of nourishment. Only opening up to the possibility of their psychic bisexuality allows men to be "real men," that is, full human beings, capable of offering compassion to themselves and others, capable of mothering themselves and others. The cure lies in men finding the mother *inside them*. (Similarly, the cure for bitterness in women is to find a father-principle, a way of expressing anger and strong passion, inside themselves.) Maybe behind Jesus' powerful statement that "unless you leave father and mother you are not worthy of me" lies the ideal that adults have to learn to father and mother themselves if they are to grow into the kind of compassion that Jesus represents.

Self-pity is not authentic self-love. It is sentimental and therefore a distorted love that looks *outside* for what ought to be found *inside*. True love requires diving deep into oneself and developing an inner life that pays attention to one's joy, grief, creativity, and compassion.

HATRED

Hatred seems to be the obverse of love. It comes from the heart—where love comes from—and therein lies its power. It is a misdirection of love energy and is clearly related to both anger and resentment. Anger, as Aquinas points out, is much less serious than hatred, because anger does not seek evil against another except as just revenge or reparation for an offense. It seeks recompense. Hatred, on the other hand, is directed indiscriminately against anyone or any group at all, not for reasons of justice but "merely because their disposition or character is not to our liking." The punishment hatred wants to mete out has no limits: "Hatred intends evil in itself to one's neighbor."The person who hates does not care if the object of his hatred is deserving of it or not.[4]

Do people take pleasure in malice? Hitler apparently did, in James Hillman's view, speaking of the "demonic call" to which Hitler seemed to have responded.[5] If the heart chakra stands for the fullest of human energies, our capacity for love, then its misdirection may unleash the fullness of its evil counterpart, our capacity for hatred. How necessary it is to guard the heart!

RESENTMENT

The stirrings of the passion that we call compassion begin in the third chakra with moral outrage. These stirrings are meant to culminate and come to fruition in the fourth chakra. The reader will recall Hildegard of Bingen's "man in sapphire blue," the "Christ in every one of us" who stands with his hands and palms extended outwards.[6] That illustration holds the key to compassion because compassion is taking the heart-energy and extending it outward to others *through our hands*. Our out-stretched hands symbolize compassion, for compassion is not just about feelings (as pity is) but about *action* as well. It is the heart-energy we put into action, whether that energy manifests itself as healing or as cele-brating energy (both of which do indeed heal). But hatred and resent-ment put the human hands to an opposite use. Instead of healing, killing; instead of compassion, hurt.

It has been said that hatred is anger oriented to the past and resent-ment is anger oriented to the present.[7] Anger stored in the memory keeps the fires of hatred going, and some cleansing of the memory is needed to calm those fires. Resentment is the simmering hatred that makes itself known in the present. We fool ourselves if we underesti-mate its power for destruction. Resentment happens when we hold hurt in a long time, and it festers and rots and seeks expression in hatred and violence. Resentment represents an advanced state of ire and anger, a situation that develops readily into bitterness and rancor. When this anger has not been purified and redirected in the third chakra, it lodges in the heart.

If resentment is ignored and not dealt with, it builds up and up over time and gives birth to many forms of hatred and revenge. A few years ago a man from Bosnia told me that the war in his country and all its awful genocide was due to one thing: the politicians who tapped into the *resentment* among the three different groups in his culture, the Roman Catholics, the Orthodox, and the Muslims. All three had long-standing complaints against the others, and the politicians, with their own agendas, exploited these resentments.

Exploitation does follow on resentment. Resentment is such a powerful force because it stems from love energies that are denied us—all the power of love propels it as a giant thrust against that which we hate. Being a great misdirection of love-energy, resentment will eventually not be denied, and those who exploit it know it. Hitler knew a lot about resentment; otherwise he could not have achieved his anti-Semitic and other programs. He appealed to his citizens' resentments, and they responded in kind.

THE REFUSAL TO FORGIVE AND LET GO

There is only one cure for resentment, and that is forgiveness. But resentment refuses to let go and refuses to forgive. It learns to cherish its hurt, its anger, and its hatred. Like a child refusing to surrender its teddy bear, a resentful person refuses to let go of the security and comfort that spite gives him or her. Like love, resentment grows, building up over the years, over the generations, over time. One can feel that quite palpably in the struggle still being waged in the Middle East. Again, certain politicians stake the success of their careers on appealing to people stuck in resentment. The violence and hatred to which resentment gives birth are only too evident both in the Middle East and in Bosnia.

Forgiveness is possible. I once met a woman whose teenage son had been murdered in a drive-by killing in Los Angeles. They found and convicted the killer, who was about the same age as her son. She visited him in prison, and gradually they became fast friends. She told me that that friendship gave meaning to her son's death. Her story also gives us meaning and hope: that the human heart is so big that it can move beyond hate and resentment to forgiveness. But it must make that choice. A young woman who had been sexually abused from the age of eight into her teen years wrote a poem to deal with her pain. Its essence is about letting go and forgiveness and moving on with her life. Forgiveness is not about altruism or about shutting one's eyes to justice and injustice. It is, however, about finding freedom from a tainted relationship so that living becomes possible again. Here is the poem of that teenager who is dealing with the reality of her abuse—*and of her freedom.*

TEARS FROM THE PAST

When I was a child and wanted to cry,
the tears were dry and I didn't know why.
Then I grew and some would flow,
But the reasons for my pain,
I wouldn't let show.
Again I grew and so did my pain,
I thought for sure I was to blame.
When I close my eyes a vision appears.
It captures my thoughts and brings back the fears
Of nights when I slept and then was awoke.
By a dark skinned man with his hands at my throat
He would say very softly. "Don't say a word."
These are the times I was never heard
An innocent child,
with tears from the past.
The silence is broken, my words heard at last.
To whom it may concern; might be you, you, and you.
My shame is no more,
because the struggle is through.
Now I look in the mirror and all that I see...
Is a beautiful woman and her destiny.
What would that be, you might ask?
She's grown from the pain, and let go of the past.

FORGIVENESS AS A PATH TO FREEDOM

The phrase "refusal to forgive" suggests that there is an invitation, per-haps even a constant invitation, to forgive. But where is this invitation coming from? It could be coming from an individual, but that would not be enough to awaken and engage the heart chakra. If it is coming from the universe itself and from the Source of all things in the uni-verse, then indeed it is enough to awaken a person to action and to love. One must presume that that is the source of the invitation, since to learn to forgive is to learn a great lesson about one's own greatness. The universe does forgive, which is one way it gets on with its own tasks. Getting on with one's tasks is a way to put issues behind us that are draining energy from the chakra committed to compassion, the fourth chakra.

Forgiveness is vast—there really is no rational reason for it. Justice by itself asks not for forgiveness but for restitution. Forgiveness requires *some great love,* a love that beckons one to another horizon, another place, another relationship. Sometimes this call is clear, and sometimes it lurks in the dark, is muffled, and requires faith even to catch a faint echo of its presence. Big love calls people to forgive bigly. When one is stuck in a place of unforgiveness, one should return to the first chakra and find big reasons for living and loving, and *go back to lis-tening again to the invitations of the cosmos.* Just as the cosmos is large enough to absorb our pain, so it is large enough to challenge us to for-giveness. In the act of forgiving, the soul grows magnanimous.

BETRAYAL

Betrayal is an affront to the fourth chakra, because we betray only what we love (or loved at one time). Betrayal does not happen between strangers but between lovers, partners, coworkers, countrymen or countrywomen, family members, co-citizens. The image of Judas betraying his friend Jesus with a kiss has a doubly powerful meaning to us. One does not kiss a stranger. Betrayal turns a friend into an enemy overnight. Love is erased by hatred—or so it seems. The revelation of betrayal produces a shock that leaves one breathless and even without words. At such a rapid metamorphosis one is filled with doubts about "what that friendship meant" and "was it real?" Memories of shared love and laughter and work get tarnished, erased, or clouded in doubt. Past experiences of abuse, especially if they occurred as a vulnerable child, inevitably rise to the surface to dance their dire shadow-dances in our psyche.

The words we use for betrayal reveal the depth of the experience, for they are as strong as any words in our vocabulary. Among them are: *treachery, treason, disloyalty, deception, breach of faith, cheating, dishonesty, perfidy, faithlessness.* The very depth of brokenheartedness when there is betrayal reveals the depth of this treachery. The fact that the heart is so vulnerable indicates how powerful the fourth chakra is: When love is misdirected in this chakra, it is a powerful force of destruction indeed.

I know no solution to betrayal except two: bringing about some kind of justice or reconciliation, and moving on, letting go, forgiving. Forgiving in this context is not about forgetting. It is about becoming free of a relationship, either by eliciting repentance from the person who has betrayed, so the relationship can start over cleanly, or by leaving the relationship altogether. So wrenching is the experience of betrayal that one never really gets over it. Betrayal marks the end of innocence in a relationship or in one's mind-set.

How one faces this end of innocence is another story in our personal and social journey: Do we face it with more hatred in the heart, returning bitterness for betrayal? Do we turn to addictions to numb the ineffable pain? Do we grow old and cynical overnight? Do we give up? Do we internalize the hurt and say "it was my fault" and thus take on the guilt of the betrayer? Or do we go into the dark night of the soul, as the mystics recommend, and let the pain teach us its valuable albeit expensive lessons? Do we pick up a drum and wail and grieve and rage? Not to do such things may constitute a great *sin of omission* for the heart chakra, for the heart needs attention at times of betrayal, for it is the heart itself that was betrayed. It is hurting, bleeding, being sapped of energy; yes, it may be broken and need fixing.

Sam Keen speaks up for forgiveness when he writes:

> Only forgiveness sets us free from the locked-in compulsive cycle
> of suspicions-hurt-retaliation and allows us to turn our gaze away
> from the single enemy to the kaleidoscopic possibilities that sur-

round us. Enmity hardens the heart, narrows the focus of the eyes, constricts muscles and blood vessels. Assume the posture of fight or flight and blood pressure goes up and everything in the nervous system is focused on a single point of danger.[8]

The alternative Keen offers to hatred is trust, which "softens the body, dilates the arteries, widens the eyes, allows us to open up and welcome the surroundings."[9]

THE BLAME GAME

We all are tempted to partake of the blame game and to fix responsibility for our injuries and hurts on others. Sometimes these accusations are justified, and sometimes the responsibility is our own or of mixed accountability. In the latter case, of course, blame is not justified. But what does blame do to the accuser? Living with blame may be a way of living in the past, recounting old hurts, picking at old scabs so they never heal. Is this good for the one doing it? What is achieved by being certain of whom is to blame? The word *blame* shares its origin with the word *blaspheme,* which means "to revile, accuse and address with irreverence." Ultimately, blasphemy is "the act of claming the attributes of deity," according to *Webster's Dictionary.*

To play the blame game may be to play God, and not a very nice God at that. There is nothing wrong with partaking of Divinity; surely our work of compassion and justice born of anger at injustice, represents such healthy activity. But blame? Something about blame includes getting stuck in the past and thereby belittling our godliness. Better to let go and not be stuck in our blame questions, which seem to surface the most when we are most tempted by cynicism and pessimism. Better to expand the heart and mind than to live around blame. "Magnanimous people deliberately determine to forget injuries they have suffered," Aquinas tells us.[10]

Instead of blame, we can use the occasion of injury to grow into greater compassion, to understand more deeply the pain and injuries of others, and to take action extending our service to others. What hurts us can teach us if we let it do so. Suffering is a teacher of compassion.

Blame is very powerful, and the alternative to magnanimity (literally, a "great soul") is getting stuck in blame. People do get addicted to blame; it may become a way of life.

PESSIMISM BORN OF SELF-HATRED

The great psychologist Otto Rank offered a profound observation when he said that pessimism is a philosophy of hatred that springs from self-hate.[11] Pessimism is indeed a philosophy—it is a way of seeing the world, of trying to understand the world, of finding our place in it. But calling it a "philosophy of hatred" is very strong language—who wants to invest in a philosophy of hatred? Who would confess to believing in such a philosophy? Therein lies Rank's wisdom and depth—that he dares to unmask where pessimism comes from. It comes from hatred: hatred of life, of possibility, of the powers of imagination and creativity to recycle bad events, hatred of hope. And yet the "philosophy of pessimism" is widespread in our culture, driving so many of us to respond to advertising and its countless promises of false hope. Is this not behind cynicism and much of the ennui and despair that we spoke of when discussing acedia in the first chakra?

But Rank takes us further and deeper into an understanding *and a cure* for a philosophy of pessimism when he points out that the true source of pessimism lies in *self-hatred.* Pessimism, he is suggesting, is the projection of our own self-worth onto the world. Where true self-love is meager, our love of the world will be meager. "Love others as you love yourself," advised Jesus—but if our love of self is shallow, the love we put into the world will be also. And the world, in its various misdirected loves, is so strong that our weak and shallow love will be easily drowned in the energies of that world.

The result? We will slink back into pessimism, the pessimism that is inevitable when love is based only on the human and is out of relation with cosmic or Divine love, including the Divine love incarnated in created things. Our self-doubts and self-hatred and self-constructed pessimism will deceive us into actually believing (for it takes an act of belief) that life is vile and that pessimism is the proper response to such vileness. Blessing is gone; melancholy reigns. And when melancholy reigns, the heart shrinks, as Aquinas observed. Our world gets smaller. Joy is rarer and rarer to be found. (Joy, said Aquinas, expands the heart, while sadness deflates it.)

The cure for self-hatred includes the purification and utilization of *all* the chakra-energy. The first chakra is the starting point: moving beyond anthropocentric self-doubt and sinfulness (the wrongs done us by human beings or societies) to the graced community of the more than human. If self-hatred causes a pessimistic philosophy, then true self-love—self in the context of the whole—can cause a blessing-oriented philosophy. A rediscovery of our *original blessing* and that of all of creation is a practical cure for self-hatred. Many persons have told me that fact.

FEAR

One cannot talk about the fourth, heart chakra, without talking about fear. Fear in itself is a danger alarm that can preserve our very existence. The person who meets a bear in the forest and is not afraid may have no skills or incentive to solve the problem imaginatively—and quickly.

But fear has another side as well. It can choke us, close us down, and paralyze us. It can result in social hysteria, including scapegoating, blaming, and hate.[12] Much fear-rendering information comes into our lives these days, from news of the demise of the planet to terrorist threats and to crime in the streets and drugs and downsizing at work. In addition, as we move into a new millennium, apocalyptic fears are rising.

How do we respond to this fear-laden information? (And do the media prey on our fear because it sells papers and television advertising?) Fear, a Lakota teacher once taught me, is the door that lets evil into the heart. True prayer is standing up to fear by strengthening the heart. Fear is about a weak heart. If we are to become the lovers and doers of compassion that constitutes the work of the fourth chakra, our frail and fragile hearts need strengthening. Dr. Gerald Jampolsky and his fine movement of attitudinal healing, a movement that touches refugees in Bosnia as well as drug addicts and others, teaches that fear is the opposite of love. Clearly, then, fear is a heart chakra issue.

I was startled a few years ago to read that Thomas Aquinas called fear a mortal, that is a deadly, sin. Obviously he was talking about fear not as an emotion but *as a choice*. People do at times choose fear and choose to make it into a worldview and build a lifestyle around it. Fear is an emotion we all feel, especially at this time in history, when so many structures of family, culture, religion, and society are in meltdown. Ignorance always feeds fear, and our species is ignorant of what will transpire in the next century around issues of world population expansion, food and water shortages, distribution of income, power, and decision-making. Anyone living today would have to be a fool *not* to harbor some fear.

Because fear is more widespread than usual, it is all the more necessary to be able to "test the spirits" and discern authentic fear from false fear, or as Aquinas put it, "chaste fear" from "servile fear."[13] The latter is what makes slaves of people. No one need harbor that kind of fear in their heart or lifestyle.

That fear pertains to the heart chakra was recognized by Aquinas when he taught that "all fear arises from love because no one fears anything except what is contrary to something he or she loves."[14] The cure for the wrong kind of fear is *courage* ("big heart," in French) or fortitude. Strength can stand up to fear and see it through. Indeed, Aquinas believes that "fear is repugnant to a magnanimous [or "big-souled"] person."[15] Fear, because it comes from the heart and can loom so large in our worldview, is a direct enemy of compassion. Aquinas said, "Those who are in great fear . . . are so intent on their own passion, that they pay no attention to the suffering of others."[16] Ignoring the suffering of others is a way of denying one's own humanity—as part of all sadism, it was intrinsic to the modus operandi of fascist powers in this century and still is.

The biblical tradition has always attacked fear as the enemy of spirit. Rabbi Heschel says that the prophet "casts out fear," and the historical Jesus talked more than once about "fearing not" and observing the sparrows and others who survive quite handsomely without great fear. The Epistle of John says that "love drives out fear." Martin Luther King, Jr., when asked how he could dare to march in areas where people wanted to kill him, replied, "We must love something more than the fear of death if we are to live." Love does drive out fear. All these teachings are proposing that love and trust are the cure for fear. Joanna Macy says, "Have confidence in the Buddha nature in all things." Realizing the

Buddha nature (or Cosmic Christ) in every being, she says, is the way to sustain ourselves when fear arises. In a self-sustaining universe the need to *use fear* as a way to control people gives way to being sustained by trust, by the deep interconnective relationships that truly sustain our shared existence. The Holy Spirit, Aquinas taught, is what makes people strong.[17]

Fear exiles people from the strength and centeredness that they achieve in the third chakra. It is a kind of surrender to an outside force. To return to our center and to the power gleaned from each of the chakras—cosmology in the first chakra, personal union in the second, and centering in the third—is a proper way to combat fear and build up courage and heart in the fourth chakra. It is very important to *face fear,* to treat it as the powerful being it is. "What do you have to teach me?" is an appropriate question to put to our fear. "Why have you come?" It is important to have ancestors, members of the communion of saints whom we love for their courage, to call upon at times of fear and temptation to fear. It is important to read the lives of people who have lived out of vision and courage and have not closed down their hearts. It is important to fill up with a sense of the joy that cosmology brings ("wonder brings joy," said Aquinas) so that we can stand firm in the presence of struggle and doubt. It is important to pass on a sense of strength to our children and young people, instead of a sense of dependency, a dependency that is acquired in a consumer-driven economic system.

In the fourth chakra, being the middle chakra, the energy and issues *from all the other chakras* find their center. Indeed, Meister Eckhart talked about the heart as a "center" from which all energy flows; I imagine a series of spirals that emanate from the heart, intersect with the other chakras, and return to the heart. A give-and-take, outer and inner, kind of dynamic ensues.

When I encounter people whose lives are driven by fear, a sadness comes over me because of what is lost. I imagine what wonders and surprises and hopes and healings these people might have brought to the community, had they not given up and settled for comfort or security or control. Fear contributes to pusillanimity, and Aquinas taught that pusillanimity ("little-souledness") is a kind of pride or arrogance, insofar as a person settles for a bad self-opinion rather than learning their gifts and what they might contribute to the greater community.

"Pusillanimity is a greater sin than presumption," he warned. It leads to sins of omission, especially as regards works of justice.

ANXIETY, A MODERN EXPLOSION OF FEAR

Protestant theologian Reinhold Niebuhr taught that anxiety is "the internal precondition of sin" and the "breeding ground for sin."[18] Anxiety is a kind of fear—though fear is of an object and anxiety is more a state of being terrified. Anxiety has no particular object.[19] Gerald May says that in the Protestant canon of sins anxiety replaced acedia. Anxiety, or a state of being afraid, may relate to the anthropocentrism of modern society in which we are not at home in the universe but terrified by it. If the universe were indeed a machine with no meaning or purpose, as the modern worldview has it, then our anxiety is understandable, and the many places of refuge we have sought to shelter us from our cosmic fear may be understood for what they are: ersatz cosmologies.

FASCISM: AN INSTITUTIONALIZING OF
FEAR AND HATRED

When fear reaches the social and political arena, it becomes very scary indeed. If Aquinas was correct when he said that fear drives compassion out because it is such a strong passion in itself, is it not true that fascism is a political system lacking all compassion? Where was the *compassion* toward children, women, men, old people, and others in the Hitler-led and Mussolini-led and Franco-led fascist systems of this century? The scapegoating and hatred and resentment that built up in hatred of the Jews became institutionalized in the pogroms and state-sponsored death camps. How much of fascism's appeal was its institutionalized hatred and resentment? Fascism invariably appeals to small-souled people.

Today fascism is in the news again, not only because many die-hard Nazis are behind the most recent atrocities in Bosnia, but because Swiss and Vatican banks are being reexamined for their economic complicity with the fascist powers of this century, a complicity that resulted in profits they made trafficking on Holocaust victims.[20] One has to wonder to what lengths people and their institutions will be driven when they are pursued by the demons of fear. For some people the pope or someone else may be substituted for the "Führer" because the issue is the same: the surrender of our powers and conscience to another in exchange for security. Fear is indeed a powerful beast. It needs careful watching and wise bridling.

GREED OR AVARICE AND THE FOURTH CHAKRA

Greed is a heart and spirit issue, destroying self and others. Hildegard of Bingen called avarice "the servant of idols . . . [that] is terribly envious. . . . It pillages with harshness and bitterness . . . it walks and plunders ferociously, sparing nothing when it pillages."[21] Avarice leads to violence and injustice because "it takes whatever riches it can, either justly or unjustly, without even asking where they are for or whom they belong to. . . . Men serving this fault are never free from care and do not trust in God, but they immerse themselves violently in different things."[22] Yet all the effort put into acquiring goods is ultimately for naught because "everything they do in their greedy work dies in death."[23] You can't take it with you.

Hildegard pictured Avarice in dialog with Contentment. Avarice speaks first: "I am not a thief or a robber, but I take all the things I want and acquire all of them with my own craftiness."

Pure Contentment responds:

Nothing is sufficient to satisfy you. I, however, sit above the stars where all of God's good things are sufficient for me and I rejoice in the sweet sound of a tambourine when I trust in him. I kiss the sun when I hold him with joy; I embrace the moon when I hold him in love and when all the things that have come into existence from the sun and moon are sufficient for me. Why should I desire more than I need?[24]

This last question sounds like E. F. Schumacher or Buddhism. Contentment is about settling the heart into what it truly needs and what will truly satisfy.

Aquinas provided a profound analysis of greed when he pointed out that "the greed for gain knows no limit and tends to infinity."[25] We all seek the infinite—that is part of our desire for God or spirit, part of our being here. But avarice looks for the infinite in the wrong places— it is misdirected love, the desire for objects that cannot satisfy. Aquinas distinguishes two basic kinds of desires: the natural and the man-made. The natural "cannot be actually infinite because it is what nature requires and nature tends to something finite and fixed. Hence a person never desires infinite meat, or infinite drink."[26] But when it comes to man-made objects of desire, a kind of quest for the infinite takes us over. Our minds are infinite in their capacity to see more and want more and invent more: "Hence, one that desires riches may desire to be rich not up to a certain limit but to be simply as rich as possible."[27] In this context we see how avarice can devour a person.

Avarice has been called an inordinate desire for money, and an inordinate love of having. It has been called the opposite of justice[28] and an obstacle to love and compassion: "One person cannot overabound in external riches without another person lacking them, for temporal goods cannot be possessed by many people at the same time."[29] Cupidity can "extinguish charity" in a person. Eckhart made the point that gold cannot go into our hearts without killing us. Our hearts are not made for gold but for relating. Often avarice is tied in with injustice because the avaricious person is so in love with his or her wealth that he will do almost anything to acquire it. Warned Aquinas, "It pertains to avarice to take or keep the goods of others unjustly and this is always a mortal sin."[30] Avarice often arises from fear because we are afraid we won't be able to pay our bills. Avarice resides *in the heart,* according to Aquinas, and restlessness and violence can derive from it, as well as perjury, fraud, and betrayal.[31] He sees Judas' betrayal as deriving from avarice. Aquinas, following the prohibitions against usury in the Hebrew Bible, believed that the making of money on money was a serious wrong because money "was devised for the purpose of exchange."

E. F. Schumacher's classic work *Small Is Beautiful* extends a prophetic call to all citizens of our planet to let avarice go. Interestingly, he calls on Buddhism, with its highly developed teachings on excess desire, to express a philosophy that can heal us of our modern-day greed. He also calls on Aquinas. It is noteworthy that he did not turn to Protestantism, which is so contemporaneous with the modern era, to critique our out-of-control avaricious economic system. Perhaps the lesson of returning to premodern solutions is that we will not cure modernism's diseases with modern medicines. Some premodern wisdom that takes us into a deeper sense of cosmology and community is necessary. Spirituality is necessary—moral nostrums alone will not do the trick.

To those who lived through the 1980s, greed is no abstract concept. Greed is about the $700 billion bill that the American taxpayers picked up for the lending abuses of the deregulated savings and loan industry. "Greed had a field day," as Korten puts it. While the number of the world's billionaires rose from 145 in 1987 to 358 in 1994, the inequality between countries and the rates of unemployment soared.[32] Korten analyzes the economic rationalists who give the free-market ideology its intellectual legitimacy as being flesh-less. That is to say, their doctrine is a species of rationalism and is derived deductively from first principles without the use of the senses. They do not and dare not *feel* the pain their work is causing.

Their philosophy of the corporation takes the privileges that accrue to a human person and leaves aside the moral responsibilities for many of their social and environmental consequences. The process is itself cannibalistic; "every member of the corporate class, no matter how powerful his or her position within the corporation, has become expendable—as growing numbers of top executives are learning."[33] Korten sees this institutionalized greed as a betrayal of Adam Smith's philosophy of capitalism. In *The Wealth of Nations*, published in 1776, Smith condemned business monopolies sustained and protected by the state and expressed a desire for a market composed solely of small buyers and sellers.

> The idea that a major corporation might have exclusive control over a lifesaving drug or device and therefore charge whatever the market will bear would have been anathema to him. . . . Smith never advocated a moral philosophy in defense of unrestrained greed. He was talking about small farmers and artisans trying to get the best price for their products to provide for themselves and their families. That is self-interest—not greed. Greed is a high-paid corporate executive firing 10,000 employees and then rewarding himself with a multimillion-dollar bonus for having saved the company so much money.[34]

In their rush to increase the GNP, neoclassical economists, stuck in their anthropocentrism and antiflesh bias, ignore the role of the eco-flesh and assume that economics is about labor, capital, and goods flowing between corporations and homes. They never allude to the environment itself. Yet there is no infinite growth on a finite planet, except in the order of the spiritual: "To accept the reality of physical limits is to accept the need to limit greed and acquisition in favor of economic justice and sufficiency."[35] Desire seeks the infinite, and misdirected desire seeks it in constant physical growth. Isn't it interesting that cancer, a response of our bodies expressing itself in unlimited growth, is so prevalent a killer at this time in history, when our social fabric is overrun with an economic philosophy based on constant growth? Is our economy also cancerous? Like cancer cells, we seem not to know or care about our limits.

In 1960 the average CEO of a major firm received forty times the pay of the average worker, but in 1992 he received 157 times as much.[36] From 1977 to 1989 the average real income of the top 1 percent of U.S. families increased by 78 percent, while the bottom 20 percent decreased by 10.4 percent.[37] With the postmodern invention of computers, Korten points out, money has become more and more an abstraction: "The creation of money has been delinked from the creation of value."[38] This has been very tempting to people who now sit at computers and make their money that way. Billions of dollars can be transacted in less than a second. This is a *fleshless* economic game "running on autopilot without regard to human [or nonhuman] consequences."[39] One expert estimates that for every dollar circulating in the productive world economy, from $20 to $50 is circulating in the economy of pure (fleshless) finance, but no one really knows for sure. Korten believes that "the global financial system has become a parasitic predator that lives off the flesh of its host—the productive economy."[40] We eat what we love. Desire drives us to it.

In 1991 flash floods hit portions of the Philippines, killing thousands of people. The parish priest reported that many asked him, "Why did God do this do us?" His response was: "Why are some people doing this to us? A lot of people are saying this happened because the forests are gone, and we have no more trees to hold the water because of the illegal loggers. These people died from a natural disaster, but they also died because of human greed."[41]

In the *Divine Comedy* Dante tells of encountering in a dream an ugly and stammering siren who nevertheless sings a seductive song. The song represents the enticements of avarice, gluttony, and lust. Dante explains that when the soul turns sad and has lost inner joy, it runs to external goods for comfort—gluttony, avarice, and lust take over. The work of the heart chakra, joy, cannot be overlooked, or worse things will follow. Avarice takes over, and its "quest for the infinite" will break out in many different ways.

We do seek the infinite, and Aquinas taught that we can find satisfaction in this quest with three faculties: with our minds (who ever knows or learns too much?); with our hearts (who ever loves too much?); and with our hands connected to our imaginations (what two artists have ever given birth to the same creative work?). Mind, heart, and imagination are the proper places to look for the infinite. The very looking and seeking requires such discipline that limits are also learned. Sacrifice matters—it is part of the gift we bring to the spiritual search.

Fear has something to do with greed since we fear the loss of our wealth or status, or we fear the insecurity built into our precarious existence on this planet. Avarice feeds fear and vice versa. Avarice also feeds the institutionalized fear that fascism is about.

HARDNESS OF HEART

Medieval theologians generally agreed that too much avarice turned the heart *cold and hard*. Aquinas commented that "the avaricious man hardens his heart so that he will not out of compassion come to the aid of anyone at the expense of his possessions."[42] Avarice results, then, in the exact opposite of compassion. For this reason Hildegard of Bingen on several occasions called hard-heartedness "the worst sin."

> Hard-heartedness is the worst sin since it shows no mercy. Neither does it think that charity is necessary nor does it do any good works. . . . Hard-heartedness should not be allowed to harden itself against God or man. For this is the worst evil of all evils. It spares no one and shows no mercy. It despises men and draws back from God. It does not rejoice with men nor does it encourage humans to do good deeds.[43]

Hildegard depicted a dialogue between Hard-heartedness and Compassion. Hard-heartedness speaks first:

If I am always busy being compassionate, what good will it do me? What kind of life will I have if I pay attention to all the happy and sad people? I will take care of myself. Let others take care of themselves.

Compassion responds:

O you of stone, what are you saying? Flowering herbs give out an aroma and a stone glitters; all creation shows its fullness in some way. All the creatures on the earth minister to humans and by doing this freely they accomplish good. You, however, are not even worthy enough to have the form of a human. Since you have no mercy you are like pungent black smoke. But I am like the sweetest plant growing in the air. I have moisture and I am green. My veins are so full that I can help others. . . . I think about what is needed and I do that. I help all the sick get healthy; my words are like salve for pain. But you are nothing but pungent smoke!⁴⁴

THREE SINS BEHIND THE SINS

Traditionally avarice, pride, and desire were not named among the capital sins. Rather, they were considered the ultimate *pre-sins,* the sins behind sins, and they are said to run through all the capital sins. We have seen that all the chakras contain arrogance, avarice, the quest for more, desire, or what is called concupiscence. Injustice, understood as lack of authentic power balancing with power, also permeates all the chakras and all the capital sins.

Rather than put these sins in an antechamber, it is time to bring them out in the open and realize their special impact on the chakras. While arrogance cuts through all the chakras, it begins in the first with anthropocentrism and solipsism and the refusal to listen. While avarice runs through all the chakras in some manner, its special home is the heart: It sets one's heart on treasures that will not satisfy and therefore must be acquired infinitely. And while concupiscence, the desire behind desires, is present in all the chakras, it seems to have a special place in the first and the fourth, the cosmic chakra and the heart.

The solution to concupiscence's capacity to overwhelm us or run away with us is not to condemn it but to steer it to what is authentically desirable, to what the mystics call "the beloved." Kabir warned against those who would choke desire by stringent ascetic practices and legalisms but end up getting angry a lot and being lustful in spite of it all. Humor also doesn't hurt for checkmating concupiscence. But what the church has often done—equating concupiscence with sex and then holding sex up as a problem—doesn't help. I prefer what Saint Teresa did with concupiscence when she observed that prayer itself is "95 percent about desire." To grasp the truth of our own desires, we have to undergo a purification and an understanding, not by running from or repressing desire but by encountering it as face-to-face as possible. Desire has so much to teach us. The lack of desire after all, so prevalent in the first chakra, is the number-one source of misdirected love in our time. The awakening of kundalini energy *is* the awakening of desire. Desire moves people to commit themselves to great things; it is not the enemy.

OFFSPRING OF THE SIN AGAINST
THE FOURTH CHAKRA: A SUMMARY

In the traditional listing of the capital sins, the fourth chakra corresponds to avarice. The "daughters" of the sin of avarice are traditionally considered to be treachery, fraud, deceit, perjury, restlessness, violence, obduracy in regards to compassion. The offspring of sin against the fourth chakra that I propose are self-pity, hatred, resentment, refusal to forgive and let go, betrayal, the blame game, pessimism born of self-hatred, fear, fascism as an institutionalizing of fear and hatred, avarice or greed, hardness of heart.

EUCHARIST, THE SACRAMENT OF
THE FOURTH CHAKRA

The tradition of the Holy Eucharist in Christianity speaks well to the issues of the fourth chakra. This chakra is about love and compassion, about bringing together cosmic and intimate love-energies and strengthening us for being instruments of compassion. The Eucharist is a meal, and like all food and drink, it is meant to make us strong, to nourish us. The fourth chakra's work is principally work of compassion, and what better strengthening for this work than to be fed by the Cosmic Christ food, a food steeped in adversity, as was the historical Jesus in his time of death? Food is not only nourishing, it is cosmic and deeply intimate. All four chakras play out in the symbolism of this sacrament of soul-food. People who are strengthened by such food need not be overcome by fear; they are imbibing cosmic food and drink (as all food and drink is, in our new cosmology), and so they are on a path of magnanimity, not pusillanimity.

The sixteenth century, in its intense anthropocentrism, fought over whether the priest at the Eucharistic table did his work by "transubstantiation" (Roman Catholics) or by "consubstantiation" (Lutherans) or some other way. Today's cosmology carries us far beyond this human-centered debate about a cosmic event (as all worship should be about cosmic connecting). Today's cosmology puts the Eucharist into a far richer context. What transpires is less the work of the priest than the work of the heart of the universe. The Eucharist is about the universe loving us unconditionally still one more time and giving itself to us in the most intimate way (as food and drink). Interconnectivity is the heart of the Eucharistic experience: God and humanity coming together, God and flesh, the flesh of wheat, wine, sunshine, soil, water, human ingenuity, stars, supernovas, galaxies, atoms, fireballs—every Eucharist has a 15-billion-year sacred story that renders it holy.

The *gratitude* from which the Eucharist derives its very name (*eucharistein* means "to give thanks" in Greek) is not just our gratitude toward the Source of all things; it is also the universe's gratitude for our presence and for our efforts at contributing, however imperfectly.

The Eucharist is heart food from the cosmos—the "mystical body of Christ" and the Cosmic Christ or Buddha nature found in all beings in the universe—to us. Christ is the light of the world, which we now know is made *only* of light. Flesh is light and light is flesh. We eat, drink, sleep, breathe, and love that light. The Eucharist is also our hearts expanding and responding generously: "Yes, we will." We will carry on the heart-work called compassion, the work of the cosmos itself.

SPIRITUAL EXERCISES APROPOS OF
THE FOURTH CHAKRA

1. Make a list of the six things you love most in the world. How do your work and lifestyle contribute (or not contribute) to your relationships with these beings? How can these relationships be improved?

2. What do you do when your desires get out of hand? Can you learn disciplines to harness them and steer them to the things you most cherish?

3. Practice breathing meditations. Breathe in; breathe out. Pay attention to your breath. Love and cherish it. How much does your breath cost? How much does breathing cost? What really matters in life?

4. Chant. Make up chants. Find chants that others do. Get tapes of chant, and spend fifteen minutes at the end of your workday chanting alone or with others. Notice what a difference this makes in your capacity to relax and enjoy the gift of the *now*.

5. About fear: What three things are you most afraid of? Draw a picture of them. Ask the picture to speak to you. Ask it, "What have you come to teach me?"

6. Make an altar of brave persons you admire. Remember them through the day. Remember them especially in the morning as your day begins. Ask for their help when you are tempted by pusillanimity.

7. What are you doing to resist institutionalized fear? What more can you do? How effective are your efforts?

8. What lessons of forgiveness have you learned? Tell stories of forgiveness by you or toward you. What difference has forgiveness made in your life? Are you growing in your capacity for forgiveness?

9. A simple lifestyle is the opposite of a life based on greed and avarice. In what ways are you simplifying your lifestyle? What people do you know who are successful at doing this, and what can you learn from them? Start a group of simple-lifestylers to give one another support.

10. Are you tempted by self-hatred and the pessimism that flows from it? What are you doing about it? What about self-pity? Read Howard Thurman's remarks about self-pity again. What can you do to improve on your authentic self-love? How does this self-love translate into compassion for others?

11. *Heart* and *hearth* come from the same word. What are you doing—and what might you be doing—to create a hearth for others, to create gathering spaces where hearts and souls can come alive with stories and music and sharings and ideas? Can you displace the pseudo-hearth of the television with a genuine hearth where people can expand their joy and forgiveness and passion and creativity? Whom can you enlist to assist you in this good work?

12. A traditional litany to the Sacred Heart of Jesus follows, but in light of a Cosmic Christ theology, it is important to translate it into a Litany to the Sacred Heart of the Christ (or the Buddha or the universe's Source). Pray this litany. Paint it. Dance it. Write poetry in response to it. "Heart of Christ, infinite in majesty, Heart of Christ, sacred temple of God, Heart of Christ, tabernacle of the Most High, Heart of Christ, house of God and gate of heaven, Heart of Christ, burning furnace of charity, Heart of Christ, abode of justice and love, Heart of Christ, full of goodness and love, Heart of Christ, abyss of all virtues, Heart of Christ, most worthy of all praise, Heart of Christ, king and center of all hearts, Heart of Christ, in whom are all the treasures of wisdom and knowledge, Heart of Christ, in whom dwells the fullness of Divinity, Heart of Christ, in whom the Father is well pleased, Heart of Christ, of whose fullness we have all received, Heart of Christ, desire of the everlasting hills, Heart of Christ, patient and most compassionate, Heart of Christ, enriching all who call upon thee, Heart of Christ, fountain of life and holiness, Heart of Christ, atonement for our sins, Heart of Christ loaded down with opprobrium, Heart of Christ, source of all consolation, Heart of Christ, our life and resurrection, Heart of Christ, our peace and reconciliation, heart of Christ, delight of all the saints."

13. In what way do you have a "heart of Christ"? How are you grow-

ing it? Which of these images for the heart of Christ most apply to your own heart? Which do you want to develop more fully?

14. Hildegard taught that contentment is the medicine for avarice. Practice contentment. Learn to savor the simple gifts of life. Make a list of the times and places that have brought you contentment. Now make a list of things that arouse avarice in you. How can you fast from these things in order to practice more contentment?

CHAPTER 12

MISDIRECTED LOVE
IN THE FIFTH CHAKRA:
GLUTTONY AND CONSUMERISM

The fifth chakra, the throat chakra, lies between the heart (fourth chakra) and the creative mind (sixth chakra). The misdirected energy here has traditionally been named as gluttony. Interestingly, the word *gluttony* comes from the word *gluttus* or "throat" in Latin. Traditionally, gluttony is defined as "an inordinate desire to eat."[1] Brought about by avarice and an excessive desire for what goes down the throat, the gluttonous person refuses to put the breaks on whatever food or drink enters their body. Often the result is that things "choke us up" or get "stuck in our throats" or gag us. Gluttony is avarice from the heart that has made it up to the throat, where it gets temporary satisfaction. I believe that the contemporary word for *gluttony* is in fact *consumerism*.

CONSUMERISM AND THE FIFTH CHAKRA

To consume is "to take into the throat." Many people would say, "Well, I may be a shopaholic, but I keep my body in good shape and don't eat too much, so I am not gluttonous." But I would say, au contraire. To consume is to eat, and we are *eating the words of advertisers* when we build our lives around shopping. Our insides are affected not just by the food we take in but by everything we take in—including ideas, values, ways to pass our time, all our relations. If shopping is a basis of our relationships, then it is our preoccupation, and we are by definition consumers. We are also in many ways eating the planet, devouring its very flesh, gobbling down its soil and trees and waters, when we pour concrete and build malls and consume gas and pollute air to drive there and back again.

When we consume, we devour, finish, deplete, exhaust, expend, dissipate, burn up, use up, ingest, squander, and spend. And spend. And spend. Like squirrels in a cage, as economist Juliet Shor puts it, we work to spend and spend and spend some more because the addiction of consumerism always needs a new hit and another fix. Clearly gluttony has many offspring—and consuming is at the heart of them all.

If gluttony is a throat issue, it raises the question of the holiness of the flesh once again: How holy are our throats? Are they *sanctuaries* where the Holy of Holies enters? If so, do we keep them clean and pure for that purpose? A warning from the Cree nation goes like this:

> Only after the last tree has been cut down,
> Only after the last river has been poisoned,
> Only after the last fish has been caught
> Only then will you find that money cannot be eaten.

THE SHOPPING ADDICTION: A PSEUDO-COSMOLOGY

The Middle Ages saw gluttony as a sin of the flesh, meaning that the pleasure of eating to excess was a bodily more than a spiritual pleasure. Today's understanding of the nature of addiction, however, reveals that all addictions are soul addictions. In this sense avarice, or misdirected desire, permeates all the chakras. It just finds a special home in the fourth chakra and then a special outlet in the fifth chakra.

The distinction between spirit sin and flesh sin is not so distinct in our time, when everything is for sale and when shopping has become practically a cosmology (a pseudo-substitute for the first chakra). One television commercial this Christmas season pictured a child saying, "I was born to shop." This worldview, this specious cosmology, surely names much that is going on in our time. Rabbi Heschel warns us that shopping will substitute for the first chakra when he says: "Forfeit your sense of awe, let your conceit diminish your ability to revere, and the universe becomes a market place for you."[2] Consumerism is a kind of cosmology that the advertising media pump into us daily. Shoving things down our throats, "gorging us." Eating or *any act of taking in* has a soullike dimension because we take in not just to feed our stomachs but to feed our souls. And our souls are very large—like a gorge or canyon.

If our souls are quite empty, then they are indeed a *chasm* into which we have to pour thing upon thing, new thing (latest model) upon new thing. The cycle is infinite, as is avarice, "a quest for the infinite that knows no limit and tends to infinity." We want to fill our souls with something very large. Lacking a cosmology, we fill our shopping carts instead. We respond to what our culture teaches us, and that is mostly about shopping (because so much of our cultural art and language derives from advertising arts).

EXCESS: ADDICTION AND AVARICE IN THE FIFTH CHAKRA

The avarice we spoke of in the fourth chakra finds a special outlet in the fifth. It is as if avarice were a cancer in our heart that spreads up into our throats. Instead of hands that heal, which is the picture of compassion emanating from the heart, gluttony creates hands that seize, hold, grab, grip, grasp, clutch, clench, clamp, buy, purchase, take, loot, plunder, snatch, steal, rifle, own, possess, and have. Furthermore, in our society the food industry and its powerful advertisers are urging us to eat constantly. "We are a society inundated with food and drink," observes one psychologist. "Our gluttony and the greed of the food industry and its advertisers are responsible for this saturation of our consciousness with eating and drinking."[3] This same psychologist reports that his clients with food-related problems report spending 40 to 85 percent of their waking hours on food-related activities![4]

Thomas Aquinas taught what Buddhism and other spiritual traditions teach when he said that the food we take in should be "commensurate with the sustenance of nature and the good condition of man and the society of those with whom one lives. When therefore a person desires and takes food according to this rule of reason he takes it according to need, but when he exceeds this limit, he transgresses the rule of reason by departing from the mean of virtue to satisfy the desire of pleasure."[5] Eating "according to need" rather than "exceeding the limit" and paying attention to the needs of the whole society: Here is a code that applies not just to the food we take in but to all the consuming we do.

Not knowing our limits is truly scary because we are a species that spreads everywhere, and with our immense creativity, we can affect all other beings on our planet. If knowing our limits is part of good health, then not knowing our limits leads to sickness of many kinds. Often the only limit is getting sick—throwing up, disgorging, bulimia, obesity, heart attack. The soul is empty, and the flesh pays the price. It fills up and up and up. And since our economic system sells us gluttony daily and is built on such cancerous growth, all this excess seems very normal—until the body becomes ill. The blessing of the flesh is that, as a last resort, it speaks out to say "Stop! Enough *is* enough! No more! Quit taking in!"

Excess in the fifth chakra leads us to punish our holy bodies. The abuse of our holy flesh results from our not loving our flesh and not paying attention to our soul's needs. Alcoholism and drug addiction are conspicuous examples of this. Many of those healed in AA and NA are healed because they have found food and drink *for their souls* that allows them to deal with their inner pain or with their anguish or yearning for the infinite. Instead of taking infinite, unending amounts of outside stimulants into their bodies to fill a cavern inside the soul, they can live from inside out again. The same holds true for drug addictions, which wreak havoc on the body and soul of self and eventually others in the form of crime and violence.

Eating and drinking are not just distractions but, for some, an *escape* from the pain of daily life and bread earning. Much of television watching and excess eating, drinking, and shopping plays the role of an escape from the pain in our souls. We can get off television by going into that pain and then operating beyond it.

THE REFUSAL TO GIVE BIRTH FROM
THE THROAT BIRTH CANAL

The throat and the fifth chakra are about not just taking in but also putting out. We speak with our throat—or at least we are meant to. But sometimes the taking can substitute for our talking, and silence overtakes us. Both our heart and our mind refuse to speak out.

In "The Transformation of Silence into Language and Action," poet Audre Lorde writes about how she was told she was dying of breast cancer. She underwent a revelation about the need to speak out. "I have come to believe over and over again that what is most important to me must be spoken, made verbal and shared, even at the risk of having it bruised or misunderstood," she writes.[6] When she faced her mortality, she realized that "what I most regretted were my silences.... My silences had not protected me. Your silence will not protect you."[7] Fear is no excuse not to speak out—unfinished work in the fourth chakra can influence our fifth chakra. "We have been socialized to respect fear more than our own needs for language and definition, and while we wait in silence...the weight of that silence will choke us."[8] Others depend on our getting over our silence and our fear of speaking out: "We can sit in our corners mute forever while our sisters and our selves are wasted, while our children are distorted and destroyed, while our earth is poisoned; we can sit in our safe corners mute as bottles, and we will still be no less afraid."[9]

The throat is like a birth canal through which pass our deepest thoughts and hopes and dreams and poems. The throat, if clean and empty, is meant to trumpet our truth, to announce good news, to bestow our wisdom, to present the gifts we carry within, to offer our wisdom. Significantly, our throat chakra lies between our heart and third eye and mind chakras: We trumpet not only what we know with our hearts but also what we know with our minds, its powers of intellect and intuition. All this constitutes "good news." All this can be a wake-up call for others. All this is the work of the prophet, which must always be fed by the work of the heart and the creative mind (the fourth and sixth chakras respectively).

Through the throat, revelation happens; "the purpose of a word is to reveal," said Meister Eckhart.[10] Think of it: *All* of the words that we intend for others pass through our throat (excepting some of the written ones). Through our throats we sing, chant, croon, carol, yodel, tune, warble, chirp, cry, moan, lament, keen, hoot, whine, murmur, groan, scream, roar, bellow, screech, shout, shriek, wail, whoop, yell, weep, speak, chatter, gossip, confer, pronounce, declare, proclaim, publicize, and announce. No wonder Meister Eckhart urged us to "pay attention to what is in you. Announce it, pronounce it, produce it, and give birth to it."[11] The throat is indeed a birth canal—we give birth to our truths through it. Passing through the throat and the larynx, they become beings in the world. But they do so only if the birth canal is open and free, and it cannot be so if we have defined our throat *not* as a birth canal but exclusively as a conduit for consumer goods.

Misdirecting the love of the fifth chakra, then, includes forsaking the throat as birth canal in favor of using it as a one-way pipe of consumption. Here avarice itself gets "stuck in the throat," which lies dangerously close to the jugular. Is consumerism "going for the jugular" in our society? Is it out of control? Is there something mortal about it? Is it killing our souls so that very soon our bodies will follow?

Talk about abortion! How many beings are stillborn in us because the throat canal is set on "taking in" due to consumerism and is not prepared to "give back"? How many beings are killed even before they reach the light of day because we are not giving birth but busy stuffing ourselves instead? Our elders should be teaching us to give back, to give away, to give out, to give birth—but, sad to say, the majority with the power to do so are busy making money and buying the things that money can buy.

GAGGING AND CONCEALING

It is no accident that the birth canal we call the throat is located just above the heart chakra. Just as compassion is meant to express itself through our hands, it is also meant to express itself through our throats. Our speech and our "word" are meant to be a Divine "word," Divine speech, a Divine revelation, a Divine utterance. From our Divine hearts is born the Christ, the Buddha, the goddess, the light of the ages, the wisdom, Sophia—so many names to give this newborn child. The birth canal of which I speak is a holy birth canal and is not restricted to women or to women at a certain age. Our praise is a giving-birth: We give birth constantly in this lifetime through our throats.

To refuse to give birth, to give birth reluctantly, to allow garbage to pile up in our throats from excessive consumption—all this misdirects the love-energy of the fifth chakra. To yield to being gagged is to give away our power—it clogs up the work of the third chakra, which needs to express itself in the fifth. This is why the prophets are people who *speak out* and *interfere*—they refuse to be muzzled, throttled, silenced, quieted, hushed, suppressed, shut up. When they see a truth about justice and compassion or its lack, they speak out so that the community listens.

Fleeing from our responsibility to give birth is a sin against the fifth chakra. Instead of *revealing* through our voices, we are *concealing*. We choose to conceal. A sin of omission takes us over. We are all meant to be prophets; mystical energy is to be invested in the healing of the community. But we are also all free to cop out, to give up, to allow ourselves to be gagged. The goodies of consumerism gag us, as do the fears that we might stir up trouble. The courage we learn in the fourth chakra is essential for our work in the fifth. There was no prophet who was not courageous. Jesus has been described as a great "announcer." Theologian Dominic Crossan describes his work this way:

He was neither broker nor mediator but, somewhat paradoxically, the *announcer* that neither should exist between humanity and divinity or between humanity and itself. Miracle and parable, healing and eating were calculated to force individuals into unmediated physical and spiritual contact with God and unmediated physical and spiritual contact with one another. He *announced,* in other words, the unmediated or brokerless Kingdom of God.[12]

The throat, then, is meant to be a two-way street. We take in the goods of this world—food and drink and air first of all (and *goods* and *blessing* are the same words)—*and* we give them out. We return blessing for blessing. We also consume other items but, we hope, with the same reverence for the sacred that we hold for food, drink, and air. The necessities of life pass through the throat—breathing, eating, drinking. We are participants and subjects but not prime movers in any of these—the air, the lungs, the food, the waters, the gullet, the stomach were all prepared for us in advance. We just show up! Hopefully, we do so with more than rapaciousness and greed in our eyes and hearts. Hopefully we do so with a fully developed sense of reverence. In many respects the fifth chakra is one that teaches us *not to take for granted.*

One way to get that reverence back is to voluntarily choose to do without. Fasting, vegetarianism, going without water—all these exercises can purify the throat, cleanse the gullet, so that the next time we take in, we do so with awareness and the proper sense of gratitude and awe.

LYING AND HYPOCRISY

The throat chakra is meant to be a holy place from which our truth emerges. Our throats are made for truth-telling, not lying or hypocrisy (which is lying by our actions). Martin Buber believes that humans alone among all earth creatures lie because humans are capable of "conceiving the being of truth."

> The lie is the specific evil which man has introduced into nature. All our deeds of violence and our misdeeds are only as it were a highly bred development of what this and that creature of nature is able to achieve in its own way. But the lie is our very one invention, different in kind from every deceit that the animals can produce.[13]

When our speech compromises truth, society collapses. "The basis of men's common life has been removed. The lie has taken the place, as a form of life, of human truth." Speech breeds delusion in people's hearts and illusions and falsifies the relation of soul to being. Duplicity or a "double heart" takes over.[14] To walk one's talk and not just talk our talk seems to be central to the survival of community. Hypocrisy comes from the Greek word for acting on a stage. The hypocrite does not walk his or her talk; he does not play his role but someone else's.

TAKING SPEECH FOR GRANTED

Our speech too needs to be guarded and careful in the sense that we owe it to our heart-truth to utter it with care and crafting and even

tenderness. People who come from oral traditions, such as tribal people, often have a reverence for words that is the opposite of the verbosity of our advertising-driven culture. Noise is something we take in
all day. It can interfere with our inner silence and therefore with our
speech. For true speech always comes from an inner space and a deep
silence, a being-with that has itself spoken to us, a contemplative place
where we *con-temple,* "share a temple with," the Divine presence, the
Cosmic Christ and Buddha nature that we have encountered in all our
experiences.

If a purpose of a word is to reveal, then with every word we utter,
we are all other Christs announcing the revelation of the Divine in the
human and in the flesh. Since we speak as well as breathe with our
breath, and since breath is also *ruah* or spirit, the throat is surely a holy
passageway for the spirit. As such, it deserves to be purified and
cleansed so as to be an appropriate passage for spirit to emerge. The
spirit and Divinity that *flows* "through all things" (Book of Wisdom) also
blows through our speech. Our speech is literally a breath. It is *ruah* or
spirit blowing. Every word we utter has the potential to be the word of
God. Who would want to take such a power for granted? Who would
want to abort or stifle such Divine incarnations? Perhaps this is what
Meister Eckhart had in mind when he said, "We are all meant to be
mothers of God."[15]

In shining light on the power of speech, we should not be too literal. Our "word" is not only our spoken word but any word that comes
from our hearts and consciences. Alice Walker, in *Living by the Word,*
addresses herself to the power of the fifth chakra when she connects the
oral tradition of our ancestors to our more recent art of writing and the
role that speech plays in representing other creatures.

> The longer I am a writer . . . the better I understand what writing is;
> what its function is, what it is supposed to do. I learn that the
> writer's pen is a microphone held up to the mouths of ancestors
> and even stones of long ago. That once given permission by the
> writers—a fool, and so why should one fear?—horses, dogs,
> rivers, and, yes, chickens can step forward and expound on their
> lives. The magic of this is not so much in the power of the micro-
> phone as in the ability of the nonhuman object or animal to *be* and
> the human animal to *perceive its being.*[16]

Ours is a species that can perceive the being of others—no wonder we have so much to say, so much to praise, so much to speak about. What a shame to waste this power of expressing the beings of others.

GAGGING OF OTHERS AND TAKING AWAY
THEIR VOICE

It used to be that avarice was a sin of the rich, but today the powerful are themselves passing on their favorite pastime to the poor and middle class. They have the influence to pass on their "values" or their oddly defined loves to people who are so poor that they may yearn for things but never be able to purchase them, much less enjoy life more if they were to purchase them.

The misdirected love energies that happen in the fifth chakra include not only our taking in too much and stifling our truth and our capacity to birth it. It also applies to those who are doing the stuffing of our throats, selling us goods we do not *need,* making a consumer atmosphere and ideology and consumer monsters. Who made that ad, for example, of a child saying, "I was born to shop"? Some cynical adult, no doubt, and some cynical company run by adults is making money, along with its shareholders, by selling such vice. Where is the vice squad when we need it? Isn't it a capital offense to use and abuse the young? Isn't adultism at work here, as well as the greed that will use anybody and anything for its grasping purposes?

To gag another and stifle their truth is surely a sinful act, and in a society where only a few control so many of the airwaves and television access, a lot of that is going on. Due to a growing movement called "democracy for hire," there are now more than four times as many public relations employees engaged in manipulating news on behalf of paying clients than there are actually news reporters. More than half of the *Wall Street Journal*'s news stories are based solely on press releases. The result? "The distinction between advertising space and news space grows less distinct with each passing day."[17]

Politics is also for hire. Television, with its immense costs to politicians, has broken down the grassroots democratic organizations of the past and substituted campaigns that need huge funding efforts. Some

law firms in Washington, it is believed, are specializing in selling political influence to monied clients and raising money for both political
parties in the process: "These firms are in the business of brokering
power to whomsoever will pay their fees."[18] The voter *has now become a*
consumer, as one observer sees is: "Voters are now viewed as a passive
assembly of 'consumers,' a mass audience of potential buyers. Research
discovers through scientific sampling what it is these consumers know
or think and, more important, what they feel, even when they do not
know their own 'feelings.' A campaign strategy is then designed to connect the candidate with these consumer attitudes. Advertising images
are created that will elicit positive responses and make the sale."[19]

Nor are other governments oblivious to the buying (and subsequent gagging) of American public opinion. In the late 1980s Japanese
corporations spent $100 million annually on political lobbying in the
United States, and another $300 million to influence public opinion.
They employed 92 Washington law, public relations, and lobbying
firms on their behalf, while Canada employed 55, Britain 42. "The
purpose is to rewrite U.S. laws in favor of foreign corporations—and
it often works."[20] Are China's lobbying efforts in the election of 1996
anything new?

The global consumer culture is gagging people everywhere. The
chairman of the Coca-Cola Company puts it clearly and without regret:
"People around the world are today connected by brand name consumer products as much as by anything else."[21] Corporate logos and the
visions they excite apparently constitute the new religious experience
of our time.

ADULTISM AND THE GAGGING OF THE YOUNG

Executives of the MTV entertainment network, which reaches 210
million households in 71 countries, describe MTV as the "most influential educator of young people on five continents." They describe what
the young are taking in from MTV as a "longing":

The performances and the ads merge to create a mood of longing—for someone to love, for something exciting to happen, for an

end to loneliness, and for things to buy—a record, a ticket to a rock concert, a T-shirt, a Thunderbird. The advertising is all the more effective because it is not acknowledged as such. . . . All across the planet, people are using the same electronic devices to watch or to listen to the same commercially produced songs and stories.[22]

This "mood of longing"—is this not the opening up of the heart chakra, a laying bare of desire and yearning? And is not such yearning especially heated in our adolescent years? What is being offered to fill the emerging adult-size soul? "Things to buy," by their own admission. *Not things to relate to, not relations with all other beings or their marvelous source.* One wonders if this artful instruction in objects to buy—the primary education of the young on five continents—is going to lead to peace and joy or to frustration and unhappy hearts. Are the adults who are delivering such goods into the minds, hearts, and throats of the young poisoning them? In the Beatitudes of Jesus, we are taught to "hunger and thirst after justice." Is this not the kind of teaching elders should be handing on to the young? Is an infinite list (for it can change daily) of tickets, automobiles, records, and other bonbons in any way a moral substitute?

Adults in the media industries, including the advertising industries, ought to be required to take courses on eldering: what it means to be an elder, and the responsibilities of being an elder. The people who stand in the secular pulpits of our time are in powerful places, and their influence ought to be humanizing, not avaricious. What parent would pour toxins down their children's throats? So what business executive would pour toxins down young people's throats and for what motivation? Let them at least come out of the dark closets where they lurk (and count their millions) to tell us who they are and why they do it.

Today the cigarette industry is being challenged in the United States (though American companies are not being challenged in their dealings abroad) to cease seducing the young. Cigarettes are clearly a throat issue, an issue of the fifth chakra. Adults are enticing youth into this addictive and harmful habit. A Japanese youth told me that his stepfather gave him cigarettes on his fifteenth birthday (a kind of "rite of passage," no doubt), and within two years he was smoking forty cigarettes a day! Today, at twenty-two, he is smoking eleven cigarettes a day. Youth around the world are being appealed to by cigarette advertisers, just as "Joe Camel" is finally being given the funeral he deserves in America.

How much of smoking and sucking on a cigarette is a yearning of the heart chakra for touch and intimacy and breathing itself? Dr. Dean Ornish defines a cigarette package as "twenty friends in a box." If adults were providing a more viable community with the young, would the young be so desperate for "friends in a box"? Wouldn't appropriate work for elders be to create community rather than to create ads for cigarettes or to give cigarettes out to our teenagers? With a cigarette one both takes in and gives out. It is a kind of secular pseudo-breathing meditation—"suck in, blow out." Perhaps a more authentic spiritual practice could help eliminate this toxic practice that so harms the body, especially at the heart chakra which is also the lung chakra.

ADVERTISING AS AN INVASION OF OUR THROATS

Advertisers manipulate our minds by appealing to our fantasy lives (sixth chakra) for the purpose of arousing our wants and desires. One remedy is to have a fantasy life of one's own and to resist that which comes from outside. Avon is selling its beauty products in the town of Santarém, Brazil, to very poor women who are for the most part illiterate and whose households make an average wage of $3 per day. A skin-renewal product called Renew, which costs $40 a jar, is pushed on TV ads as being able to make women appear younger and solve their problems. The result? "Women do everything to buy it. They stop buying other things like clothes, like shoes. If they feel good with their skin they prefer to stop buying clothes and buy something that is on the television. People think it is a real miracle."[23] These are the words of the communications director for Avon of Brazil.

New electronic media have given powerful industries *access to the intimacy of our throats*—not just our personal throats but our family and community throats. The *hearth* is being affected as well as the heart. The hearth represents the family heart, the family or community gathering place for stories, and a vast number of today's stories are manufactured by the advertising industry. The hearth is heartlike, it is warm and fiery and cozy and intimate. Yet a hearth is so lacking in the lives of so many today, warns Michael Meade, that young people, whose hearts so yearn for the community fire, may just burn down our society in order to feel the warmth.

One indigenous person comments on life in her village:

> Our village was prosperous. . . . The real foundation of our pros-
> perity . . . was the deep and enduring sense of community that
> enabled us to make the best use of these resources. . . We had all the
> things we needed—well-crafted, beautiful things that lasted a long
> time—but we did not do much "consuming."[24]

We, as a species, are so immature about handling such intimate power pouring into our personal and collective throats that we need to stop and critique what we and our children are receiving and failing to receive. We would jump to action if our child swallowed Drāno; so too we ought to be moved to action by some of the ideological toxins that are being forced down their gullets. We also need to develop an inner life and our own voice so we are not just taking in but also putting out. In this way our creativity and values may be heard and trumpeted. Participation is key. We are to be subjects, not objects; sharers, not consumers. We were not born to shop. We were born to share and to celebrate the sharing.

OFFSPRING OF THE SINS OF THE FIFTH CHAKRA

Traditionally, the "daughters" of the sin of gluttony were uncleanness of body or soul (which includes dulling of the mind and senses), unseemly joy or emotional excess at what we consume, garrulousness, verbosity, the misuse of speech, scurrility, and a lack of physical composure.[25]

I am suggesting the following offspring of the sins of the fifth chakra: consumerism, the shopping addiction as a pseudo-cosmology, excess, addiction and avarice, refusal to give birth through the birth channel of the throat, gagging and concealing, lying and hypocrisy, taking speech for granted, the gagging of others and taking away their voice, adultism and the gagging of the young, advertising as invasion.

PRIESTHOOD, THE SACRAMENT OF THE FIFTH CHAKRA

The priesthood is the archetype of spiritual leadership in a community. The priest is meant to preach and teach as an inspirer, a prophet who interferes with whatever is blocking compassion from happening in the community. The priest is the one who knows something from experience (not just from academic texts) about the word of God in the *context* of the daily flesh of people's lives. The priest knows how sacred all the chakras are and how to honor them, to purify them, to awaken them so that their energy can stir into the greater community. The priest is meant to be prophetic—to speak out in the name of justice and healing and thereby usher in a God of compassion. The priest is meant to tell the creation story that gives a context to our lives and a reverence and joy at living. The priest also helps us to reconcile and forgive and start anew.

Who is a priest? Where do we find leadership like this? In *The Reinvention of Work* I proposed that *all workers are priests* (an adaptation of Luther's teaching that all believers are priests). All work worthy of the name is meant to bring the sacred alive in the world. Thus, its practitioners are priests.

To bring about this kind of priesthood, one that truly honors and engages the fifth chakra along with all the other chakras that feed into it, we need training grounds different from most seminaries today. We need training grounds where spiritual experience is at least as attended to as textual studies and where the new cosmology is sung, danced, studied, debated, rapped, and practiced. And where all the words of God—not just the human ones—are reverenced. And where the mystic *and* the prophet are elicited from each person.

I believe that at least one model exists for such a training ground; I have been involved in its ongoing creation for twenty-one years. It began as the Institute in Culture and Creation Spirituality in Chicago in 1977, and it has now evolved to be the University of Creation Spirituality in Oakland. Here we have developed a learning model where "getting one's voice" is at the heart of the curriculum, along with cosmology, mysticism, art, and justice-making. Our Doctor of Ministry program, the first ever oriented to *all* kinds of workers (not just clergy or theologians), is returning the excitement to education, work, and spirituality. It does so because, with a living cosmology, it puts the context back into education. Someday it will be imitated by the churches and seminaries. I hope it will not be too late.

Today many young people are being called by Gaia, by the spirit, by the future itself to be priests, but not in the traditional seminary-going and text-oriented ways. They are being called through their hearts, and their arts of ritual-making and artistry can call community together to celebrate. The priest, after all, leads the *celebration* of the community in praise and thanksgiving. At our Techno Ritual Center, located two blocks from our university in downtown Oakland, we are working with the priests of our culture who, being artists drawn to the new cosmology, are way ahead of academicians passing out degrees in theological studies. The stirrings of the human heart for healthy, hearty celebration will not be denied. A new kind of priest is emerging. It dwells in every one of us potentially, and in the form of worship we have devised, wherein all participants dance, we all share the priesthood. The posse is the priest. We all share the priesthood because we are all breathing deep, praying deep, and participating fully. The priesthood, after all, is not a *state* or *condition;* it is a living process, an alive happening, real authorship, bringing out the priest inside all of us. True celebration does that.

Authentic priesthood is the direct opposite of gagging others and taking away their voice: It is empowering others to find their voice and utter it, beginning with a voice of praise and continuing with a voice of emergence of one's truth—the truth of one's heart (fourth chakra) and of one's mind (sixth chakra). Eliciting creativity and compassion from others for the sake of the greater community—this is the work of the priesthood, and no one is exempt from it.

SPIRITUAL EXERCISES APROPOS OF THE FIFTH CHAKRA

The fifth chakra calls for finding our own voice and giving birth to our inner selves. Some ways to awaken the fifth chakra include the following:

1. Take voice lessons. Learn to sing, chant, speak your voice—literally.

2. Learn to paint, draw, write, dance, sculpt, rap, or take up a musical instrument. Tell your story and your lessons from life in one or more of these media.

3. Do numbers 2 and 3 with others and on behalf of others. In other words, teach others to do the same—especially the young ones.

4. Turn off your television. Cut your hours first by a quarter; then by half; then by three-quarters. And then???

5. Read Jerry Mander's *Four Arguments for the Elimination of Television* and Bill McKibben's *The Age of Missing Information*. Get neighbors and friends and coworkers to discuss these books and the issues raised in them.

6. Start your own radio program or television work. Go into journalism and become a spiritual warrior there, bringing values that are truly yours, including cosmology and all the seven chakra values discussed in this book.

7. Make a list of *what you take in every day* from sources you did not participate in creating:
   a. Food
   b. Drink
   c. Information
   d. Television

   Now ask: How much of this was toxic? How much of it was healthy? What can I do to lessen the former and increase the latter?

8. Keep a list of how many trips you make to a shopping mall over a week or two and what you purchase there. Then ask: How necessary are these trips? What am I actually doing when I'm there? What am I really looking for there? Might I spend my time differently—for example, assisting some nonprofit with my volunteer labor? Or reading? Or making my own things? Or gardening? Or bicycling?

9. Commit yourself to a family hearth, a gathering place for stories and music and dance and celebration among your family and neighbors. Keep track of the results.

10. Create a Television Anonymous group (TA) that agrees to keep television watching to a moderate amount and supports one another in the process of going cold turkey. Keep a log of TV

commercials you and your children watch (have them help keep the log) for one week. Discuss as a family what is entering your throat here: How much of what is offered is something you (a) need? (b) want? (c) can afford? What can you as a family be doing with your shared time that is *more fun and invigorating* than TV?

11. Simplify your lifestyle. Get help in doing so. Create a "green ceiling," a limit on your income, and try to live within it. Are you living more fully? What are you learning?

12. Grow an organic garden. What changes does this make in your life?

13. Try fasting. Try vegetarianism or semivegetarianism. How does this diet affect your appreciation of things you eat?

CHAPTER 13

MISDIRECTED LOVE
IN THE SIXTH CHAKRA:
RATIONALISM, REDUCTIONISM,
AND PESSIMISM

The sixth chakra concerns our "third eye," intuition, and
the bringing together of our left and right hemispheres of
the brain in creativity. To misdirect its energy is to deprive
ourselves both personally and communally of our most
powerful gift to the world: our creativity.

One might say that the sixth chakra is the marriage not only of the
proverbial left and right hemispheres but also of the Divine and the
human. For creativity is indeed our link to the Divine as well as
the Divine's link to us. It is, in biblical language, the "image of God"
coming alive in us, for God is the Creator par excellence, the "Artist of
artists" (Aquinas), the Source of all things, the "Mother of all worlds
who dwells within all of us" *(Tao Te Ching),* the Holy Spirit that birthed
and continues to birth the universe. This same Spirit, this same Cosmic
Mother, this same Creative One who "lies on a maternity bed all day
giving birth" (Eckhart) is present within us. "We can use it any way we
want," warns the *Tao Te Ching.*

OMISSION OF CREATIVITY

This is indeed a warning—to use our creativity and let the spirit of creation flow through us. Not to use it, not to let the spirit flow through us, is also a choice. It is not a wise one, for we are made for creativity, we all have a sixth chakra, blessed and nourished and sustained by all five preceding ones. This chakra has much to do on our behalf and on the large community's behalf, and to let it sit idle and go unused is a grievous act of omission. Since every moral choice and every act of creativity is an *act,* every time we refuse to give birth we are committing an act of omission. Omit or create: that seems to be our moral option. "The same Spirit that hovered over the waters at the beginning of creation hovers over the artist's mind at work," Thomas Aquinas taught. That is an amazing teaching: The universe is *still being created* and yet we are on such intimate terms with the Creator Spirit that we are *cocreators* if we choose to respond to that Spirit of Creativity. What an opportunity! What a blessing! What a great need we have to tap into the flowing lava—waters and fires flowing from the inner depths of the previous five chakras—in order to bring forth the images and energy appropriate to this chakra.

Lewis Mumford spoke of the power and impact of creative intuition when he said: "Every transformation of humanity has rested upon deep stirrings of the intuition, whose rationalized expression amounts to a new vision of the cosmos and the nature of the human." To ignore these "deep stirrings of the intuition" would be tantamount to aborting the transformations of humanity. At a time like ours, when so many transformations are called for, stifling creativity would seem to be the last action our species can afford.

I often meditate on the following story, which I have adapted from my scientist friend Brian Swimme. Apparently our species began about 2 million years ago in the hot savannas of eastern Africa. There we discovered fire, and armed with it, our curiosity got the best of us and we set out to see the world. After about a million years, some of our ancestors arrived at the edge of what we call Europe and Asia today. But as soon as they arrived from the African savannas, the ice age struck! Retreating to caves for shelter, our forebears hid inside for 700,000 years waiting for the ice to melt. Imagine—from the heat of Africa to the cold of the ice age. Surely they spent the first 100,000 years asking: "Who turned off the heat?" Meanwhile, they had to learn all new things to survive—how to hunt and skin a woolly mammoth, how to keep predators away from the cave, how to track animals in the snow while keeping their feet from freezing.

My amazement in this story is that the only thing that saved our ancestors from extinction was their creativity. Imagine what well-developed sixth chakras these people had! They were tough. They did not dwell on self-pity or pusillanimity—they could not afford to—and if they had, we would not be here to tell their story. We are made of hearty stock—and creative stock. We ought to be developing our creativity as never before. Instead, as we saw in the previous chapter, our self-expression is often being gagged and silenced and dictated to by the great powers of our time.

SUPPRESSION OF THE PROPHETIC

Meister Eckhart put it marvelously when he said, "Whatever can be truly expressed in its proper meaning must emerge from inside a person and pass through the inner form. It cannot come from outside a person but must emerge from within."[1] Truth must indeed come *from our insides.* Creativity is the prophetic work of a healthy throat chakra working in tandem with an alive sixth chakra. Aquinas tells us that "metaphor and symbol" are the language of the prophets. Prophets appeal *to the imagination,* as Walter Brueggeman has also written in *The Prophetic Imagination.*[2]

The stirring of the imagination has the potential to awaken and arouse a community that is off center or imbalanced. When prophets stir it by their symbols and metaphors, they are speaking sixth chakra to sixth chakra, "eye to eye" in the sense of third eye to third eye. This is a powerful communication, face-to-face, and promises great things. Here truth can happen. Here creativity begets creativity and intuition begets intuition. From this potential much can be given birth to. Jesus felt that the Kingdom of God itself could be given birth to—and he was not alone.

This invitation of creativity that the sixth chakra extends to us all is rejected by certain currents of pseudo-Christianity today. When fundamentalists took over a school board in New Hampshire recently, their first declaration was that no teacher was allowed to use the word *imagination* in the classroom. Apparently God-given imagination is just too much for these self-proclaimed judges. See to what distances control and fascism will carry people who are afraid.

Every one of the chakras inspires fear because every one of them is about awakening power. Spirit power takes discipline in order to be bridled. Without this discipline we are lost, and without courage we are stuck in fear. Robbing children and teachers of their God-given right and responsibility to creativity represents a new low in adultism. Wherever there is fear, there is power, and the fear of these adults is evidence of the power of the imagination and indeed of the child in all of us to share in the Divine creativity of this universe.

To cleanse and awaken and utilize our sixth chakra effectively, we need to effect a new kind of union between the child within and the adult. Jesus recognized this when he said, "Become like a child; receive the kingdom." The child presumably still holds fast to a sense of awe, wonder, and spontaneity—all graces from the first chakra. In that statement Jesus recognized the connection between the first and sixth chakra. Kabir also recognized the connection when he wrote: "O seeker / To see the face of thy Beloved / cleanse the eye that is within / And then behold how like a child / You have become!"[3] The cleansing of the third eye restores a kind of childlikeness, a necessary ingredient to creativity.

A good example of the prophetic nature of creativity is laid out by bell hooks, in an essay on "Postmodern Blackness":

> Much postmodern engagement with culture emerges from the yearning to do intellectual work that connects with habits of being, forms of artistic expression, and aesthetics that inform the daily life of writers and scholars as well as a mass population. On the terrain of culture, one can participate in critical dialogue with the uneducated poor, the black underclass who are thinking about aesthetics. One can talk about what we are seeing, thinking, or listening to; a space is there for a critical exchange. It's exciting to think, write, talk about, and create art that reflects passionate engagement with popular culture, because this may very well be "the" central future location of resistance struggle, a meeting place where new and radical happenings can occur.[4]

INJUSTICE AND IGNORANCE IN THE SIXTH CHAKRA

If the sixth chakra is about the prophetic imagination, then to fail to develop the imagination is to stifle justice as well. The prophets struggle for justice. Justice is, after all, a work of balancing power with power, and the sixth chakra is a balancing chakra. Is injustice not a lack of balance? Is the work to eliminate injustice not the work to right what is unbalanced? Is an underdeveloped sixth chakra, then, not a breeding ground for injustice, personally and culturally understood? The struggle for justice requires analysis as well as imagination—it requires a marriage of our intellectual and intuitive sides. To fail to develop either of these, to settle for *ignorance* therefore, is a failing of the sixth chakra, a missing of the mark.

LIVING IN SAFETY VS. DEVELOPING OUR INTUITION

In developing our intuition and creative powers, we do not remain forever in a childlike state. Indeed, there is much about childhood that we have to set aside if we are to learn to connect intelligence and intuition. Clarissa Pinkola Estés points this out when she summons people to "be the keepers of the creative fire" by using "all our senses to wring the truth from things, to extract nourishment from ideas, to see what there is to see, know what there is to know."[5] She names several steps along the journey of growing into our intuition, and the first is to "allow the too-good mother to die." The instinctual life cannot come alive if we are in a codependent relationship with an overly protective and hovering mother. Learning to be our own mother means "developing one's own consciousness about anger, intrigue, politic. Becoming alert by oneself, for oneself. Letting die what must die. As the too-good mother dies, the new woman is born."[6]

The developing intuition has to question those "long-held tenets which make life too safe, which overprotect, which make women walk with a scurry instead of a stride."[7] Perhaps the metaphor of "Mother Church," which often overprotects and overscolds while itself underperforms, ought to be included among those mothers that one must move beyond in order that spiritual maturity might happen. New

mothers beckon us with risks and with goals worthy of risks. As Estés
puts it, the new mother is not just loving but also "fierce and demanding." We must move on—"we are off the teat and learning to hunt."[8]

A second and third step in coming into our creativity and intuition
that Estés names is going into the darkness to perceive "the cruelty
whirling around us—be it within our psyches or without in the culture." It is about moving from being nice to being knowing.[9] Learn to
navigate in that darkness and to feed intuition there. This is done especially by listening to the intuition—"one feeds it life by listening to it"
and acting on its advice.[10]

We often feel before we see, and good listening pays attention to
this reality. The fourth task is one of learning to "face great power—in
others, and subsequently one's own power." We move from a "lifeless
life" that neglects intuition and puts the light of the psyche out, to one
of respect—"respect in the face of great power is a crucial lesson."[11]
Power has a habit of rubbing off on others. The experience makes one
strong—but in what sense? "To be strong does not mean to sprout muscles and flex. It means meeting one's own numinosity without fleeing,
actively living with the wild nature in one's own way. It means to be
able to learn, to be able to stand what we know. It means to stand and
live."[12]

A strength is required of all creativity—strength not only to
endure labor pains and give birth but to undergo criticism from those
threatened by what is new. It is the strength, as Otto Rank points out,
to endure the inner guilt that is often internalized from *artistes manqués,*
of which there are so many in our society, with its underdeveloped sixth
chakra (among others).

Still another task that Estés insists is necessary for awakening the
intuitive is what she calls "serving the nonrational." We must make
room for contemplation in our lives, cleansing ourselves so as to get in
touch with our deepest values again and prepare to put ourselves at the
service of something or someone great. There we learn "not to cringe
away from the big, the mighty, the cyclical, the unforeseen, the unex-
pected, the vast and grand scale which is the size of nature, the odd, the
strange, and the unusual."[13] The artist entertains diversity and does not
run from it. Our imagination is fed by what we have not previously seen,
what is too large or too interesting for us to control. It takes us beyond

the rational. There we learn important lessons, such as to cleanse our thinking, renew our values, sweep the self, and clean up our thinking and feeling states on a regular basis. It is kind of a retreat mode to which we are invited. I think it has a lot to do with solitude. The artist in us must learn to be at home with solitude, not running from aloneness by busyness, noisiness, or even constant companionship.

RATIONALISM

Paul Ricoeur observes that "one lives only that which one imagines."[14] Does this mean that if we stifle our imagination, we stifle our living? Rationalism by definition stifles the imagination. It kills alternatives. It is one-sidedness in the mind. Rank believes that rationalism is what killed the Roman Empire and that it is the number-one plague of the twentieth century. Instead of an emphasis on the "dynamic forces governing life and human behaviour," our rationalistic psychology serves only to increase "the power of irrational forces operating in modern life." In other words, too much of the rational makes us crazy. It dehumanizes us. It drives us to war for the silliest ideological reasons.[15]

Life itself, after all, is not rational. It is the ultimate marvel of the more-than-rational. Certainly the modern era, with its dependency on the Cartesian philosophical model of "clear and distinct ideas" and the quantitative methods of science, ignored feeling and intuition. It preferred obedience to creativity. In an era of computers and microchips, this rationalism easily translates into *faceless and fleshless statistics* that encourage greed and exploitation of people and earthlings while creating pseudo-ecstasies of money and power and other abstractions.

The sixth chakra has the potential to *melt these idols down* into real life once again. When we accept ideologies and abstractions as rational, we invite deep pathology, as Rank points out. "While natural forces operating in the human being have been stigmatized as irrational because they seem uncontrollable," we have learned to accept "certain powerful ideologies which have been accepted or interpreted as purely rational, when in reality they are emotional."[16] Behind much rationalism lies ideology and uncritiqued emotionalism. Body counts are a good example. So too is excessive flag-waving and money-making at the expense of the "body counts" of trees that die and ozone that is punctured and species that go extinct and prisoners that overcrowd our prisons and children who languish in front of television.

Mathematics professor and chaos theorist Ralph Abraham warns of the need to implement in our lives the new grasp of chaos in the universe. He warns:

> Our passion for order and control is throttling the life out of Nature.... In the Chaos Revolution of the sciences, we are now learning that chaos is essential to the survival of life. For example, the healthy heartbeat is more chaotic than the diseased heartbeat, and the normal brain is more chaotic than the dysfunctional brain. ... Our challenge now is to restore goodness to chaos and disorder to a degree, and to reestablish the partnership of Cosmos and Chaos, so necessary to nature, to health, and to creation.[17]

Behind much rationalism is a quest for control. Rationalism is part of a strategy in psychic and social control. Theologian Dominic Crossan comments on the supposed "value-freeness" of 19th century rationalism when he writes: "The way in which the nineteenth century dreamed of uncommitted, objective, dispassionate historical study should be clearly seen for what it was—a methodological screen to cover various forms of social power and imperialistic control."[18]

David Korten warns that the next frontier for colonization by transnational corporations is the mind itself, what we are calling the sixth chakra. Corporations including Pizza Hut, Taco Bell and Coca-Cola are getting their junk food into our school lunch programs and 20 million U.S. schoolchildren used some form of corporate-sponsored teaching materials in their classrooms in 1990. A vice president of Scholastic, Inc., wrote that corporations must find ways to "build share of mind and market into the 21st century" and challenged executives to "devise promotions that take students from the aisles in school rooms to the aisles in supermarkets" and to build "brand and product loyalties through classroom-centered" activities.[19]

The mass media have the wherewithal to enter our sixth chakras and imaginations with the highly sophisticated art form we call advertising. Resistance is required.

KNOWLEDGE AT THE EXPENSE OF WISDOM

Wisdom is the great accomplishment of the sixth chakra—finding a balance between intellect and intuition and giving birth to new truths. A distorted sixth chakra settles for knowledge over wisdom; it dispenses with wisdom altogether, leaving aside the important lower chakra work that culminates in the heart. Wisdom is knowledge and awareness of the heart and of connections to the cosmos (the fourth and first chakras respectively). Wisdom is never anthropocentric; she sits on a throne ruling *the universe* with justice and compassion *for the poor.* She "encircled the vaults of the sky" and she "walked on the bottom of the deeps" (Sirach 24:5,8). She knows eros, for she *plays* with God before the creation of the world—"ever at play in the Divine presence, at play everywhere in the world" (Proverbs 8:30,31). Invariably she is pictured as female and often with a Divine son in her lap, as in the ancient tradition of the goddess Isis and the Black Madonna—a tradition that gave birth in the Middle Ages to the very name *cathedral,* which meant a throne where the goddess sits (her name in the West being Mary) bringing peace and harmony to the central city. As Erich Neumann put it: "It is no accident that the greatest Mother Goddess of the early cults was named Isis, 'the seat,' 'the throne,' the symbol of which she bears on her head."[20] How telling that patriarchy distorted the meaning of *throne* in the cathedral and reduced it to a male bishop's seat. Our ancestors knew better: It was the goddess sitting on her throne. It was a promise of eros and compassion ruling the city.

Patriarchy distorts wisdom and settles for knowledge exclusively. Much of current-day educational philosophy and practice is still committed to knowledge at the expense of wisdom. Wisdom requires art to teach and learn because art is the proper language of heartfelt truth and the truths of the lower chakras, such as moral outrage and cosmic connection and erotic love and passion for justice.[21]

Emerson in the nineteenth century and James Hillman in our times raise the question of "intuition versus tuition."[22] Are academia and organized education capable of and willing to train our intuition and not just the informational sides of our mind? Must "tuition" or formal education succumb to knowledge-only learning? Is wisdom possible within our "universities"? Can "universe" be returned to the university? Is the first chakra possible there? I believe that one can blend tuition and intuition, but it takes a conscious effort to do so. For starters, one must bring the previous five chakras back to education. One must bring the universe back and the body back. All this we are trying to do in our new University of Creation Spirituality.

PESSIMISM BORN OF DESPAIR

The alternative to awakening our intuition and creativity in the sixth chakra is spreading still more pessimism into the world. The traditional sin of the spirit that most corresponds to the sixth chakra is that of *despair* or *pessimism*. Rabbi Schimmel makes the point that "because we are accustomed to view depression from a medical rather than a moral or spiritual perspective, we may not even recognize the spiritual roots of our despair."[23] Hildegard pictured Despair and Bountifulness in dialogue with each other. Despair says: "What else is left for me, unless death? I do not rejoice in any good things nor find any consolation in sins; I do not find any good in other creatures."[24] Bountifulness responds: "You do not want to respond to God or his precepts, but you instead want to stay bitter. But I am bountiful in rain and dew and in ointment and medicine so that I bring about pleasant things in the rain, joy in the dew, mercy in the ointment, and consolation for all sorrows in the medicine."[25] Bitterness, Hildegard observed, accompanies despair: "Bitterness does not desire any joy out of life, but only embraces sorrowful work that does not embrace God."[26]

Despair permeates our culture. Pessimism wafts over our patriarchal and war-oriented civilization like a cloud of poisonous radiation. We all breathe it daily. Its toxins begin in the first chakra, where awe and wonder can be lost or at least stifled. But it reaches a certain climax in the sixth chakra, because creativity is the energy force with which we have to wash ourselves of despair and pessimism.

When Rank says pessimism comes from "a repression of creativity," he might also be saying that pessimism comes from a repression of the sixth chakra. People who are out of touch with their creativity are set up for pessimism. Their hope is blighted; no light feeds it. They must live in the dark.

Aquinas warned that despair is more dangerous than sins against faith or love, because when despair takes over a person or a culture, there are no limits to rein in their excess wickedness. Nothing is more dangerous than "to teach despair," he warned.[27] We live in a pessimistic and even cynical time, in what Rank has called a "morbid civilization,"[28] one that prefers thanatos to eros, love of death to love of life. At a time like ours, adults and those with power must bend over backward *not to teach despair.* Unfortunately, rationalism and reductionism are contributing to passing on despair and not instilling hope.

A new school of biology, for example, is preaching an old and familiar sermon of original sin, only blaming it on our original genes, which they call "selfish genes." The anthropomorphism (and projection?) of this phrase hardly sounds "scientific" to me. But suppose we have inherited "selfish genes" from our ancestors, including early primates and others—have we not also inherited generous genes and even compassionate ones? Must we dig up yet another version of Augustine's original sin ideology with which to scare the next generation? Can we at least learn about original blessing and teach that also? And our Divine capacities for creativity and compassion? And mysticism? Is it not possible that we inherit *both* "seeds" of violence *and* "seeds" of Divinity, as mystics like Meister Eckhart, Thich Nhat Hanh, and the author of the Letter of Peter teach?

In Lyall Watson's *Dark Nature: A Natural History of Evil,* the author, who lacks a cosmology expresses no gratitude or reverence for what the universe has accomplished on behalf of life, including human life. He exhibits only a kind of mass media "gotcha" mentality when he lists harrowing examples of animals hurting other animals. Yet terror-filled or not, the unfolding of life on this planet was and is obviously an amazing and beautiful accomplishment, and at least at times, order does reign among the chaos. What architect Charles Jencks calls the "jumping universe" is the profound surprises that the universe has birthed over its multibillion-year story. Watson expresses no wonder. His only context is planetary, yet our entire planetary life-system depends on the sun and the aeons of time and the fabric of space that is our authentic home. At this time in our history, we cannot afford such a déjà vu, typically male attitude of pessimism. We need what is possible, not what is impossible, to move us—and even to save us. To teach despair is indeed dangerous.

All the chakras I have considered, if properly engaged in, point the way to healthy and life-giving and erotic living. The sixth chakra *inherits* this power and is a certain gathering point wherein all our learning and all our intuition come together to create something new: hope for a pessimistic world; birth for a dying world; love for a hateful world; and creativity for a boring world of bored souls. Cosmology, feminism, courage, love, prophetic speaking-out—all feed our creativity and are in turn fed by it.

Significantly, the first three chakras are the more *inner* chakras in the sense that they take in and build up inner habits of living deeply in the world. But the fifth, sixth, and seventh chakras are in many ways the *outgoing* chakras—they take our heart-energy and soul-learnings into the world. Into the fourth chakra the lower chakras bank their graces, and from it the higher chakras derive their graces to bestow upon the world. The upper chakras are more community-oriented in the sense that they are outgoing. One might say that the lower chakras are more introverted and the upper more extroverted. The weaknesses of the extroverted chakras are exposed if we ignore the inner work of the introverted chakras, while the introverted go into their weak side if we do not reach out to the community at large. Once again, the heart chakra, the middle chakra, seems key: Can it harness introvert-energy "from below" and extend it "outside" to the community at large? Can it harness extrovert-energy "from above" and infuse the lower chakras with it?

REDUCTIONISM: A KIND OF BLINDNESS

Rationalism and one-sidedness of the brain easily lead to reductionism. When we are reductionistic, we lessen diversity, we diminish greatness, and we decrease the complexity of what is to a morsel of its authentic scope. Settling for reductionism is like putting blinders on our eyes. We do not see well. In fact, the inner eye goes dormant; we go blind, just as in the first chakra we go deaf when we refuse to listen.

Aquinas said that pessimism comes from a "contraction of the mind." So rich are our imaginations that we are capable even of shrinking and contracting our own minds by putting blinders on them. If we choose, we can constrict this vastness and bind it, just as certain Chinese customs of old bound the feet of girls so they would remain tiny (in the process distorting the bone structure of these women's feet). Dogmas (as opposed to doctrines or agreed-on basic teachings) are a kind of binding and constriction and reductionism that pepper the history of both religion and warfare in the West. Today's fundamentalist sects continue in this tradition of contracting and shrinking of the mind.

A year ago a fundamentalist interviewed on British television was confronted with a dinosaur egg that was carbon-dated to 60 million years ago. How did he reconcile this with his dogma that the earth is six thousand years old? "God created that egg to test my faith," he replied. On American radio recently a fundamentalist insisted the world is six thousand years old; he was debating another to whom it had been revealed that it is two thousand years old (which, by the way, leaves the Hebrew Bible—which was put together beginning about 2,500 years ago—out in the cold before creation itself).

Dogmatism and the reductionism that goes with it are by no means restricted to religion. Science has itself been involved in dogmas and attitudes that have restricted our capacities to feel, experience, sense, know, perceive, savor, observe, taste, and enjoy.

If, as Theodore Roszak tells us, mysticism was anathema in the Age of Enlightenment, then the right hemisphere of our brain was practically closed down. Without a marriage of left and right hemispheres, no balanced creativity can emerge. Academia institutionalized this scientific prejudice and reductionism, robbing so many more people of their sense of awe, wonder, playfulness, and eros. The corporate and military and governmental power brokers to which academia often and regularly sold its soul also did little to develop the latent side of our minds. If they gave birth to anything, it was seldom to spiritually balanced beings. Whenever mysticism is ignored, reductionism is the result.

When greed and avarice feed into the sixth chakra, a kind of economic reductionism takes over. We use our great capacity for creativity not to struggle for justice or to celebrate but to make money. The idols that greed brings in its wake are often very trivial. The powers of avarice married to the powers of creativity do not build up community but steal it.

ANTI-ANGEL BIASES

Another example of reductionism during the machine era has been the ignoring of angelic spirits. A machine cosmology left as little room for angels as it did for artists, children, or mystics. Who needed angels if the universe happened all by chance, and was lonely and desperate, and lacked shared ideas and shared love, and we humans were the only intelligences in the universe? Modern theologians abandoned angels just as swiftly as did scientists, only with an added dimension of guilt and shame.

But today even scientists are talking about angels, as I know from having written a book with British scientist Rupert Sheldrake called *The Physics of Angels*. His ideas stretch the mind—for example, the sun, which is more complex than the human brain, might be an angel or be watched over by angels, since it is part of teachings on angels that angels and intelligences go together.[29] The courage of scientists like Sheldrake is impressive—he is allowing a fuller discourse and larger questions back into scientific dogma. He has taken many hits for it—one scientific journal said that his books should be burned (a page from religious history, no doubt, and a bit of an eye-opener to those of us who were led to believe that science is "value-free" and scientists are emotionless. To desire to burn others' books seems quite an emotional desire indeed.).

The return of angels to public and scientific and even academic discourse is a sign that reductionism might itself become less constricted. And that may make room for more joy and hope. Sheldrake invokes the memory of Alfred Russel Wallace, who copublished the theory of evolution with Darwin but who chose a divergent path. The "gloomy materialism" of Darwin held that all evolution happened by chance and lacked any meaning or purpose. "By contrast, Wallace came to the conclusion that evolution involved more than natural selection and was guided by creative intelligences, which he identified with angels."[30] Maybe the angels, with their optimism, can make up for the gloom that reductionistic scientists and theologians have brought to our culture. One of the positive features of the recent Mars landing was how joyful and childlike and (dare I use the word?) mystical the scientists at NASA were as they walked us through the Rover's doings on Mars. It seemed as if a new generation of scientists had actually brought their *heart chakras to their work.* Bravo!

Aquinas taught that angels have a special gift for *intuition*—indeed, they learn only from intuition. (They don't have to go to school, get degrees, or study.) Thus they are especially attuned to issues of intuition, including the work of artists. This insight may help to explain why so many artists paint angels or work with them in music they compose or listen to, or experience them in the act of writing. Angels travel on the highway of intuition, and artists and others who also travel that highway will no doubt encounter some angels on their way. Why not? Very often the high point of the creative process happens to the artist when she loses a sense of place and time and gets "taken over" by the spirit working through her. No doubt the angels are working there as well.

Indeed, Aquinas taught that angels "carry ideas from prophet to prophet." If we are in tune with our fifth or prophetic chakra, the angels will carry things beyond to the sixth. The sixth chakra is a special doorway through which angels enter our imaginations and intuitions. (The seventh chakra, as we shall see, is a special doorway where we reach out to the angels.) If it is true that angels play a special role in intuition, then to repress angelic awareness is to stifle intuition as well. The modern era smothered both angels and intuition.

SUPERSTITION AND ANTI-INTELLECTUALISM

Another instance of misdirected love in the sixth chakra is the opposite of rationalism: the denigration and neglect of the rational or intellectual. Superstition and anti-intellectualism ignore the analytical side of our brains. We are not creative without an intellectual life of some kind. Ideas count. Logic has its place. For centuries a kind of putrid preoccupation with the unreal and the fabulous dominated Western religion, and witch burnings and other atrocities followed. Indeed, the very rationalism of modern science was in many ways a response to the excess of flights of imagination that were undertaken at the expense of intelligent observation, often in the name of religion.

Religion, then, is not without blame for the rationalism and even some of the reductionism of modern science. It was religious leaders and churchmen, after all, who refused to look into Galileo's telescope and took the easy way out of condemning him instead. Control was the name of the game then, too, but it was the control that self-willed ignorance brings and fear of learning something new about the universe. The sixth chakra requires a balance of intelligence *and* intuition. It is not easy to come by; it takes some spiritual practice to hold that kind of equilibrium, a spiritual maturity that in turn depends on five healthy chakras supporting the sixth.

TECHNOLOGY

Technology is the use of the amazing human mind and imagination to solve problems and give birth to possibilities. Technology is as old as the oldest ax chopped from stone, the flint that gave birth to the first fire, the first paints with which our ancestors depicted animals on the walls of wet caves, the boomerang or the pot or the potter's wheel or the woof or needle and thread. Technology itself is not evil—in fact, its potential for helping us to survive is not only awesome but often beautiful and salutary. I marvel at bridges and those who make them; at airplanes and those who conceive them; at the Rover on Mars and the pictures it sent us so many millions of miles away. Technology in itself is part of the *doxa* and glory of our species. It is a sixth chakra accomplishment because it is the work of the creative mind, the coming-together of intellect and ingenuity.

But since technology was born in a moral vacuum and a reductionistic ethic, its power is profoundly dangerous. Goethe's *Faust* is an apt story of the unleashing of that one-sided power. Prometheus is a more ancient metaphor for the same unleashing. Much of technology today is driven by reductionistic and rationalistic motives, whether of the money-making or nation-conquering or ego-tripping or people-hating kind. When technology has not passed through the healthy and balanced work of the other five chakras, it is dangerous indeed. By the time it arrives at the sixth chakra, it is a weapon for the use of forces of hate and destruction. And that, in this century, has more often than not been the case.

WAR

War is many things. It is technology put to the service of hate. It is universities and politicians and media propagandists teaming up with the military. It is invariably an advancing of an ideology, such as nationalism or racism (which relates it to the first chakra). It displays a one-sidedness that is often very patriarchal. Mothers are trained to want to send their sons to war to kill and be killed, maim and be maimed, for the glory of the native land or the reigning ideology. War is also very adultist—older men send younger men to war, holding it up as a rite of passage and an adventure that appeals to the spirits of youth, especially in a culture that offers them no rites of passage or true adventures by which to test their spirits. In this way war is second chakra fodder. It embraces the third chakra because it is about power-against-power and victor-over-vanquished. It works out of the fourth chakra because if it is at all justified, it is about rescuing the oppressed and therefore about compassion; if it is unjustified, it is about carrying hate and revenge and recrimination and resentment to their logical conclusion (kill the enemy). War involves the fifth chakra because no one can deny that propaganda and preaching to get people aroused is part and parcel of a successful war effort. In the twelfth century Bernard of Clairvaux played this dubious role in the crusades, of which he was the first propagandist.

The sixth chakra offers a special home for war, however, a home where all these negative energies from previous chakras can gather and circle like ravenous wolves seeking to devour their prey. Why is the sixth chakra so key to a successful war effort? Because the sixth chakra is about creativity and intuition. Wars are fought and won by creativity and intuition and hunches; they are a kind of art form—bloody, but arty nonetheless. We talk about the "genius" of Napoleon or of Alexander the Great, and from a strictly goal-oriented value system, their achievements cannot be denied. In addition, much genius and creativity go into the ingenious weapons of war—Leonardo da Vinci invented helicopters and the equivalent of machine guns. The atomic bomb, the nuclear bomb, the nuclear submarine, radar, sonar, all inventions of this century—while horrible to behold—are, from a reductionistic perspective, amazing things for us to have birthed.

When war is not tempered by heart and mind and wisdom, however, it becomes what it has become in this century: a monument to the cruelty of which humans are capable when we operate out of our one-sidedness, a monument to evil working its way through the human imagination. War is the sixth chakra without the right brain or the middle eye. It is raw power, raw creative power, unleashed on "the enemy." War bypasses the healthy side of the chakras; it mows them over as a tank mows over peasants in their fields. Cosmology, feminism, empowerment of the powerless, compassion, truth-telling, creativity on behalf of compassion—these dimensions to our existence have no chance under the onslaught of technological warfare.

The wars of our century have not just been fought against humans—it would be anthropocentric even to think they had. We are currently making war against the soil and the ozone, the forests and the waters, the other species and our children yet unborn. We have unleashed technological warfare of untested chemicals on the soil, into the rivers, over the plants, and into the bloodstreams of living animals, which we then take into ourselves. Like any war, these wars are ideological—they derive from uncritically accepted dogmas such as the one that says humans can do anything to anybody as long as they make money and don't get caught.

SADISM AND CRUELTY

Sadism is a misuse of imagination; it is using our imagination to torture others and to take pleasure in watching others in pain. Sadism is a distortion of the sixth chakra, an energy center that is dedicated to creativity and imagination—but creativity meant to be put to the use of compassion, not destruction. Judith Shklar, in *Ordinary Vices,* considers cruelty the worst evil and defines it as the "willful inflicting of physical pain on a weaker being in order to cause anguish or fear."[31] She feels it should be first on the list of deadly sins. Cruelty and its patent misuse of the power of creativity needs all the ingenuity of the other chakras to work. Like some of the others sins, such as consumerism, cruelty did not make it onto the monastic agenda developed in the Egyptian desert by hermit monks.[32]

War unleashes the worst side of humanity's energies. Consider Pol Pot and his Khmer Rouge, who turned the fields of Cambodia red with the blood of his countrymen and women and children. He and his followers killed 1.7 million people—one-quarter of the population—in the "killing fields." These killings were sadistic. Pol Pot's methods included slow death by starvation, overwork, disease, torture, and execution. The institutionalized brutality of the sadist in war atrocities is not about playing with the enemy but gloating over his or her suffering. It is difficult to imagine any action more opposed to compassion.

The sadism of the Nazi tormentors and executioners, of the Stalinist brigades, of the Bosnian murderers and rapists and torturers, and of those among warring African tribes and slaveowners and Indian haters—all this sad history tells us something of the *power of the sixth chakra* gone awry. (The sixth chakra could not succumb to this abuse were it not fed by the hatred and anger and close-mindedness derived from the other chakras, also off center and unbalanced.)

The sadist is always in control. The sadist does not see the eyes of the other, much less the Divine light that enters his own third eye. The sadist is too much in control to let light in from the outside. The sadist truly lives in the dark.

OFFSPRING OF MISDIRECTED LOVE IN THE SIXTH CHAKRA: A SUMMARY

The tradition of the seven capital sins has no direct parallel to the sins of reductionism and rationalism that I name in this chapter, and thus there are no traditional "offspring" to enumerate. The rational did not dominate the monastic communities of the Egyptian desert or southern France sixteen hundred years ago. Superstition may have played a role there, but it is unlikely that rationalism did, and if it did, it was probably named as part of the sin of pride. The pessimism named in this chapter, however, does correspond to the sin of the spirit that Aquinas names as despair.

The offspring of the powers of misdirected love that I name in the sixth chakra include omission of creativity, suppression of the prophetic, injustice and ignorance, living in safety and refusing to develop intuition, rationalism, knowledge at the expense of wisdom, pessimism born of despair, reductionism as a kind of blindness, a bias against the angels (and therefore intuition and other spirits), superstition and anti-intellectualism, technology serving misdirected powers of the other chakras, war, sadism and cruelty.

MARRIAGE, THE SACRAMENT OF THE SIXTH CHAKRA

Among the traditional seven sacraments, marriage most corresponds to the sixth chakra. Of course, the second chakra is also about union and communion and sexuality, but marriage, as opposed to sexual union itself, has a broader community scope. In marriage people often choose to have children. In marriage people manifest a relationship that the whole community can bless and endorse and support. In marriage offspring learn the ways of living in the world and of contributing fully and imaginatively to the larger community.

The marriage of the sixth chakra is the marriage of right and left brain hemispheres, the union of intellect and intuition, of inner and outer into a third eye, a new realization of the in-depth illumination of things. In the sixth chakra the dualisms cease and the inner becomes the outer. This holy union births ideas and movements, truths and art forms that will go into the world and bless it. It is a union "until death do us part," but it is not a static union. Creativity is never static; it may get one up often in the middle of the night; it may drive one to do unparalleled and daring things; it may disturb the peace. But it is never static. Both parts of the brain—intellect and visionary—need to be fed and nourished in this union. Sharing is what keeps the relationship going—sharing of time, space, meals, ideas, feelings, fears, dreams.

SPIRITUAL EXERCISES APROPOS OF THE SIXTH CHAKRA

1. Listen to your intellect. Find an idea there. Now sing the idea or paint it or dance it or render it into poetry.

2. Take a picture or a photo or a painting or a poem or a letter or a paragraph that you have written. Analyze it for the ideas that are there. Share them with others. Notice how the sharing deepens the ideas.

3. In what ways are you prophetic? Have you used imagination lately to express your prophetic contribution to your community?

4. Do you prefer to live in safety or to trust your intuition and build it up? Have you left the "too secure mother" of your family? of your religion? of your government? What was that leave-taking like? How difficult was it? How did you accomplish it? Share these questions and stories with others.

5. Give an example of "head trips" or rationalism that you have encountered in your life. Why would Otto Rank say that rationalism killed the Roman Empire? How do you see it affecting our civilization as regards (a) the media, or (b) the economic system, or (c) the education system?

6. What things make you pessimistic? What do you do when pessimism strikes? What new things have you learned to do as a result of this book on the chakras?

7. Give examples of the teaching of despair going on in our culture at this time. What can we do about it?

8. Give examples of superstition or anti-intellectualism that you have witnessed in your life. What can we do about this?

9. How is reductionism a kind of blindness? Are we all born blind? What are you doing to open the eyes of one another? to open your third eye?

10. Have you experienced angels at any time in your life? Do you know others who have? What is the relation of your experience of the creative process and the experience of spirit in your life?

11. Have you ever met angels on the highway of intuition? Explain the encounter. What did you learn from it?

12. List the good things technology brings to you. Then list the destructive things it does to us. Weigh the two. How can we bring them more in line?

13. Discuss war as a destructive but creative act. What war stories

can you tell or do you recall from others who were in war? What do you learn from these stories?

14. What examples of sadism and cruelty do you see in today's world? How can you contribute to healing this attitude of control and domination? Is play a solution to sadism? What is the relation between sadism and war?

15. Mary is a wisdom figure and a goddess figure in the West. Meditate on these images of Mary taken from the traditional litany in her name, and respond with dance or song, poetry or painting, discussion or journal keeping to what moves you. "Mother of God, Mother of Christ, Mother of Divine grace, Mother most amiable, Mother most admirable, Mother of good counsel, Mother of our Creator, Mother of Our Savior, Mirror of justice, Seat of wisdom, Cause of our joy, Spiritual vessel, Vessel of honor, Singular vessel of devotion, Mystical rose, Tower of David, Tower of ivory, House of gold, Ark of the covenant, Gate of heaven, Morning star, Health of the sick, Refuge of sinners, Comforter of the afflicted, Queen of angels, Queen of patriarchs, Queen of prophets, Queen of martyrs, Queen of peace."

CHAPTER 14

MISDIRECTED LOVE
IN THE SEVENTH CHAKRA:
ENVY AND RESENTMENT

The seventh chakra is about directing our love to the outside world, to building community. It is a kind of *culmination point*. It takes all the heat and light and warmth and energy awakened in the previous six chakras to the great community that lies beyond—the community of all light beings. This energy in turn recycles back to the first chakra and begins anew. The seventh chakra is about linking up with and affiliating with others and building community. But envy ruins all that. Envy is the distortion of the seventh chakra and the misuse and misdirection of its love energy. There is something supreme and culminating about envy if it truly takes over our soul. Writer Angus Wilson claims that envy "wears an uglier face than lust's bloodshot eyes, or gluttony's paunch, or pride's camel nose, or avarice's thin lips."[1]

ENVY AS COMPETITION

Competition that resides deep in the heart of individuals or movements may be the opposite of community. Envy is a damaged relationship; it sees the other as a problem, as an obstacle, as competition. Instead of cooperation flowing from community, envy gives rise to estrangement and antagonism, rivalry and contention, strife and opposition. Instead of striving for unity and a common effort, we have jealousy, spite, morbid suspicions; instead of shared trust that grows, we have insecurity, distrust, mistrust, ill will, and malice. Instead of care and shared compassion, we have possessiveness, resentfulness, contesting, covetousness, hostility, and obstruction. Patriarchy, by zeroing in on dualism and strife, often breeds competition and with it envy. The amount of envy that wafts around the corridors of patriarchal power should never be underestimated.

ENVY AS THE REFUSAL TO PRAISE

Meister Eckhart offers an amazingly simple but usable test of goodness when he says: "A good person is one who praises good people." Praise is what we are about on this earth—it is how community happens. "Praising is what matters!" shouts the poet Rilke.[2] Rilke also warns of the relation between doing praise and doing justice when he says: "We do justice only where we praise."[3] Competition and a competitive attitude of shooting down the goodness in others thwart our capacities for praise. Injustice and indifference to injustice thwart praise. Praise might be called the opposite of envy: Both praising people and envious people recognize the good in others. But one appreciates it enough to honor it; the other wants to do it in. So much of community building and community making is about praising and allowing persons to recognize their beauty.

We are called to praise not just human goodness but all goodness, as we saw in chapters one to three. This is how we create "kinship" with the scents and juices of the earth.[4]

ENVY AS ANTI-ECUMENICAL

In our discussion of the seventh chakra in Part I, we talked about ecumenism as a reaching-out for unity among groups that seem to differ. But the energies that envy arouses make it very different from ecumenism: envy scores much during anti-ecumenical times. How much religious antagonism and war in the past four hundred years, for example, has been due to envy? Deep Ecumenism is a search for the light, glory, radiance, wisdom, and Christ or Buddha nature in other people and religions and races and ethnic traditions; one does not abandon one's own roots but deepens them in the process. This process cannot happen where envy holds sway.

Envy is the opposite of ecumenism; it is anti-ecumenical. Bishop William Swing, the Episcopal bishop of California, has recently started a movement to bring world religions together under an umbrella called United Religions, mirroring the United Nations. So far, in its initial stages, he is receiving much support from a great variety of religious people. Interestingly, however, the Vatican has not responded favorably. Might some envy be afoot in the Vatican? It would not be the first time in its rather checkered history. Envy is indeed a powerful force both personally and socially—it is almost as powerful as love itself, and like anger, it derives from love, since all the effects of the soul derive from love.

ENVY: SORROW THAT LEADS TO HATRED

What then is envy? It has been defined as "sorrow over another's good insofar as it impedes one's own excellence." Aquinas said, "Envy is felt when someone is sorry that his neighbor possesses good things which he does not have."[5] When we feel this sorrow at others' blessings, we can end up refusing to contribute to them or even hating them. Envy gives birth to hatred because an envious person does not stop with jealousy; it can lead to harming the other or wishing them harm.

In the sixth chakra we considered the role of pessimism and sadness when creativity is missing. A damaged sixth chakra sets us up for a damaged seventh chakra. A distorted first chakra is about sadness too—acedia is sadness at the divine goodness or at life itself. But envy's sadness is more anthropocentric—it is directed toward one's neighbor's goodness. Obviously, they feed each other. An ill-directed or unattended first chakra, one where sadness is not healed by some cosmic joy, will contaminate the seventh chakra as well.

RESENTMENT

Envy is born of hurt and hatred and injustice. It is all the more reason why societies must pay attention to injustice early, for without justice visible and active, the human heart will settle for resentment. Envy breeds resentment, and resentment can lead to war and hatred, scapegoating and projection. Resentment *provokes* people and tribes and nations and groups to anger, bitterness, rancor, ill will, indignation, ire, rage, animosity, fury, wrath, vengeance, hostility, antagonism, and revenge. We saw this in Bosnia; we have seen it with Cardinal Ratzinger in the Vatican and with his countrymen a generation ago in Nazi Germany. Like a cancer, resentment festers and grows, often hidden under wraps, until one day it explodes into the light of day. Many a killer has operated out of resentment, and perhaps the king of them all was Hitler.

WHEN ENVY CONNECTS TO EVIL SPIRITS OR DEMONS IN THE SEVENTH CHAKRA

The seventh chakra is about *connecting* to the "outside world." It is an outreach to the angels, our light encountering their light, light meeting light, *doxa* ("glory and radiance") meeting *doxa*. But when the chakra system is thoroughly misdirected and unbalanced, light does not meet light; rather, darkness meets darkness, gloom meets gloom, spirit meets evil spirit. Traditionally it is said that the devil rides waves of envy. Hildegard of Bingen represented this tradition when she taught that "the devil does all his work out of envy and begrudges men obtaining the highest blessedness."[6]

Envy is in some ways more powerful than hatred, for it feeds hatred and gives birth to it and is more subtle. Hatred tends to be more out in the open; it is as if people are more ashamed of their envy than of their hatred, so they keep it inside, where it rankles and rots, decays and putrefies, all the time seeping bile into the imagination, which works it over and over until it gives birth to shadowy beings that come into existence by way of projections. Traditionally these beings have been called *demons.*

Who, what, is Satan? The role of Satan in the Hebrew Bible is that of adversary. *Satan* is not the name of a particular personage; its meaning in Hebrew is "one who opposes, obstructs, or acts as an adversary." Satan, who plays a very minor role in the Hebrew Bible, is alive and well in the first century, both among the Essenes, who were an ascetic Jewish community of about four thousand men living in the desert, and among the followers of Jesus. Each of these movements saw Satan (or Beelzebub or Belial or Mastema, "hatred") as very important. In the gospels Jesus wrestles between God's spirit and the demons, between God's kingdom and Satan's. According to Elaine Pagels, in her fine study on *The Origin of Satan,* the key issue raised by the image of Satan in both Mark's gospel and Matthew's is

> above all, the issue of human violence. The gospel writers want to locate and identify the specific ways in which the forces of evil act through certain people to effect violent destruction, above all, in Matthew's words, the righteous blood shed on earth, from the blood of innocent Abel to the blood of Zechariah the son of Barachiah (23:35)—violence epitomized in the execution of Jesus, which Matthew sees as the culmination of all evils. The subject of cosmic war serves primarily to interpret human relationship—especially all-too-human conflict—in supernatural form.[7]

Satan in the Jewish tradition is a power that assails not from without *but from within the community*—"not the distant enemy but the intimate enemy—one's trusted colleague, close associate, brother—one who turns unexpectedly jealous and hostile."[8] The worldview of the Essenes placed the cosmic battle between angels and demons at "the very center of their cosmology and politics," according to Pagels.[9]

John's gospel also sees the struggle of Jesus as a supernatural battle between forces of good and evil, and the setting is cosmological. "By the end of the gospel, Jesus' epiphany will have accomplished in human society what God accomplished cosmologically in creation: the separation of light from darkness—that is, of the 'sons of light' from the offspring of darkness and the devil." [10]

In the Book of Revelation the Roman Empire is equated with Satan. At the time the book was written, Christians were being persecuted for refusing to pay homage to that empire. Early Christian theologians like Justin and Origen saw the Christian community as an alternative to the "satanic" powers of the Roman Empire, which, in fact, had executed Origen's father when he was seventeen and left Origen's mother destitute with seven children. "Persecuted Christians like Origen forged a radical tradition that undermined religious sanction for the state, claiming it instead for the religious conscience," Pagels notes. [11]

In the tradition of Satan, the seventh chakra thus plays a prominent role. The issue is community versus destruction of community. The conflict includes cosmological powers of light warring with powers of darkness; envy, hostility, and resentment that lead to violence expressed in "cosmic" warfare of good versus evil; and energy being sent into the larger community (including the prophetic energy of resisting certain values in the human society). As Pagels puts it, "Satan evokes more than the greed, envy, lust, and anger we identify with our own worst impulses, and more than what we call brutality. [He is a] spirit . . . in his frustrated rage he mirrors aspects of our own confrontations with otherness." [12] We might say that Satan sums up all the negative energies of which an unbalanced chakra is capable. It is the culminating force at the pinnacle chakra where, instead of connecting to light beings and benign ones in the universe, we connect to malevolent powers—powers of cosmic nihilism.

All this is summarized in a fashion by the author of the Letter to the Ephesians, who wrote: "Our struggle is not against flesh and blood, but against powers, principalities and the world-rulers of the present darkness, against spiritual forces of evil in heavenly places" (Ephesians 6:12). The powers that be in the heavens and on the earth are the powers against which our awakened energies struggle. Theologian Walter Wink understands the "powers" to stand for "ideologies, the *zeitgeist,* customs, public opinion, peer pressure, institutional expectations, mob psychology, jingoistic patriotism, and negative vibes," which bring about "the quality of alienated existence, the general spiritual climate that influences humanity, in which we live, and move, and lose our beings."[13] These realities are not hosts in the sky but an "atmosphere that envelops people and seals their fate." It is something we breathe, absorb, and drink.[14] *Satan* means the "actual power that congeals around collective idolatry, injustice, or inhumanity, a power that increases or decreases according to the degree of collective refusal to choose higher values."[15] All this is work of the seventh chakra.

CONSUMER SOCIETY AND ADVERTISERS: AROUSERS OF ENVY

We can all participate in evil spirits. The seventh chakra warns us that our powers go into the world to encounter either angels or demons, life or death, creativity or destruction. Through our crown chakra our energy passes *out into the world, out into the universe,* for better or worse.

Today's dominant energy of avarice feeds on envy, resentment, and advertising, which awakens these same activities. British economist E. F. Schumacher warned us, "What is the great bulk of advertising other than the stimulation of greed, envy, and avarice? It cannot be denied that industrialism, certainly in its capitalist form, openly employs these human failings—at least three of the seven deadly sins—as its very motive force."[16] The stimulation of envy lies at the very heart of the "motive force" behind consumerism. The fantasy life that advertising creates for us arouses consumer addictions and connects the misdirected yearnings of the heart (the fourth chakra) to the gluttonous addictions of a misdirected fifth chakra.

As the powerful forces of consumerism, advertising, and the media have increased their influence in our lives, one has to ask: How much has envy also increased? Is consumerism driven by the engine of envy? Isn't envy behind the bulk of the advertising industry? According to David Korten, today's economic system creates an "intense competition between the more powerful and weaker members" of society for a shrinking pool of basic resources.[17] Even while more millionaires and billionaires than ever before are stalking the globe, the numbers of poor and unemployed and those living in impoverished conditions are rising.

As Tom Hayden puts it, we are eliminating welfare as we know it but not poverty as we know it or unemployment as we know it. Soup kitchen sponsors report that their lines are longer than ever and contain more women and children than ever before.[18] This at a time when the stock market is at an "all-time high." High for whom? High for those who need it the most? Or high for those who need it the least? *Business Week* magazine reveals what goes on when raw competition drives the economy: "Modern multinationals are not social institutions. They will play governments off one another, shift pricing to minimize taxes, seek to sway opinion, export jobs, or withhold technology to maintain a competitive edge."[19]

DISCONNECTING FROM THE ANCESTORS: A SIN OF OMISSION

Our ancestors who are *luminaries* are among those light beings with whom we are invited to link up in the seventh chakra. A sin of omission in the seventh chakra is to ignore or be disconnected from our ancestors in the communion of saints. To forget them or ignore them is to fail to make connections; it is a failure in community. And when we fail to establish community and praise those light beings that have preceded us, then we run out of energy and courage ourselves, and we lack the imagination that these spirit beings can pass on to us. The deceased are present in our hearts and prayers as well as literally in our bodies; after all, we carry their DNA and genes within us.

It is not just our ancestors from whom we can choose to disconnect. It may also be our own brothers and sisters. We can also choose to ignore our relationships to those in pain and trouble, as many Christians and others did when they turned their backs on their Jewish brothers and sisters and the sins perpetrated against them by the Nazis. They refused to acknowledge the demonic energies that were coming into culture and society at their behest. James Hillman says they were stuck in a kind of pseudo-innocence that heard nothing, saw nothing, and felt nothing: "The Jews, the Western statesmen, the Intellectuals and democrats, the church, could not see the demonic. . . . We hid in denial and wide-eyed innocence, that openness which also opens wide the gate to the worst. . . . Innocence seems to ask for evil."[20] It is as if we cut off our crown chakras to hide in our chosen cellars of ignorance and denial.

OFFSPRING OF SINS OF THE SEVENTH CHAKRA: A SUMMARY

The tradition names the following "daughters" of the sin of envy: hatred, tale-bearing or gossip, detraction (speaking evil about another in an open way), exulting over another's misfortune, sorrow over another's prosperity.

In this chapter we have considered these offspring of the misdirected love energy of the seventh chakra: envy as competition, envy as anti-ecumenism, envy as sorrow that festers into hatred, resentment, envy and resentment connecting with evil spirits or demons, consumer society and advertising as arousers of envy, and disconnecting from the ancestors, a sin of omission.

ANOINTING THE SICK, THE SACRAMENT APROPOS OF THE SEVENTH CHAKRA

Traditionally the sacrament of anointing the sick was called *extreme unction* because it anointed with oil those who were dying, or in their "extreme" state before passing from this life. Pictures from antiquity abound depicting the soul at death leaving the body through the crown chakra. The seventh chakra is said to unite us to different realms and different worlds, including those of angels and our ancestors. In light of the more recent theology of the sacrament as being a healing sacrament for the sick (and not just for the dying), it has parallels with the seventh chakra insofar as the healing of relationships is important in this chakra. Community itself heals, spreading oils and balms of refreshment for soul and body alike, while envy distances itself and destroys community.

Envy eats a person up from the inside and prepares the way for actions that are violent, hateful, and irreversible. To heal envy would be to put a balm on much that poisons human hearts and relationships, especially when so much of our lives are inundated with advertising and the subsequent arousal of envy and avarice. The sickness that this sacrament heals, then, is not just physical sickness but spiritual sickness—a virus that engenders envy in us. It is a sickness "unto death" in our culture, for it is killing our planet and our children and our own hearts and souls.

Another dimension to this sacrament as traditionally understood is the role of angels and demons at the time of death. As we have seen, demons are indeed encountered in the seventh chakra—or their counterpart, angels. So here too is a parallel between the seventh chakra and the sacrament of anointing the sick. This sacrament steels one for encounters with the foe. It strengthens the heart for struggle. Given the demons of envy, greed, and hatred loose in our culture today, it is never too soon for such spiritual support.

SPIRITUAL EXERCISES APROPOS OF
THE SEVENTH CHAKRA

The following are exercises to withstand the unbalanced forces that gather at the seventh chakra:

1. Regarding anti-ecumenism, what have you done for ecumenism lately? What are you doing to encourage relations between churches, synagogues and mosques with spirituality as their common base?
2. Are you studying the mystics of your own and others' traditions? With what results?
3. What examples of sorrow festering into hatred and resentment do you detect in our culture? Where does it show itself? What can we do to diffuse it?
4. Create a puppet that names Resentment in our time. Create skits with it yourself and then with others. What do you learn?
5. Create rituals that can cleanse us of our various resentments.
6. Do you agree that Hitler was a master at feeding into resentment? Do you sense any politicians in our day feeding on

the same energy? Who and how do they operate? What can you do to interfere? What lessons are to be learned from Hitler?

7. Have you ever encountered evil spirits in your life? Under what circumstances? What can you do about it?

8. Under what circumstances have you encountered angels in your life? How did they assist you or move you to greater love and sense of community?

9. What are you doing or can you do to create community a. where you work? b. where you live? c. where you learn and celebrate?

10. Make a list of advertising claims on television for three evenings or days. How do each of these advertisements either (a) arouse envy and resentment or (b) not do so? What can you do to lessen their arousal of resentment?

11. Are you connected to your luminary ancestors? How or how not? How present to you are these beings? Do you connect with the communion of saints? How can you make these connections more real?

12. Create an altar to honor you ancestors. Pray there daily. How does it affect your courage and your energy?

13. Practice turning envy into emulation. Instead of stewing about another's success, ask yourself: How can I learn from this person's work and success?

14. Practice praise. Each day, find something to praise in the people you live with and the people you work with. Praise them to their face. Learn to accept praise yourself. Hold it in your heart as a gift from the gift-giver of life itself.

7 CAPITAL SINS AND THE CHAKRAS

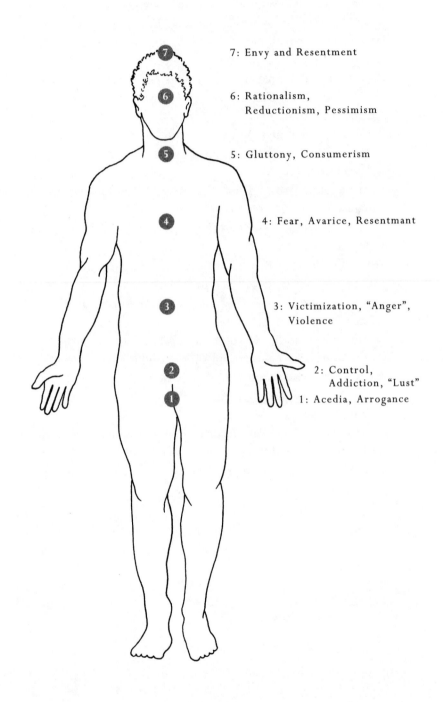

7: Envy and Resentment

6: Rationalism, Reductionism, Pessimism

5: Gluttony, Consumerism

4: Fear, Avarice, Resentmant

3: Victimization, "Anger", Violence

2: Control, Addiction, "Lust"

1: Acedia, Arrogance

OFFSPRING OF THE 7 CAPITAL SINS WITH 7 CHAKRAS

6: Omission of creativity, suppression of the prophetic, injustice and ignorance, living in safety and refusing to develop intuition, rationalism, knowledge at the expense of wisdom, pessimism born of despair, reductionism, kind of blindness, a bias against the angels (and therefore intuition and other spirits), superstition and anti-intellectualism, technology serving misdirected powers of other chakras, war, sadism and cruelty.

4: Self-pity, hatred, resentment, refusal to forgive and let go, betrayal, the blame game, pessimism born of self-hatred, fear, fascism as an institutionalizing of fear and hatred, avarice or greed, hardness of heart.

7: Envy as competition, envy as anti-ecumenism, envy as sorrow that festers into hatred, resentment, envy and resentment connecting with evil spirits or demons, consumer society and advertising as arousers of envy, disconnecting from the ancestors, a sin of omission.

5: Consumerism, shopping as cosmology, excess, addiction and avarice, refusal to give birth through the birth channel of the throat, gagging and concealing, lying and hypocrisy, taking speech for granted, the gagging of others and taking away their voice, adultism and the gagging of the young, advertising as invasion.

3: Bitterness and passive-aggressive behavior, resistance to spiritual warriorhood, victimhood, surrendering our power, self-destruction, violence and destruction, pursuit of unhealthy power, adultism, insecurity.

2: Control, objectifying the other, patriarchy, addiction, one-sidedness, dualism, imbalance, barrenness, sentimentalism, humorlessness, homophobia, institutional desire, pride and disobedience, sadomasochism, and corporate violence.

1: Couchpotatoitis, despair, boredom, cosmic loneliness, restlessness of spirit, disobedience understood as not listening, trivia, autism and the refusal to listen, arrogance, racism, anthropocentrism, denominationalism, idolatry, pusillanimity, injustice, lack of healthy curiosity and ambition, ecocide, sins of omission, ignorance, vainglory, anthropocentrism, domesticating the wild, television's trivializing and colonizing, media titillation, denial, ingratitude, sadness, sloth, wasting waste.

CONCLUSION:

THE BLESSINGS OF FLESH *AND* SPIRIT

AND THE LAUNCHING OF A MORAL WAVE

FOR OUR FUTURE

> If we were to weigh all the living things on earth, humans
> would constitute by weight only one one-millionth of the
> total biomass. We are so *tiny a part* of what is going on
> here on earth (and within it). Yet do we account for only
> one one-millionth of the destruction?

Therein lies the issue in this book: How can one species—our own—
do so much destruction? How can we slow the havoc we are wreaking?
Are there ways to move "beyond sin"? Our species is "in the middle"
between the macro beings and the micro beings. Given our profound
powers of creativity, which can be *misused* for destructive purposes,
we have a serious responsibility. What can we do about our direst tendencies?

The modern era and the twentieth century have dulled us both to
grace and to the exercise of our powers of destruction. Sin achieved
its apogee in Hitler, Stalin, Pol Pot, and others, armed with twentieth-
century technologies and media propaganda and attuned to resentments. Their history is a warning about what humans can let loose when
the chakra powers are ignored. "Technology exacerbates everything.
...It intensifies every form of dissociation," warns psychiatrist Robert
Jay Lifton.[1] The Nazis working the gas chambers had undergone
"extreme and gross forms of psychic numbing," as one expert puts it.[2]
We too can easily succumb to "psychic numbing," as we learn almost

daily about the peril that the earth is in. Just recently a biologist told me that she thinks most biologists have in fact given up on the human race and on any hope that the earth as we know it will survive.

But Meister Eckhart and the mystical traditions of East and West think otherwise. When Eckhart said, "Everything praises God. Darkness, privations, defects, and evil praise God and bless God," he was admonishing us not to give up hope.[3] There are positive steps that our species can take as we enter a new millennium. Joy and excellence are not beyond our capacity. If sin is *missing the mark,* then excellence is *finding the mark.*

I present in this concluding chapter some basic directions to help us find our way in the future. First I offer a reflection on the blessings of flesh and spirit, then propose seven positive precepts for our species living a spiritual life. I close by proposing one virtue that summarizes a new cosmology and how it can, if we commit to it, lead us to fulfill our potential for excellence.

BRINGING BLESSED FLESH AND BLESSED SPIRIT TOGETHER

Flesh and spirit are both so powerful and so amazing and so intertwined that they frighten us. When blessed flesh and blessed spirit merge, great joy happens. That joy also can frighten us.

Some people want to live without living flesh, and to control it because it so threatens them; others want to live without spirit because it too is threatening. Among the former are all the flesh-haters of history. That our attitudes toward flesh are part of the history of human treachery is evident.

Without a cosmology, we cherish neither cosmic flesh nor earth flesh nor human flesh. All flesh is expendable. Hitler, like many arch-conservative Catholics, did not cherish the flesh—he scorched it, hated it, reviled it. Race was the basis of his ideology. Only Aryan flesh was worth saving. Slavery too was race-based, as well as economically based; so was the genocide done to Native peoples in the Americas and beyond; and the Vietnam War was deeply affected by race. Sexism too is a denigration of certain flesh, that of women. Homophobia and all the "hate crimes" of which we are capable share in the hatred of flesh, as does the destruction of habitats and other species.

Descartes, the philosopher of the modern era, stripped flesh of its soul and rendered flesh inert, setting it up for attack and conquest. Before Descartes, the fourth-century theologian Augustine set flesh and women up for attack. Descartes killed the flesh—that was his way to control it: dead flesh, dead meat, dead everything. Hitler would advance this reality in the manner he learned from World War I, the expendability of flesh. Flesh is no longer alive, no longer sacred, no breath, no *ruah* or spirit. Today's environmental assaults are also wars against the flesh—against the flesh of the soil and of animals and fish and waters and also against our own flesh and blood—the future of our grandchildren and theirs, who inherit a planet wounded profoundly.

Meister Eckhart named the power of this spirit that can threaten us:

> Consider the divine spirit in the human soul. This spirit is not eas-ily satisfied. It storms the firmament and scales the heavens trying to reach the Spirit that drives the heavens. Because of this energy everything in the world grows green, flourishes, and bursts into leaf. But the spirit is never satisfied. It presses on deeper and deeper into the vortex, further and further into the whirlpool, the primary source in which the spirit has its origin. This spirit seeks to be bro-ken through by God. God leads this spirit into a desert into the wilderness and solitude of the divinity where God is pure unity and where God gushes up within himself or herself.[4]
>
> The divine countenance is capable of maddening and driving all souls out of their senses with longing for it. When it does this by its very divine nature it is thereby drawing all things to itself.[5]

Clearly, a spiritual life is not for the feint of heart. Timidity is not a spiritual position. Sin is the misdirected powers of spirit and flesh gone awry; it is power off center. It takes greatness of soul, magnanimity, to allow both flesh and spirit their proper place in our lives and not to shrink from that marriage. We need that magnanimity now.

SEVEN POSITIVE PRECEPTS FOR LIVING
A FULL AND SPIRITED LIFE

If the seven chakras and the seven principles of Creation Spirituality have anything to teach us, it is that we humans have, as Hildegard of Bingen put it, "everything we need within us already." Instead of commandments of "Thou shalt not," we can learn the positive lessons of living well on this planet. The chakras and the principles teach us how to direct the love-energies we all possess. These well-directed energies might be summarized in the precepts that follow. They constitute a path for the next millennium that can draw the human race together rather than apart. They name what a graced life, a life of the spirit, consists of. They enumerate the magic that happens when blessings of the spirit and blessings of the flesh come together.

1. Live with the wonders of cosmology (a relation to the whole), and live grounded to the earth and ecology. Resist acedia, which guarantees arrogance and laziness.
2. Live with passion (better lustful than listless), which derives from our yearning for union on the personal level.
3. Live with moral outrage and stand up to injustice.
4. Live with compassion and resist fear.
5. Live with telling your truth and resist being gagged by consumerism and its sellers.
6. Live with giving birth and develop *all* of your creative powers of intellect and imagination.
7. Live for the building of community among all light beings. Resist competitive and envious relations with others.

These seven precepts for living positively in the spirit turn the tables on the capital sins, those misdirected loves that diminish us. These precepts guide and *direct* the spiritual powers we all harbor within us. For human beings to work from these common precepts and to gather all our work and citizenship, relations, and efforts around them irrespective of national or religious differences would herald a new era. It would demonstrate that we have, after all, learned something from the sins of our fathers (and mothers). Future generations would thank us for it. We would be more grateful for living, and therefore we would live more simply and more joyfully on this blessed earth-flesh we call home.

GENEROSITY, THE MORAL WAVE OF THE FUTURE

Might there be a way to recognize the moral future bearing down upon us? Is there one virtue that might capture all the energy of the seven chakras and the seven principles of Creation Spirituality? Can we simplify our moral lives without being simplistic? I propose a rediscovery of the virtue of *generosity.*

The older I get, the more I am impressed with generosity as a sure sign of the spirit (and the more I recognize hoarding as its opposite). Where there is generosity, there is spirit. Ask me, "Who is a spiritual person?" and I reply, "A generous person." Look for generosity. Look for it in yourself. Think of the people you most admire—whether public figures or personal acquaintances. How often is generosity a part of their character? Think of Gandhi or Jesus; Martin Luther King, Jr., or Dorothy Day; Maya Angelou or Hildegard of Bingen. Your parents or grandparents; your teacher or your counselor. A good teacher is generous—giving of time and self to students. A good monk is generous; a good politician; a good parent; a good spouse; a good carpenter; a good artist. It seems to me that they all have generosity in common.

Generosity is about giving from one's abundance, from the depth of one's heart, from one's very soul. Generosity is about giving without a guaranteed return—it is about the "giveaway." I believe that the true moral path of the twenty-first century will be very different from the path of the modern era because it will be marked by generosity: not "Everyone for himself (or herself)" but "Who can give away the most?"—the most time, the most of one's gifts, the most of one's dreams and hopes and accomplishments of hands, head, and heart. Generosity takes trust; it takes a willingness to fail. Generosity and spirit go together.

If we have learned anything from our new creation story today, it is how *generous* the universe is. The sun, we are told, is giving out so much energy that the entire earth system runs on just one-billionth of that energy! So much generosity in the universe; so much abundance and giving-away. Has our species learned to follow this same path? Will we be at peace or become peacemakers until we do?

Was Jesus not speaking of generosity when he said, "From those to whom much has been given, much will be expected." Our species has been given much—15 billion years of giving. Every meal, every glass of water, every inhalation of air is a generous giving. We need to rediscover how to become both generous receivers and generous givers ourselves.

Each of the seven chakras can be summarized in terms of generosity. Living with cosmology, in preference to living with anthropocentrism or group egoism or racism, is about living generously. It is about expanding our souls to become larger. (Meister Eckhart said, "God is delighted to watch your soul enlarge.") Living with passion and with finding a balance between sexuality and mysticism is about living generously. Living with being grounded and centered and finding a place for your moral outrage is about living generously. So too is living with compassion and providing relief for the pain of others, whether that pain be ignorance or abuse or physical suffering or emotional distress or vulnerability due to age or class or social condition.

Living by telling your truth and putting it into the world, by finding your wisdom within and making it known—this takes generosity. Choosing to give birth regularly by utilizing all the creative gifts of mind and imagination you have been given—this takes generosity. And finally, building community when so much dissection and division and isolation and loneliness have overtaken our species in the recent past—this is also living generously. Truly each of the seven chakras calls us to develop our generosity. There is ample evidence that a good life is a generous life. Our species, if it is to survive, must rediscover its latent and powerful capacities for generosity.

GENEROSITY, THE TRUE MEANING OF EXCELLENCE

The word *generous* comes from two Latin words: *genero,* which means "to beget, produce, create, cause to exist, bring to life or generate," and *genus,* which means "birth, descent, origin (especially of high birth), father, family, nation, stock, offspring, race, kind, class, sort." The words *generate* and *generative* also derive from the word *genus,* or "kind." To be part of a kind, part of a genus, is to have brought being into existence, to have procreated and given birth. What an affirmation of our powers of creativity in *generosity* and its related terms! It takes generosity to be generative.

According to *Webster's Dictionary,* the English word *generous* means "to be magnanimous, kindly, liberal in giving, openhanded, marked by abundance or ample proportions, copious." Aquinas taught that magnanimity is the greatest of all the virtues—it comes from two Latin words for "large soul" *(magna anima).* It implies excellence and derives from gratitude. We give away when we are grateful. Yet "it is difficult to be magnanimous; no evil person is magnanimous."[6] Trust is essential for magnanimity and courage—trust in oneself as well as in the spirit. Indeed, "magnanimity strengthens a person to take on good tasks" and brave tasks.[7]

> Magnanimity is the expansion of the soul to great things.... Magnanimous people do not expose themselves to dangers for trifles, nor are they lovers of danger, as it were exposing themselves to dangers hastily or lightly. However, magnanimous people brave great dangers for great things because they put themselves in all kinds of danger for great things, for instance, the common welfare, justice, divine worship, and so forth.[8]

A magnanimous person is not bitter but has learned to let go and to forgive. Such people "deliberately determine to forget injuries they have suffered." Such people are "more solicitous about the truth than about the opinions of others" and do not leave their path of virtue "because of what people think."[9]

The virtue of generosity is very appropriate for a time of discovering a new cosmology. The word *generous* in English, which is related to the words *gene, geneology, genus, genuine, genesis, generate,* and *generative,* is also related to *kin* and *kind* and *kindly.* Clearly, the etymology of the word *generous* is deeply cosmological. It is therefore a very appropriate virtue for the recovery of a cosmology and the first chakra.

We saw in Part I that in light of today's creation story, the word *flesh* needs to be expanded to include all matter. Because it derives from one moment in time and makes up one space that we call the universe (from the Latin word *unus,* or "one"), all matter is kin or of one kind (or genus). *Kin* means "a group of persons of common ancestry, one's relatives," according to *Webster's.* Today we know that *all being is kin, all flesh is kin,* all the beings of the universe are our relatives. We all derive from the same ancestry, after all. We are all of one kind, one kin. What a moment for reinventing and recelebrating community! Community motivates for generosity—in community people find ways to give with greater abundance.

The word *kind* as a noun derives from the Old English word *cyn* or *kin.* It too denotes "family and lineage, the fundamental nature or essence of a group united by common traits or interests." (The Latin word for this is *genus.)* Who can deny the common interests we share with our kin today? The fundamentalist emphasis on "family values" is correct in one sense and off-base in another. It is correct to seek out the common interests and traits and therefore morality of a united group. But it is wrong to narrow the term *family* to only one's "blood" ancestors. Our true family is the family of being, the family of creation, the family of our Creator and the Source of all being. Is this not why so many traditions have called the Creator "Father" or "Mother"? The new cosmology has broadened our understanding of family considerably.

The word *kind* as an adjective, which means "affectionate, loving, gentle or agreeable," also derives from *kin* and *kind* as nouns. To be kind goes naturally with being family, with being related, with being kin or of a kind. Families survive by caring and by kindness. Kinship leads to kindness, or ought to. One can expect kindness therefore to take on fuller expression as we live out our true family more fully.

We genuinely begin to live out the blessing of our shared flesh with all of its implications. Truth is related to genuineness (which comes from the same root as *generous* and *genus),* lack of hypocrisy, the living-out of authentic family values. In this context community can take on new depth and strength, and that which opposes community will be unmasked for what it is: a lie.

Jesus gave us sound and simple advice about testing spirits: "By their fruits you will know them," he said. The fruits of healthy spirituality are the peace and joy that come from authentic kinship and kindness and generosity and genuineness.

Part of generosity is sacrifice. This word has been badly abused during the patriarchal period, when *sacrifice* often meant "You sacrifice for me." But it is a word worth redeeming. Etymologically, *sacrifice* means "to make holy." Who would want to throw out a word like that? Traditionally, a sacrifice was an offering that was burnt up and presented to the Holy One. All lovers sacrifice, be they parents sacrificing for their children, or children for their aging parents, or spouses for each other, or artists for their work and those who will derive joy from it. Sacrifice is a kind of giveaway.

The word *sacrifice* confronts the idol of our culture known as Comfort. A culture with an economic system that runs on consumerism is a culture whose true God is the god of comfort. Sacrifice implies choosing generosity over comfort. (Jesus never said, "Blessed are the comfortable," and neither did Buddha.)

In this family of words from which we derive our word *generosity,* there is a constant echo in both Latin and Old English of being "highborn," that is, of *excellence.* According to *Webster's,* the English word *generous* in its archaic use meant "to be highborn" and "to be characterized by a noble or forbearing spirit." Generosity has something to do with excellence and nobility. Generosity, like magnanimity, is about a great soul, a large soul, a giving heart, an abundance within us that gets called outside us. Generosity allows us to democratize highbornness or nobility, if you will. It is how each of us expresses the true nobility of our nature.

Nobility ought not signify birth in a noble class; rather, it is being born, as Meister Eckhart put it, "from the noblest foundation of all," that is, from the Godhead which is itself so generous and so giving and so excellent and so much in pursuit of beauty and the sharing of beauty that creation itself is also abundant and beautiful, after the very image of its Creator. *Genius* derives from the same root word as generosity. Perhaps a generous spirit is our true *genius* as a species. Perhaps that is why spiritual teachers East and West call our species to that excellence called compassion. All of us are born from sacred stock—15 billion years of generous giving and generous receiving. We are all noble and in a real sense Divine. We will know this from the fruits of our activities, for as Jesus observed, a good tree bears good fruit and a bad one bad fruit.

THE SPECIAL ROLE OF GRACE IN BUILDING RESPONSIBILITY

Evil does enter the world through human activity. From Cain to Hitler, bad things *do* occur. The passage from the stone that Cain used to kill his brother to today's missiles, bombs, and bacterial warfare that kill en masse is not a sign of "progress" but a warning that the major threats to our survival come from within us.

Paul wrote that "where sin abounds, grace does more abound," but Christian theologians—and even worse, Christian history—have more often than not put the emphasis on sin and left out grace. Grace is the appropriate *context* for living and for understanding our sinning. The context can be spelled out as (1) cosmology and its graced history; (2) the *blessing* or goodness of existence and the powers that go with it that makes even sin possible; (3) creativity—every malicious choice, as a choice, being in some way an act of creativity, and cleaning up sin being tantamount to critiquing our creativity; (4) the quest for goodness and blessing that is inherent in all our choices, even our sinful ones (Aquinas believed that every choice we make is in some way based on love); (5) a sociopolitical context, since sin is not only a personal matter but a rupture of social, ecological, and political relationships—and therefore is about injustice.

We are responsible in a special way today to *pay attention to grace* and to pass on the good news of grace to self and others. The primary source for grace is creation itself, cosmology, and the awe it brings in its wake. It is flesh itself. We humans, being part of nature and cosmology, are also sources of grace even to ourselves.[10]

What else are we responsible for? The four paths of Creation Spirituality lay out the following map: (1) The responsibility to savor, to not take for granted, to experience awe, reverence, and gratitude, that is, grace. (2) The responsibility to let go and trust the darkness. (3) The responsibility to create and thus contribute gracefully. (4) The responsibility to critique our creativity with tests of justice, celebration, and compassion.

To be responsible is to realize that we have inherited a treasure, a gift of great price, a beauty. Aquinas ushered in the age of sin as a refusal to be responsible when he defined salvation as "preserving things in the good."[11] We do preserve not by freezing things but by cocreating and evolving with things.

A conscious or unconscious refusal to be responsible emanates from an *indifference to goodness itself.* It is a taking-for-granted, a profound cynicism, a denial of how we got here, the sacrifices that the universe *and* our ancestors made for us to be here, a preference for blame over living, a closing of our eyes and ears and minds and bodies to the goodness of things even in the midst of the real evil in the world, a coldness of heart. I discussed this idea in Chapter 8. The sin of acedia is clearly, to me, the number-one sin in our civilization—indeed, during the modern era we are so oblivious to it that we have reduced its meaning to "sloth," understood as a refusal to contribute to the industrial engine.

How can we cut through this denial? How do we awaken our capacity for blessing-awareness, goodness-awareness? Cosmology does it, and art, and ritual wherein art and cosmology come together. For all this to come about both education and worship must be reborn. We need all the chakras to be aflame. We need generosity to return.

If we are generous, then our ways will be generous. And if we as a species can grow in generosity, then we will be worthy to continue and indeed to thrive on this kindly planet in this kindly though tumultuous universe where all—flesh and spirit, creation and Creator—are kin.

APPENDIX A:

HITLER AS A RELIGIOUS FIGURE

No one can reflect on evil and sin at the end of the twentieth century without reflecting on Adolf Hitler *and* on the success he "enjoyed" for fifteen years among his ardent followers and countrymen and -women. Many of these followers were churchgoing Christians or claimed to be Christian as they went to church. This man united evil forces of anti-Semitism and of seven misguided chakras, together with technology and modern media, to accomplish the greatest genocide, the greatest killing, the greatest destruction ever achieved by a human against other humans.

The Holocaust is about sin and, more than sin, it is about expiation, scapegoating (a ritual act), rituals, propaganda, the media, technology, racism, religious bigotry, and sins of omission. The old sins of hatred and resentment and racism and religious competition take on a new evolutionary power when married to cyanide ovens, panzer tank divisions, modern railroad boxcars, submarine warfare, V-2s, bombings of cities, nationalism, suspension of civilization, and rewarding of sadism. Modern creativity in the sciences, technology, and warfare take us beyond sin to collective guilt and ultimately to questions of responsibility.

Cain got into trouble for killing one man, his brother; Hitler, who killed twenty million German brothers and sisters alone, was heralded as a hero in the media of his land for fifteen years. Hitler, who killed untold Catholic brothers and sisters, was never excommunicated by the head of his church, the pope in Rome. Hitler, who exterminated six million Jews in concentration camps as well as gays and the mentally ill and anyone else labeled as "unfit," never wore an X on his forehead, as did Cain for killing one brother. What forces were behind Hitler's success in his lifetime?

HITLER AND THE RELIGION OF DEFILEMENT

Psychologist Alice Miller proposes that Hitler's complicity with evil stems from his abuse as a child. James Hillman prefers to see his evil as that of a "bad seed" in league with demonic powers. Without discounting either of these analyses, I propose considering how Hitler's "success" may have been a projection of an internalized religious sentiment derived from his (admittedly perverted) form of Austrian Catholicism. His greatest electoral successes were among Catholics, first in Austria and then in Bavaria, and the pope never excommunicated him—perhaps because he was in fact, *as he declared,* carrying the "ghetto" to its logical conclusion, the ghetto being an invention of sixteenth-century popes.

The work of Paul Ricoeur, in particular, contributes to this explanation (see Appendix C). In analyzing the first level of human evil as *defilement* and the fight against impurity, Ricoeur also names the first tenet of belief in Hitler's religion: "Some are pure and others are impure; preserve yourself from all impurities. Non-Aryans are impure. Therefore do what it takes to rid yourself of non-Aryans. They have no rights anyway because they are defiled." This religious appeal on Hitler's part helps explain his success: It profoundly appealed to the uncommon self-loathing of *a defiled race* following on the defeat of the imperial German people in the First World War, as well as the guilty conscience of pseudo-Christianity. Hitler promised and delivered religious rites of *purification* that ranged from setting the Reichstag on fire, to sacrificing young men to the gods of war and nationalism, to performing mass rituals, and finally to instituting the "ultimate solution." Scapegoating Jews, homosexuals, gypsies, and other "defiled ones" was a *rite of purification* to rid him and his followers of their *defilement.* The murder of the Jews was a "magical ritual slaughtering," says James Rhodes in his study *The Hitler Movement.*[1]

Hitler's work was a pseudo-religious deed—therein lay its power.

Rituals of purgation, purging, cleansing, uniting, communing, chanting, processing, bowing, adulating, invoking cosmic powers of hatred and battling—all of it appealed to the first level of evil cleansing, as Ricoeur defines *defilement*. This quest to purify a defilement even overrode the war effort. Morris Berman sees this clearly:

> The Nazis' fanatical eagerness to exterminate the Jews even when it was detrimental to the war effort (as was the case by 1944) becomes much more understandable. We are talking about cosmology, eschatology, world-myth, and ultimate salvation. In a cosmic battle between Aryan and Jew, victory could usher in a thousand-year reign, in which the "righteous" would redeem the earth.[2]

Hitler's "religion" was base in every sense of the word. It appealed to the first level of religion's promise to cleanse and save from defilement, and it stopped there. It provided no sense of sin, of ethics, of conscience, and no sense of guilt or even shame—at least, none that drove large numbers of people to resistance. Call it denial, call it desperation, call it fear, call it the trapped wounded child, but whatever it is called, it is real evil. Its appeal was religious because Hitler promised salvation and healing to a wounded and despised and self-loathing people eager to escape defilement.

If the Christianity of this century had had a cosmology, a sense of creation, instead of just redemption, might it have mounted more resistance to Hitler? Hitler chose to replace Hildegard's awareness of *viriditas* or "greening power" with a scorched-earth policy. He effectively killed spirit and replaced it with hatred, even of the earth.

Was Hitler listened to disproportionately because he preached a familiar religion of salvation and redemption, with no sense of the blessedness of existence and little love of flesh? He replaced creation with Nazism and nationalism. Why did the churches not stand up for creation? Why are they still not doing so? It may be that the churches, like Hitler, lack a healthy first chakra—that is to say, they too were and are anthropocentric.

The deep evil of Hitler raises questions about organized, institutional religion that will not go away. Besides the obvious questions of the pope's role in all this and the seized assets of Holocaust victims, and the anti-Semitism of Christianity that seemed to go unabated for centuries, other issues rise to the surface. Principal among them seem to be: If Christian churches had been doing their work properly, clearing the soul of defilement through ritual and rites and preaching, then would this generation of Christians have been so attracted by Hitler's heresies? The failure of ecclesial liturgies and theologies and even the seminary training of ministers and priests to turn out prophets and creation-centered mystics—is this not one of the greatest lessons learned from Hitler's success?

Four centuries earlier Luther had decried Rome as Babylon and the antichrist from his theological chair in Wittenberg, but under Hitler Berlin became the new Babylon, and neither religion—Roman or Lutheran—can claim innocence in that debacle.

A lesson learned from the Hitlerian nightmare, then, is the import of the sins of omission of the Christian academic, seminary, and church systems. These sins helped create a vacuum for the pseudo-rites and pseudo-religious appeal of Hitler. He was the country's favorite preacher. If religion cannot deal effectively with defilement, someone else will. What a powerful lesson for our future as a species! It awakens our consciences to the potential of sins of omission in today's cultural and global context.

HITLER, EXEMPLAR OF MISDIRECTED CHAKRAS

Hitler is a case study in misdirected chakras. For the first chakra, he unquestionably had zeal, but his zeal was narrowly focused. It was not a zeal for creation or the Source of creation or beauty, but a zeal for his version of a very narrow nation-state, one that excluded all races except the so-called Aryan race and all religions that preached justice. He replaced cosmology with Nazism, which was both his cosmology and the source of his zeal. Lacking a genuine cosmology, his racism built a religion around defilement and hatred of the "other," the non-Aryan.

As for the second chakra, dualism was what drove Hitler and his anti-Semitism. He carried out to its gross end the philosophy of Houston Stewart Chamberlain, whose *Die Grundlagen des XIX Jahrhunderts (Foundations of the Nineteenth Century),* published in Germany in

1900, argued that race was the key to history and that God was incarnated in the Germans and the Devil was embodied in the Jews. Because these were the only two pure races left on the earth, struggle was necessary to decide which one was the chosen people. This dualism drove Hitler to his extermination mania.

In addition, Hitler exercised male dominance in the militarizing of his nation and in his personal relationships—indeed, six of his girlfriends committed suicide. He was attractive to women and set himself up on a pedestal for their idolization. At this chakra something even more ugly may have been operating in Hitler: his lust turned to *bloodlust*. Witnesses speak of a kind of sexual frenzy that accompanied his speeches, which were aimed at stirring the masses to follow him and his Nazi cosmology into the gore of battle and slaughter. The Nazi ritual ceremonies (see sixth chakra, below) were described by eyewitnesses as having an "orgiastic atmosphere," and Hitler's exhaustion was described "in sexual terms."

As for the third chakra, Hitler's anger was so externalized that it expressed itself in storm troopers and SS commandants, in panzer divisions and submarines, in bombings and the subjugation of millions. His was not a power from within but a kind of "possession," as Jung and others commented. Jung wrote: "One man, who is obviously 'possessed,' has possessed a whole nation."[3] Hitler's power-over mania did not stop with conquests of Poland and Czechoslovakia, Belgium, the Netherlands, France, or Russia. It was a quest for global conquest.

As for the fourth chakra, one sometimes saw a sentimental kind of pity, but no one could accuse Hitler of compassion. His heart was dedicated fiercely to the Nazi cosmology, which was a philosophy of hatred—a hatred that caused him to exterminate six million Jews in concentration camps and 36 million other human beings in the Second World War. This hatred drove him to destroy cities and history, museums and cultures, religions and countries.

As for the fifth chakra, Hitler had seizures while preaching from the podium, where he would both writhe in fury and charm the crowds. A believer in propaganda, he utilized the twentieth-century media of radio and film to preach his version of truth. "There would be no Third Reich without the media," he declared. He appointed Josef Goebbels and others to propagandize. But they were not announcing good news:

they were spreading the hate of the fourth chakra and the injustice of the other chakras. Hitler was described by Hermann Rauschning as being "the master-enchanter and the high priest of the religious mysteries of Nazidom." Thus Hitler found not only a pulpit but a kind of priestly role that went beyond the preaching itself.

As for the sixth chakra, there was no awakening of the third eye in Hitler, no marriage of light and darkness to serve the cause of wisdom. He put the vast technological knowledge of the twentieth century at the disposal of war, cruelty, and sadism. Heinz Hohne describes Hitler's attack on the Jews as a "murderous wave of unbridled sadism. . . . Hour by hour, day by day, week by week, the SS and their local auxiliaries drove the Jews into the gas chambers, beating, tormenting, insulting and torturing."[4]

A survivor of Auschwitz reported seeing a pile of female corpses with breasts cut off and flesh sliced from the thighs with deep incisions. "We were wading in blood way above our ankles," the observer reported. Hitler was driven by war, not by union; by division, not by ecumenism; by conquering, not by balancing; by armed conflict, slaughter, and bloodshed, not by peace. Hitler took "pleasure in malice," notes James Hillman.

A perverse kind of response to the rationalism of the modern era was evident in Hitler's success in manipulating the irrational. Jung recognized this when he wrote: "Despite their crankiness, the Wotan-worshippers seem to have judged things more correctly than the worshippers of reason. . . . A hurricane has broken loose in Germany while we still believe it is fine weather."[5] The imbalance of modern rationalism left a hole in the mystical psyche that Hitler obligingly filled.

Nor did the Hitlerian worldview ignore an inverted kind of religious creativity. He called for a new crusading order after the model of the Knights Templar of old, and Himmler actually compared the SS to the Jesuit Order on several occasions. Creativity was put to powerful effect in rituals where as many as 140,000 people would gather at night for ceremonies "soaked in mysticism and Wagnerian ritual," as Morris Berman puts it.[6]

The party boasted its own liturgical handbook written by Franz Hermann Woweries called *Nationalsozialistische Feier-Stunden (National Socialist Ceremonials),* published in 1932. Its guidance included the use of lights, a stage draped in black, an altar with steps covered with helmets, weapons, candles, and more. Hitler was the preacher at these services, and his oratory evoked a "hysterical response...a mutual frenzy" in his audience. At the annual Nuremberg rally 130 searchlights were placed around a field at forty-foot intervals. The light beams extended 25,000 feet into the air and merged at the top to create "a luminous dome effect, a cathedral of light." This light hovered over Hitler in the darkness and was accompanied by music, flags, and colors. A newspaper in 1937 reported the spectacle:

> From out of the night [the spotlights] cut and then build a baldachin of light which stretches over the entire stadium. For a moment there is dead silence.... The wide stadium now acts as a mighty gothic tower of light. From the spotlights there emanates a bluish-violet light.... A hundred and forty thousand—there are at least that many gathered here—cannot free themselves from this moment.[7]

The light of the sixth chakra was indeed evoked—but for what purpose?

HITLER: CONNECTOR TO THE DEMONIC

Hitler's journey of misdirected chakras culminates at the seventh chakra. We see a misappropriation of the seventh chakra in this master of envy and resentment. How did Hitler get to be so powerful? What did he project that got him elected to office and supported by so many for so long? I don't think it is possible to understand Hitler and his feats without grasping his success at *awakening resentment and feeding on it*. I believe that it was envy and resentment that made Hitler succeed.

Hitler seems to have had some deep relationship to demonic spirits. James Hillman talks of Hitler's *daimon* becoming a demon, about the "bad seed" and "demonic call" that drew Hitler, a call that included transgression as transcendence, taking pleasure in malice, a "dizziness of deviance," and "opening the door to a suprahuman condition where devil and divinity are indistinguishable."[8] (Indeed, Hitler was compared to Christ by many of his followers.) Hillman lists seven characteristics of evil, death, and destruction that fit Hitler's persona: a cold heart; hellfire; wolf; anality; suicides of six women who knew him; freaks; and humorlessness.[9] In addition, the demonic showed itself in Hitler in his eyes; in his life being spared on several occasions; in his absolute certainty; in his insomnia; in his lack of time; and in the lack of exchange of ideas.[10]

Instead of building community, Hitler destroyed community upon community upon community. He seems to have built *an inversion of what we would mean by community.* Instead of building solidarity, the personified hatred of evil spirits builds dissension. Not love but hate; not sharing but competition; not celebration but brooding over the success of others and raining terror and death on others; not letting others be themselves (even their successful selves) but conjuring up ways to tear others down. All this marks the trail that envy and resentment pursue.

Morris Berman talks of the SS being demonic and says "the whole of Germany during these years was pervaded by a kind of demonic atmosphere."[11] The language of "demons" and "devils" was actually invoked by Hitler on numerous occasions. Said Hitler, "The personification of the devil as the symbol of all evil assumes the living shape of the Jew." This was a constant refrain in his "demonization" (Berman's word) of the Jewish people. Berman says: "All this was *cosmological* for Hitler, and he said as much on several occasions."[12] The Jewish people became the devil incarnate. "They had to find *human* devils because they were living in a secular society; the age of *actual* demons was long over."[13] Demonology was the "main theme" in Hitler's rantings.[14] Hitler saw his work in a perverted way as a new kind of humanity and a bigger religion than religion itself: "Man is becoming God—that is the simple fact. Man is God in the mankind. . . . Those who see in National Socialism nothing more than a political movement know scarcely anything of it. It is more even than a religion: it is the will to create mankind anew."[15]

Berman says Nazism "seems unavoidably demonic in character, a different level of evil from that of mere administrative violence."[16] He sees Hitler's goal as a "demonic attempt to reenchant the world. The language of National Socialism was that of transcendence. Hitler recognized instinctively a religious need on the part of the masses."[17]

One wonders why the masses had such a religious need. Why were

the churches so failing in their job that Hitler was so successful in filling the gap? One must ask: How many of the chakras was the church
nourishing and awakening? How could so many fall for such a pseudo-
religion?

And fall they did. "An entire nation followed him and furnished a
legion of executioners," notes Karl Bracher.[18]

Even today we could once again make those connections or travel
on that highway. It takes vigilance to develop *each* of the chakras we
have been discussing. For we can miss the mark about any of them, and
mindfulness and attention are required. How important it is to guard
our own chakras lest they be distorted and misdirected by others who
are as off center as was Hitler. It could happen again, warns Berman:
"Frankly, I see nothing to prevent the emergence of some form of race
ideology, and certainly nothing to prevent massive economic depression . . . and when this happens, the search will be on for convenient
scapegoats."[19]

APPENDIX B:

SYNONYMS FOR *SIN* IN ENGLISH

I have long subscribed to the thesis that a culture reveals a lot about itself by the number of words it has for certain realities. Inuit peoples living at the North Pole are said to have some twenty words for *snow,* while many equatorial peoples have none at all. But they do have many words for *camel* and *sunshine* and *desert.* In America we have many words for the automobile. Consider these for starters: *car, jalopy, wheels, auto, vehicle, bomb, lemon, clunker, roadster, wreck.*

SIN AS A NOUN AND AS AN ADJECTIVE

The English language also has many words for *sin.* Even if we don't like using that particular word in our times, the *concept* (and perhaps the experience) seems nevertheless quite common. One thesaurus I consulted contains at least ninety-five synonyms for *sin* in our culture. Among the nouns are: *transgression, offense, iniquity, error, misdeed, peccadillo, vice, wrongdoing, depravity, disaster, trespass, evil, misdemeanor, misbehavior, violation, infraction, mistake, blooper, faux pas, boner, oversight, corruption, lechery, immorality, debauchery, fault, wickedness, defect, vileness, viciousness, degeneracy, sordidness, baseness, meanness, rudeness, debasement.* Among adjectives for sinful, we have: *amoral, harmful, unfortunate, baneful, unfavorable, bad, corrupt, depraved, flagitious, immoral, wicked, vile, sinister, base, wrong, hurtful, harmful, adverse, inferior, ill, naughty, disagreeable, severe, diseased, dissolute, impenitent, incorrigible, licentious, nefarious, heinous, abandoned, villainous, profligate, erring, dishonest, impure, bribable, exploiting, mercenary, underhanded, praetorian, false, shady, unfair, unjust, reprobate, crooked, iniquitous.*

SIN AS A VERB

Among the sinning verbs we have: *transgress, break a law, err, go astray, misbehave, do wrong, offend, blunder, miscalculate, fail, be wrong, be mistaken, insult, irritate, slight, affront, fall short, gall, slur, antagonize, mortify, pollute, pervert, lure, falsify, infringe, encroach, intrude.* No one could conclude that our culture, however fed up with the word *sin,* ignores its reality and experience in its language. Nor can we attribute all our languaging to theologians, however preoccupied with sinfulness some of them appear to be.

The very richness of this vocabulary suggests that theology may be the least of the arts dedicated to exploring the immoral (or amoral or baneful or ...) sides to human existence. Please note that these hundred-plus synonyms for human misbehavior do not even begin to list *the actual acts themselves!* These are mere synonyms for the generic concept. To list the specific acts might take an encyclopedia or two and many years of study of human history. The word *sin* and the concept behind it is vast. That is why I have chosen to focus this book on the seven capital sins and sins of the spirit.

APPENDIX C:

PAUL RICOEUR ON THE EVOLUTION OF SIN

Religious anthropologist Paul Ricoeur demonstrates in
The Symbolism of Evil that humanity has always been developing its awareness of its own powers for mischief. It is
part of the fascination of being human to reflect on the
pain we cause ourselves and others. According to
Ricoeur, however, there has been a "progress of conscience."[1] Human history also provides evidence of a
"growing wickedness of men"—at least, that is the way
the Bible portrays it in the stories of Cain and Abel, the
Flood, the Tower of Babel, and ultimately the enslavement
under Egyptian pharaohs. All are illustrations of the evolution and growth of human depravity. Ricoeur places sin
in an evolutionary context.[2] Sin and our awareness of sin
have evolved along with culture, history, self-awareness,
religion, powers of technology, science, and creativity.

In the unfolding of our species, Ricoeur detects three layers of sin-
consciousness and delineates this evolution as a movement from (1)
defilement, to (2) sin and conscience, to (3) guilt and grace. Each stage
incorporates the previous ones. We never *leave behind* a former age.
Rather, we incorporate it and take it with us, for better or for worse.

DEFILEMENT: PRIMORDIAL NOTIONS OF SIN

For Ricoeur, the rites of purification that are found everywhere among
ancient humanity are explained by a "dread of the impure," feelings of

impurity or defilement.[3] This "dread of the impure" goes way back in our collective history: "The primitive dread deserves to be interrogated as our oldest memory," Ricoeur proposes.[4] "Every evil is symbolically a stain. The stain is the first 'schema' of evil."[5] Sexual defilement remains in our memory as an early stage of sinfulness. So omnipresent are prohibitions against incest, sodomy, abortion, and sexual relations at specific times and places that "the inflation of the sexual is characteristic of the whole system of defilement."[6] The Greeks also addressed themselves to issues of defilement and purification, though for them "the essential purification [was] that of wisdom and philosophy."[7]

Along with defilement came the dread brought on by the fear of suffering: "Suffering is the price for the violation of order; suffering is to 'satisfy' the claim of purity for revenge."[8] Fear and trembling accompany dread: "Man suffers because he is impure."[9] For a long time humanity equated suffering with defilement and a failure to be pure, but it took Job to question that equation. When he challenged the inevitability of linking the ethical world of sin with the physical world of suffering, he advanced our understanding of defilement.

SIN AND CONSCIENCE:
THE HEBREW BIBLE

For Ricoeur, sin differs from defilement in that sin involves a relationship to a transcendent source. In the Babylonian confession of sins, for example, "the penitent becomes conscious of his sin as a dimension of his existence and no longer only as a reality that haunts him; the examination of conscience and the interrogative thinking that it gives rise to are already there."[10]

Defilement became incorporated into the new sin-consciousness, as for example in the Levitical proscriptions in the Bible. In Hebrew thought what lies at the heart of a sin-awareness is the "before God" awareness: "The category that dominates the notion of sin is the category of 'before God.'"[11] Humans standing before the covenant become aware of sin. The prophetic tradition of Amos denounces sin through wrath and indignation against injustice. Nor is sin about externals. Rather, "the prophet aims at the wicked heart from which iniquity comes forth."[12] A radical level of conversion is sought. Deuteronomy "internalizes sin in the most radical fashion" when Moses, promulgating the moral charter for the promised people in a promised land, appeals to "the inner obedience of the heart"[13] (Deuteronomy 6:4–6). A tension exists between the role of the heart and the actual transgression of particular laws. This tension constitutes a relation between God and the people of the covenant.

In the context of sin, dread and anxiety take on a new meaning. "In rising from the consciousness of defilement to the consciousness of sin," says Ricoeur, "fear and anguish did not disappear; rather, they changed their quality."[14] A kind of terror constitutes the relation of sinful humans before God. The symbol of the wrath of God or the Day of Yahweh concerns "the political fate of the community." There lies the crux of sin: it threatens the community. This wrath is not the vindication of taboos or the resurgence of a primordial chaos "but the Wrath of Holiness itself."

Time will reveal that it is also a wrath born of the sadness of love— one might say a *grief* that God feels at several stages over human sin. Grief has both an angry or wrathful dimension *and* a sorrowful dimension. The threat that goes with this anger is not about eternal punishment or hell but "remains a threat internal to history," internal to the evolution of the people.[15] The psalmist who prays to God "Out of the depths I cried out to thee" (Psalm 130) reveals a tenderness that sin cannot destroy: "The Wrath of holiness might be only the Wrath of Love, if one dare say so."[16]

Sin reveals both a negative and a positive side, as Ricoeur sees it. Defilement is one thing, but sin rupturing a relation is another. Idolatry, like vanity, is the pursuit of false sacredness—pursuit of what does not exist, and in this sense a pursuit of nothingness. Nevertheless, real pardon exists on God's part—God is said to repent (Exodus 34:6f.)—and real return is available on humanity's part:

> I will not execute the fierceness of my wrath,
> I will not return to destroy Ephraim;
> For I am God, and not man
> I am the Holy One in the midst of thee,
>   and I do not love to destroy. (Hosea 11:9)

"The biblical writers read this repenting of wrath into history itself," says Ricoeur.[17] The return of humans is the repentance of humans.

GUILT AND GRACE

The growing awareness of guilt alters the evolution of sin-awareness. "The consciousness of guilt constitutes a veritable revolution in the experience of evil: that which is primary is . . . the evil use of liberty, felt as an internal diminution of the value of the self."[18] With guilt, humanity moves beyond ritual to the ethical since "guilt represents an internalization and a personalization of the consciousness of sin."[19] When conscience emerges, responsibility and consciousness advance. With this stage of evolution, conscience "becomes the *measure* of evil in a completely solitary experience," and the discovery and development of guilt "expresses above all the promotion of 'conscience' as supreme."[20] Guilt and sin can now actually be separated. When the Jewish people were enslaved in Babylon, the community itself could not be saved; the individual was the door to hope. Collective reform became "a cause for despair" and yielded to prophetic preaching about individual sin and personal guilt. Here there was still hope. In the framework of sin, evil is a situation in which humans are caught as a single collective; but in the framework of guilt, evil "is an act that each individual 'begins.' A loneliness accompanies the guilty conscience."[21]

Each human being has two "inclinations" or tendencies or impulses (called *yetzer):* a good one and an evil one. Both are planted in humans by the Creator, who made things "very good." Thus it follows that "the evil inclination . . . is not a radical evil, engendered by man, from which he is radically powerless to free himself; it is rather a permanent temptation that gives opportunity for the exercise of freedom of choice."[22] This is why repentance-as-return is so primal to Jewish piety.

One also sees this idea in the early preaching of the historical Jesus: Repent! Return. Start over. *Metanoia:* Change your ways, change your heart. Ultimately, Ricoeur believes, Jesus and Paul brought a new and startling dimension to the issue of sin and guilt: the belief in grace.

NOTES

INTRODUCTION:
A SPECIES WANTING ATTENTION

1. M. Scott Peck, *The People of the Lie* (New York: Touchstone, 1985), 263.
2. Ibid., 129.
3. Martin Buber, *Good and Evil* (Upper Saddle River, New Jersey: Prentice Hall, 1953), 64.
4. Solomon Schimmel, *The Seven Deadly Sins* (New York: The Free Press, 1992), 1, 4.
5. Ibid., 5.
6. Matthew Fox, ed., *Hildegard of Bingen's Book of Divine Works* (Santa Fe: Bear & Co., 1987), 117.
7. Lyall Watson, *Dark Nature: A Natural History of Evil* (New York: HarperPerennial, 1997), 290.
8. Matthew Fox, *Hildegard of Bingen's Book of Divine Works*, 117.
9. Paul Ricoeur, *The Symbolism of Evil* (Boston: Beacon Press, 1967), 6.
10. Consider the question raised by psychologist Karl Menninger in *Whatever Became of Sin?* (New York: Hawthorn Books, 1973).
11. Norman Pittenger, *Cosmic Love and Human Wrong* (New York: Paulist Press, 1978), 8.
12. Ibid., 3.
13. Ivone Gebara, "Cosmic Theology: Ecofeminism and Panentheism," *Creation Spirituality* (Winter: 1993): 9.
14. Coleman Barks, trans., *The Essential Rumi* (New York: HarperCollins, 1995), 36.
15. See Matthew Fox, *The Coming of the Cosmic Christ* (San Francisco: Harper-SanFrancisco, 1988), 228–244.
16. Buber, *Good and Evil*, 96, 95.
17. Erich Fromm, *The Anatomy of Human Destructiveness* (New York: Holt, Rinehart and Winston, 1973), 254.
18. Ricoeur, *Symbolism of Evil*, 8.
19. Fromm, *The Anatomy of Human Destructiveness*, 432f.
20. Morton W. Bloomfield, *The Seven Deadly Sins* (Ann Arbor, Michigan: State College Press, 1952), 182.
21. Erich Fromm says that humans are "the only primate who can feel intense pleasure in killing and torturing." Furthermore, "what is unique in man is that he can be

driven by impulses to kill and to torture, and that he feels lust in doing so; he is the only animal that can be a killer and destroyer of his own species without any rational gain, either biological or economic. Malignant aggression...is specifically human and not derived from animal instinct" (Erich Fromm, *The Anatomy of Human Destructiveness,* 181, 218).

22. Jon D. Levenson, *Creation and the Persistence of Evil* (Princeton, NJ: Princeton University Press, 1987), 44.

23. Martin Buber, *Good and Evil,* 66.

24. Charles Jencks, *The Post-Modern Reader* (London: St. Martin's Press, 1992), 31.

25. Robert Funk, *Honest to Jesus* (San Francisco: HarperSanFrancisco, 1996), 299.

26. The papal silence has come to the fore again with the publication of *The Hidden Encyclical of Pius XI,* a study that documents that Pope Pius XI prepared an encyclical that condemned Hitler's racist policies but that Pope Pius XII, who inherited the document when Pius XI died, never published it and never truly condemned Hitler. See Georges Passelecq and Bernard Suchecky, *The Hidden Encyclical of Pius XI* (New York: Harcourt Brace, 1997).

27. Cited in Matthew Fox, *Sheer Joy: Conversations with Thomas Aquinas on Creation Spirituality* (San Francisco: HarperSanFrancisco, 1992), 423.

28. David C. Korten, *When Corporations Rule the World* (West Hartford, CT: Kumarian Press, 1995).

29. William Julius Wilson, *When Work Disappears: The World of the New Urban Poor* (New York: Alfred A. Knopf, 1996).

30. Dominic Crossan, *The Birth of Christianity* (San Francisco: HarperSanFrancisco, 1998), 38, 46. Unfortunately, Crossan sees the Bible as the Word of God made text and Jesus as the Word of God made flesh but he underplays the role of *creation as the Word of God made flesh* (page 45). Cosmology deserves to play a larger role in the solution to sarcophobia than he allows.

31. Cited in Ted Peters, *Sin: Radical Evil in Soul and Society* (Grand Rapids, MI: William B. Eerdmans, 1994), 323.

32. John Calvin, *Institutes of the Christian Religion,* 2.1.8.

33. Ricoeur, *Symbolism of Evil,* 156.

34. Cited in ibid., 304, n. 19.

35. Schimmel, *Seven Deadly Sins,* 1.

36. Martin Buber, *Good and Evil,* 28.

37. Erich Fromm, *The Anatomy of Human Destructiveness,* 366, 368.

PART I: BLESSINGS OF THE FLESH

1. Ernesto Cardinale, *Cosmic Canticle* (Willimantic, CT: Curbstone Press, 1993).

2. James Lovelock, *The Ages of Gaia* (New York: W.W. Norton, 1988), 40.

3. Paul Ricoeur, *The Symbolism of Evil,* 10f.

4. Jon D. Levenson, *Creation and the Persistence of Evil,* 90.

5. Ibid., 127.

CHAPTER 1: REDEEMING THE WORD *FLESH*

1. Thomas Aquinas, *On Evil* (Notre Dame, IN: University of Notre Dame Press, 1995), 170.
2. Ibid., 169.
3. David Abram, *The Spell of the Sensuous: Perception and Language in a More-Than-Human World* (New York: Pantheon, 1996), 41.
4. Matthew Fox and Rupert Sheldrake, *Natural Grace* (New York: Doubleday, 1996), 19.
5. In Abram, *The Spell of the Sensuous,* 60.
6. Cited in Matthew Fox, *On Becoming a Musical, Mystical Bear: Spirituality American Style* (New York: Paulist Press, 1976), xvi.
7. Cited in Ken Wilbur, *Sex, Ecology, Spirituality: The Spirit of Evolution* (Boston: Shambhala, 1995), 440.
8. Diane Ackerman, *A Natural History of the Senses* (New York: Vintage, 1991), 145.
9. Bishop John A. T. Robinson insists that the West has been misunderstanding Paul by reading him too much through the glasses of Greek philosophy and not enough through Paul's own eyes as a Jew. Since the basis of Paul's thought is Hebrew and not Greek, to understand Paul in Greek terms is "simply misleading.... When it is remembered that our modern use of the terms 'body' and 'flesh' is almost wholly conditioned by these Hellenic presuppositions, it is clear that great care must be observed if we are not to read into Paul's thought ideas which are foreign to him." Unfortunately, this "great care" has rarely been observed by subsequent Christian writers. (John A.T. Robinson, *The Body: A Study in Pauline Theology* [London: SCM Press, 1961], 12).
10. Ibid., 13.
11. Ibid., 14.
12. Ibid., note 1.
13. Ibid., 15.
14. Ibid., 17f.
15. Ibid., 24.
16. Ricoeur, *Symbolism of Evil,* 142f.
17. Robinson, *The Body: A Study in Pauline Theology,* 25.
18. "In essence, *sarx* and *soma* designate different aspects of the human relationship to God. *While sarx stands for man, in the solidarity of creation, in his distance from God, soma stands for man, in the solidarity of creation, as made for God*" (Ibid., 31).
19. Ibid., 9.
20. Crossan, *The Birth of Christianity,* xxxi.
21. Ibid., xxxii. Crossan believes that overcoming the dualism between flesh and spirit constitutes "the most important reason why historical Jesus research is necessary" (p. 30).
22. Schimmel, *Seven Deadly Sins,* 20.
23. Ibid.

24. Plato, *The Last Days of Socrates,* trans. Hugh Frederick (Harmondsworth, England: Penguin, 1969), 112.
25. Ibid., 110.
26. Ricoeur, *Symbolism of Evil,* 338.
27. Ibid., 335.
28. James B. Nelson, *Embodiment: An Approach to Sexuality and Christian Theology* (Minneapolis, MN: Augsburg, 1979), 51.
29. Ibid., 52.
30. Ibid., 53.
31. Ibid., 33.
32. David Abram, *The Spell of the Sensuous,* 66.
33. Ibid., 67. Italics his.
34. Ibid., 68f.
35. Ibid., 65.
36. Cited in Harry F. Gaugh, *Willem De Kooning* (New York: Abbeville Press, 1983), 101. I am indebted to my artist friend, Mark Roth, for conversations about the depth of de Kooning's work.
37. Gabrielle Roth, *Sweat Your Prayers: Movement as Spiritual Practice* (New York: Jeremy P. Tarcher, 1997), xviif. Similar stories are told of women overcoming sexual abuse through bodywork in Carol A. Wiley, *Women in the Martial Arts* (Berkeley, CA: Atlantic Books, 1992).
38. Ibid., xviii.
39. Ibid., 1.
40. Abram, *Spell of the Sensuous,* 252f.
41. Ibid., 253.
42. Ibid., 248.
43. Matthew Fox, *Breakthrough: Meister Eckhart's Creation Spirituality in New Translation* (New York: Doubleday, 1980), 79.
44. Yet the text-preoccupations of education and religion alike in the modern era have coopted the word *spell* to mean getting letters right on a page. Much of the magic has been take from *spell*. We are seldom "spell-bound" by our relations to matter and flesh any longer. Awe dwindles when flesh's wonder is denigrated or forgotten or reduced to letters on a page.
45. Fox, *Breakthrough,* 217.

CHAPTER 2: UNIVERSE FLESH

1. "Mars: Beauty and Mystery," *San Francisco Chronicle,* July 6, 1997, A1.
2. Ricoeur, *The Symbolism of Evil* (Boston: Beacon Press, 1967), 12.
3. Walt Whitman, *Leaves of Grass,* Edwin Weston, ed. (New York: Paddington Press, 1976), 179f.
4. Cited in Galen Rowell, *The Yosemite: Photography and Annotation* (San Francisco: Sierra Club Books, 1990), 26.

5. Cited in Barbara Ardinger, "Yorro Yorro: Aboriginal Creation and the Renewal of Nature," *Creation Spirituality* (Spring 1995), 57.

6. Howard Thurman, *The Search for Common Ground* (Richmond, IN: Friends United Press, 1986), 7f.

7. Ibid., 15.

8. Madge Midley, *Beast and Man: The Roots of Human Nature* (Ithaca, NY: Cornell University Press, 1978).

9. Theodore Roszak, *The Voice of the Earth* (New York: Simon & Schuster, 1992), 17.

10. Ibid., 113.

11. Vaclav Havel, "The New Measure of Man," *New York Times,* July 8, 1994.

12. Stephen Mitchell, trans., *The Selected Poetry of Rainer Maria Rilke* (New York: Vintage, 1984), 69.

13. Michael Talbot, *Mysticism and the New Physics* (London: Arkana/Penguin, 1993), 50.

14. Ibid., 85.

15. Jack Sarfatti, cited in ibid., 87.

16. Arne A. Wyller, *The Planetary Mind* (Aspen, CO: MacMurray & Beck, 1996), 218f.

17. Ibid., 219.

18. Ibid., 26.

19. Ibid., 27.

20. Ibid., 219.

21. Ibid., 219, 27.

22. Ibid., 218.

23. Ibid., 220.

24. Ibid., 26.

25. Brian Swimme and Thomas Berry, *The Universe Story* (San Francisco: HarperSanFrancisco, 1992), 83.

26. Ibid., 70.

27. Ibid., 64.

28. Neil McAleer, *The Cosmic Mind-boggling Book* (New York: Warner Books, 1982), 93.

29. Ibid., 91.

30. Ibid.

31. Ibid., 101.

32. Ibid., 102.

33. Ibid., 110.

34. Ibid., 112.

35. Annie Dillard, *Pilgrim at Tinker Creek* (New York: Harper & Row, 1985), 21.

36. McAleer, *Cosmic Mind-boggling Book,* 126f.

37. Ibid., 128.

38. Ibid., 2, 4.

39. Ibid., 9.

40. Ibid., 10.

41. Ibid., 21.

42. Ibid., 56.

43. Ibid., 129.
44. Ibid., 141.
45. Ibid., 155.
46. Ibid., 157.
47. Ibid.
48. Ibid., 173.
49. Ibid., 184.
50. Ibid., 189.
51. Ibid., 188.
52. Ibid., 191.
53. James Lovelock, *The Ages of Gaia,* xiv.
54. Ibid., xivf.
55. Cited in Fox, *Sheer Joy,* 75.

CHAPTER 3: EARTH FLESH

1. Mary Oliver, *New & Selected Poems* (Boston: Beacon Press, 1992), 110.
2. Theodore Roszak, *The Voice of the Earth,* 116.
3. Ibid., 130f.
4. Arne A. Wyller, *The Planetary Mind,* 157.
5. Ibid., 6.
6. Ibid.
7. Cited in Lennart Nilsson, *Behold Man: A Photographic Journey of Discovery Inside the Body* (Boston: Little, Brown, 1974), 1.
8. Kevin Kelley, ed., *The Home Planet* (New York: Addison-Wesley, 1988), 38.
9. Ibid., 47.
10. Ibid., 120.
11. Ibid., 138.
12. Ibid., 52.
13. Ibid., 60.
14. Ibid., 88.
15. Ibid., 126.
16. Ibid., 140.
17. Ibid., 58.
18. James Lovelock, *The Ages of Gaia,* 31.
19. Ibid., x.
20. Ibid., 39f.
21. Claus Westermann, *Blessing in the Bible and the Life of the Church* (Philadelphia: Fortress, 1978), 28.
22. Lyall Watson, *Lifetide* (New York: Bantam, 1980), 166.
23. Wyller, *Planetary Mind,* 106.
24. Ibid., 117.
25. David Abram, *The Spell of the Sensuous,* 65.

26. Ibid., 80.
27. Matthew Fox, *Breakthrough: Meister Eckhart's Creation Spirituality in New Translation,* 59.
28. Diane Ackerman, *A Natural History of the Senses,* 55.
29. Jeffrey Moussaieff Masson and Susan McCarthy, *When Elephants Weep: The Emotional Lives of Animals* (New York: Delta, 1995), 78.
30. Annie Dillard, *Pilgrim at Tinker Creek,* 94.
31. Guy Murchie, *The Seven Mysteries of Life* (Boston: Houghton Mifflin Co., 1978), 95.
32. Sim Van Der Ryn and Stuart Cowan, *Ecological Design* (Cavelo, CA: Island Press, 1996), 117.
33. Dillard, *Pilgrim at Tinker Creek,* 164.
34. Ibid., 164.
35. Ibid., 198.

CHAPTER 4: HUMAN FLESH

1. Wendell Berry, "The Pleasures of Eating," *Our Sustainable Table,* Robert Clark, ed. (San Francisco: North Point Press, 1990), 125.
2. Ibid., 131.
3. Arne A. Wyller, *The Planetary Mind,* 26f.
4. Pierre Teilhard de Chardin, *Human Energy* (New York: Harcourt Brace Jovanovich, 1969), 23, 130.
5. Lennart Nillson, *Behold Man: A Photographic Journey of Discovery Inside the Body,* 1.
6. Wyller, *Planetary Mind,* 27.
7. James Lovelock, *The Ages of Gaia,* 69.
8. Wyller, *Planetary Mind,* 80f.
9. Ibid., 136.
10. Marc McCutcheon, *The Compass in Your Nose and Other Astonishing Facts about Humans* (Los Angeles: Jeremy P. Tarcher, 1989), 135, 139.
11. Ibid., 151.
12. Ibid., 141.
13. Ibid., 115.
14. Ibid., 127.
15. Deane Juhan, *Job's Body: A Handbook for Bodywork* (Barrytown, NY: Station Hill Press, 1987), 93.
16. McCutcheon, *Compass in Your Nose,* 129.
17. Ibid., 131.
18. Juhan, *Job's Body,* 109f.
19. Ibid., 115f.
20. Ibid., 133.
21. Ibid., 114.
22. Diane Ackerman, *A Natural History of the Senses,* 5.
23. Ibid., 10.

24. Ibid., 11.

25. Ibid., 9.

26. Ibid., 13.

27. Ibid., 16.

28. Ibid., 20.

29. Ibid., 26.

30. Ibid., 31.

31. Ibid., 51.

32. McCutcheon, *Compass in Your Nose*, 154.

33. Ibid., 152.

34. Guy Murchie, *The Seven Mysteries of Life*, 119.

35. Ackerman, *Natural History of the Senses*, 236.

36. Ibid., 236.

37. Juhan, *Job's Body*, 24.

38. Ibid., 35.

39. Ibid., 43.

40. Ibid., 49.

41. Ackerman, *Natural History of the Senses*, 80.

42. Ibid., 121.

43. Ibid., 139.

44. McCutcheon, *Compass in Your Nose*, 165f.

45. Ackerman, *Natural History of the Senses*, 132.

46. Ibid., 178.

47. McCutcheon, *Compass in Your Nose*, 90.

48. Ibid., 27.

49. Ackerman, *Natural History of the Senses*, 212.

50. Ibid., 224.

51. Wyller, *Planetary Mind*, 109.

52. Ibid., 112.

53. Ibid., 115.

54. Ackerman, *Natural History of the Senses*, 235.

55. Ibid., 116.

56. Ibid., 117.

57. Murchie, *Seven Mysteries of Life*, 492.

58. McCutcheon, *Compass in Your Nose*, 27.

59. Wyller, *Planetary Mind*, 121.

60. Ibid., 131.

61. Ibid., 132.

62. Ibid., 133.

63. Ibid., 136.

64. Ibid., 138f.

65. Ibid., 139.

66. Ibid., 140.

67 McCutcheon, *Compass in Your Nose,* 68.

68. Ibid., 66.

69. Murchie, *Seven Mysteries of Life,* 146.

70. Ibid., 150.

CHAPTER 5: THE SEVEN CHAKRAS

1. Matthew Fox, *Breakthrough: Meister Eckhart's Creation Spirituality in New Translation,* 118.

2. Ibid., 289.

3. Ibid., 373f.

4. Ibid., 108.

5. Matthew Fox, ed., *Hildegard of Bingen's Book of Divine Works,* 106.

6. Ibid., 10.

7. Jonathan Star, trans., *A Garden Beyond Paradise* (New York: Bantam Doubleday Dell, 1992), 112.

8. Richard Gerber, M.D., *Vibrational Medicine* (Santa Fe: Bear & Co., 1996), 369. Gerber continues: "Recent scientific research in the field of psychoneuroimmunology has begun to hint at deeper connections between the brain, endocrine, and immune systems than had been previously recognized. The relationships between stress, depression, and immune suppression are only now finding increased recognition." (369f).

9. Sigmund Mowinckel, cited in Claus Westermann, *Blessing in the Bible and the Life of the Church,* 20.

10. Kay Gardner, *Sounding the Inner Landscape: Music as Medicine* (Stonington, ME: Caduceus Publications, 1990), 16. I am indebted for this section on the chakras in particular to this work of Kay Gardner. See also Swami Sivananda Radha, *Kundalini Yoga for the West* (Berkeley: Shambhala, 1985).

11. Diane Ackerman, *A Natural History of the Senses,* 255.

12. Raghavan Iyer, *The Moral and Political Thought of Mahatma Gandhi* (New York: Oxford University Press, 1973), 91.

13. See Otto Rank, *Beyond Psychology* (New York: Dover Publications, 1958).

14. For example, Matthew Fox, *The Coming of the Cosmic Christ,* 163–79 and Matthew Fox, *Whee! We, wee All the Way Home: A Guide to a Sensual, Prophetic Spirituality* (Santa Fe: Bear & Co., 1981).

15. See Fox, *Breakthrough,* 335–37.

16. See Deng Ming-Dao, *Scholar Warrior: An Introduction to the Tao in Everyday Life* (San Francisco: HarperSanFrancisco, 1990).

17. Caroline Myss does an excellent job of connecting the chakras to the loss of power so widely felt in our society in *Anatomy of the Spirit: The Seven Stages of Power and Healing* (New York: Harmony Books, 1996).

18. Fox, *Breakthrough,* 267f.

19. Cited in Anodea Judith, *Wheels of Life* (St. Paul: Llewellyn Publications, 1992), 237.

20. Marc McCutcheon, *The Compass in Your Nose and Other Astonishing Facts about Humans,* 152.

21. See Fox, *Breakthrough,* 213–25.

22. Matthew Fox, *Sheer Joy: Conversations with Thomas Aquinas on Creation Spirituality,* 112f.

23. Richard J. Finneran, ed., *The Collected Works of W. B. Yeats: Volume I, The Poems (Revised),* (New York: Macmillan, 1989).

24. See Christiane Northrup, M.D., *Women's Bodies, Women's Wisdom* (New York: Bantam, 1995).

25. McCutcheon, *Compass in Your Nose,* 52.

26. Arne A. Wyller, *The Planetary Mind,* 127.

27. Deane Juhan, *Job's Body: A Handbook for Bodywork,* 48.

28. See Matthew Fox, "Deep Ecumenism, Ecojustice, and Art as Mediation," in Matthew Fox, *Wrestling with the Prophets* (San Francisco: HarperSanFrancisco, 1995), 215–42.

29. Ackerman, *Natural History of the Senses,* 250.

30. McCutcheon, *Compass in Your Nose,* 45.

31. Wyller, *Planetary Mind,* 107.

CHAPTER 6: WHAT THE MYSTICS SAY ABOUT SIN

1. Sehdev Kumar, *The Vision of Kabir: Love Poems of a 15th Century Weaver-sage* (Concord, Ontario, 1984), 32.

2. Coleman Barks, trans., *The Essential Rumi,* 36.

3. Jonathan Star, *A Garden Beyond Paradise: The Mystical Poetry of Rumi,* 57.

4. Ibid.

5. Edmund Helminski, *The Ruins of the Heart: Selected Lyric Poetry of Jelaluddin Rumi* (Putney, VT: Threshold Books, 1981), 46.

6. Ibid., 49.

7. Coleman Barks, *One-Handed Basket-Weaving* (Athens, GA: Maypop, 1991), 27f.

8. Ibid., 40.

9. Ibid., 47.

10. Ibid., 79.

11. Ibid., 96.

12. Kumar, *Vision of Kabir,* 9.

13. Ibid., 16.

14. Ibid., 109.

15. Ibid., 110.

16. Ibid., 109.

17. Ibid., 152.

18. Ibid., 106.

19. Ibid., 152.

20. Ibid., 150.

21. Ibid., 157.

20. Ibid., 254.
21. Ibid., 99.
22. Ibid., 100f.
23. Ibid., 101.
24. Ibid.
25. Pittenger, *Cosmic Love and Human Wrong,* 65f.
26. Ibid., 26.
27. Ibid., 85.
28. William F. May, *A Catalogue of Sins* (New York: Holt, Rinehart and Winston, 1967), 10.
29. Langdon Gilkey, *Shantung Compound* (NY: Harper & Row, 1966), 233.
30. Howard Thurman, *Deep River and the Negro Spiritual Speaks of Life and Death* (Richmond, Indiana: Howard Thurman Books, 1975), 60.
31. Ricoeur, *The Symbolism of Evil,* 155.
32. Ibid.
33. Ibid., 156.
34. Duncan E. Littlefair, *Sin Comes of Age* (Philadelphia: The Westminster Press, 1975), 47, 38.
35. M. Scott Peck, *People of the Lie,* 42f.
36. Ibid., 69, 71.
37. Angela West, *Deadly Innocence: Feminist Theology and the Mythology of Sin* (London: Wellington House, 1995), 109, 110.
38. Valerie Saiving Goldstein, "The Human Situation: A Feminine View," in *The Journal of Religion,* 1960, vol. 40, 100.
39. Ibid., 109.
40. Susan Brooks Thistlethwaite, *Sex, Race, and God: Christian Feminism in Black and White* (New York: Crossroad, 1989), 87, 88.
41. Rosemary Radford Ruether, *Gaia & God: An Ecofeminist Theology of Earth Healing* (San Francisco: HarperSanFrancisco, 1992), 141, 142.
42. Carter Heyward, *Our Passion for Justice* (New York: The Pilgrim Press, 1984), 210.
43. Clarissa Pinkola Estés, *Women Who Run With the Wolves* (New York: Ballantine Books, 1992, 1995), 11.
44. Ibid.
45. Jean Delumeau, *Sin and Fear: The Emergence of a Western Guilt Culture, 13th–18th Centuries* (New York: St. Martin's Press, 1990), 1.
46. Ibid., 4, 5.
47. Ibid., 31.
48. Ibid., 29.
49. Ibid.
50. Ibid., 27.
51. Ibid., 28.
52. Ibid., 27.
53. Ibid., 246f. In keeping with this tradition, Aquinas would strongly disagree with

those Reformation theologians who taught the depravity of the human. He says: "In no one is natural justice [is this comparable to "original blessing"?] totally corrupt. ...It is impossible that the good of the nature which is suitability or aptitude for grace be totally taken away by sin" (Thomas Aquinas, *On Evil*, 97, 99).

54. Matthew Fox, *Original Blessing* (Santa Fe: Bear & Co., 1983).

55. Delumeau, *Sin and Fear: The Emergence of a Western Guilt Culture 13th–18th Centuries*, 248.

56. Lecture at the University of Creation Spirituality, Oakland, April, 1998.

57. Delumeau, *Sin and Fear*, 248.

58. Ibid., 245.

59. Watson, *Dark Nature: A Natural History of Evil* (New York: HarperPerennial, 1997), 140.

60. Ibid., 89.

61. Ibid., 261.

62. Ibid., 85.

63. Ibid., 138f.

64. Ibid., 260.

65. Ibid., 45.

66. Ibid., 277.

67. Ibid., 54.

68. Ibid., 264.

69. Ibid., 135.

70. Ibid.

71. Ibid., 290.

72. Ibid., 87f.

73. Ibid., 291.

74. Ibid., 285.

75. Ibid.

76. Ibid., 46.

77. Ibid., 134.

78. Ibid., 46.

79. Ibid., 276.

80. Jeffrey Moussaieff Masson and Susan McCarthy, *When Elephants Weep: The Emotional Lives of Animals* (New York: Delta, 1995), xviii.

81. Ibid., xxi.

82. Ibid., 163.

83. Ibid., 175.

84. Ibid., 176.

85. Ibid., 136f.

86. Rank, *Beyond Psychology*, 35.

87. Ibid., 283.

88. Fox, *Breakthrough: Meister Eckhart's Creation Spirituality in New Translation*, 75–82.

89. See Korten, *When Corporations Rule the World*.

90. Bill McKibben, *The Age of Missing Information* (New York: Plume, 1993).
91. Aquinas, *On Evil,* 350.
92. Ibid., 332.
93. Ibid., 321.
94. Ibid., 387.
95. Ibid., 338.

PART III: SINS OF THE SPIRIT

1. Siegfried Wenzel, *The Sin of Sloth: Acedia* (Chapel Hill: University of North Carolina Press, 1960), 129.
2. Bloomfield, *The Seven Deadly Sins,* 23.
3. Ibid.
4. See ibid., 233ff.
5. V. Palachovsky and C. Vogel, *Sin in the Orthodox Church and in the Protestant Churches* (Belgium: Desclee & Cie, 1960), 44.
6. Morton W. Bloomfield, *The Seven Deadly Sins,* 78.
7. Thomas Aquinas, *Summa Theologica,* II–II, q. 36.
8. Wenzel, *Sin of Sloth: Acedia,* 40.
9. Daniel McGuire, "Review of Solomon Schimmel, *The Seven Deadly Sins,*" *Horizons,* Spring, 1994, vol. 21, 214.
10. Wenzel, *The Sin of Sloth,* 168f.
11. Ibid., 39.
12. Ibid., 181f.

CHAPTER 8: MISDIRECTED LOVE IN THE FIRST CHAKRA

1. Dante, *Paradiso,* 33, 145.
2. Siegfried Wenzel, *The Sin of Sloth: Acedia,* 129.
3. Solomon Schimmel, *The Seven Deadly Sins,* 197.
4. Matthew Fox, *Hildegard of Bingen's Book of Divine Works,* 64.
5. Ibid., 110.
6. Hildegard of Bingen, *The Book of the Rewards of Life,* Bruce W. Hozeski, trans. (New York: Oxford University Press, 1994), 203f.
7. Thomas Aquinas, *On Evil,* 90.
8. Josef Pieper, *On Hope* (San Francisco: Ignatius Press, 1986), 52.
9. Cornel West, *Race Matters* (New York: Vintage, 1994), 22f.
10. Ibid., 23.
11. Ibid., 29.
12. Ibid., 27.
13. Matthew Fox, *Sheer Joy: Conversations with Thomas Aquinas on Creation Spirituality,* 114f.
14. Wenzel, *Sin of Sloth: Acedia,* 158f.

15. Ibid., 157.
16. Ibid., 159.
17. Erich Fromm, *The Anatomy of Human Destructiveness,* 243.
18. Ibid., 248.
19. Ibid., 244.
20. Sam Keen, *What to Do When You're Bored and Blue* (USA: Wyden Books, 1980), 112.
21. Ibid., 202.
22. Ibid., 223.
23. Ibid., 223f.
24. Ibid., 100.
25. Fox, *Hildegard of Bingen's Book of Divine Works,* 297.
26. Keen, *What to Do When You're Bored and Blue,* 100.
27. Howard Thurman, *The Search for Common Ground* (Richmond, IN: Friends United Press, 1986), 83.
28. Aquinas, *On Evil,* 346.
29. Fox, *Sheer Joy,* 99.
30. West, *Race Matters,* 27.
31. Ken Wilbur, *Sex, Ecology, Spirituality,* 422.
32. Dorothee Soelle, *Beyond Mere Obedience* (New York: The Pilgrim Press, 1982), xiii.
33. Ibid., 6.
34. Ibid., 9f.
35. Ibid., xiv.
36. Ibid., xx.
37. Bill McKibben, *The Age of Missing Information,* 147.
38. Ibid., 149.
39. Ibid., 26.
40. Wendell Berry, *The Hidden Wound* (San Francisco: North Point Press, 1989), 112.
41. Ibid., 123.
42. Lisa See, *On Gold Mountain* (New York: Vintage, 1995), 42.
43. Ibid., 43.
44. Ibid., 62.
45. Ibid., 45.
46. Ibid., 85.
47. Alan Boesak, "Spirituality and the 'New World Order,'" talk given at the University of Creation Spirituality, Feb. 7, 1997.
48. Sehdev Kumar, *The Vision of Kabir: Love Poems of a 15th Century Weaver-sage,* 14.
49. Ibid., 31.
50. Ibid.
51. Ibid., 32.
52. Ibid.
53. Jonathan Star, *A Garden Beyond Paradise,* 51.
54. Matthew Fox, *Meditations with Meister Eckhart* (Santa Fe: Bear & Co., 1981), 64.
55. Aquinas, *On Evil,* 344.
56. Ibid., 90.

57. Josef Pieper, *Fortitude and Temperance* (New York: Pantheon Books, 1954), 112.

58. Wenzel, *The Sin of Sloth: Acedia,* 184.

59. Ibid., 185.

60. Ibid., 110.

61. Fox, *Sheer Joy,* 280.

62. Thurman, *Search for Common Ground,* 104.

63. Alistair Service and Jean Bradbery, *The Standing Stones of Europe: A Guide to the Great Megalithic Monuments* (London: J. M. Dent, 1993), 40.

64. Ibid.

65. Ibid., 41.

66. Ibid., 43. The quote is from Erich Neumann.

67. Ibid., 50.

68. Ibid., 60.

69. Fox, *Sheer Joy,* 279.

70. Aquinas, *On Evil,* 130.

71. Clarissa Pinkola Estés, *Women Who Run With the Wolves,* 129.

72. Theodore Roszak, *The Voice of the Earth,* 41.

73. Ibid., 80.

74. Wenzel, *Sin of Sloth: Acedia,* 111.

75. McKibben, *Age of Missing Information,* 188f.

76. Ibid., 75.

77. Ibid., 77.

78. Fox, *Sheer Joy,* 354.

79. McKibben, *Age of Missing Information,* 21.

80. Ibid., 18.

81. Ibid., 80.

82. Ibid., 84.

83. Ibid., 20.

84. Wenzel, *Sin of Sloth: Acedia,* 33.

85. Fox, *Sheer Joy,* 281.

86. Aquinas, *On Evil,* 324.

87. Aquinas, *Summa Theologica,* II–II, q. 106, a. 1, ad 1.

88. Fox, *Breakthrough,* 501.

89. Thich Nhat Hanh, *Living Buddha, Living Christ* (New York: Riverhead Books, 1996), 140.

90. Morton W. Bloomfield, *The Seven Deadly Sins,* 201.

91. Wenzel, *Sin of Sloth: Acedia,* 186.

92. Ibid., 135–42.

93. Ibid., 142.

94. Brendan Doyle, *Meditations with Julian of Norwich,* 28.

95. Sim Van Der Ryn and Stuart Cowan, *Ecological Design,* 106f.

96. Ibid.

97. Ibid., 109.

98. Ibid., 109f.

99. Ibid., 112.
100. Wenzel, *Sin of Sloth: Acedia,* 187.
101. Fox, *Sheer Joy,* 184.
102. Aquinas, *On Evil,* 368f. These "daughters" are from Gregory the Great. Aquinas added ignorance to them; see p. 315.
103. Ibid., 344. See Aquinas, *Summa Theologica,* II–II, q. 132, a. 5.
104. Estés, *Women Who Run With the Wolves,* 95.
105. Keen, *What To Do When You're Bored and Blue,* 123.

CHAPTER 9: MISDIRECTED LOVE IN THE SECOND CHAKRA

1. Matthew Fox, ed., *Hildegard of Bingen's Book of Divine Works,* 114.
2. Solomon Schimmel, *The Seven Deadly Sins,* 120.
3. Ibid., 116.
4. Ibid., 120.
5. Ibid., 121.
6. Ibid., 119.
7. Ibid., 137.
8. Ibid., 124. Paul Ricoeur says that it is characteristic of the system of defilement to inflate the sexual. See Appendix C below.
9. Lyall Watson, *Dark Matter: A Natural History of Evil,* 104f.
10. Ibid., 105, 109.
11. Ibid., 109.
12. Ibid., 118.
13. Ibid., 124.
14. Cornel West, *Race Matters,* 27.
15. Ibid., 45.
16. Dorothee Soelle, *Beyond Mere Obedience,* (New York: The Pilgrim Press, 1982), xix.
17. Ibid., 20f.
18. Ibid., 23.
19. Ibid., xviii–xx.
20. Charlene Spretnak, *States of Grace* (San Francisco: HarperSanFrancisco, 1991), 136f.
21. Rosemary Radford Ruether, *New Woman, New Earth: Sexist Ideologies and Human Liberation* (New York: Seabury, 1975), 3f.
22. Adrienne Rich, *The Dream of a Common Language: Poems, 1974–1977* (New York: W.W. Norton, 1978), 64.
23. Suzi Gablik, *The Reenchantment of Art* (New York: Thames & Hudson, 1991), 176.
24. Mary E. Giles, ed., *The Feminist Mystic and Other Essays on Women and Spirituality* (New York: Crossroads, 1985).
25. bell hooks, *killing rage: Ending Racism* (New York: Henry Holt & Co., 1995), 73.
26. Ibid., 74.
27. Ibid., 66.
28. Schimmel, *Seven Deadly Sins,* 129.

29. Ibid.

30. Clarissa Pinkola Estés, *Women Who Run With the Wolves,* 10f.

31. Matthew Fox, *Breakthrough: Meister Eckhart's Creation Spirituality in New Translation,* 70f.

32. See ibid., 81.

33. Gerald G. May, *Addiction and Grace* (San Francisco: Harper & Row, 1988), 3.

34. Thomas Aquinas, *On Evil,* 438.

35. Estés, *Women Who Run With the Wolves,* 12f.

36. Ibid., 13.

37. Ann Douglas, *The Feminization of American Culture* (New York: Knopf, 1977), 254.

38. Ibid., 46. For more on sentimentalism, see my article "On Desentimentalizing Spirituality," in Matthew Fox, *Wrestling with the Prophets* (San Francisco: HarperSanFrancisco, 1995), 297–316.

39. Estés, *Women Who Run With the Wolves,* 128f.

40. Ibid., 129.

41. Ibid., 121.

42. Anne Wilson Schaeff, *When Society Becomes an Addict* (San Francisco: Harper & Row, 1987), 47.

43. Gregory Bateson, *Steps to an Ecology of Mind* (New York: Ballantine, 1972), 326, 313.

44. Ibid., 330.

45. Ibid., 335.

46. Erich Fromm, *The Anatomy of Human Destructiveness,* 288.

47. Ibid., 292.

48. Ibid., 289f.

49. Ibid., 291.

50. Ibid., 290.

51. David C. Korten, *When Corporations Rule the World,* 7f.

52. Ibid., 59.

53. William Leach cited in ibid., 149.

54. Ibid., 67.

55. Ibid., 176.

56. Ibid., 241.

57. Ibid., 243.

58. Aquinas, *On Evil,* 438; he is citing Gregory the Great.

CHAPTER 10: MISDIRECTED LOVE IN THE THIRD CHAKRA

1. Sam Keen, *What to Do When You're Bored and Blue,* 101.

2. Ibid.

3. Howard Thurman, *For the Inward Journey* (Richmond, IN: Friends United Meeting, 1984), 132.

4. Howard Thurman, *The Creative Encounter* (Richmond, IN: Friends United Press), 53.

5. Adrienne Rich, *The Dream of a Common Language: Poems, 1974–77*, 64.

6. Ibid., 29.

7. Cynthia Tucker, "Racism Rages On, Without Apology," *San Francisco Chronicle*, Aug. 9, 1997, A18.

8. David C. Korten, *When Corporations Rule the World*, 307.

9. Ibid., 308.

10. Ibid., 312.

11. Ibid., 313.

12. Hildegard of Bingen, *Scivias*, Adelgundis Fuhrkotter, ed. (Turnnholti: Brepols, 1978), 550.

13. Hildegard of Bingen, *The Book of the Rewards of Life*, 43.

14. Matthew Fox, *Breakthrough: Meister Eckhart's Creation Spirituality in New Translation*, 423.

15. Hildegard of Bingen, *Book of the Rewards of Life*, 64.

16. Ibid., 42f.

17. Solomon Schimmel, *The Seven Deadly Sins*, 83.

18. Ibid.

19. Ibid., 91.

20. Korten, *When Corporations Rule the World*, 257.

21. Caroline Myss emphasizes this, with good reason, in her work on the chakras and the "Seven Stages of Power and Healing." See Caroline Myss, *Anatomy of the Spirit: The Seven Stages of Power and Healing*.

22. Thomas Aquinas, *On Evil*, 97.

CHAPTER 11: MISDIRECTED LOVE IN THE FOURTH CHAKRA

1. Clarissa Pinkola Estés, *Women Who Run With the Wolves*, 159.

2. Ibid.

3. Ibid., 158.

4. Thomas Aquinas, *On Evil*, 387f.

5. James Hillman, *The Soul's Code: In Search of Character and Calling* (New York: Random House, 1996), 234.

6. Matthew Fox, *Illuminations of Hildegard of Bingen*, 22–25.

7. William F. May, *A Catalogue of Sins*, 90.

8. Sam Keen, *What to Do When You're Bored and Blue*, 221.

9. Ibid.

10. Matthew Fox, *Sheer Joy: Conversations with Thomas Aquinas on Creation Spirituality*, 351.

11. Otto Rank, *Beyond Psychology*, 191.

12. I am indebted to Joanna Macy for a workshop on fear that we co-facilitated in Munich, Germany, and for her inspiring ideas and challenges.

13. Fox, *Sheer Joy*, 344.

14. Ibid., 339.

15. Ibid., 341.

16. Ibid., 338.

17. Ibid., 348.

18. Ted Peters, *Sin: Radical Evil in Soul and Society,* 64.

19. Ibid., 34 note.

20. "U.S. Spy Documents Implicate Vatican Bank in Nazi Dealings," *San Francisco Chronicle,* Aug. 4, 1997, A10.

21. Hildegard of Bingen, *The Book of the Rewards of Life,* 238.

22. Ibid., 239.

23. Ibid., 240.

24. Ibid., 224f.

25. Fox, *Sheer Joy,* 488.

26. Ibid.

27. Ibid.

28. Aquinas, *On Evil,* 393.

29. Ibid., 490.

30. Ibid., 396.

31. Ibid., 400.

32. David C. Korten, *When Corporations Rule the World,* 65.

33. Ibid., 74.

34. Ibid., 75.

35. Ibid., 81.

36. Ibid., 108.

37. Ibid., 109.

38. Ibid., 187.

39. Ibid., 189.

40. Ibid., 193.

41. "Searches Continue for Storm Victims in Philippine Town," *Dallas Morning News,* Nov. 8, 1991, 7A.

42. Aquinas, *On Evil,* 399f.

43. Hildegard of Bingen, *Book of the Rewards of Life,* 53, 41.

44. Ibid., 14f.

CHAPTER 12: MISDIRECTED LOVE IN THE FIFTH CHAKRA

1. Hugh of St. Victor cited by Thomas Aquinas, *On Evil,* 411.

2. Abraham Joshua Heschel, *God in Search of Man: A Philosophy of Judaism* (New York: Farrar, Straus, & Cudahy, 1955), 78.

3. Solomon Schimmel, *The Seven Deadly Sins,* 139.

4. Ibid., 140.

5. Aquinas, *On Evil,* 412.

6. Audre Lorde, *Sister Outsider* (Trumansburg, NY: Crossing Press, 1984), 40.

7. Ibid., 41.

8. Ibid., 44.

9. Ibid., 42.

10. Matthew Fox, *Breakthrough: Meister Eckhart's Creation Spirituality in New Translation*, 61.

11. Ibid., 64.

12. John Dominic Crossan, *Jesus: A Revolutionary Biography* (San Francisco: HarperSanFrancisco, 1994), 198. Italics mine.

13. Martin Buber, *Good and Evil*, 7.

14. Ibid., 9.

15. Fox, *Breakthrough*, 335f.

16. Alice Walker, *Living By the Word* (New York: Harcourt Brace & Co., 1989), 170.

17. David C. Korten, *When Corporations Rule the World*, 146.

18. Ibid., 147.

19. Cited in ibid., 147.

20. Ibid.

21. Ibid., 153.

22. Cited in ibid., 153f.

23. The story is told in ibid., 154.

24. Ibid., 277.

25. From Gregory the Great and Aquinas, *On Evil*, 422f.

CHAPTER 13: MISDIRECTED LOVE IN
THE SIXTH CHAKRA

1. Matthew Fox, *Breakthrough: Meister Eckhart's Creation Spirituality in New Translation*, 407.

2. Walter Brueggeman, *The Prophetic Imagination* (Philadelphia: Fortress Press, 1978).

3. Sehdev Kumar, *The Vision of Kabir: Love Poems of a 15th Century Weaver-sage*, 93.

4. bell hooks, *Yearning: Race, Gender and Cultural Politics* (Boston: South End Press, 1990), 31.

5. Clarissa Pinkola Estés, *Women Who Run With the Wolves*, 75.

6. Ibid., 81.

7. Ibid., 82.

8. Ibid., 84.

9. Ibid., 86.

10. Ibid., 90.

11. Ibid., 92.

12. Ibid., 94.

13. Ibid., 98.

14. Paul Ricoeur, *The Symbolism of Evil*, 178.

15. Otto Rank, *Beyond Psychology*, 23.

16. Ibid., 24.

17. Ralph Abraham, *Chaos, Gaia, Eros* (New York: HarperSanFrancisco, 1994), 120, 141.

18. Crossan, *Jesus: A Revolutionary Biography,* 200.

19. David C. Korten, *When Corporations Rule the World,* 156.

20. See Eloise McKinney-Johnson, "Egypt's Isis: The Original Black Madonna," in Ivan Van Sertima, ed., *Black Women in Antiquity* (New Brunswick, NJ: Transaction Books, 1984), 68.

21. See Susan Cady, Marian Ronan, Hal Taussig, *Wisdom's Feast* (San Francisco: Harper & Row, 1989); and Ana Castillo, *Goddess of the Americas, La Diosa de las Americas: Writings on the Virgin of Guadalupe* (New York: Riverhead Books, 1996).

22. James Hillman, *The Soul's Code: In Search of Character and Calling,* 100f.

23. Solomon Schimmel, *The Seven Deadly Sins,* 201.

24. Hildegard of Bingen, *The Book of the Rewards of Everyday Life,* 132.

25. Ibid., 75.

26. Ibid., 108.

27. Matthew Fox, *Sheer Joy: Conversations with Thomas Aquinas on Creation Spirituality,* 186.

28. Rank, *Beyond Psychology,* 26.

29. See Matthew Fox and Rupert Sheldrake, *The Physics of Angels* (San Francisco: HarperSanFrancisco, 1996).

30. Ibid., 23.

31. Judith Shklar, *Ordinary Vices* (Cambridge: Harvard University Press, 1984), 8.

32. See Jean Delumeau, *Sin and Fear: The Emergence of a Western Guilt Culture, 13th–18th Centuries,* 243: "This omission on the part of cloistered monks was natural...and all to their honorable credit. They could well have felt the temptations of pride, envy, jealousy, anger, and sorrow, of lust and gluttony. It is hard, however, to think of them as inordinately cruel: hence they neglected to include malice in the list of major sins."

CHAPTER 14: MISDIRECTED LOVE IN THE SEVENTH CHAKRA

1. Angus Wilson, et al., *The Seven Deadly Sins* (New York: William Morrow & Co., 1962), 10.

2. Rainer Maria Rilke, *The Sonnets to Orpheus,* Stephen Mitchell, trans. (New York: Touchstone Book, 1985), 31.

3. Ibid., 117.

4. Ibid., 43–47.

5. Thomas Aquinas, *On Evil,* 349–51.

6. Hildegard of Bingen, *The Book of the Rewards of Life,* 142.

7. Elaine Pagels, *The Origin of Satan* (New York: Vintage, 1995), 13.

8. Ibid., 49.

9. Ibid., 56.

10. Ibid., 100.

11. Ibid., 146.
12. Ibid., xvii.
13. Walter Wink, *Naming the Powers: The Language of Power in the New Testament,* vol. 1 (Philadelphia: Fortress Press, 1984), 84.
14. Ibid., 83.
15. Ibid., 105.
16. E. F. Schumacher, *Good Work* (London: Abacus, 1980), 26.
17. Hildegard of Bingen, *Book of the Rewards of Life,* 238.
18. David C. Korten, *When Corporations Rule the World,* 26.
19. Stephanie Slater, "Down and Out in the Land of Billionaires," *San Francisco Chronicle,* Aug. 10, 1997, B11.
20. Korten, *When Corporations Rule the World,* 157.
21. James Hillman, *The Soul's Code: In Search of Character and Calling,* 239.

CONCLUSION: THE BLESSINGS OF FLESH *AND* SPIRIT

1. Robert Jay Lifton, in Derrick Jensen, ed., *Listening to the Land: Conversations about Nature, Culture and Eros* (San Francisco: Sierra Club Books, 1995), 143.
2. Ibid.
3. Matthew Fox, *Breakthrough: Meister Eckhart's Creation Spirituality in New Translation,* 197.
4. Matthew Fox, *Meditations with Meister Eckhart,* 70.
5. Ibid., 86.
6. Matthew Fox, *Sheer Joy: Conversations with Thomas Aquinas on Creation Spirituality,* 353, 352.
7. Ibid., 352.
8. Ibid., 350, 351.
9. Ibid., 351.
10. A frightening example of what happens when we lack a cosmology can be found in the words of Ernest Becker: "What are we to make of a creation in which the routine activity is for organisms to be tearing others apart with teeth of all types. ... Creation is a nightmare spectacular taking place on a planet that has been soaked for hundreds of millions of years in the blood of all its creatures.... Whatever man does on this planet has to be done in the lived truth of the terror of creation, of the grotesque, of the rumble of panic underneath everything." Cited in Theodore Roszak, *The Voice of the Earth,* 59.
11. Matthew Fox, *Sheer Joy,* 412.

APPENDIX A: HITLER AS A RELIGIOUS FIGURE

1. Morris Berman, *Coming to Our Senses: Body and Spirit in the Hidden History of the West* (New York: Simon & Schuster, 1989), 271, 269, note 33.
2. Ibid., 271f.

3. Ibid., 274. What follows draws on Berman's chapter "The Twisted Cross."
4. Ibid., 289.
5. Ibid., 274.
6. Ibid., 285.
7. Ibid., 287.
8. James Hillman, *The Soul's Code: In Search of Character and Calling*, 236.
9. Ibid., 217ff.
10. Ibid., 222ff.
11. Berman, *Coming to Our Senses*, 284.
12. Ibid., 267.
13. Ibid., 271.
14. Ibid., 273.
15. Ibid., 253.
16. Ibid., 256f.
17. Ibid., 269.
18. Ibid., 272.
19. Ibid., 291.

APPENDIX C: PAUL RICOEUR ON THE EVOLUTION OF SIN

1. Paul Ricoeur, *The Symbolism of Evil*, 46.
2. Ibid., 184.
3. Ibid., 25.
4. Ibid., 30.
5. Ibid., 46.
6. Ibid., 28.
7. Ibid., 38.
8. Ibid., 30.
9. Ibid., 32.
10. Ibid., 48.
11. Ibid., 50.
12. Ibid., 56.
13. Ibid., 61.
14. Ibid., 63.
15. Ibid., 67.
16. Ibid., 70.
17. Ibid., 79.
18. Ibid., 102.
19. Ibid., 64.
20. Ibid., 104.
21. Ibid., 107.
22. Ibid.

INDEX

Abraham, Ralph, 300
Abram, David, 15, 32–33, 39, 63
Acedia, 124, 167–79, 183–208, 228, 318, 338
Ackerman, Diane, 15, 25–26, 63–64, 76–78, 81–84, 86
Addiction, 186, 213, 218–21, 226, 276–78
Adultism, 179, 245–46, 284, 285–87, 296
Advertising, 213, 277, 287–88, 300
Altruism, 148, 149, 152, 153
Ancestors, disconnection from, 322–23
Angels, 4–5, 306–7, 324
Anger, 104, 106–7, 234–43, 252–54
Anointing the sick, 323–24
Anthony, 198
Anthropocentrism, 5, 53, 151, 179, 183–84, 192–95, 204, 263
Aristotle, 20, 21, 150, 165
Arrogance, 176, 179–85, 199, 269, 331
Augustine, 23, 24, 30–31, 38, 101, 135, 145, 147, 226, 303, 330
Avarice, 264–69, 276–78, 284, 305, 321
Awe, 5, 15, 20, 21, 40–41, 43–47, 54

Baptism, 205–6
Bateson, Gregory, 226–27
Berry, Thomas, 100, 147, 159, 178, 194
Berry, Wendell, 69, 179–80
Betrayal, 256–58
Bitterness, 234–35, 252, 302
Blame, 258–59
Blessings of the flesh, 2, 12–17, 19–116
Bloomfield, Morton W., 9, 12, 162
Boredom, 172–74, 197, 235–36
Borg, Marcus J., 130–31, 134
Bossuet, Cardinal, 25
Brain, 77, 80, 87–90
Breathing, 39, 76, 78–79, 105–6
Brow (sixth) chakra, 108–11, 114, 293–314
Buber, Martin, 2, 8, 11, 17, 139, 282
Buddhism, 138, 158, 160, 264, 265, 278

Calvin, John, 16, 145–46
Capital sins, 2–3, 9–10, 14, 15, 161–327
Cardinale, Ernesto, 19
Carver, George Washington, 66–67

Cassian, John, 163–65, 187, 198, 200
Chakras, 2–3, 9, 14, 93, 94–119, 161–327
Chodron, Pema, 138
Chopra, Deepak, 84
Christianity, 11, 14, 25–32, 94–96, 140–47, 154, 162, 200, 221, 229, 320, 337
Community, 111–12, 188–91, 240, 315–16, 320, 323, 331, 333, 335, 336
Compassion, 96, 104–7, 153, 236–37, 243, 251–53, 258, 263, 268–69, 331, 333
Concealment, 280–82
Concupiscence, 220, 269–70
Confirmation (sacrament), 247–48
Consumerism, 168, 220, 275–77, 280, 284–86, 321–22, 331, 336
Control, 225–32, 240, 300, 308
Corporate violence, 230–32, 266–67
Cosmology, 10–11, 54, 45, 333, 337, 338, 331, 238
    first chakra, 99–101, 170–71, 188, 199, 204, 334
    flesh understanding, 4, 19–21, 38–40
Cowan, Stuart, 100, 203
Creation Spirituality, 9, 14, 98–114, 289–90, 302, 331, 337
Creativity, 9, 96, 108–11, 238, 293–98, 302–3, 305, 310, 312, 331, 333, 337
Crossan, Dominic, 14, 28–29, 131–34, 281, 300
Cruelty, 310–11
Curiosity, 191–92, 200

Dante, 9, 162, 167, 172, 201, 268
Darwin, Charles, 63, 148, 154, 306
Dawkins, Richard, 148, 153
Deep Ecumenism, 8–10, 98, 137–45, 165, 317
De Koonig, Willem, 33, 55
Delumeau, Jean, 145, 146
Demons, 318–21, 324
Denial, 198–99
Denominationalism, 179, 184–85, 186
Descartes, Rene, 23, 147, 330
Despair, 127, 145, 151, 169–72, 176, 200, 302–4, 311

Destruction, 241–43, 328
Disobedience, 176–77, 228–30, 231
Douglas, Ann, 222, 240
Dualism, 159, 221–22
Dugger, William, 231
Duve, Christian de, 58

Earth, blessings of, 57–68
Eckhart, Meister, 39, 41, 63, 95, 103–5, 107,
    110, 128–30, 136, 155, 185, 199, 200,
    218, 242, 262, 265, 279–80, 283, 293,
    295, 303, 316, 329, 330, 333, 336
Ecology, 36–37, 118–19, 179, 191, 194,
    203–4, 229, 310, 330
Emerson, Ralph Waldo, 148, 301
Empowerment, 104, 123, 234, 235, 241, 252
Endocrine system, 97–101, 106, 108–9, 112,
    219
Envy, 164, 315–24, 331
Estés, Clarissa Pinkola, 144, 159, 192, 206,
    217, 222–24, 250, 297, 298
Eucharist, 270–71
Evagirus of Pontus, 163, 164, 168
Evil, 2, 3–5, 9, 11, 17, 160, 253
    biologists' view, 147–51
    demons and, 318–21
    mystics' view, 121, 125–30, 136
    sin's evolution and, 154–58
    theologian's view, 92, 139, 142–43
    See also Sin
Eyes, 62–63, 85–87

Fascism, 186, 263–64, 268
Fear, 43, 260–64, 268, 296, 331
Feminism, 103, 149, 209, 214–17
Fire (metaphorical), 95–97, 175
Flesh, extended meaning of 4, 23–41; See also
    Blessings of the flesh
Food, 81–83, 271, 277–78
Forgiveness, 106–7, 254–58
Fromm, Erich, 8, 9, 17, 139, 172, 227
Fundamentalism, 6, 146, 155, 157, 223,
    295–96, 305, 335
Funk, Robert, 12

Gablik, Suzi, 216
Gaia, 33, 61–62, 76, 189, 246, 290
Galileo, 25, 308
Gandhi, Mahatma, 101, 137
Gebara, Ivone, 6
Generosity, 9, 332–36, 338
Gerber, Richard, 97
Giles, Mary, 216
Gilkey, Langdon, 142
Gluttony, 219, 268, 275–78

Goodness, 2, 92, 316, 337–38
    biologists' view, 147–48, 150
    mystics' view, 121, 125, 128, 136
    theologian's view, 139, 142
Grace, 127, 129, 135, 141, 171, 219, 328,
    337–38
Gratitude, 40, 199–200, 271
Gregory the Great, pope, 163–65, 193, 200
Guilt, 135, 146, 157, 158, 229, 242
Gutierrez, Gustavo, 141

Hamilton, William, 212
Hard-heartedness, 268–69
Hatred, 164, 252–53, 259–60, 263–64,
    317–19
Havel, Vaclav, 46
Hayden, Tom, 322
Hearing, sense of, 83–84, 100–101
Heart
    fourth chakra, 104–7, 114, 250–74
    hardness of, 268–69
    purity of, 139
Heschel, Abraham, 4, 46, 92, 139, 235, 261,
    277
Heyward, Carter, 144
Hildegard of Bingen, 3, 39, 95, 105, 106, 141,
    168, 174, 179, 187, 210, 241, 242, 253,
    264, 268–69, 302, 318, 331
Hillman, James, 253, 301, 322–23
Hinduism, 101, 119, 137, 158, 250
Hitler, Adolf, 9, 155, 177, 253, 254, 318,
    328–30
Hobbes, Thomas, 151
Hobday, Jose, 193
Holy Spirit, 95–96, 221, 262
Homosexuality, 108, 228, 238, 329
Hooks, bell, 216, 296
Hoyle, Fred, 58
Hugh of St. Victor, 141, 164
Human flesh, blessings of, 69–93
Humorlessness, 224–25
Hypocrisy, 282

Idolatry, 185–86
Ignorance, 119, 137, 138, 158–59, 184,
    191–92, 198, 261, 297
Imbalance, 159, 187–88, 222
Incarnation, 14, 24, 37–38
Infinite, 265, 267, 268, 277
Injustice, 130, 159, 187–88, 269, 297, 316,
    331
Insecurity, 246–47
Interdependence, 8–9, 53, 183, 193, 216
Intuition, 294, 297–99, 301–2, 307, 308
Irwin, James, 60

Jampolsky, Gerald, 260
Jencks, Charles, 12, 151, 303
Jerome, 26, 30
Jesus Christ, 14, 26, 29, 31–32, 37–39, 53,
    92, 94–95, 102, 130–36, 140, 147, 153,
    176, 184, 206, 214–15, 226, 229, 237,
    252, 259, 261, 281, 295, 296, 319–20,
    333, 335
Judaism, 2, 27, 29, 39, 95, 106, 133–34,
    138–40, 146–47, 319
Juhan, Deane, 109
Julian of Norwich, 126–28, 136, 202–3
Jung, Carl, 17, 223
Justice, 104, 191; See also Injustice

Kabir, 121, 125–26, 136, 184–85, 270, 296
Keen, Sam, 173–74, 236, 257–58
Keller, Helen, 77, 80, 84
King, Martin Luther, Jr., 261
Knowledge, 301–2
Korten, David, 13, 14, 156, 229–30, 240, 243,
    266, 267, 300, 321
Kundalini, 94, 95, 99, 159, 270

Langland, William, 9, 201, 202
L'Engle, Madeleine, 215
Levenson, Jon D., 11
Liberation, 103–4, 106–7, 140
Lifton, Jay, 328
Light, 47–48, 69–70, 85, 96, 112, 129–30
Littlefair, Duncan, 142
Loneliness, cosmic, 174–75, 247
Lorde, Audre, 279
Love, 5, 31, 107, 109, 221, 250, 256; See also
    Misdirected love; Self-love
Lovelock, James, 20, 53–54, 61–62
Lust, 96, 209–14, 218, 219, 228–30, 268
Luther, Martin, 135, 146, 147, 289
Lying, 282

Magnanimity, 9, 330, 334
Maguire, Daniel, 164
Mander, Jerry, 291
Marriage, 30, 38, 133–34, 312
Masson, Jeffrey Moussaieff, 152–54
May, Gerald, 219, 263
May, William, 142
McCarthy, Susan, 152–54
McKibben, Bill, 157, 178, 195, 197, 207, 220,
    291
Meade, Michael, 288
Media, 171, 195–98, 213, 216
Meditation, 138, 200
Merbold, Ulf, 61
Merleau-Ponty, Maurice, 25, 32

Midley, Madge, 45
Miracles, 43–44
Misdirected love, 2, 98, 114, 159–62,
    167–327
Mitchell, Edgar, 60
Morality, 122–23, 152, 155
Mowinckel, Sigmund, 62, 97
Muir, John, 44–45
Mumford, Lewis, 294
Murchie, Guy, 90
Mysticism, 94–98, 121–36, 184–85, 305

Nature, 63–67, 132–33, 147–54, 178
Nelson, Paul, 30
Neumann, Erich, 301
Niebuhr, Reinhold, 141, 143, 263
Nillson, Lennart, 71
Northrup, Christiane, 107
Nygren, Anders, 143

Obedience, 176–77
Objectification, 211–14, 221
Ockels, Wubbo, 60
O'Keeffe, Georgia, 33, 55
Oliver, Mary, 57
Omission, sins of, 191, 195, 257, 322–23
One-sidedness, 220–21, 225
Origen, 31, 320
Original sin, 16, 145–47, 149, 151, 303
Ornish, Dean, 174, 287

Pagels, Elaine, 319–20
Passion, 96, 138, 331, 333
Passive-aggression, 235
Patriarchy, 103, 133–34, 214–17, 251, 252,
    301, 316
Paul, 16, 21, 26–32, 38, 135–36, 147, 337
Peck, M. Scott, 1–2, 142
Peraldus, 186
Pessimism, 145–52, 201, 259–60, 302–4,
    311
Petrarch, 172, 201
Philo, 103
Pieper, Josef, 186
Pittenger, Norman, 6, 141
Plato, 29–30, 31, 156
Power, 96–98, 239–41, 243–47
Pride, 176, 179, 183, 228–30, 311
Priesthood, 289–90
Prigogine, Ilya, 47, 70
Procreation, 30, 31
Prophecy, 107–8, 295–96
Protestantism, 145, 146, 147, 265–66
Purity, 132, 134
Pusillanimity, 186–87, 262–63

Racism, 179–83, 186, 227, 329

Rank, Otto, 101, 154, 224, 238, 259, 298, 299, 302, 303, 313

Rationalism, 299–300, 303, 307–8, 311

Reconciliation, 232–33

Reductionism, 159, 303, 304–6, 311

Repentance, 140

Resentment, 253–54, 263, 318

Responsibility, 337–38

Restlessness of spirit, 175

Rich, Adrienne, 216, 238, 239

Ricoeur, Paul, 5, 8, 16, 21, 28, 30, 42, 43, 135, 140, 142, 155, 299

Rilke, Rainer Maria, 47, 92, 316

Roman Catholicism, 30–31, 106, 251, 317

Root (first) chakra, 99, 114, 167–208

Roszak, Theodore, 46, 122, 192, 305

Roth, Gabrielle, 33–34

Ruether, Rosemary Radford, 143 215–16

Rumi, 7, 97, 122–25, 136, 185

Sacraments, 3, 205–6, 232–33, 247–48, 270–71, 289–90, 312, 323–24

Sacred, 4–5, 43, 158

Sacrifice, 336

Sadism, 227–28, 310–11

Sadness, 200–201, 204, 317–18

Sadomasochism, 230–32, 239

Saiving Goldstein, Valerie, 143

Satan, 319–21

Savage-Rumbaugh, Sue, 152

Schachter, Zalman, 16

Schaeff, Anne Wilson, 218, 226

Schimmel, Solomon, 3, 17, 29, 164, 168, 211–12, 216, 242, 302

Schumacher, E. F., 264, 265, 321

Science, 24, 54, 147–55, 303

Seeing, 62–63, 85–87

Self-destruction, 241

Self-hatred, 259–60

"Selfish genes," 148–49, 151, 153, 303

Self-love, 176, 252

Self-pity, 251–52

Senses, 76–91

Sentimentalism, 222–24, 235, 236, 239–40

Sexism, 5, 179, 186, 329

Sexuality, 13, 30–31, 38, 83, 90
  second chakra, 101–3, 114, 209–33

Shatalov, Vladimir, 60–61

Sheldrake, Rupert, 4, 24, 46, 306

Shklar, Judith, 310

Shor, Juliet, 276

Sim Van der Ryn, 203

Sin, 5–17, 96–97, 117–60, 330
  capital, 2–3, 9–10, 14, 15, 161–327
  of spirit vs. flesh, 164–65, 172, 219–20

Sloth, 127, 201–2, 219, 338

Smell, sense of, 76–78

Smith, Adam, 266

Soelle, Dorothee, 177, 214–15

Solar plexus (third) chakra, 103, 114, 234–49

Solzhenitsyn, Aleksandr, 3

Soul, 3, 7, 15, 20, 23, 27, 95, 277, 330

Speech, 84, 280–87, 331

Spirit, 329–38
  sins of, 2, 6, 13, 15, 161–327

Spirituality, 6, 122, 134, 246, 266

Spiritual warriorhood, 236–37, 247–48

Spretnak, Charlene, 215

Suffering, causing of, 158

Superstition, 307–8, 311

Swimme, Brian, 294

Swing, William, 317

Szent-Györgyi, Albert, 59

Taoism, 104, 138, 159, 243

Taste, 81–83

Technology, 4, 17, 155–57, 308, 328

Teilhard de Chardin, Pierre, 71

Television, 85, 156–57, 178, 195–97, 284

Teresa of Avila, 229, 270

Theologians, 6, 92, 137–47

Thich Nhat Hanh, 8, 136, 138, 200, 201, 207, 303

Thistlethwaite, Susan Brooks, 143

Thomas, Lewis, 61

Thomas Aquinas, 2, 4, 10, 15, 20, 23, 39, 40, 42, 54, 98, 103, 104, 107, 114, 119, 127, 141, 147, 160–62, 164, 165, 167–70, 176, 186, 187, 191, 195, 197, 199–201, 205, 222, 234–36, 243, 247, 252, 258, 260–65, 268, 278, 293–95, 303, 304, 307, 311, 317, 334, 337–38

Thought, 87–90

Throat (fifth) chakra, 107–8, 114, 275–92

Thurman, Howard, 45, 142, 174–75, 188, 237, 238–39

Tillich, Paul, 141

Touch, sense of, 79–81

Trust, 226, 247, 258

Truth, 96, 108, 137, 282, 295, 331, 333

Tucker, Cynthia, 239

Universe, blessings of, 42–56, 332–33

Vainglory, 193

Victimhood, 237–39, 251

Violence, 211–14, 223, 241–43
  corporate, 230–32, 266–67
Volynon, Boris, 60

Walker, Alice, 283
Wallace, Alfred Russel, 306
Wang, Taylor, 60
War, 309–11
Waste, 202–4
Watson, Lyall, 62–63, 148–53, 212–13
Wenzel, Siegfried, 204
West, Angela, 142
West, Cornel, 169–70, 176, 213

West, Rebecca, 215
Whitehead, Alfred North, 25
Whitman, Walt, 43–44
Wickramasinghe, Chandra, 58
Wilbur, Ken, 176
Williams, William Carlos, 69
Wilson, Angus, 315
Wink, Walter, 320–21
Wisdom, 96, 108, 184, 301–2, 333
Wyller, Arne, 58–59, 63, 86–90,
  109

Yeats, William Butler, 107

For more information about the Doctor of Ministry degree in work and spirituality offered at the University of Creation Spirituality or about the master's of liberal arts degree in creation spirituality offered by Naropa Institute in Oakland, California, contact:

University of Creation Spirituality
2141 Broadway Ave.
Oakland, Ca. 94612
510-8354827
ucs@csnet.org www.netser.com/ucs

Naropa Oakland
2141 Broadway Ave.
Oakland, Ca. 94612
510-8354827
ucs@csnet.org www.netser.com/ucs